The Complete Scotland 1999-2000

The Complete Scotland
1999-2000

Carrick Media

The information in The Complete Scotland, in particular the statistical material, has been gathered from a vast range and number of sources, and space does not permit us to credit all concerned, but we must single out the Government information services and their annual publications, the Scottish Abstract of Statistics and the Annual Report of the Registrar General for Scotland, both of which we recommend to serious students of Scottish public affairs.

Published by Carrick Media
1/4 Galt House, 31 Bank Street, Irvine KA12 0LL
01294 311322

Copyright 1999 Carrick Media

Printed in England by Redwood Books

British Library Cataloguing-in-Publication Data
A catalogue record for this book is available from the British Library

ISBN 0 946724 44 X

Contents

THE WAY WE LIVE

PEOPLE

Preface

The year under review in this, the second annual edition of *The Complete Scotland*, was one of momentous change: preparations for and elections to the Scottish Parliament, followed by ministerial appointments and the assumption of devolved power by the Scottish Executive. It was our original intention to publish the book in the early summer, but such was the scope and importance of the constitutional reforms we decided that this would have been counter-productive. By delaying publication until the autumn, we have been able to include a major section devoted to the new government of Scotland, its machinery, personalities and legislative programme. The Parliament has had an extremely hostile press in its first few months, which has made it easy to overlook the profound long-term significance of all that it represents.

The Complete Scotland has itself been restructured to take account of the new Scotland – with a generous chunk of the book devoted to a detailed exposition of the Parliament and the Executive. Elsewhere, however, it offers the same eclectic range of knowledge, practical and curious, for readers who need to know all there is to know about the country and who would prefer to have the facts at their fingertips. It provides quick, reliable access to such diverse information as the coldest day in Scotland's history, how to become a crofter, and the clear-up rate for housebreaking (a profession recommended if only because its practitioners are so rarely detected). It also includes the turnout for every Council area in the 1999 local elections. Why mention this mundane matter? Because no one in Scotland (not even COSLA) knew how many had voted. We had to go to Lancaster University for the figures.

The heart of the book is "The Way We Live Now" – for which we have selected illuminating examples of the work of the organisations which most influence our lives. Our thanks to all those who have helped us to bring the book to press.

Kenneth Roy, October 1999

Government

The Scottish Parliament

Background

On 24 July 1997 the Secretary of State (Donald Dewar) presented a White Paper to Parliament outlining a scheme for the establishment of a Scottish Parliament, provided the Government's policy on devolution was supported in a referendum. The White Paper proposed a 129-member parliament to be elected in 1999, 73 members of which would each represent a constituency elected by majority vote, the remaining 56 members to be elected by proportional representation on the basis of lists submitted by political parties. Elections would be held every four years. The Scottish Parliament would have powers to raise or reduce the basic rate of income tax by up to 3p, provided that this specific proposal was supported in the referendum.

On 11 September 1997 there was a decisive endorsement both of the Parliament and of the tax varying power, 74.3% of those who voted supporting the Parliament and 63.5% declaring in favour of the tax varying power. The electorate in only two of the 32 unitary authorities registered disapproval of either proposition, those being Orkney and Dumfries and Galloway, which voted against the tax varying power.

On 6 May 1999 the first election to the Scottish Parliament produced no overall majority for the largest single party, Labour, which subsequently entered a coalition with the Liberal Democrats.

The Parliament was opened by the Queen on 1 July 1999.

Devolved Powers

The Parliament has "legislative competence" to make primary legislation – Acts of the Scottish Parliament – on a wide range of devolved matters, including:

Agriculture	Health
Economic development	Housing
Education	Local government
Environment	Planning
Fisheries	Social work
Food standards	Transport (some aspects)
Forestry	Tourism

Acts of the Scottish Parliament will require to comply with rights under the European Convention on Human Rights and with European community law.

Reserved Powers

The UK Parliament continues to be the sovereign parliament of the UK and retains the power to legislate about any matter. However, a convention is expected to be established that the UK Parliament will not normally legislate on devolved matters in Scotland without the consent of the Scottish Parliament.

The Scottish Parliament will not be able to legislate about certain reserved matters, including: the constitution; defence; foreign affairs; electricity, coal, oil and gas, nuclear energy; employment; financial and economic affairs; social security.

There are provisions in the Scotland Act to ensure that the Scottish Parliament can legislate on devolved matters even if this has an ancillary effect on reserved matters. The Parliament can also legislate to apply certain general rules of Scots law consistently to reserved and devolved matters. Questions about whether the Scottish Parliament can legislate about a matter can be referred to the judicial committee of the Privy Council.

The UK Government has a limited power to intervene to prevent the submission of a Scottish bill for royal assent if it has reasonable grounds to believe that it contains provisions which would be incompatible with an international obligation, or the interests of defence or national security, or that it would have an adverse effect on the operation of the law as it applies to reserved matters.

The Scottish Executive

The Scottish Parliament nominates one of its number to be the First Minister, who is appointed by the Queen. With the Parliament's agreement, the First Minister in turn appoints or nominates to the Queen the other members of the Scottish Executive.

The Scottish Executive is the government of Scotland for all devolved matters. The members of the Executive, collectively referred to as "the Scottish Ministers" are:

The First Minister (Donald Dewar); the Lord Advocate and the Solicitor General for Scotland (the Scottish Law Officers); and other ministers appointed by the First Minister. The First Minister also appoints junior ministers to assist the Scottish Ministers.

The Scottish Parliament and the Scottish Executive assumed their full powers on 1 July 1999. On that date, the powers and duties exercised by UK ministers in Scotland relating to devolved matters transferred to the Scottish Ministers.

The Permanent Secretary to the Scottish Executive is Muir Russell.

Secretary of State for Scotland

Before devolution, the Secretary of State for Scotland was responsible to the UK Parliament for the operations of the Scottish Office, which formerly discharged most of the functions of the UK government in Scotland, excluding defence, foreign policy, taxation, and social security. After devolution, a Secretary of State continues to be appointed as a member of the UK Government. He or she is not a member of the Scottish Executive but remains a member of the UK cabinet, representing Scottish interests in matters that are reserved to the UK Parliament.

Programme for Government

In autumn 1999, the Scottish Executive published its programme for government. Included are the following commitments, each with a target date for accomplishment:

Advertising
Ban tobacco advertising, end 1999

Agriculture
Package of measures to "assist the integration of agriculture with a wider and more diverse rural economy", early 2000
Introduce independent appeals mechanism for farmers suffering penalties in relation to EU subsidy claims, autumn 2000

Business
Introduce business mentoring scheme, 2000
Set up the Scottish University for Industry, 2000
Develop a manufacturing strategy and start to implement it, 2000
Support the establishment of a Scottish Institute of Enterprise, 2001, to encourage the transformation of ideas from laboratories into successful businesses
Create 100,000 new Scottish businesses, 2009

Childcare
Set up a new National Childcare Information Line, end 1999
Set up a new independent regulatory body to ensure high quality care for children, 2001
Ensure a nursery place for every 3-year-old whose parents want it, 2002
Out of school care places for 100,000 children, 2003

Community Care
Introduce a Carers' Strategy to help unpaid carers, 2000

Culture
National Culture Strategy, summer 2000

Drugs
Set up a Scottish Drug Enforcement Agency to target dealers and the supply of drugs, summer 2000

Education
Increase student numbers by 42,000, 2002
Double loan funding for mature part-time students on low incomes, 2001

Environment
New urban wastewater treatment systems in Edinburgh and Glasgow, end 2000

Food and food standards
Introduce a Butchers' Licensing Scheme for Scotland, 2000
New schemes to help Scottish food and drink industry, autumn 2000

Football
Set up a Scottish Football Academy, 2002

Health
Launch Scottish NHS Direct to provide 24-hour telephone health advice service, early 2000
Create network of Healthy Living Centres to improve health in areas of poverty and deprivation, 2002

Hospitals
Ensure that patients know the time of their hospital appointment before leaving their local surgery, 2002
Launch walk-in/walk-out hospitals in which patients will be assessed and treated by specialist staff offering same day treatment, 2002
80 One-Stop Clinics where patients will get diagnosis and treatment in the same day, 2002
Deliver biggest-ever hospital building programme in Scotland and provide 8 major new modern hospital developments, 2003

Housing
Empty Homes Initiative to bring 900 empty houses back into use for people in need, 2000
Three-year programme to build 18,000 houses for affordable renting or low-cost owner occupation, 2002
New accommodation and better support services for homeless so that "no one has to sleep rough", 2003
Large-scale investment to improve council houses through schemes to encourage community ownership, 2003
Improve 100,000 houses suffering from dampness and condensation through Healthy Homes Initiative, 2003

Land
Legislation to abolish feudal tenure, 1999
Legislation to provide a community right of purchase when land comes to be sold, spring 2000
Legislation to provide a right of responsible access to the land, spring 2000
Legislation to modernise crofting tenure, autumn 2000

Local Government
Set up Community Leadership Forum to encourage modernisation of local government, end 1999
Set up Scottish Standards Commission and a code of conduct for local government, summer 2000

Museums
Free admission to National Museums of Scotland, spring 2001

National Parks
Establish first National Park for Scotland, in Loch Lomond and the Trossachs, summer 2001

Policing
Use information technology to free up police officers for front-line duties and develop a Scottish Police Information Strategy, end 1999

Poverty
New Social Inclusion Partnerships supporting the regeneration of Scotland's most deprived neighbourhoods, end 1999
60,000 children "raised out of poverty", 2002

Schools
New framework for continuing professional development of teachers, 2000
Reduce class sizes in P1, P2 and P3 to 30 or fewer, summer 2001
60 new Community Schools, 2002
1,000 additional teachers and 5,000 classroom assistants, 2002
e-mail address for every school child, 2002
Build or substantially renovate 100 schools, 2003
Four modern computers for each class, 2003
Personal Learning Plan for every school age child, 2003

Skills
Initiate a Scottish Labour Market Unit to highlight the skills the country needs, end 1999
Create 20,000 Modern Apprenticeships, 2003

Stalking
Review the law on harassment and stalking, 2001

Transport
Legislation to invest in transport and encourage bus use, early 2000
Implement national transport timetable system, end 2000
Public Transport Fund to provide alternatives to car use, 1999-2002
Increase Freight Facilities Grant with aim of moving freight off the roads, spring 2002

Ministers of the Scottish Executive

First Minister
Donald Dewar, MP, MSP
Ministerial responsibilities
Head of the Scottish Executive. With the Deputy First Minister, responsible for the development, implementation and presentation of Scottish Executive policies.
Biographical notes
Labour Member for Glasgow Anniesland; b 1937, Glasgow; educ Glasgow Academy and Glasgow University; divorced; 1 son, 1 daughter; lives in Glasgow; before entering (UK) Parliament, practised as a solicitor in Glasgow; MP, Aberdeen South, 1966-70, and Glasgow Garscadden, since 1978; Opposition Spokesman on Scottish Affairs, 1981-92, and Social Security, 1992-95; Secretary of State for Scotland, since 1997.

Deputy First Minister and Minister for Justice
Jim Wallace, QC, MP, MSP
Ministerial responsibilities
With the First Minister, responsible for the development, implementation and presentation of Scottish Executive policies. Responsible for Home Affairs, including civil law and criminal justice, criminal justice social work services, police, fire, prisons and courts, law reform, land reform policy and freedom of information.
Biographical notes
Liberal Democrat Member for Orkney; b 1954, Annan; educ Annan Academy, Downing College Cambridge, and Edinburgh University; married; 2 daughters; lives in Orkney; called to the Scottish Bar, 1979; MP, Orkney and Shetland, since 1983.

Minister for Enterprise and Lifelong Learning
Henry McLeish, MP, MSP
Ministerial responsibilities
Responsible for the economy, business and industry, including Scottish Enterprise, Highlands and Islands Enterprise, tourism, trade and inward investment, further and higher education, science, lifelong learning, training and delivery of the New Deal.
Biographical notes
Labour Member for Fife Central; b 1948, Methil; educ Buckhaven High School and Heriot-Watt University; married; 1 son, 1 daughter, 1 step-son, 1 step-daughter; former research officer, Social Work Department, Edinburgh Corporation; elected to Kirkcaldy District Council, 1973, and Fife Regional Council, 1978; Leader, Fife Regional Council, 1982-87; MP, Fife Central, since 1987; former Minister of State, Scottish Office.

Minister for Children and Education
Sam Galbraith, MP, MSP, FRCS(Glas)
Ministerial responsibilities
Responsible for pre-school and school education, children and young people, culture and the arts, the built heritage, architecture, sport and lottery funding.
Biographical notes
Labour Member for Strathkelvin and Bearsden; b 1945, Clitheroe; married; 3 children; educ Greenock High School and Glasgow University; before entering (UK) Parliament, was a consultant in neurosurgery with Greater Glasgow Health Board, 1978-87; MP, Strathkelvin and Bearsden, since 1987; former Minister for Health, Social Work, Sport, the Arts and Children, Scottish Office.

Minister for Finance
Jack McConnell, MSP
Ministerial responsibilities
Responsible for the Scottish budget, including local government finance, resource allocation and accounting; for modernising government; and for assisting the First Minister and Deputy First Minister on the development and co-ordination of Scottish Executive policy.
Biographical notes
Labour Member for Motherwell and Wishaw; b 1960, Irvine; married; 1 son; 1 daughter; educ Arran High School and Stirling University; teacher of mathematics, 1983-92; Member, Stirling District Council, 1984-92, Leader of the Council, 1990-92; General Secretary, Scottish Labour Party, 1992-98.

Minister for Health and Community Care
Susan Deacon, MSP
Ministerial responsibilities
Responsible for health policy, the National Health Service in Scotland, community care, and food safety.
Biographical notes
Labour Member for Edinburgh East and Musselburgh; aged 35; b Musselburgh; lives in Musselburgh with partner and 1 daughter; educ Musselburgh Grammar School and Edinburgh University; former research officer, West Lothian District Council and East Lothian District Council; became a senior training consultant, 1994, before joining the Edinburgh Business School at Heriot-Watt University as Director of MBA programmes.

Minister for Rural Affairs
Ross Finnie, MSP
Ministerial responsibilities
Responsible for policy in relation to rural development, including agriculture, fisheries and forestry.

Biographical notes
Liberal Democrat Member for West of Scotland; b 1947, Greenock; educ Greenock Academy; married; 1 son; 1 daughter; chartered accountant; Member, Inverclyde District Council and Inverclyde Council, 1977-99; Chairman, Scottish Liberal Party, 1982-86.

Minister for Communities
Wendy Alexander, MSP
Ministerial responsibilities
Responsible for social inclusion, local government, and housing. Lead responsibility for Scottish Executive policy on equality issues and the voluntary sector.
Biographical notes
Labour Member for Paisley North; b 1963, Glasgow; educ Park Mains High School (Erskine), Glasgow University, Warwick University, INSEAD Business School, France; worked as a management consultant, Europe, America, and Asia; also worked as a research officer for the Labour Party; former Special Adviser to Secretary of State for Scotland.

Minister for Transport and the Environment
Sarah Boyack, MSP
Ministerial responsibilities
Responsible for transport, including the development of integrated transport policies for rural areas, the environment, natural heritage, sustainable development, strategic environmental assessments, and land-use planning.
Biographical notes
Labour Member for Edinburgh Central; aged 38; lecturer in planning; former Convener, Royal Town Planning Institute, Scotland, and chaired its women's panel; Scottish Co-ordinator, Socialist Environmental Resource Association; Chair, National Organisation of Labour Students, 1985; Board Member, Scottish Centre for Public Policy.

Minister for Parliament
Tom McCabe, MSP
Ministerial responsibilities
Responsible for Parliamentary affairs and the management of Executive business in the Parliament.
Biographical notes
Labour Member for Hamilton South; b 1954, Hamilton; educ St Martin's Secondary School, Hamilton, and Bell College of Technology; former welfare rights officer; Leader, Hamilton District Council, 1992-96, and of South Lanarkshire Council, 1996-99; former Board Member, Lanarkshire Development Agency; former Convener, Strathclyde Joint Fire Board.

Junior Ministers of the Scottish Executive

Deputy Minister for Justice
Angus MacKay, MSP
Ministerial responsibilities
Deputy to the Minister of Justice with particular responsibility for land reform and co-ordination of policy on drugs.
Biographical notes
Labour Member for Edinburgh South; b 1964, Edinburgh; educ St Augustine's High School; degree in politics and modern history; elected Member, City of Edinburgh Council, 1995.

Deputy Minister for Enterprise and Lifelong Learning
Nicol Stephen, MSP
Ministerial responsibilities
Deputy to the Minister for Enterprise and Lifelong Learning, with particular responsibility for training, further and higher education.
Biographical notes
Liberal Democrat Member for Aberdeen South; b 1960; educ Robert Gordon's College, Aberdeen, Aberdeen University and Edinburgh University; married; 2 children; qualified as a solicitor; Member, Grampian Regional Council, 1982-92; MP, Kincardine and Deeside, 1991-92.

Deputy Minister for Highlands and Islands and Gaelic
Alasdair Morrison, MSP
Ministerial responsibilities
Deputy to the Minister for Enterprise and Lifelong Learning, with particular responsibility for Highlands and Highlands Enterprise, University of the Highlands and Islands, tourism, and Gaelic.
Biographical notes
Labour Member for Western Isles; former journalist, BBC Stornoway, and editor, An Gaidheal Ur.

Deputy Minister for Children and Education
Peter Peacock, CBE, MSP
Ministerial responsibilities
Deputy to the Minister for Children and Education, with particular responsibility for pre-school and school education, children and young people.
Biographical notes
Labour Member for Highlands and Islands; b 1952, Edinburgh; married; 2 sons; educ Hawick High School, Jordanhill College of Education; former community worker; former area officer, Citizens Advice Bureau; self-employed consultant; elected to Highland Regional Council, 1982; Convener, Highland Council.

Deputy Minister for Culture and Sport
Rhona Brankin, MSP
Ministerial responsibilities
Deputy to the Minister for Children and Education, with particular responsibility for culture and the arts, the built heritage, architecture, sport and lottery funding.
Biographical notes
Labour Member for Midlothian; educ Aberdeen University; former teacher and lecturer on educational needs; former Chair, Scottish Labour Party.

Deputy Minister for Community Care
Iain Gray, MSP
Ministerial responsibilities
Deputy to the Minister for Health and Community Care, with particular responsibility for community care.
Biographical notes
Labour Member for Edinburgh Pentlands; b 1957, Edinburgh; educ Inverness Royal Academy and George Watson's College, Edinburgh; degree in physics; twice married; 1 daughter; 2 step-daughters; former school teacher; worked for Oxfam, 12 years.

Deputy Minister for Rural Affairs
John Home Robertson, MSP
Ministerial responsibilities
Deputy to the Minister for Rural Affairs, with particular responsibility for fisheries, forestry and research. Assists the Minister for Rural Affairs on policy in relation to rural development.
Biographical notes
Labour Member for East Lothian; b 1948, Edinburgh; educ Ampleforth

College and West of Scotland Agricultural College; married; 2 sons; MP, East Lothian, since 1983; former MP, Berwick and East Lothian; former Opposition Whip.

Deputy Minister for Local Government
Frank McAveety, MSP
Ministerial responsibilities
Deputy to the Minister for Communities, with particular responsibility for local government.
Biographical notes
Labour Member for Glasgow Shettleston; b 1962, Glasgow; educ Strathclyde University; married; 1 son, 1 daughter; secondary school teacher, 1984-98; Member, Glasgow District Council, 1988-95, Glasgow City Council, 1995-99; youngest-ever Leader of the Council.

Deputy Minister for Communities
Jackie Baillie, MSP
Ministerial responsibilities
Deputy to the Minister for Communities, with particular responsibility for social inclusion and for co-ordination of Executive policy on equality and the voluntary sector.
Biographical notes
Labour Member for Dumbarton; b 1964, Hong Kong; educ St Anne's School, Windermere, Cumbernauld College, Strathclyde University; married; 1 daughter; former community economic development manager, Dunbartonshire District Council; former resource centre manager, Strathkelvin District Council.

Deputy Minister for Parliament
Iain Smith, MSP
Ministerial responsibilities
Deputy to the Minister for Parliament, with particular responsibility for the Parliamentary handling of the legislative programme.
Biographical notes
Liberal Democrat Member for North East Fife; b 1992; educ Newcastle University; elected Member, Fife Regional Council, 1992; former advice centre manager.

Law Officers

Lord Advocate
Rt Hon Lord Hardie (Andrew Rutherford Hardie), QC
Lord Advocate, since 1997; b 1946, Alloa; educ St Modan's High School, Stirling, and Edinburgh University; married; 2 sons, 1 daughter; Member, Faculty of Advocates, since 1973; Advocate Depute, 1979-83; Dean, Faculty of Advocates, 1994-97.
Solicitor General for Scotland
Colin Boyd, QC
Solicitor General for Scotland, since 1997; b 1953, Falkirk; educ Wick High School, George Watson's College (Edinburgh), Manchester University, Edinburgh University; married; 2 sons, 1 daughter; Solicitor, 1978-82; called to the Bar, 1983; Advocate Depute, 1993-95.

Presiding Officers of the Scottish Parliament

Presiding Officer
Rt Hon Sir David Steel, KBE, MSP
Liberal Democrat Member for Lothians; b 1938, Kirkcaldy; educ George Watson's College, Edinburgh, and Edinburgh University; married; 3 children; former MP for Roxburgh, Selkirk and Peebles and, later, Tweeddale, Ettrick and Lauderdale; Leader of the Liberal Party, 1976-88; returned to (UK) Parliament, 1997, as Lord Steel of Aikwood.

Deputy Presiding Officer
George Reid, MSP
Scottish National Party Member for Mid Scotland and Fife; b 1939, Tullibody; married; 2 daughters; former MP, Clackmannan and East Stirling; journalist and television producer; former Director of Public Affairs, Intrenational Red Cross.

Deputy Presiding Officer
Patricia Ferguson, MSP
Labour Member for Glasgow Maryhill; b 1958, Glasgow; educ Garnethill Convent Secondary School, Glasgow; married.

Departments of the Scottish Executive

Development Department

Address: Victoria Quay, Edinburgh EH6 6QQ
Telephone: 0131-556 8400
Head of Department: John Graham

Administers a wide range of Government responsibilities, including social inclusion, housing and area regeneration, local government finance, land use planning, building control, European Structural Funds management, roads and transport, and planning and building control. The department (SEDD) also provides economic and statistical advice for various parts of the Scottish Executive.

SEDD's primary housing aim is to ensure an adequate supply of housing in Scotland, in particular by encouraging private finance. The department sponsors Scottish Homes, the national housing agency. SEDD provides advice and guidance to local authorities and other housing agencies on securing an adequate supply of housing for community care groups as part of the Government's policy for Care in the Community, and for homeless people in priority need. Improvements in Scotland's housing stock are promoted through targeting local authority and Scottish Homes resources. SEDD promotes improvements in housing management and in rights of tenants.

SEDD is responsible for social inclusion policies, including area regeneration: i.e., the economic, social and environmental improvement of disadvantaged urban areas. The department manages the Social Inclusion Partnership, a special grant scheme.

It is further responsible for developing and administering policy on local government: its structure, powers, conduct and finance (including Council Tax and non-domestic rates). SEDD sponsors the Local Government Boundary Commission for Scotland and the Accounts Commission for Scotland.

SEDD advises the First Minister on national planning guidance and advice, local authority structure plans, and on development proposals of national importance, and deals with planning appeals. It is also responsible for policies on building control which ensure that the construction, use and demolition of buildings pose no threat to health and safety.

SEDD has responsibility for transport policy in Scotland, including the trunk road network, and shipping and air services in the Highlands and Islands.

It provides economic advice and statistical information to some other departments in the Scottish Executive, and prepares the Scottish Abstract of Statistics and other economic and statistical publications.

Education Department

Address: Victoria Quay, Edinburgh EH6 6QQ
Telephone: 0131-556 8400
Head of Department: John Elvidge

Administers Government policy for education, children and young people, and arts, culture and sport.

SEED promotes a high-quality education service in schools and administers Government policy for school education in co-operation with local authorities, which are responsible for providing school education in their areas. It gives guidance on the content of education and on the key elements in initial teacher-education courses, seeking to match the supply of teachers to demand.

The department funds the Scottish Council for Educational Technology, a non-departmental public body which promotes the application of new technology in education and training. It works closely with the Superhighways Task Force in taking forward Government initiatives in information and communications technologies in education.

Just over £1m is spent annually on directly commissioned policy-related research. The Scottish Council for Research in Education is also contracted to provide national services in educational research.

HM Inspectorate of Schools, a distinct part of the department, has responsibility for promoting quality assurance within the education system as a whole. HM Senior Chief Inspector is the principal professional adviser on education to ministers. HMI inspect and report across a wide range of educational establishments and education services, from pre-school to aspects of teacher education, higher education and community education services.

SEED administers government policy for pre-school and nursery education, childcare, social work and legal provision for young people, including youth justice. It funds the Scottish Children's Reporter Administration, a non-departmental public body which administers the Children's Hearing system for young offenders. The department also administers the development of community education, youth work, community development and community-based adult education. It administers a grant scheme to support national voluntary organisations in the community education sector and funds the Scottish Community Education Council, a non-departmental public body which is responsible for the promotion and development of community education in both the statutory and voluntary sectors.

The Chief Social Work Inspector is ministers' principal professional adviser on social work services. He co-ordinates and manages the work of the Social Work Services Inspectorate across all departments of the Scottish Executive, reporting annually to the Scottish Parliament on the performance and quality of these services. The Inspectorate is also responsible for policy and development of social work training and education, and of workforce regulation. Social Work Services Inspectorate staff in the department are responsible for professional advice and inspection of social work services for children and young people. Staff in other departments provide advice and inspection of community care and criminal justice services.

SEED encourages the development of the arts and architecture, cultural and built heritage, and sports and recreation. It funds the National Galleries, National Library and National Museums of Scotland, and provides funds to support the work of the Scottish Arts Council, Scottish Screen, Sport Scotland, and a wide range of other bodies including the Scottish Museums Council. The department is also responsible for architectural policy, policy on Gaelic and on Scottish broadcasting. Historic Scotland, an executive agency, is responsible for care of, and public access to, public monuments and historic buildings.

Another executive agency, the Scottish Public Pensions Agency, administers pension arrangements for some 370,000 people, mainly NHS and teaching service employees and pensioners.

Enterprise and Lifelong Learning Department

Address: Meridian Court, Cadogan Street, Glasgow G2 6AT
Telephone: 0141-248 4774
Head of Department: Eddie Frizzell

Administers Government policy for industry and energy issues, enterprise and tourism, delivery of the New Deal, lifelong learning and higher and further education, work-based training and careers guidance.

Through the Scottish Further Education Funding Council and the Scottish Higher Education Funding Council, the department pays grants to further and higher education institutions in Scotland.

One of the department's agencies – the Student Awards Agency for Scotland – is also responsible for administering grants and loans for Scottish-domiciled students in higher education. Further information on the agency can be found at www.student-support-saas.gov.uk

The department (SEELLD) promotes quality standards in further and higher education institutions to meet the needs of individuals, society and employers.

SEELLD is also concerned with general policy towards industry, and it is through the department that the First Minister carries out his statutory responsibilities for Scottish Enterprise and Highlands and Islands Enterprise. The department takes a special interest in measures to stimulate the growth of business, including start-ups, innovation, the knowledge economy, and technology transfer, and supports trade activity and export promotion through Scottish Trade International. The department co-operates with Scottish Enterprise in sponsoring Locate in

Scotland, which aims to attract inward investment.

SEELLD carries out the First Minister's responsibilities for energy policy. The department is also responsible for the work of the Scottish Tourist Board.

Health Department

Address: St Andrew's House, Regent Road, Edinburgh EH1 3DG
Telephone: 0131-556 8400
Chief Executive: Geoff Scaife

Responsible for health policy and the administration of the National Health Service in Scotland.

The Chief Executive of the Scottish Executive Health Department leads the central management of the NHS, is accountable to ministers for the efficiency and performance of the service, and heads a Management Executive which oversees the work of 15 area health boards responsible for planning health services for people in their area, and 28 self-governing NHS Trusts responsible for providing services to patients and to the community.

The Public Health Policy Unit of the Health Department is responsible for promoting the health of the people of Scotland.

The department has a further responsibility for the State Hospital, which cares for patients who require treatment under conditions of special security, and the Health Education Board for Scotland, which promotes positive attitudes to health and encourages healthy lifestyles.

It is also responsible for social work policy and in particular for community care and voluntary issues.

Justice Department

Address: Saughton House, Broomhouse Drive, Edinburgh EH11 3XD
Telephone: 0131-556 8400
Head of Department: Hamish Hamill, CB

Brings together the Scottish Office Home Department and the Scottish Court Administration. Responsible for: police and fire services; criminal justice, including criminal justice social work; aspects of civil law; courts administration; legal aid; liaison with the legal profession in Scotland.

The department (SEJD), in partnership with chief constables and local police authorities, discharges the First Minister's responsibilities for administration of an efficient police service, including provision of training at the Scottish Police College. It has similar responsibilities for the fire service, including provision of training at the Scottish Fire Service Training School. The department promotes emergency planning by both government and local authorities, and co-ordinates preparation for civil emergencies.

SEJD is responsible for criminal justice policy and procedure in Scotland, including the early release of prisoners, and such civil law matters as matrimonial and family law, policy on victims of crime, and regulation of charities.

It is further responsible for the legal aid system and aspects of the work of District Courts. It supports the operations of a number of courts and tribunals, including the Scottish Land Court and the VAT and Duties Tribunal. It also has a role in administering the system of appointments of the judiciary in Scotland (other than appointments to the District Courts).

The department deals with electoral procedures, including registration of electors, and with Royal, church and ceremonial matters.

There are two agencies within the department: the Scottish Prison Service, which was established as an executive agency in 1993, and the Scottish Court Service, which was established as an executive agency in 1995.

Rural Affairs Department

Address: Pentland House, 47 Robb's Loan, Edinburgh EH14 1TY
Telephone: 0131-556 8400
Head of Department: John Graham

Responsible for advising ministers on United Kingdom and European Community policy relating to agriculture, environment issues and fisheries, and for the implementation of those policies in Scotland.

The department's main aim is to help improve the economic performance of Scotland's agriculture, fishing, and food industries while safeguarding the interests of consumers, protecting the environment, and ensuring a fair deal for taxpayers. The department (SERAD) also helps to promote agricultural, biological and environmental research.

SERAD works for the effective implementation of EC Common Agricultural Policy and Common Fisheries Policy obligations, and promotes further reform of these policies.

The department is responsible for assisting the development and structural adjustment of the agriculture, aquaculture and fishing industries; developing conservation measures to protect fish stocks; and taking action against plant diseases and pests, and animal and fish diseases. It also encourages high animal welfare standards on farms and in transport.

SERAD aims to protect and enhance the environment by promoting environmentally sensitive farming, farm woodlands and sustainable development, by securing the conservation and enhancement of Scotland's natural heritage and by improving scientific understanding of our terrestrial and aquatic environment.

The department is responsible for ensuring that UK and EC objectives for pollution control and drinking water are met, including appropriate control over the use and disposal of radioactive substances, and the regulation of environmental aspects of nuclear installations.

It further aims to promote the well-being of Scotland's countryside by protecting the rural economy, particularly remote communities and less favoured areas. The department is responsible for supporting an appropriate balance of development and conservation, for securing the active involvement of all members of rural communities, and for encouraging a wider appreciation of natural heritage.

The department aims to support the core research work of Government-funded research agencies and a programme of research commissioned on a competitive basis.

In addition to the six main departments, the Scottish Executive has three other departments:

Corporate Services
Principal Establishment Officer: Colin MacDonald
Provides central support for Ministers and staff of the Executive, covering such matters as human resources, employee relations, training and development, equal opportunities, accommodation and estate management, communications and information, and security.

Executive Secretariat
Chief Executive: Robert Gordon
Responsible for parliamentary liaison and co-ordination of relations with the UK Government and Europe. Provides support to the Scottish Cabinet.

Addresses:
St Andrew's House
Regent Road, Edinburgh EH1 3DG
Telephone: 0131-556 8400

Scottish Executive EU Office
6 Rond Point Schuman
1040 Brussels
Telephone: +32.2.282.83.20

Finance Department
Head of Group: Dr Peter Collings
Advises Ministers on the allocation of the Scottish budget. Advises other departments on financial matters, and issues guidance to the Executive, non-departmental public bodies, and other public bodies on propriety and regularity in financial affairs. It includes the internal audit of the Executive.

The Scottish Parliamentary Constituencies

May 1999

CENTRAL SCOTLAND

AIRDRIE AND SHOTTS
Electorate 58,481 Poll 56.79%

K Whitefield, Lab	18,338
G Paterson, SNP	9,353
P Ross-Taylor, Con	3,177
D Miller, LD	2,345
Lab majority	8,985

COATBRIDGE AND CHRYSTON
Electorate 52,178 Poll 57.87%

E Smith, Lab	17,923
P Kearney, SNP	7,519
G Lind, Con	2,867
J Hook, LD	1,889
Lab majority	10,404

CUMBERNAULD AND KILSYTH
Electorate 49,395 Poll 61.97%

C Craigie, Lab	15,182
A Wilson, SNP	10,923
H O'Donnell, LD	2,029
R Slack, Con	1,362
K McEwan, SSP	1,116
Lab majority	4,259

EAST KILBRIDE
Electorate 66,111 Poll 62.49%

A Kerr, Lab	19,987
L Fabiani, SNP	13,488
C Stevenson, Con	4,465
E Hawthorn, LD	3,373
Lab majority	6,499

FALKIRK EAST
Electorate 57,345 Poll 61.40%

C Peattie, Lab	15,721
K Brown, SNP	11,582
A Orr, Con	3,399
G McDonald, LD	2,509
R Stead	1643
Others	358
Lab majority	4,139

FALKIRK WEST
Electorate 53,404 Poll 63.04%

D Canavan, Falkirk W	18,511
R Martin, Lab	6,319
M Matheson, SNP	5,986
G Miller, Con	1,897
A Smith, LD	954
Falkirk W majority	12,192

HAMILTON NORTH AND BELLSHILL
Electorate 53,992 Poll 57.82%

M McMahon, Lab	15,227
K McAlorum, SNP	9,621
S Thomson, Con	3,199
J Struthers, LD	2,105
K McGavigan, Soc Lab	1,064
Lab majority	5,606

HAMILTON SOUTH
Electorate 46,765 Poll 55.43%

T McCabe, Lab	14,098
A Ardrey, SNP	6,922
M Mitchell, Con	2,918
J Oswald, LD	1,982
Lab majority	7,176

KILMARNOCK AND LOUDOUN
Electorate 61,454 Poll 64.03%

M Jamieson, Lab	17,345
A Neil, SNP	14,585
L McIntosh, Con	4,589
J Stewart, LD	2,830
Lab majority	2,760

MOTHERWELL AND WISHAW
Electorate 52,613 Poll 57.71%

J McConnell, Lab	13,955
J McGuigan, SNP	8,879
W Gibson, Con	3,694
J Milligan, Soc Lab	1,941
R Spillane, LD	1,895
Lab majority	5,076

ADDITIONAL MEMBERS ELECTED BY PR
L McIntosh, Con
D Gorrie, LD
A Neil, SNP
M Matheson, SNP
L Fabiani, SNP
A Wilson, SNP
G Paterson, SNP

GLASGOW

GLASGOW ANNIESLAND
Electorate 54,378 Poll 52.37%

D Dewar, Lab	16,749
K Stewart, SNP	5,756
W Aitken, Con	3,032
I Brown, LD	1,804
A Lynch, SSP	1,000
Others	139
Lab majority	10,993

GLASGOW BAILLIESTON
Electorate 49,068 Poll 48.32%

M Curran, Lab	11,289
D Elder, SNP	8,217
J McVicar, SSP	1,864
K Pickering, Con	1,526
J Fryer, LD	813
Lab majority	3,072

GLASGOW CATHCART
Electorate 51,338 Poll 52.55%

M Watson, Lab	12,966
M Whitehead, SNP	7,592
M Leishman, Con	3,311
C Dick, LD	2,187
Others	920
Lab majority	5,374

GLASGOW GOVAN
Electorate 53,257 Poll 49.52%

G Jackson, Lab	11,421
N Sturgeon, SNP	9,665
T Ahmed-Sheikh, Con	2,343
M Aslam Khan, LD	1,479
C McCarthy, SSP	1,275
Others	190
Lab majority	1,756

GLASGOW KELVIN
Electorate 61,207 Poll 46.34%

P McNeill, Lab	12,711
S White, SNP	8,303
M Craig, LD	3,720
A Rasul, Con	2,253
H Ritchie, SSP	1,375
Lab majority	4,408

GLASGOW MARYHILL
Electorate 56,469 Poll 40.75%

P Ferguson, Lab	11,455
B Wilson, SNP	7,129
C Hamblen, LD	1,793
G Scott, SSP	1,439
M Fry, Con	1,194
Lab majority	4,326

GLASGOW POLLOK
Electorate 47,970 Poll 54.37%

J Lamont, Lab Co-op	11,405
K Gibson, SNP	6,763
T Sheridan, SSP	5,611
R O'Brien, Con	1,370
J King, LD	931
Lab Co-op majority	4,642

GLASGOW RUTHERGLEN
Electorate 51,012 Poll 56.89%

J Hughes, Lab	13,442
T Chalmers, SNP	6,155
R Brown, LD	5,798
I Stewart, Con	2,315
W Bonnar, SSP	832
Others	481
Lab majority	7,287

GLASGOW SHETTLESTON
Electorate 50,592 Poll 40.58%

F McAveety, Lab Co-op	11,078
J Byrne, SNP	5,611
R Kane, SSP	1,640
C Bain, Con	1,260
L Clarke, LD	943
Lab Co-op majority	5,467

GLASGOW SPRINGBURN
Electorate 55,670 Poll 43.77%

P Martin, Lab	14,268
J Brady, SNP	6,375
M Roxburgh, Con	1,293
M Dunnigan, LD	1,288
J Friel, SSP	1,141
Lab majority	7,893

ADDITIONAL MEMBERS ELECTED BY PR
W Aitken, Con
R Brown, LD
D Elder, SNP
S White, SNP
N Sturgeon, SNP
K Gibson, SNP
T Sheridan, SSP

HIGHLANDS AND ISLANDS

ARGYLL AND BUTE
Electorate 49,609 Poll 64.86%

G Lyon, LD	11,226
D Hamilton, SNP	9,169
H Raven, Lab	6,470
D Petrie, Con	5,312
LD majority	2,057

CAITHNESS, SUTHERLAND AND EASTER ROSS
Electorate 41,581 Poll 62.60%

J Stone, LD	10,691
J Hendry, Lab	6,300
J Urquhart, SNP	6,035
R Jenkins, Con	2,167
Others	836
LD majority	4,391

INVERNESS EAST, NAIRN AND LOCHABER
Electorate 66,285 Poll 63.10%

F Ewing, SNP	13,825
J Aitken, Lab	13,384
D Fraser, LD	8,508
M Scanlon, Con	6,107
SNP majority	441

MORAY
Electorate 58,388 Poll 57.50%

M Ewing, SNP	13,027
A Farquharson, Lab	8,898
A Findlay, Con	8,595
P Kenton, LD	3,056
SNP majority	4,129

ORKNEY
Electorate 15,658 Poll 56.95%

J Wallace, LD	6,010
C Zawadzki, Con	1,391
J Mowat, SNP	917
A Macleod, Lab	600
LD majority	4,619

ROSS, SKYE AND INVERNESS WEST
Electorate 55,845 Poll 63.42%

J Farquhar-Munro, LD	11,652
D Munro, Lab	10,113
J Mather, SNP	7,997
J Scott, Con	3,351
D Briggs, Ind	2,302
LD majority	1,539

SHETLAND
Electorate 16,978 Poll 58.77%

T Scott, LD	5,435
J Wills, Lab	2,241
W Ross, SNP	1,430
G Robinson, Con	872
LD majority	3,194

WESTERN ISLES
Electorate 22,412 Poll 62.26%

A Morrison, Lab	7,248
A Nicholson, SNP	5,155
J MacGrigor, Con	1,095
J Horne, LD	456
Lab majority	2,093

ADDITIONAL MEMBERS ELECTED BY PR
J MacGrigor, Con
M Scanlon, Con
M MacMillan, Lab
P Peacock, Lab
R Grant, Lab
W Ewing, SNP
D Hamilton, SNP

LOTHIANS

EDINBURGH CENTRAL
Electorate 65,945 Poll 56.73%

S Boyack, Lab	14,224
I McKee, SNP	9,598
A Myles, LD	6,187
J Low, Con	6,018
K Williamson, SSP	830
Others	555
Lab majority	4,626

EDINBURGH EAST AND MUSSELBURGH
Electorate 60,167 Poll 61.48%

S Deacon, Lab	17,086
K MacAskill, SNP	10,372
J Balfour, Con	4,600
M Thomas, LD	4,100
D White, SSP	697
Others	134
Lab majority	6,714

EDINBURGH NORTH AND LEITH
Electorate 62,976 Poll 58.19%

M Chisholm, Lab	17,203

A Dana, SNP	9,467
J Sempill, Con	5,030
S Tombs, LD	4,039
R Brown, SSP	907
Lab majority	7,736

EDINBURGH PENTLANDS
Electorate 60,029 Poll 65.97%

I Gray, Lab	14,343
D McLetchie, Con	11,458
S Gibb, SNP	8,770
I Gibson, LD	5,029
Lab majority	2,885

EDINBURGH SOUTH
Electorate 64,100 Poll 62.61%

A MacKay, Lab	14,869
M MacDonald, SNP	9,445
M Pringle, LD	8,961
I Whyte, Con	6,378
Others	482
Lab majority	5,424

EDINBURGH WEST
Electorate 61,747 Poll 67.34%

M Smith, LD	15,161
J Douglas-Hamilton, Con	10,578
C Fox, Lab	8,860
G Sutherland, SNP	6,984
LD majority	4,583

LINLITHGOW
Electorate 54,262 Poll 62.26%

M Mulligan, Lab	15,247
S Stevenson, SNP	12,319
G Lindhurst, Con	3,158
J Barrett, LD	2,643
Others	415
Lab majority	2,928

LIVINGSTON
Electorate 62,060 Poll 58.93%

B Muldoon, Lab	17,313
G McCarra, SNP	13,409
D Younger, Con	3,014
M Oliver, LD	2,834
Lab majority	3,904

MIDLOTHIAN
Electorate 48,374 Poll 61.51%

R Brankin, Lab Co-op	14,467
A Robertson, SNP	8,942
J Elder, LD	3,184

G Turnbull, Con	2,544
Others	618
Lab Co-op majority	5,525

ADDITIONAL MEMBERS ELECTED BY PR
J Douglas-Hamilton, Con
D McLetchie, Con
D Steel, LD
K MacAskill, SNP
M MacDonald, SNP
F Hyslop, SNP
R Harper, Green

MID SCOTLAND AND FIFE

DUNFERMLINE EAST
Electorate 52,087 Poll 56.94%

H Eadie, Lab Co-op	16,576
D McCarthy, SNP	7,877
C Ruxton, Con	2,931
F Lawson, LD	2,275
Lab Co-op majority	8,699

DUNFERMLINE WEST
Electorate 53,112 Poll 57.75%

S Barrie, Lab	13,560
D Chapman, SNP	8,539
E Harris, LD	5,591
J Mackie, Con	2,981
Lab majority	5,021

FIFE CENTRAL
Electorate 58,850 Poll 55.82%

H McLeish, Lab	18,828
T Marwick, SNP	10,153
JA Liston, LD	1,953
K Harding, Con	1,918
Lab majority	8,675

FIFE NORTH EAST
Electorate 60,886 Poll 59.03%

I Smith, LD	13,590
E Brocklebank, Con	8,526
C Welsh, SNP	6,373
C Milne, Lab	5,175
Others	2,277
LD majority	5,064

KIRKCALDY
Electorate 51,640 Poll 54.88%

M Livingstone, Lab Co-op	13,645
S Hosie, SNP	9,170

M Scott-Hayward, Con	2,907
J Mainland, LD	2,620
Lab Co-op majority	4,475

OCHIL
Electorate 57,083 Poll 64.58%

R Simpson, Lab	15,385
G Reid, SNP	14,082
N Johnston, Con	4,151
J Mar and Kellie, LD	3,249
Lab majority	1,303

PERTH
Electorate 61,034 Poll 61.27%

R Cunningham, SNP	13,570
I Stevenson, Con	11,543
J Richards, Lab	8,725
C Brodie, LD	3,558
SNP majority	2,027

STIRLING
Electorate 52,904 Poll 67.68%

S Jackson, Lab	13,533
A Ewing, SNP	9,552
B Monteith, Con	9,158
I Macfarlane, LD	3,407
Others	155
Lab majority	3,981

TAYSIDE NORTH
Electorate 61,795 Poll 61.58%

J Swinney, SNP	16,786
M Fraser, Con	12,594
M Dingwall, Lab	5,727
P Regent, LD	2,948
SNP majority	4,192

ADDITIONAL MEMBERS ELECTED BY PR
N Johnston, Con
B Monteith, Con
K Harding, Con
K Raffan, LD
B Crawford, SNP
G Reid, SNP
T Marwick, SNP

NORTH-EAST SCOTLAND

ABERDEEN CENTRAL
Electorate 52,715 Poll 50.26%

L Macdonald, Lab	10,305
R Lochhead, SNP	7,609
E Anderson, LD	4,403
T Mason, Con	3,655
A Cumbers, SSP	523
Lab majority	2,696

ABERDEEN NORTH
Electorate 54,553 Poll 51.00%

E Thomson, Lab	10,340
B Adam, SNP	9,942
J Donaldson, LD	4,767
I Haughie, Con	2,772
Lab majority	398

ABERDEEN SOUTH
Electorate 60,579 Poll 57.26%

N Stephen, LD	11,300
M Elrick, Lab	9,540
N Milne, Con	6,993
I McGugan, SNP	6,651
Others	206
LD majority	1,760

ABERDEENSHIRE WEST AND KINCARDINE
Electorate 60,702 Poll 58.87%

M Rumbles, LD	12,838
B Wallace, Con	10,549
M Watt, SNP	7,699
G Guthrie, Lab	4,650
LD majority	2,289

ANGUS
Electorate 59,891 Poll 57.66%

A Welsh, SNP	16,055
R Harris, Con	7,154
I McFatridge, Lab	6,914
D Speirs, LD	4,413
SNP majority	8,901

BANFF AND BUCHAN
Electorate 57,639 Poll 55.06%

A Salmond, SNP	16,695
D Davidson, Con	5,403
M Mackie, LD	5,315
M Harris, Lab	4,321
SNP majority	11,292

DUNDEE EAST
Electorate 57,222 Poll 55.33%

J McAllion, Lab	13,703
S Robison, SNP	10,849
I Mitchell, Con	4,428

R Lawrie, LD	2,153
H Duke, SSP	530
Lab majority	2,854

DUNDEE WEST
Electorate 55,725 Poll 52.19%

K MacLean, Lab	10,925
C Cashley, SNP	10,804
G Buchan, Con	3,345
E Dick, LD	2,998
J McFarlane, SSP	1,010
Lab majority	121

GORDON
Electorate 59,497 Poll 56.51%

N Radcliffe, LD	12,353
S Stronach, SNP	8,158
A Johnstone, Con	6,602
G Carlin-Kulwicki, Lab	3,950
Others	2,559
LD majority	4,195

ADDITIONAL MEMBERS ELECTED BY PR
D Davidson, Con
A Johnstone, Con
B Wallace, Con
R Lochhead, SNP
S Robison, SNP
B Adam, SNP
I McGugan, SNP

SOUTH SCOTLAND

AYR
Electorate 56,338 Poll 66.48%

I Welsh, Lab	14,263
P Gallie, Con	14,238
R Mullin, SNP	7,291
E Morris, LD	1,662
Lab majority	25

CARRICK, CUMNOCK AND DOON VALLEY
Electorate 65,580 Poll 62.66%

C Jamieson, Lab Co-op	19,667
A Ingram, SNP	10,864
J Scott, Con	8,123
D Hannay, LD	2,441
Lab Co-op majority	8,803

CLYDESDALE
Electorate 64,262 Poll 60.61%

K Turnbull, Lab	16,755

A Winning, SNP	12,875
C Cormack, Con	5,814
S Grieve, LD	3,503
Lab majority	3,880

CUNNINGHAME SOUTH
Electorate 50,443 Poll 56.06%

I Oldfather, Lab	14,936
M Russell, SNP	8,395
M Tosh, Con	3,229
S Ritchie, LD	1,717
Lab majority	6,541

DUMFRIES
Electorate 63,162 Poll 60.93%

E Murray, Lab	14,101
D Mundell, Con	10,447
S Norris, SNP	7,625
N Wallace, LD	6,309
Lab majority	3,654

EAST LOTHIAN
Electorate 58,579 Poll 60.74%

J Home Robertson, Lab	19,220
C Miller, SNP	8,274
C Richard, Con	5,941
J Hayman, LD	2,147
Lab majority	10,946

GALLOWAY AND UPPER NITHSDALE
Electorate 53,057 Poll 66.56%

A Morgan, SNP	13,873
A Fergusson, Con	10,672
J Stevens, Lab	7,209
J Mitchell, LD	3,562
SNP majority	3,201

ROXBURGH AND BERWICKSHIRE
Electorate 47,639 Poll 58.52%

E Robson, LD	11,320
A Hutton, Con	7,735
S Crawford, SNP	4,719
S McLeod, Lab	4,102
LD majority	3,585

TWEEDDALE, ETTRICK AND LAUDERDALE
Electorate 51,577 Poll 65.37%

I Jenkins, LD	12,078
C Creech, SNP	7,600

G McGregor, Lab	7,546
J Campbell, Con	6,491
LD majority	4,478

ADDITIONAL MEMBERS ELECTED BY PR
P Gallie, Con
D Mundell, Con
M Tosh, Con
A Fergusson, Con
M Russell, SNP
A Ingram, SNP
C Creech, SNP

WEST SCOTLAND

CLYDEBANK AND MILNGAVIE
Electorate 52,461 Poll 63.55%

D McNulty, Lab	15,105
J Yuill, SNP	10,395
R Ackland, LD	4,149
D Luckhurst, Con	3,688
Lab majority	4,710

CUNNINGHAME NORTH
Electorate 55,867 Poll 59.95%

A Wilson, Lab	14,369
K Ullrich, SNP	9,573
M Johnston, Con	6,649
C Irving, LD	2,900
Lab majority	4,796

DUMBARTON
Electorate 56,090 Poll 61.86%

J Baillie, Lab	15,181
L Quinan, SNP	10,423
D Reece, Con	5,060
P Coleshill, LD	4,035
Lab majority	4,758

EASTWOOD
Electorate 67,248 Poll 67.51%

K Macintosh, Lab	16,970
J Young, Con	14,845
R Findlay, SNP	8,760
A McCurley, LD	4,472
Others	349
Lab majority	2,125

GREENOCK AND INVERCLYDE
Electorate 48,584 Poll 58.95%

D McNeil, Lab	11,817

R Finnie, LD	7,504
I Hamilton, SNP	6,762
R Wilkinson, Con	1,699
D Landels, SSP	857
Lab majority	4,313

PAISLEY NORTH
Electorate 49,020 Poll 56.61%

W Alexander, Lab	13,492
I Mackay, SNP	8,876
P Ramsay, Con	2,242
T Mayberry, LD	2,133
F Macdonald, SSP	1,007
Lab majority	4,616

PAISLEY SOUTH
Electorate 53,637 Poll 57.15%

H Henry, Lab	13,899
B Martin, SNP	9,404
S Callison, LD	2,974
S Laidlaw, Con	2,433
Others	1,946
Lab majority	4,495

RENFREWSHIRE WEST
Electorate 52,452 Poll 64.89%

P Godman, Lab	12,708
C Campbell, SNP	9,815
A Goldie, Con	7,243
N Ascherson, LD	2,659
Others	1,612
Lab majority	2,893

STRATHKELVIN AND BEARSDEN
Electorate 63,111 Poll 67.17%

S Galbraith, Lab	21,505
F McLeod, SNP	9,384
C Ferguson, Con	6,934
A Howarth, LD	4,144
Others	423
Lab majority	12,121

ADDITIONAL MEMBERS ELECTED BY PR
A Goldie, Con
J Young, Con
R Finnie, LD
L Quinan, SNP
F McLeod, SNP
K Ullrich, SNP
C Campbell, SNP

Scottish Parliamentary Election

May 1999

VOTING SYSTEM

The Scottish Parliament was elected using the Additional Member System, a type of proportional representation intended to ensure that the share of seats each party received would reflect as closely as possible its level of support among voters. Each voter had two votes, the first to elect a constituency member by the traditional "first past the post" method, the second for a polical party, or candidate standing as an individual, within a larger electoral area called a Scottish Parliament region. Each of the eight regions was allocated seven additional seats, the members chosen to fill these additional seats being known as "regional members".

CONSTITUENCY (FIRST) VOTE

Labour	908,346
Scottish National Party	672,768
Scottish Conservative	364,425
Liberal Democrat	333,269
Others	63,770

Party share of the constituency vote: Labour, 38.8%; Scottish National Party, 28.7%; Scottish Conservative, 14.0%; Liberal Democrat, 13.2%; Others, 2.7%. *Allocation of seats on constituency vote:* Labour 53; Scottish National Party, 7; Scottish Conservative, 0; Liberal Democrat, 12; Independent, 1.

REGIONAL (SECOND) VOTE

Party share of the regional vote: Labour, 33.6%; Scottish National Party, 27.3%; Scottish Conservative, 15.4%; Liberal Democrat, 12.4%; Others, 11.2%. *Allocation of seats on regional vote:* Labour 3; Scottish National Party, 28; Scottish Conservative, 18; Liberal Democrat, 5; Green, 1; Scottish Socialist Party 1.

REGIONAL RESULTS

Central Scotland

Labour	129,822
Scottish National Party	91,802
Scottish Conservative	30,243
Falkirk West	27,700
Liberal Democrat	20,505
Socialist Labour	10,956
Others	19,458

Glasgow

Labour	112,588
Scottish National Party	65,360
Scottish Conservative	20,239
Scottish Socialist Party	18,581
Liberal Democrat	18,473
Others	21,107

Highlands and Islands

Scottish National Party	55,933
Labour	51,371
Liberal Democrat	43,226
Scottish Conservative	30,122
Green	7,560
Others	13,460

Lothians

Labour	99,908
Scottish National Party	85,085
Scottish Conservative	52,067
Liberal Democrat	47,565
Green	22,848
Socialist Labour	10,895
Scottish Socialist Party	5,237
Others	6,908

Mid Scotland and Fife

Labour	101,964
Scottish National Party	87,659
Scottish Conservative	56,719
Liberal Democrat	38,896
Others	20,424

North-East Scotland

Scottish National Party	92,329
Labour	72,666
Scottish Conservative	52,149
Liberal Democrat	49,843
Others	18,459

South Scotland

Labour	98,836
Scottish National Party	80,059
Scottish Conservative	68,904
Liberal Democrat	38,157
Others	32,414

West Scotland

Labour	119,663
Scottish National Party	80,417
Scottish Conservative	48,666
Liberal Democrat	34,095
Others	27,573

Members of Scottish Parliament

Name	Party	Constituency
denotes Additional Member elected by PR		
*Adam, Brian	SNP	North East Scotland
*Aitken, Bill	Con	Glasgow
Alexander, Wendy	Lab	Paisley North
Baillie, Jackie	Lab	Dumbarton
Barrie, Scott	Lab	Dunfermline West
Boyack, Sarah	Lab	Edinburgh Central
Brankin, Rhona	Lab	Midlothian
*Brown, Robert	LD	Glasgow
*Campbell, Colin	SNP	West of Scotland
Canavan, Denis	Ind	Falkirk West
Chisholm, Malcolm	Lab	Edinburgh North & Leith
Craigie, Cathie	Lab	Cumbernauld & Kilsyth
*Crawford, Bruce	SNP	Mid Scotland & Fife
Cunningham, Roseanna	SNP	Perth
Curran, Margaret	Lab	Glasgow Baillieston
*Davidson, David	Con	North East Scotland
Deacon, Susan	Lab	Edinburgh East & Musselburgh
Dewar, Rt Hon Donald	Lab	Glasgow Anniesland
*Douglas-Hamilton, Rt Hon Lord James	Con	Lothians
Eadie, Helen	Lab	Dunfermline East
*Elder, Dorothy-Grace	SNP	Glasgow
Ewing, Fergus	SNP	Inverness East, Nairn & Lochaber
Ewing, Margaret	SNP	Moray
*Ewing, Dr Winnie	SNP	Highlands and Islands
*Fabiani, Linda	SNP	Central Scotland
Ferguson, Patricia	Lab	Glasgow Maryhill
*Fergusson, Alex	Con	South of Scotland
*Finnie, Ross	LD	West of Scotland
Galbraith, Sam	Lab	Strathkelvin & Bearsden
*Gallie, Phil	Con	South of Scotland
*Gibson, Kenneth	SNP	Glasgow
Gillon, Karen	Lab	Clydesdale
Godman, Trish	Lab	West Renfrewshire
*Goldie, Annabel	Con	West of Scotland
*Gorrie, Donald, OBE	LD	Central Scotland
*Grahame, Christine	SNP	South of Scotland
*Grant, Rhoda	Lab	Highlands & Islands
Gray, Iain	Lab	Edinburgh Pentlands

*Hamilton, Duncan	SNP	Highlands and Islands
*Harding, Keith	Con	Mid Scotland & Fife
*Harper, Robin	Green	Lothians
Henry, Hugh	Lab	Paisley South
Home Robertson, John	Lab	East Lothian
Hughes, Janis	Lab	Glasgow Rutherglen
*Hyslop, Fiona	SNP	Lothians
*Ingram, Adam	SNP	South of Scotland
Jackson, Gordon, QC	Lab	Glasgow Govan
Jackson, Dr Sylvia	Lab	Stirling
Jamieson, Cathy	Lab	Carrick, Cumnock & Doon Valley
Jamieson, Margaret	Lab	Kilmarnock & Loudoun
Jenkins, Ian	LD	Tweeddale, Ettrick & Lauderdale
*Johnston, Nick	Con	Mid Scotland & Fife
*Johnstone, Alex	Con	North East Scotland
Kerr, Andy	Lab	East Kilbride
Lamont, Johann	Lab	Glasgow Pollok
Livingstone, Marilyn	Lab	Kirkcaldy
*Lochhead, Richard	SNP	North East Scotland
Lyon, George	LD	Argyll and Bute
McAllion, John	Lab	Dundee East
*MacAskill, Kenny	SNP	Lothians
McAveety, Frank	Lab	Glasgow Shettleston
McCabe, Tom	Lab	Hamilton South
McConnell, Jack	Lab	Motherwell & Wishaw
Macdonald, Lewis	Lab	Aberdeen Central
*MacDonald, Margo	SNP	Lothians
*McGrigor, Jamie	Con	Highlands & Islands
*McGugan, Irene	SNP	North East Scotland
Macintosh, Kenneth	Lab	Eastwood
*McIntosh, Lyndsay	Con	Central Scotland
MacKay, Angus	Lab	Edinburgh South
MacLean, Kate	Lab	Dundee West
McLeish, Henry	Lab	Central Fife
*McLeod, Fiona	SNP	West of Scotland
*McLetchie, David	Con	Lothians
McMahon, Michael	Lab	Hamilton North & Bellshill
*Macmillan, Maureen	Lab	Highlands & Islands
McNeil, Duncan	Lab	Greenock & Inverclyde
McNeill, Pauline	Lab	Glasgow Kelvin
McNulty, Des	Lab	Clydebank & Milngavie
Martin, Paul	Lab	Glasgow Springburn
*Marwick, Tricia	SNP	Mid Scotland & Fife
*Matheson, Michael	SNP	Central Scotland
*Monteith, Brian	Con	Mid Scotland & Fife
Morgan, Alasdair	SNP	Galloway & Upper Nithsdale

Morrison, Alasdair	Lab	Western Isles
Muldoon, Bristow	Lab	Livingston
Mulligan, Mary	Lab	Linlithgow
*Mundell, David	Con	South of Scotland
Munro, John	LD	Ross, Skye & Inverness West
Murray, Dr Elaine	Lab	Dumfries
*Neil, Alex	SNP	Central Scotland
Oldfather, Irene	Lab	Cunninghame South
*Paterson, Gil	SNP	Central Scotland
*Peacock, Peter	Lab	Highlands & Islands
Peattie, Cathy	Lab	Falkirk East
*Quinan, Lloyd	SNP	West of Scotland
Radcliffe, Nora	LD	Gordon
*Raffan, Keith	LD	Mid Scotland & Fife
*Reid, George	SNP	Mid Scotland & Fife
*Robison, Shona	SNP	North East Scotland
Robson, Euan	LD	Roxburgh & Berwickshire
Rumbles, Mike	LD	West Aberdeenshire & Kincardine
*Russell, Michael	SNP	South of Scotland
Salmond, Alex	SNP	Banff & Buchan
*Scanlon, Mary	Con	Highland & Islands
Scott, Tavish	LD	Shetland
*Sheridan, Tommy	SSP	Glasgow
Simpson, Dr Richard	Lab	Ochil
Smith, Elaine	Lab	Coatbridge & Chryston
Smith, Iain	LD	North East Fife
Smith, Margaret	LD	Edinburgh West
*Steel, Rt Hon Sir David	LD	Lothians
Stephen, Nicol	LD	Aberdeen South
Stone, Jamie	LD	Caithness, Sutherland & Easter Ross
*Sturgeon, Nicola	SNP	Glasgow
Swinney, John	SNP	North Tayside
Thomson, Elaine	Lab	Aberdeen North
*Tosh, Murray	Con	South of Scotland
*Ullrich, Kay	SNP	West of Scotland
*Wallace, Ben	Con	North East Scotland
Wallace, Jim, QC	LD	Orkney
Watson, Mike	Lab	Glasgow Cathcart
Welsh, Andrew	SNP	Angus
Welsh, Ian	Lab	Ayr
*White, Sandra	SNP	Glasgow
Whitefield, Karen	Lab	Airdrie & Shotts
Wilson, Allan	Lab	Cunninghame North
*Wilson, Andrew	SNP	Central Scotland
*Young, John, OBE	Con	West of Scotland

Parliamentary Committees

Audit
Convener: Andrew Welsh (SNP)
Members: Brian Adam, Scott Barrie, Cathie Craigie, Annabel Goldie, Margaret Jamieson, Nick Johnston, Lewis Macdonald, Paul Martin, Euan Robson, Andrew Wilson

Education, Culture and Sport
Convener: Mary Mulligan (Labour)
Members: Karen Gillon, Ian Jenkins, Kenneth Macintosh, Fiona McLeod, Brian Monteith, Cathy Peattie, Michael Russell, Jamie Stone, Nicola Sturgeon, Ian Welsh

Enterprise and Lifelong Learning
Convener: John Swinney (Scottish National Party)
Members: Fergus Ewing, Annabel Goldie, Nick Johnston, Marilyn Livingstone, George Lyon, Margo MacDonald, Duncan McNeil, Elaine Murray, Elaine Thomson, Allan Wilson

Equal Opportunities
Convener: Kate MacLean (Labour)
Members: Malcolm Chisholm, Johann Lamont, Marilyn Livingstone, Jamie McGrigor, Irene McGugan, Michael McMahon, Michael Matheson, John Munro, Nora Radcliffe, Shona Robison, Tommy Sheridan, Elaine Smith

European
Convener: Hugh Henry (Labour)
Members: Dennis Canavan, Bruce Crawford, Winnie Ewing, Sylvia Jackson, Cathy Jamieson, Margo MacDonald, Maureen Macmillan, David Mundell, Irene Oldfather, Tavish Scott, Ben Wallace, Allan Wilson

Finance
Convener: Mike Watson (Labour)
Members: David Davidson, Rhoda Grant, Adam Ingram, George Lyon, Kenneth Macintosh, Keith Raffan, Richard Simpson, John Swinney, Elaine Thomson, Andrew Wilson

Health and Community Care
Convener: Margaret Smith (Liberal Democrat)
Members: Malcolm Chisholm, Dorothy-Grace Elder, Duncan Hamilton, Hugh Henry, Margaret Jamieson, Irene Oldfather, Mary Scanlon, Richard Simpson, Kay Ullrich, Ben Wallace

Justice and Home Affairs
Convener: Roseanna Cunningham (Scottish National Party)
Members: Scott Barrie, Phil Gallie, Christine Graham, Gordon Jackson, Lyndsay McIntosh, Kate MacLelan, Maureen Macmillan, Pauline McNeill, Tricia Marwick, Euan Robson

Local Government
Convener: Trish Godman (Labour)
Members: Colin Campbell, Kenneth Gibson, Donald Gorrie, Keith Harding, Sylvia Jackson, Johann Lamont, Michael McMahon, Bristow Muldoon, Gil Paterson, Jamie Stone

Procedures
Convener: Murray Tosh (Conservative)
Members: Donald Gorrie, Janis Hughes, Gordon Jackson, Andy Kerr, Gil Paterson, Michael Russell

Public Petitions
Convener: John McAllion (Labour)
Members: Helen Eadie, Phil Gallie, Christine Grahame, Pauline McNeill, Margaret Smith, Sandra White

Rural Affairs
Convener: Alex Johnstone (Conservative)
Members: Alex Fergusson, Rhoda Grant, Richard Lochhead, Lewis Macdonald, Irene McGugan, Alasdair Morgan, John Munro, Elaine Murray, Cathy Peattie, Mike Rumbles

Social Inclusion, Housing and Voluntary Sector
Convener: Margaret Curran (Labour)
Members: Bill Aitken, Robert Brown, Cathie Craigie, Fiona Hyslop, John McAllion, Alex Neil, Lloyd Quinan, Keith Raffan, Mike Watson, Karen Whitefield

Standards
Convener: Mike Rumbles (Liberal Democrat)
Members: Patricia Ferguson, Karen Gillon, Lord James Douglas-Hamilton, Adam Ingram, Des McNulty, Tricia Marwick

Subordinate Legislation
Convener: Kenny MacAskill (Scottish National Party)
Members: Fergus Ewing, Trish Godman, Ian Jenkins, Bristow Muldoon, David Mundell, Ian Welsh

Transport and Environment
Convener: Andy Kerr (Labour)
Members: Helen Eadie, Linda Fabiani, Robin Harper, Janis Hughes, Cathy Jamieson, Kenny MacAskill, Des McNulty, Nora Radcliffe, Tavish Scott, Murray Tosh

The UK Government

The Cabinet

*Prime Minister, First Lord of the
Treasury and Minister for
the Civil Service*
Rt Hon Tony Blair

*Deputy Prime Minister and Secretary
of State for the Environment,
Transport and the Regions*
Rt Hon John Prescott

Chancellor of the Exchequer
Rt Hon Gordon Brown

*Secretary of State for Foreign and
Commonwealth Affairs*
Rt Hon Robin Cook

Lord High Chancellor
Rt Hon Lord Irvine of Lairg, PC,
QC

*Secretary of State for the
Home Department*
Rt Hon Jack Straw

*Secretary of State for Education and
Employment*
Rt Hon David Blunkett

*President of the Council and Leader of
the House of Commons*
Rt Hon Margaret Beckett

Minister for the Cabinet Office
Rt Hon Dr Mo Mowlam

Secretary of State for Scotland
Rt Hon Dr John Reid

Secretary of State for Defence
Geoff Hoon

Secretary of State for Health
Rt Hon Alan Milburn

Chief Whip
Rt Hon Ann Taylor

*Secretary of State for Culture,
Media and Sport*
Rt Hon Chris Smith

*Secretary of State for
Northern Ireland*
Rt Hon Peter Mandelson

Secretary of State for Wales
Rt Hon Paul Murphy

*Secretary of State for
International Development*
Rt Hon Clare Short

Secretary of State for Social Security
Rt Hon Alistair Darling

*Minister of Agriculture,
Fisheries and Food*
Rt Hon Nick Brown

*Leader of the Lords and
Minister for Women*
Rt Hon Baroness Jay of Paddington

*Secretary of State for
Trade and Industry*
Rt Hon Stephen Byers

Chief Secretary to the Treasury
Rt Hon Andrew Smith

*Minister of State, Department of the
Environment, Transport and the
Regions* (non-Cabinet member
invited to Cabinet)
Lord MacDonald of Tradeston

List revised 12 October 1999

The UK Parliamentary Constituencies
May 1997

* denotes member of the previous parliament

ABERDEEN CENTRAL
Electorate 54,257 Poll 65.64%

F Doran, Lab	17,745
Mrs J Wisely, Con	6,944
B Topping, SNP	5,767
J BROWN, LD	4,714
Others	446
Lab majority	10,801

ABERDEEN NORTH
Electorate 54,302 Poll 70.74%

M Savidge, Lab	13,389
B Adam, SNP	8,379
J Gifford, Con	5,763
M Rumbles, LD	5,421
Others	463
Lab majority	10,010

ABERDEEN SOUTH
Electorate 60,490 Poll 72.84%

Ms A Begg, Lab	15,541
N Stephen, LD	12,176
*R Robertson, Con	11,621
J Towers, SNP	4,299
Others	425
Lab majority	3,365

ABERDEENSHIRE WEST AND KINCARDINE
Electorate 59,123 Poll 73.05%

Sir R Smith, LD	17,742
*G Kynoch, Con	15,080
Ms J Mowatt, SNP	5,639
Ms Q Khan, Lab	3,923
Others	805
LD majority	2,662

AIRDRIE AND SHOTTS
Electorate 57,673 Poll 71.40%

*Mrs H Liddell, Lab	25,460
K Robertson, SNP	10,048
Dr N Brook, Con	3,660
R Wolseley, LD	1,719
Others	294
Lab majority	15,412

ANGUS
Electorate 59,708 Poll: 72.14%

*A Welsh, SNP	20,792
S Leslie, Con	10,603
Ms C Taylor, Lab	6,733
Dr R Speirs, LD	4,065
B Taylor, Ref	883
SNP majority	10,189

ARGYLL AND BUTE
Electorate 49,451 Poll 72.23%

*Mrs R Michie, LD	14,359
Prof N MacCormick, SNP	8,278
R Leishman, Con	6,774
A Syed, Lab	5,596
Others	713
LD majority	6,081

AYR
Electorate 55,829 Poll 80.17%

Mrs S Osborne, Lab	21,679
*P Gallie, Con	15,136
I Blackford, SNP	5,625
Ms C Hamblen, LD	2,116
Others	200
Lab majority	6,543

BANFF AND BUCHAN
Electorate 58,493 Poll 68.69%

*A Salmond, SNP	22,409
W Frain-Bell, Con	9,564
Ms M Harris, Lab	4,747
N Fletcher, LD	2,398
Others	1,060
SNP majority	12,845

CAITHNESS, SUTHERLAND AND EASTER ROSS
Electorate 41,566 Poll 70.18%

*R Maclennan, LD	10,381
J Hendry, Lab	8,122
E Harper, SNP	6,710
T Miers, Con	3,148
Others	811
LD majority	2,259

CARRICK, CUMNOCK AND DOON VALLEY
Electorate 65,593 Poll 74.96%

* G Foulkes, Lab Co-op	29,398
A Marshall, Con	8,336
Mrs C Hutchison, SNP	8,190
D Young, LD	2,613
Others	634
Lab Co-op majority	21,062

CLYDEBANK AND MILNGAVIE
Electorate 52,092 Poll 75.03%

*A Worthington, Lab	21,583
J Yuill, SNP	8,263
Ms N Morgan, Con	4,885
K Moody, LD	4,086
Others	269
Lab majority	13,320

CLYDESDALE
Electorate 63,428 Poll 71.60%

*J Hood, Lab	23,859
A Doig, SNP	10,050
M Izatt, Con	7,396
Mrs S Grieve, LD	3,796
Others	311
Lab majority	13,809

COATBRIDGE AND CHRYSTON
Electorate 52,024 Poll 72.30%

*T Clarke, Lab	25,697
B Nugent, SNP	6,402
A Wauchope, Con	3,216
Mrs M Daly, LD	2,048
Others	249
Lab majority	19,295

CUMBERNAULD AND KILSYTH
Electorate 48,032 Poll 75.00%

Mrs R McKenna, Lab	21,141
C Barrie, SNP	10,013
I Sewell, Con	2,441
J Biggam, LD	1,368
Others	1,061
Lab majority	11,128

CUNNINGHAME NORTH
Electorate 55,526 Poll 74.07%

*B Wilson, Lab	20,686
Mrs M Mitchell, Con	9,647
Ms K Nicoll, SNP	7,584
Ms K Freel, LD	2,271
Others	941
Lab majority	11,039

CUNNINGHAME SOUTH
Electorate 49,543 Poll 71.54%

*B Donohoe, Lab	22,233
Mrs M Burgess, SNP	7,364
Mrs P Paterson, Con	3,571
E Watson, LD	1,604
Others	672
Lab majority	14,869

DUMBARTON
Electorate 56,229 Poll 73.39%

*J McFall, Lab Co-op	20,470
W MacKechnie, SNP	9,587
P Ramsay, Con	7,283
A Reid, LD	3,144
Others	780
Lab Co-op majority	10,883

DUMFRIES
Electorate 62,759 Poll 78.92%

R Brown, Lab	23,528
S Stevenson, Con	13,885
R Higgins, SNP	5,977
N Wallace, LD	5,487
Others	650
Lab majority	9,643

DUNDEE EAST
Electorate 58,388 Poll 69.41%

*J McAllion, Lab	20,718
Ms S Robison, SNP	10,757
B Mackie, Con	6,397
Dr G Saluja, LD	1,677
Others	979
Lab majority	9,961

DUNDEE WEST
Electorate 57,346 Poll 67.67%

*E Ross, Lab	20,875
J Dorward, SNP	9,016
N Powrie, Con	5,105
Dr E Dick, LD	2,972
Others	839
Lab majority	11,859

DUNFERMLINE EAST
Electorate 52,072 Poll 70.25%

*Rt Hon G Brown, Lab	24,441
J Ramage, SNP	5,690
I Mitchell, Con	3,656
J Tolson, LD	2,164
Others	632
Lab majority	18,751

DUNFERMLINE WEST
Electorate 52,467 Poll 69.44%

*Ms R Squire, Lab	19,338
J Lloyd, SNP	6,984
Mrs E Harris, LD	4,963
K Newton, Con	4,606
Others	543
Lab majority	12,354

EAST KILBRIDE
Electorate 65,229 Poll 74.81%

*A Ingram, Lab	27,584
G Gebbie, SNP	10,200
C Herbertson, Con	5,863
Mrs K Philbrick, LD	3,527
Others	1,622
Lab majority	17,384

EAST LOTHIAN
Electorate 57,441 Poll 75.61%

*J Home Robertson, Lab	22,881
M Fraser, Con	8,660
D McCarthy, SNP	6,825
Ms A MacAskill, LD	4,575
Others	491
Lab majority	14,221

EASTWOOD
Electorate 66,697 Poll 78.32%

J Murphy, Lab	20,766
P Cullen, Con	17,530
D Yates, SNP	6,826
Dr C Mason, LD	6,110
Others	1,003
Lab majority	3,236

EDINBURGH CENTRAL
Electorate 63,695 Poll 67.09%

*A Darling, Lab	20,125
M Scott-Hayward, Con	9,055
Ms F Hyslop, SNP	6,750
Ms K Utting, LD	5,605
Others	1,200
Lab majority	11,070

EDINBURGH EAST AND MUSSELBURGH
Electorate 59,648 Poll 70.61%

*Rt Hon G Strang, Lab	22,564
D White, SNP	8,034
K Ward, Con	6,483
Dr C MacKellar, LD	4,511
Others	526
Lab majority	14,530

EDINBURGH NORTH AND LEITH
Electorate 61,617 Poll 66.45%

*M Chisholm, Lab	19,209
Ms A Dana, SNP	8,231
E Stewart, Con	7,312
Ms H Campbell, LD	5,335
Others	858
Lab majority	10,978

EDINBURGH PENTLANDS
Electorate 59,635 Poll 76.70%

Ms L Clark, Lab	19,675
*Rt Hon M Rifkind, Con	14,813
S Gibb, SNP	5,952
Dr J Dawe, LD	4,575
Others	727
Lab majority	4,862

EDINBURGH SOUTH
Electorate 62,467 Poll 71.78%

*N Griffiths, Lab	20,993
Miss E Smith, Con	9,541
M Pringle, LD	7,911
Dr J Hargreaves, SNP	5,791
Others	602
Lab majority	11,452

EDINBURGH WEST
Electorate 61,133 Poll 77.91%

D Gorrie, LD	20,578
*Lord J Douglas-Hamilton, Con	13,325
Ms L Hinds, Lab	8,948
G Sutherland, SNP	4,210
Others	570
LD majority	7,253

FALKIRK EAST
Electorate 56,792 Poll 73.24%

*M Connarty, Lab	23,344
K Brown, SNP	9,959
M Nicol, Con	5,813
R Spillane, LD	2,153
Others	326
Lab majority	13,385

FALKIRK WEST
Electorate 52,850 Poll 72.60%

*D Canavan, Lab	22,772
D Alexander, SNP	8,989
Mrs C Buchanan, Con	4,639
D Houston, LD	1,970
Lab majority	13,783

FIFE CENTRAL
Electorate 58,315 Poll 69.90%

*H McLeish, Lab	23,912
Mrs P Marwick, SNP	10,199
J Rees-Mogg, Con	3,669
R Laird, LD	2,610
Others	375
Lab majority	13,713

FIFE NORTH EAST
Electorate 58,794 Poll 71.16%

*M Campbell, LD	21,432
A Bruce, Con	11,076
C Welsh, SNP	4,545
C Milne, Lab	4,301
Others	485
LD majority	10,356

GALLOWAY AND UPPER NITHSDALE
Electorate 52,751 Poll 79.65%

A Morgan, SNP	18,449
* Rt Hon I Lang, Con	12,825
Ms K Clark, Lab	6,861
J McKerchar, LD	2,700
Others	1,283
SNP majority	5,624

GLASGOW ANNIESLAND
Electorate 52,955 Poll 63.98%

*Rt Hon D Dewar, Lab	20,951
Dr W Wilson, SNP	5,797
A Brocklehurst, Con	3,881
C McGinty, LD	2,453
Others	797
Lab majority	15,154

GLASGOW BAILLIESTON
Electorate 51,152 Poll 62.27%

*J Wray, Lab	20,925
Mrs P Thomson, SNP	6,085
M Kelly, Con	2,468
Ms S Rainger, LD	1,217
Others	1,158
Lab majority	14,840

GLASGOW CATHCART
Electorate 49,312 Poll 69.17%

*J Maxton, Lab	19,158
Ms M Whitehead, SNP	6,913
A Muir, Con	4,248
C Dick, LD	2,302
Others	1,489
Lab majority	12,245

GLASGOW GOVAN
Electorate 49,836 Poll 64.70%

M Sarwar, Lab	14,216
Ms N Sturgeon, SNP	11,302
W Thomas, Con	2,839
R Stewart, LD	1,915
Others	1,970
Lab majority	2,914

GLASGOW KELVIN
Electorate 57,438 Poll 56.85%

*G Galloway, Lab	16,643
Ms S White, SNP	6,978
Ms E Buchanan, LD	4,629
D McPhie, Con	3,539
Others	865
Lab majority	9,665

GLASGOW MARYHILL
Electorate 52,523 Poll 56.59%

*Ms M Fyfe, Lab	19,301
J Wailes, SNP	5,037
Ms E Attwooll, LD	2,119
S Baldwin, Con	1,747
Others	1,517
Lab majority	14,264

GLASGOW POLLOK
Electorate 49,284 Poll 66.56%

*I Davidson, Lab Co-op	19,653
D Logan, SNP	5,862
T Sheridan, SSA	3,639
E Hamilton, Con	1,979
D Jago, LD	1,137
Others	532
Lab Co-op majority	13,791

GLASGOW RUTHERGLEN
Electorate 50,646 Poll 70.14%

*T McAvoy, Lab Co-op	20,430
I Gray, SNP	5,423
R Brown, LD	5,167
D Campbell-Bannerman, Con	3,288
Others	1,213
Lab Co-op majority	15,007

GLASGOW SHETTLESTON
Electorate 47,990 Poll 55.87%

*D Marshall, Lab	19,616
H Hanif, SNP	3,748
C Simpson, Con	1,484
Ms K Hiles, LD	1,061
Others	904
Lab majority	15,868

GLASGOW SPRINGBURN
Electorate 53,473 Poll 59.05%

*M Martin, Lab	22,534
J Brady, SNP	5,208
M Holdsworth, Con	1,893
J Alexander, LD	1,349
Others	593
Lab majority	17,326

GORDON
Electorate 58,767 Poll 71.89%

*M Bruce, LD	17,999
J Porter, Con	11,002
R Lochhead, SNP	8,435
Ms L Kirkhill, Lab	4,350
Others	459
LD majority	6,997

GREENOCK AND INVERCLYDE
Electorate 48,818 Poll 71.05%

*Dr N Godman, Lab	19,480
B Goodall, SNP	6,440
R Ackland, LD	4,791
H Swire, Con	3,976
Lab majority	13,040

HAMILTON NORTH AND BELLSHILL
Electorate 53,607 Poll 70.88%

*Dr J Reid, Lab	24,322
M Matheson, SNP	7,255
G McIntosh, Con	3,944
K Legg, LD	1,924
Others	554
Lab majority	17,067

HAMILTON SOUTH
Electorate 46,562 Poll 71.07%

*G Robertson, Lab	21,709
I Black, SNP	5,831
R Kilgour, Con	2,858
R Pitts, LD	1,693
Others	1,000
Lab majority	15,878

INVERNESS EAST, NAIRN AND LOCHABER
Electorate 65,701 Poll 72.71%

D Stewart, Lab	16,187
F Ewing, SNP	13,848
S Gallagher, LD	8,364
Mrs M Scanlon, Con	8,355
Others	1,014
Lab majority	2,339

KILMARNOCK AND LOUDOUN
Electorate 61,376 Poll 77.24%

D Browne, Lab	23,621
A Neil, SNP	16,365
D Taylor, Con	5,125
J Stewart, LD	1,891
Others	407
Lab majority	7,256

KIRKCALDY
Electorate 52,186 Poll 67.02%

*L Moonie, Lab Co-op	18,730
S Hosie, SNP	8,020
Miss C Black, Con	4,779
J Mainland, LD	3,031
Others	413
Lab Co-op majority	10,710

LINLITHGOW
Electorate 53,706 Poll 73.84%

*T Dalyell, Lab	21,469
K MacAskill, SNP	10,631
T Kerr, Con	4,964
A Duncan, LD	2,331
Others	259
Lab majority	10,838

LIVINGSTON
Electorate 60,296 Poll 71.04%

* Rt Hon R Cook, Lab	23,510
P Johnston, SNP	11,763
H Craigie Halkett, Con	4,028
E Hawthorn, LD	2,876
Others	657
Lab majority	11,747

MIDLOTHIAN
Electorate 47,552 Poll 74.13%

*E Clarke, Lab	18,861
L Millar, SNP	8,991
Miss A Harper, Con	3,842
R Pinnock, LD	3,235
Others	320
Lab majority	9,870

MORAY
Electorate 58,302 Poll 68.21%

*Mrs M Ewing, SNP	16,529
A Findlay, Con	10,963
L Macdonald, Lab	7,886
Ms D Storr, LD	3,548
Others	840
SNP majority	5,566

MOTHERWELL AND WISHAW
Electorate 52,252 Poll 70.08%

F Roy, Lab	21,020
J McGuigan, SNP	8,229
S Dickson, Con	4,024
A Mackie, LD	2,331
Others	1,015
Lab majority	12,791

OCHIL
Electorate 56,572 Poll 77.40%

*M O'Neill, Lab	19,707
G Reid, SNP	15,055
A Hogarth, Con	6,383
Mrs A Watters, LD	2,262
Others	379
Lab majority	4,652

ORKNEY AND SHETLAND
Electorate 32,291 Poll 64.00%

*J Wallace, LD	10,743
J Paton, Lab	3,775
W Ross, SNP	2,624
H Vere Anderson, Con	2,527
Others	996
LD majority	6,968

PAISLEY NORTH
Electorate 49,725 Poll 68.65%

*Mrs I Adams, Lab	20,295
I Mackay, SNP	7,481
K Brookes, Con	3,267
A Jelfs, LD	2,365
Others	727
Lab majority	12,814

PAISLEY SOUTH
Electorate 54,040 Poll 69.12%

*G McMaster, Lab Co-op	21,482
W Martin, SNP	8,732
Ms E McCartin, LD	3,500
R Reid, Con	3,237
Others	400
Lab Co-op majority	12,750

PERTH
Electorate 60,313 Poll 73.87%

*Ms R Cunningham, SNP	16,209
J Godfrey, Con	13,068
D Alexander, Lab	11,036
C Brodie, LD	3,583
Others	655
SNP majority	3,141

RENFREWSHIRE WEST
Electorate 52,348 Poll 76.00%

*T Graham, Lab	18,525
C Campbell, SNP	10,546
C Cormack, Con	7,387
B MacPherson, LD	3,045
Others	283
Lab majority	7,979

ROSS, SKYE AND INVERNESS WEST
Electorate 55,639 Poll 71.81%

*C Kennedy, LD	15,472
D Munro, Lab	11,453
Mrs M Paterson, SNP	7,821
Miss M Macleod, Con	4,368
Others	841
LD majority	4,019

ROXBURGH AND BERWICKSHIRE
Electorate 47,259 Poll 73.91%

*A Kirkwood, LD	16,243
D Younger, Con	8,337
Ms H Eadie, Lab	5,226
M Balfour, SNP	3,959
Others	1,166
LD majority	7,906

STIRLING
Electorate 52,491 Poll 81.84%

Mrs A McGuire, Lab	20,382
*Rt Hon M Forsyth, Con	13,971
E Dow, SNP	5,752
A Tough, LD	2,675
Others	178
Lab majority	6,411

STRATHKELVIN AND BEARSDEN
Electorate 62,974 Poll 78.94%

*S Galbraith, Lab	26,278
D Sharpe, Con	9,986
G McCormick, SNP	8,111
J Morrison, LD	4,843
Others	494
Lab majority	16,292

TAYSIDE NORTH
Electorate 61,398 Poll 74.25%

J Swinney, SNP	20,447
*W Walker, Con	16,287
I McFatridge, Lab	5,141
P Regent, LD	3,716
SNP majority	4,160

TWEEDDALE, ETTRICK AND LAUDERDALE
Electorate 50,891 Poll 76.64%

M Moore, LD	12,178
K Geddes, Lab	10,689
A Jack, Con	8,623
I Goldie, SNP	6,671
Others	840
LD majority	1,489

WESTERN ISLES
Electorate 22,983 Poll 70.08%
*C Macdonald, Lab	8,955
Dr A Lorne Gillies, SNP	5,379
J McGrigor, Con	1,071
N Mitchison, LD	495
Others	206
Lab majority	3,576

By-election 6 November 1997

PAISLEY SOUTH
D Alexander, Lab	10,346
I Blackford, SNP	7,615
E McCartin, LD	2,582

S Laidlaw, Con	1,643
Others	671
Lab majority	2,731

By-Election 23 September 1999

HAMILTON SOUTH
B Tynan, Lab	7,172
A Ewing, SNP	6,616
S Blackall, SSP	1,847
C Ferguson, Con	1,406
S Mungall, Accies	1,075
M MacLaren, LD	634
Lab majority	556

1997 General Election in Scotland

Party	Votes cast	Share of poll
Labour	1,283,353	45.6%
SNP	621,540	22.1%
Conservative	493,059	17.5%
Liberal Democrat	365,359	13.0%
Others	53,425	1.9%

In the last nine general elections, the Scottish constituencies have been represented as follows:

Year	Lab	Con	Lib	SNP	Party in power UK
1966	46	20	5	0	Labour
1970	44	23	3	1	Conservative
1974 Feb	40	21	3	7	Labour
1974 Oct	41	16	3	11	Labour
1979	44	22	3	2	Conservative
1983	41	21	8	2	Conservative
1987	50	10	9	3	Conservative
1992	49	11	9	3	Conservative
1997	56	0	10	6	Labour

The Scotland Office

Dover House, Whitehall, London SW1A 2AU *Telephone*: 0171-270 6758
Secretary of State for Scotland: Rt Hon Dr John Reid
Minister of State for Scotland: Brian Wilson
The Secretary of State for Scotland represents Scottish interests within the UK Government in matters that are reserved to the UK Parliament, promotes the devolution settlement, pays grant to the Scottish Consolidated Fund (SCF) and is responsible for other financial transactions; and exercises certain residual functions in reserved matters.

European Parliamentary Election in Scotland

June 1999

The result of the 1999 European election in Scotland was as follows:

Labour 283,490 (28.6%)
Scottish National Party 268,528 (27.1%)
Scottish Conservative 195,296 (19.7%)
Liberal Democrat 96,971 (9.8%)
Green 57,142 (5.8%)
Scottish Socialist Party 39,720 (4.0%)
Pro Euro Conservative 17,781 (1.7%)
UK Independence Party 12,549 (1.2%)
Socialist Labour Party 9,385 (0.9%)
British National Party 3,729 (0.3%)
Natural Law Party 2,087 (0.2%)
Charles F Y Lawson 1,632 (0.1%)

The allocation of seats was decided by proportional representation, resulting in the following allocation of seats: Labour, 3; Scottish National Party, 2; Conservative, 2; Liberal Democrats 1.

In the constituencies, the Conservatives polled the highest number of votes in 12 constituencies: Ayr; Dumfries; Eastwood; Edinburgh Pentlands; Edinburgh West; Galloway & Upper Nithsdale; North East Fife; Perth; Roxburgh & Berwickshire; Stirling; Tweeddale, Ettrick & Lauderdale; West Aberdeenshire & Kincardine. The SNP polled the highest number of votes in 15 constituencies: Aberdeen North; Aberdeen South; Angus; Argyll & Bute; Banff & Buchan; Caithness, Sutherland & Easter Ross; Dundee East; Dundee West; Gordon; Inverness East, Nairn & Lochaber; Moray; North Tayside; Ochil; Ross, Skye & Inverness West; Western Isles. The Liberal Democrats polled the highest number of votes in 1 constituency: Orkney & Shetland. Labour polled the highest number of votes in the remaining 44 constituencies.

The turnout in Scotland was 24.8%.

Members of the European Parliament for Scotland 1999-2004

Labour
David Martin, PO Box 27030, Edinburgh EH10 7YP
Bill Miller, 9 Chisholm Street, Glasgow G1 5HA
Catherine Taylor, 5a Alexandra Place, St Andrews KY16 9XD

Liberal Democrats
Elspeth Attwooll, Scottish Liberal Democrats, 4 Clifton Terrace, Edinburgh EH12 5DR

Conservative
Struan Stevenson, Scottish Conservative and Unionist Central Office, 14 Links Place, Edinburgh EH6 6EZ
John Purvis, CBE, Scottish Conservative and Unionist Central Office, 14 Links Place, Edinburgh EH6 6EZ

Scottish National Party
Ian Hudghton, 70 Rosemount Place, Aberdeen AB2 4XJ
Professor Neil MacCormick, Scottish National Party, 6 North Charlotte Street, Edinburgh EH2 4JH

Profile of Local Authorities

Aberdeen City Council
Population: 213,070
Electorate: 169,203
Election 1995: poll 38.0%; Con 9; Lab 30; LD, 10; SNP 1
Election 1999: poll 52.6%; Con 6; Lab 22; LD 12; SNP 3
Referendum 1997: poll 53.0%; for parliament 71.8%; for tax power 60.3%
Council Tax (Band D): £712
Rateable value per head of population: £1,218
Weekly rent of council house: £28

Aberdeenshire Council
Population: 226,260
Electorate: 173,574
Election 1995: poll 39.7%; Con 4; Lab 0; LD 15; SNP 15; Ind 13
Election 1999: poll 57.3%; Con 7; Lab 0; LD 28; SNP 23; Ind 10
Referendum 1997: poll 57.0%; for parliament 63.9%; for tax power 52.3%
Council Tax (Band D): £643
Rateable value per head of population: £519
Weekly rent of council house: £30

Angus Council
Population: 110,070
Electorate: 87,153
Election 1995: poll 43.7%; Con 2; Lab 0; LD 2; SNP 21; Ind 1
Election 1999: poll 56.7%; Con 2; Lab 1; LD 2; SNP 21; Ind 2
Referendum 1997: poll 60.2%; for parliament 64.7%; for tax power 53.4%
Council Tax (Band D): £679
Rateable value per head of population: £466
Weekly rent of council house: £25

Argyll and Bute Council
Population: 89,980
Electorate: 70,000
Election 1995: poll 51.2%; Con 3; Lab 2; LD 3; SNP 4; Ind 21
Election 1999: poll 63.1%; Con 3; Lab 1; LD 6; SNP 5; Ind 21
Referendum 1997: poll 65.0%; for parliament 67.3%; for tax power 57.0%
Council Tax (Band D): £801
Rateable value per head of population: £729
Weekly rent of council house: £35

Clackmannanshire Council
Population: 48,560
Electorate: 36,870

Election 1995: poll 46.9%; Con 1; Lab 8; LD 0; SNP 3; Ind 0
Election 1999: poll 63.3%; Con 1; Lab 8; LD 0; SNP 9; Ind 0
Referendum 1997: poll 66.1%; for parliament 80.0%; for tax power 68.7%
Council Tax (Band D): £753
Rateable value per head of population: £572
Weekly rent of council house: £29

Dumfries and Galloway Council
Population: 147,300
Electorate: 117,430
Election 1995: poll 50.2%; Con 2; Lab 21; LD 10; SNP 9; Ind 28
Election 1999: poll 62.4%; Con 8; Lab 13; LD 6; SNP 5; Ind 14; Others 1
Referendum 1997: poll 63.4%; for parliament 60.7%; for tax power 48.8%
Council Tax (Band D): £714
Rateable value per head of population: £558
Weekly rent of council house: £32

Dundee City Council
Population: 146,690
Electorate: 115,546
Election 1995: poll 43.8%; Con 4; Lab 28; SNP 3; Others 1
Election 1999: poll 53.7%; Con 0; Lab 14; SNP 10; Ind Lab 1
Referendum 1997: poll 55.7%; for parliament 76.0%; for tax power: 65.5%
Council Tax (Band D): £920
Rateable value per head of population: £829
Weekly rent of council house: £36

East Ayrshire Council
Population: 121,300
Electorate: 94,309
Election 1995: poll 53.2%; Con 0; Lab 22; LD 0; SNP 8
Election 1999: poll 62.8%; Con 1; Lab 17; LD 0; SNP 14
Referendum 1997: poll 64.8%; for parliament 81.1%; for tax power 70.5%
Council Tax (Band D): £779
Rateable value per head of population: £455
Weekly rent of council house: £27

East Dunbartonshire Council
Population: 109,570
Electorate: 85,388
Election 1995: poll 52.8%; Con 2; Lab 15; LD9; SNP 0
Election 1999: poll 67.1%; Con 3; Lab 11; LD 10; SNP 0; Ind 0
Referendum 1997: poll 62.7%; for parliament 69.8%; for tax power 59.1%
Council Tax (Band D): £771
Rateable value per head of population: £373
Weekly rent of council house: £30

East Lothian Council
Population: 89,570
Electorate: 71,103
Election 1995: Poll 48.4%; Con 3; Lab 15; LD 0; SNP 0
Election 1999: Poll 63.2%; Con 5; Lab 17; LD 0; SNP 1
Referendum 1997: Poll 65.0%; for parliament 74.2%; for tax power 62.7%
Council Tax (Band D): £724
Rateable value per head of population: £696
Weekly rent of council house: £29

East Renfrewshire Council
Population: 87,980
Electorate: 68,122
Election 1995: Poll 49.2%; Con 9; Lab 8; LD 2; SNP 0; Others 1
Election 1999: Poll 67.8%; Con 8; Lab 9; LD 2; SNP 0; Others 1
Referendum 1997: Poll 68.2%; for parliament 61.7%; for tax power 51.6%
Council Tax (Band D): £682
Rateable value per head of population: £307
Weekly rent of council house: £27

City of Edinburgh Council
Population: 450,180
Electorate: 366,088
Election 1995: poll 44.5%; Con 14; Lab 33; LD 10; SNP 1
Election 1999: poll 61.0%; Con 13; Lab 31; LD 13; SNP 1
Referendum 1997: poll 60.1%; for parliament 71.9%; for tax power 62.0%
Council Tax (Band D): £837
Rateable value per head of population: £1,156
Weekly rent of council house: £45

Falkirk Council
Population: 144,110
Electorate: 112,129
Election 1995: poll 45.8%; Con 2; Lab 23; LD 0; SNP 8; Ind 3
Election 1999: poll 61.2%; Con 2; Lab 15; LD 0; SNP 9; Ind 6
Referendum 1997: poll 63.7%; for parliament 80.0%; for tax power 69.2%
Council Tax (Band D): £680
Rateable value per head of population: £810
Weekly rent of council house: £30

Fife Council
Population: 348,900
Electorate: 279,808
Election 1995: poll: 42.6%; Con 0; Lab 54; LD 25; SNP 9; Ind 3; Others 1
Election 1999: poll: 56.1%; Con 1; Lab 43; LD 21; SNP 9; Ind 2; Others 2
Referendum 1997: poll 60.7%; for parliament 76.1%; for tax power 64.7%

Council Tax (Band D): £747
Rateable value per head of population: £741
Weekly rent of council house: £30

Glasgow City Council
Population: 619,680
Electorate: 493,033
Election 1995: poll 38.9%; Con 3; Lab 77; LD 1; SNP 1; Others 1
Election 1999: poll 47.0%; Con 1; Lab 74; LD 1; SNP 2; Others 1
Referendum 1997: poll 51.6%; for parliament 83.6%; for tax power 75.0%
Council Tax (Band D): £982
Rateable value per head of population: £1,023
Weekly rent of council house: £40

Highland Council
Population: 208,300
Electorate: 165,333
Election 1995: poll 46.4%; Con 1; Lab 7; LD 6; SNP 9; Ind 49
Election 1999: poll 62.4%; Con 0; Lab 10; LD 12; SNP 8; Ind 50
Referendum 1997: poll 60.3%; for parliament 72.6%; for tax power 62.1%
Council Tax (Band D): £718
Rateable value per head of population: £656
Weekly rent of council house: £38

Inverclyde Council
Population: 85,400
Electorate: 67,110
Election 1995: poll 47.0%; Con 1; Lab 14; LD 5; SNP 0
Election 1999: poll 58.6%; Con 1; Lab 11; LD 8; SNP 0
Referendum 1997: poll 60.4%; for parliament 78.0%; for tax power 67.2%
Council Tax (Band D): £831
Rateable value per head of population: £553
Weekly rent of council house: £34

Midlothian Council
Population: 80,860
Electorate: 62,443
Election 1995: poll 44.9%; Con 0; Lab 13; LD 0; SNP 2
Election 1999: poll 62.0%; Con 0; Lab 17; LD 1; SNP 0
Referendum 1997: poll 65.1%; for parliament 79.9%; for tax power 67.7%
Council Tax (Band D): £858
Rateable value per head of population: £433
Weekly rent of council house: £25

Moray Council
Population: 85,870
Electorate: 65,352

Election 1995: poll 40.1%; Con 0; Lab 3; LD 0; SNP 13; Ind 2
Election 1999: poll 56%; Con 1; Lab 6; LD 2; SNP 2; Ind/Non Aligned 15
Referendum 1997: poll 57.8%; for parliament 67.2%; for tax power 52.7%
Council Tax (Band D): £652
Rateable value per head of population: £567
Weekly rent of council house: £28

North Ayrshire Council
Population: 139,660
Electorate: 107,630
Election 1995: poll: 49.4%; Con 1; Lab 27; LD 0; SNP 1; Ind 1
Election 1999: poll 58.5%; Con 2; Lab 25; LD 0; SNP 2; Ind 1
Referendum 1997: poll 63.4%; for parliament 76.3%; for tax power 65.7%
Council Tax (Band D): £718
Rateable value per head of population: £658
Weekly rent of council house: £30

North Lanarkshire Council
Population: 326,740
Electorate: 228,905
Election 1995: poll 48.1%; Con 0; Lab 60; LD 0; SNP 7; Ind 2
Election 1999: poll 57.3%; Con 0; Lab 56; LD 0; SNP 12; Ind 2
Referendum 1997: poll 60.8%; for parliament 82.6%; for tax power 72.2%
Council Tax (Band D): £699.56
Rateable value per head of population: £544
Weekly rent of council house: £30

Orkney Islands Council
Population: 19,550
Electorate 15,468
No election in 1995; Con 0; Lab 0; LD 0; SNP 0; Ind 28
Election 1999: poll 59.6%; Con 0; Lab 0; LD 0; SNP 0; Ind 21
Referendum 1997: poll 53.4%; for parliament 57.3%; for tax power 47.4%
Council Tax (Band D): £515
Rateable value per head of population: £738
Weekly rent of council house: £33

Perth and Kinross Council
Population: 133,040
Electorate: 105,653
Election 1995: poll 51.3%; Con 2; Lab 6; LD 5; SNP 18; Ind 1
Election 1999: poll 63.3%; Con 11; Lab 6; LD 6; SNP 16; Ind 2
Referendum 1997: poll 63.1%; for parliament 61.7%; for tax power 51.3%
Council Tax (Band D): £732
Rateable value per head of population: £708
Weekly rent of council house: £28

Renfrewshire Council
Population: 177,830
Electorate: 139,095
Election 1995: poll 47.4%; Con 2; Lab 22; LD 3; SNP 13
Election 1999: poll 58.7%; Con 1; Lab 22; LD 3; SNP 14
Referendum 1997: poll 62.8%; for parliament 79.0%; for tax power 63.6%
Council Tax (Band D): £783
Rateable value per head of population: £759
Weekly rent of council house: £32

Scottish Borders Council
Population: 106,300
Electorate: 86,726
Election 1995: poll 40.3%; Con 3; Lab 2; LD 15; SNP 8; Ind 30
Election 1999: poll 60.6%; Con 1; Lab 1; LD 14; SNP 4; Ind 12
Referendum 1997: poll 64.8%; for parliament 62.8%; for tax power 50.7%
Council Tax (Band D): £612
Rateable value per head of population: £471
Weekly rent of council house: £29

Shetland Islands Council
Population: 22,910
Electorate: 17,149
No election in 1995; Con 0; Lab 2; LD 2; SNP 0; Ind 15; Others 7
Election 1999: poll 62.1%; Con 0; Lab 0; LD 8; SNP 0; Ind 14
Referendum 1997: poll 51.5%; for parliament 62.4%; for tax power 51.6%
Council Tax (Band D): £486
Rateable value per head of population: £1,626
Weekly rent of council house: £36

South Ayrshire Council
Population: 114,440
Electorate: 91,349
Election 1995: poll 55.5%; Con 4; Lab 21; LD 0; SNP 0
Election 1999: poll 65.4%; Con 13; Lab 17; LD 0; SNP 0
Referendum 1997: poll 66.7%; for parliament 66.9%; for tax power 56.2%
Council Tax (Band D): £765
Rateable value per head of population: £625
Weekly rent of council house: £32

South Lanarkshire Council
Population: 306,860
Electorate: 237,934
Election 1995: poll 46.8%; Con 2; Lab 62; LD 2; SNP 8
Election 1999: poll 59.2%; Con 2; Lab 54; LD 1; SNP 10
Referendum 1997: poll 63.1%; for parliament 77.8%; for tax power 67.6%

Council Tax (Band D): £793
Rateable value per head of population: £573
Weekly rent of council house: £35

Stirling Council
Population: 83,130
Electorate: 66,068
Election 1995: poll 54.2%;Con 7; Lab 13; LD 0; SNP 2
Election 1999: poll 65.9%; Con 9; Lab 11; LD 0; SNP 2
Referendum 1997: poll 65.8%; for parliament 68.5%; for tax power 58.9%
Council Tax (Band D): £776
Rateable value per head of population: £801
Weekly rent of council house: £34

West Dunbartonshire Council
Population: 94,880
Electorate: 72,554
Election 1995: Poll: 49.7% Con 0; Lab 14; LD 0; SNP 7; Ind 1
Election 1999: Poll 59.8%; Con 0; Lab 14; LD 0; SNP 7; Ind 1
Referendum 1997: poll 63.7%; for parliament 84.7%; for tax power 74.7%
Council Tax (Band D): £978
Rateable value per head of population: £607
Weekly rent of council house: £33

West Lothian Council
Population: 153,090
Electorate: 117,491
Election 1995: poll 46.7%; Con 1; Lab 15; LD 0; SNP 11
Election 1999: poll 59.9%; Con 1; Lab 20; LD 0; SNP 11
Referendum 1997: poll 62.6%; for parliament 79.6%; for tax power 67.3%
Council Tax (Band D): £792
Rateable value per head of population: £711
Weekly rent of council house: £32

Western Isles Council
Population: 27,940
Electorate: 22,626
No election in 1995; Con 0; Lab 5; LD 0; SNP 0; Ind 25
Election 1999: poll 64.2%; Con 0; Lab 6; LD 0; SNP 3; Ind 21
Referendum 1997: poll 55.8%; for parliament 79.4%; for tax power 68.4%
Council Tax (Band D): £599
Rateable value per head of population: £445
Weekly rent of council house: £37

The Directory

A Classified Guide to Scottish Organisations

ADDICTION

ALCOHOLICS ANONYMOUS
50 Wellington Street, Glasgow G2 6HJ
0141-226 2214

SCOTTISH COUNCIL ON ALCOHOL
2nd Floor, 166 Buchanan Street, Glasgow G1 2NH
0141-333 9677

SCOTTISH DRUGS FORUM
Shaftesbury House, 5 Waterloo Street, Glasgow G2 6AY
0141-221 1175
Director: David Liddell; *Chairperson:* Anne Thomson
Founded in 1986 to provide a voice for those concerned about the effects of drug use in Scotland. A membership organisation funded by the government and by grants and donations, SDF arranges conferences and seminars; deals with inquiries from drug workers and users, the general public and the media; publishes material aimed at dispelling the myths surrounding drugs and their use; provides drug action teams to support local and regional initiatives; organises training. Its general aim has been to co-ordinate action on drug issues.

AGRICULTURE, FORESTRY AND LAND

ABERDEEN-ANGUS CATTLE SOCIETY
6 King's Place, Perth PH2 8AD
01738 622477
Chief Executive: Ronald McHattie; *President:* Martin Leslie, CVO
Maintains the pedigrees of Aberdeen-Angus cattle and preserves and publishes these along with other relevant information in the Herd Book. Promotes the breeding of Aberdeen-Angus cattle for the production of Aberdeen-Angus beef.

AYRSHIRE CATTLE SOCIETY OF GREAT BRITAIN AND IRELAND
1 Racecourse Road, Ayr KA7 2DE
01292 267123
Chief Executive: Stuart Thomson; *President:* D M Stevenson
Breed society for Ayrshire dairy cows. Provides pedigrees, promotes the breed, tests progeny, and markets milk and dairy products under the "Ayrshires" brand.

CROFTERS COMMISSION
4/6 Castle Wynd, Inverness IV2 3EQ
01463 663450
Secretary: Mike Grantham; *Chairman:* Iain MacAskill
Government-funded organisation responsible for the reorganisation, development and regulation of crofting. Works with communities towards improvement and stability in rural areas. The commission delivers the crofting counties agricultural grants scheme.

DEER COMMISSION FOR SCOTLAND
Knowsley, 82 Fairfield Road, Inverness IV3 5LH
01463 231751
Director: Andy Rinning; *Chairman:* Andrew Raven
Established in 1959 to further the conservation and control of red deer and to keep under review all matters concerning them.

Its responsibilities were extended in 1982 to include sika deer and roe deer. As a result of legislation which came into effect in 1996, the commission's general functions were defined as the sustainable management of deer and their welfare, taking into account the impact on the natural heritage, the needs of agriculture and forestry, and the interests of owners and occupiers of land; and the protection of unenclosed woodlands and the natural heritage from damage by deer. Voluntary control agreements give the commission responsibility for co-ordinated deer control and management over wider areas than before. Under the new law, night shooting of any species of deer by any person must be authorised by the commission.

FORESTRY COMMISSION
231 Corstorphine Road, Edinburgh
EH12 7AT
0131-334 0303
Director General: David Bills
Government department responsible for forestry throughout Great Britain. Its aims are to protect Britain's forests and woodlands and to encourage their management and expansion in a way that increases their value to society and the environment. It is responsible for providing support and advice to ministers.

Its internal department, the Forestry Authority, implements the government's forestry policy, including the control of tree felling, administering grants for planting and restocking, and setting standards for the industry. The commission's forests are managed by its executive agency, Forest Enterprise.

GALLOWAY CATTLE SOCIETY OF GB AND IRELAND
15 New Market Street, Castle Douglas
DG7 1HY
01556 502753
Secretary: A J McDonald; *President:* Duke of Buccleuch and Queensberry, KT
Maintains pedigree Herd Book and promotes the breed of cattle known as Galloways, one of the oldest and purest breeds of cattle in the world.

HILL FARMING ADVISORY COMMITTEE FOR SCOTLAND
Room 235, Pentland House, 47 Robb's Loan, Edinburgh EH14 1TW
0131-244 6374

INSTITUTE OF CHARTERED FORESTERS
7a St Colme Street, Edinburgh EH3 6AA
0131-225 2705
Executive Director: Mrs M W Dick; *President:* George M McRobbie
Exists to maintain and improve the standards of professional practice. The representative body for the forestry profession throughout the UK.

MEAT AND LIVESTOCK COMMISSION
Rural Centre, Ingliston, Newbridge
EH28 8NZ

0131-472 4111
General Manager: A Donaldson; *Chairman:* D T Y Curry, CBE
Exists to help improve the efficiency of the meat and livestock industry, having due regard to consumer interests.

NATIONAL FARMERS' UNION OF SCOTLAND
Rural Centre, Ingliston, Newbridge
EH28 8LT
0131-472 4000
Chief Executive: Ed Rainy Brown
Provides an authoritative voice for the Scottish agricultural community in Edinburgh, Westminster and Europe. It speaks for farmers, growers and crofters as a united whole. In Scotland it has regular meetings with ministers. Its Brussels office gathers information, lobbies commissioners and MEPs, and maintains dialogue with other EU farming organisations.

A network of 66 area and branch secretaries, backed by headquarters, enables the union to offer a locally based service to its 12,500 members – including, for example, help in obtaining compensation for the effects of major roadworks, support for co-operative ventures, the resolution of landlord-tenant problems, and advice on employment legislation. The NFU Mutual is Scotland's leading agricultural insurer.

ROYAL HIGHLAND AND AGRICULTURAL SOCIETY OF SCOTLAND
Royal Highland Centre, Ingliston, Newbridge EH28 8NF
0131-333 2444
Chief Executive: Ray Jones
Established in 1784 as the Highland Society of Edinburgh, an association for the improvement of the Highlands, receiving its first royal charter in 1787 as the Highland Society of Scotland at Edinburgh. From its inception, the society promoted education and the arts in Scotland. In its first year a professor of Gaelic was elected and competitions in music were held.

The society's interest in agriculture dates from January 1785 when medals for essays on agricultural subjects were first offered. In 1790, the chair of agriculture at Edinburgh University was founded on the society's initiative, and in 1840 William Dick was installed as the first professor of veterinary studies at Edinburgh, under the society's auspices. These initiatives led to a change of title to the Highland and Agricultural Society of Scotland, and a second royal charter, in 1834. The final change of name came in 1948.

The present-day objectives of the society are the promotion of Scottish agriculture, allied industries and the rural economy. It has a membership of 14,000. Each June it organises the Royal Highland Show, which promotes all facets of the agricultural industry from livestock to crafts. It also awards medals and certificates for achievement and administers the Scottish woods and forest awards scheme.

ROYAL SCOTTISH AGRICULTURAL BENEVOLENT INSTITUTION

Ingliston, Edinburgh EH28 8NB
0131-333 1023/1027
Director: Ian Purves-Hume; *President:* Duke of Buccleuch and Queensberry, KT
Exists to provide financial and/or in-kind help, welfare advice and support to anyone in distress who is, or has been, in farming, forestry, fish farming, horticulture and rural estate work in Scotland, and their dependants.

ROYAL SCOTTISH FORESTRY SOCIETY

Hagg-on-Esk, Canonbie, Dumfriesshire DG14 0XE
013873 71518
Administrative Director: Andrew G Little; *President:* Alan F Bloomfield

SCOTCH QUALITY BEEF AND LAMB ASSOCIATION

Rural Centre, Ingliston, Newbridge EH28 8NZ
0131-472 4040
Chief Executive: Brian M Simpson; *Chairman:* John A Ross, CBE
Promotional and marketing body for Scotch beef and lamb.

SCOTTISH AGRICULTURAL SCIENCE AGENCY

82 Craigs Road, East Craigs, Edinburgh EH12 8NJ
0131-244 8890
Director: Dr R K M Hay
Provides government with expert scientific information and advice on agricultural and horticultural crops and aspects of the environment. It also performs statutory and regulatory work in relation to national, EU and other international legislation and agreements on plant health, bee health, variety registration and crop improvement, genetically manipulated organisms, and the protection of crops, food and the environment.

SCOTTISH AGRICULTURAL WAGES BOARD

Pentland House, 47 Robb's Loan, Edinburgh EH14 1TY
0131-244 6392
Secretary: Miss F H Anderson; *Chairperson:* Mrs C A M Davis, CBE
Exists to make Orders fixing minimum wage rates, holiday entitlement and other terms and conditions of service for workers employed in agriculture in Scotland.

SCOTTISH ASSOCIATION OF YOUNG FARMERS' CLUBS

Young Farmers' Centre, Ingliston, Newbridge EH28 8NE
0131-333 2445
National Secretary: Fiona Bain

SCOTTISH CROFTERS UNION

Old Mill, Broadford, Isle of Skye IV49 9AQ
01471 822529
Director: Rory Dutton; *President:* John MacKintosh
Promotes and preserves crofting.

SCOTTISH DAIRY ASSOCIATION

46 Underwood Road, Paisley PA3 1TL
0141-848 0009

SCOTTISH LANDOWNERS' FEDERATION

25 Maritime Street, Edinburgh EH6 5PW
0131-555 1031

Director: Maurice S Hankey; *President:* Alexander R Trotter

Membership organisation representing those who own and/or manage land in Scotland.

SCOTTISH MILK RECORDS ASSOCIATION
46 Underwood Road, Paisley PA3 1TJ
0141-848 0404
Director: Duncan Todd; *Chairman:* Charles Gibb

Provides milk recording service and information concerning dairy herds.

AMBULANCES

ST ANDREW'S AMBULANCE ASSOCIATION
St Andrew's House, 48 Milton Street, Glasgow G4 0HR
0141-332 4031
Chief Executive: Brendan Healy; *Chairman:* Dr E R Robinson

Provides first aid training and associated supplies.

SCOTTISH AMBULANCE SERVICE
Tipperlinn Road, Edinburgh EH10 5UU
0131-446 7000
Chief Executive: Adrian Lucas

In 1775 two sedan chairs were acquired on behalf of doctors at Edinburgh Royal Infirmary for the "swift and commodious carriage of persons needful of medicinal enquiry yet unable to proceed thereto". This was the first organised ambulance service in Scotland. In 1882 the St Andrew's Ambulance Association was formed, starting with two horse-drawn wagons in Glasgow. The ambulance service was incorporated into the NHS in 1948, the name "St Andrew's" was dropped from the title in 1974, and the service acquired trust status in 1995, giving it the freedom to manage its own affairs.

Scotland's is the only national ambulance service in the UK and the largest in Europe, employing 3,000 people and an operational fleet of 1,000 vehicles. It operates the UK's only integrated air ambulance service, co-ordinating 2,000 flights a year to ensure that even patients in the remotest parts of Scotland can have swift access to hospital and high-quality patient care on the way.

ANGLING

SCOTTISH ANGLERS NATIONAL ASSOCIATION
Caledonia House, South Gyle, Edinburgh EH12 9DQ
0131-339 8808
Honorary Secretary: Jane Wright; *President:* Sandy Forgan

Governing body for the sport of game fishing in Scotland.

SCOTTISH FEDERATION OF SEA ANGLERS
Caledonia House, South Gyle, Edinburgh EH12 9DQ
0131-317 7192
Secretary: David Wilkie

Governing body for the sport of sea fishing in Scotland.

ANIMALS AND WILDLIFE

ADVOCATES FOR ANIMALS
10 Queensferry Street, Edinburgh EH2 4PG
0131-225 6039
Director: Les Ward; *President:* Jane Goodall, CBE

Exists to protect animals from cruelty, prevent the infliction of suffering, and promote the abolition of vivisection.

ANIMAL CONCERN
PO Box 3982, Glasgow G51 4WD
0141-445 3570
Campaigns Consultant: John Robins; *Chairperson:* Dr Macdonald Daly

Promotes the abolition of animal exploitation.

FAIR ISLE BIRD OBSERVATORY TRUST
Fair Isle, Shetland ZE2 9JU
01595 760258
Administrator: Hollie Craib

NATIONAL CANINE DEFENCE LEAGUE
Rescue Centre, Dovecotwell, by Glencaple, Dumfries DG1 4RH
01387 770346
Protects and defends dogs from abuse, cruelty, abandonment and any form of mistreatment.

PEOPLE'S DISPENSARY FOR SICK ANIMALS
Muiryfauld Drive, Tollcross, Glasgow G31 5RT
0141-778 9229

RSPB (ROYAL SOCIETY FOR THE PROTECTION OF BIRDS)
Dunedin House, 25 Ravelston Terrace, Edinburgh EH4 3TP
0131-311 6500
Director, Scotland: Stuart Housden

ROYAL ZOOLOGICAL SOCIETY OF SCOTLAND
Murrayfield, Edinburgh EH12 6TS
0131-334 9171
Director: Dr D Waugh
Founded in 1909, a private society existing in the terms of its royal charter "to promote, facilitate and encourage the study of zoology and kindred subjects and to foster and develop among the people an interest in and a knowledge of animal life". The society promotes, through the presentation of its living collections, the conservation of animal species and wild places by captive breeding, environmental education and scientific research. The society maintains the Edinburgh Zoological Park and the Highland Wildlife Park.

SCOTTISH KENNEL CLUB
3 Brunswick Place, Edinburgh EH7 5HP
0131-557 2877
Secretary General: I A Sim; *Convener:* Dr A E T Sneeded
The prime source of canine information in Scotland, with responsible dog ownership at the core of its activities. Breeders' register provides comprehensive source of information on pedigree dogs. Licenses most dog shows and runs two in Edinburgh each year. Training, rescue and welfare information.

SCOTTISH SOCIETY FOR THE PREVENTION OF CRUELTY TO ANIMALS
Braehead Mains, 603 Queensferry Road, Edinburgh EH4 6EA
0131-339 0222
Chief Executive: James Morris; *Chairman:* Adam R Thomson
Established in its present form from a merger of the Scottish and the Glasgow and West of Scotland societies and later mergers with the Glasgow Dog and Cat Home and the Aberdeen Association for the Prevention of Cruelty to Animals. Exists to prevent cruelty to animals and to promote kindness and humanity in their treatment.

Its inspectorate acts as the society's frontline in policing animal welfare legislation, rescuing animals in distress and providing advice and guidance to those in charge of animals. Animal welfare centres offer refuge to injured, abused and abandoned pets, farm animals and wildlife.

The society campaigns to improve animal welfare legislation both in the UK and the EU, provides an education programme in schools, and promotes improved animal husbandry systems.

SCOTTISH SOCIETY FOR THE PROTECTION OF WILD BIRDS
Foremount House, Kilbarchan PA10 2EZ
01505 702419
Secretary: Dr J A Gibson

SCOTTISH WILDLIFE TRUST
Cramond House, Cramond Glebe Road, Edinburgh EH4 6BT
0131-312 7765
Chief Executive: Steve Sankey
Works to protect wildlife in town and country. Through education, training and campaigning, surveying and managing wildlife habitats, looking after reserves, and partnerships with other organisations, it aims to safeguard the biodiversity of Scotland for the benefit of all. It is supported financially by its 14,000 members and by grants, donations and contracts from a variety of sources, including central and local government.

ARBITRATION

ADVISORY, CONCILIATION AND ARBITRATION SERVICE (ACAS) SCOTLAND
Franborough House, 123-157 Bothwell Street, Glasgow G2 7JR
0141-248 1400
Director Scotland: Frank Blair
Seeks to improve industrial relations and employment practice, to minimise conflict and to encourage people at work to be included in, and committed to, the greater effectiveness and success of their organisations. In preventing and resolving collective disputes, aims to identify disputes at the earliest possible stage.

ACAS has a statutory remit to promote statutory settlement of claims arising on most issues within the jurisdiction of industrial tribunals, such conciliation helping to avoid the cost of hearings. It also offers free, confidential and impartial information and advice on all aspects of employment relationships, including the rights of individual employees in matters of discipline, pay and deductions, and redundancy.

CHARTERED INSTITUTE OF ARBITRATORS (SCOTTISH BRANCH)
Whittinghame House, 1099 Great Western Road, Glasgow G12 0AA
0141-334 7222
Honorary Secretary: Bruce L Smith; *Chairman:* Gordon Bathgate
Exists to promote arbitration in Scotland and educate prospective and current arbitrators.

SCOTTISH COUNCIL FOR INTERNATIONAL ARBITRATION
27 Melville Street, Edinburgh EH3 7JF
0131-220 4776
Director/Secretary: J M Arnott; *Chairman:* Hon Lord Dervaird

ARCHAEOLOGY

COUNCIL FOR SCOTTISH ARCHAEOLOGY
c/o National Museums of Scotland, Chambers Street, Edinburgh EH1 1JF
0131-247 4119
Secretary: Mrs L Ferguson; *President:* Professor I B M Ralston
Membership organisation which works to advance the study and care of Scotland's historic environment and improve public awareness of its past.

SCOTTISH URBAN ARCHAEOLOGICAL TRUST
55 South Methven Street, Perth PH1 5NX
01738 622393
Director: David Bowler; *Chairman:* David R Penman
Concerned with archaeology in Scottish towns and their hinterlands.

SOCIETY OF ANTIQUARIES OF SCOTLAND
Royal Museum of Scotland, Chambers Street, Edinburgh EH1 1JF
0131-225 7534
Director: Fionna Ashmore
Founded in 1780 and incorporated by royal charter in 1783, the second oldest antiquarian society in Britain. Its purpose, as set out in the first of its laws, is the study of the antiquities and history of Scotland, more especially by means of archaeological research. The society is concerned with every aspect of the human past in Scotland.

Members have, from the beginning, been known as fellows. There are now some 3,000 around the world, as well as 21 honorary fellows elected for their outstanding scholarship. Membership is by election, held annually on St Andrew's Day, and is open to all with an interest in Scottish history and archaeology.

The society organises an annual programme of meetings, including monthly lectures in Edinburgh from October to June, a conference, and various seminars and excursions. All fellows receive the *Proceedings of the Society*, an annual record of research. A major part of its programme is the sponsorship of research, from survey and excavation to finds analysis and archival research.

In 1780 the society started to collect antiquities, manuscripts and books which formed the nucleus of the National Museums of Scotland. As the senior antiquarian body in Scotland, it has an important role in the cultural life and heritage of the country and is often consulted on heritage matters.

ARMED SERVICES AND EX-SERVICES

ARMY IN SCOTLAND
Craigie Hall, South Queensferry EH30 9TN
0131-310 2013
General Officer Commanding, Scotland: Major General M J Strudwick, CBE

EARL HAIG FUND SCOTLAND
New Haig House, Logie Green Road, Edinburgh EH7 4HR
0131-557 2782
Secretary: Major General J D MacDonald, CB, CBE, DL; *President:* Admiral Sir Michael Livesay, KCB
Benevolent organisation concerned with ex-Service men and women. Funds raised from Scottish Poppy Appeal.

OFFICERS' ASSOCIATION SCOTLAND
Haig House, 1 Fitzroy Place, Glasgow G3 7RG
0141-221 8141
Secretary: Lt Col J S D Robertson, DL
Provides financial assistance or advice to ex-officers, their widows, widowers and dependants, and assists ex-officers to find suitable employment.

ROYAL AIR FORCES ASSOCIATION
20 Queen Street, Edinburgh EH2 1JX
0131-225 5221
Director: G M Halloran; *President:* Air Vice Marshal J Morris, CBE
Service charity providing welfare assistance to former and serving RAF members, their widows and dependants. Offers nursing care, convalescence, war pensions advice and comradeship too, through its network of branches and clubs.

ROYAL BRITISH LEGION SCOTLAND
New Haig House, Logie Green Road, Edinburgh EH7 4HR
0131-557 2782
Director: Major General J D MacDonald; *President:* Admiral Sir Michael Livesay, KCB
Set up to look after the social and legislative needs of the ex-Service community.

SCOTTISH NATIONAL WAR MEMORIAL
The Castle, Edinburgh EH1 2YT
0131-310 5130
Secretary to the Trustees: Lt-Col H D R MacKay; *Chairman of Trustees:* Major General Sir John Swinton, KCVO, OBE
Commemorates and keeps the Rolls of Honour of Scottish war dead, 1914–18, 1939–45, and since 1945. Provides information to relatives and amends Rolls. The Memorial is a basilica type of building designed and built by Scots.

SCOTTISH SOCIETY FOR EMPLOYMENT OF EX-REGULAR SAILORS, SOLDIERS & AIRMEN
New Haig House, Logie Green Road, Edinburgh EH7 4HR
0131-557 1747
Secretary/Treasurer: Frank McGuinness; *Chairman:* Lt-Col (Retd) P J Rettie
Finds employment for regular ex-Service personnel.

ARTS
See also: Arts Centres; Dance; Museums and Galleries; Music; Theatre; Theatres and Concert Halls

SCOTTISH ARTS COUNCIL
12 Manor Place, Edinburgh EH3 7DD
0131-226 6051
Director: Tessa Jackson; *Chairman:* Magnus Linklater
One of the main funding sources for arts organisations in Scotland, an autonomous organisation operating under a royal charter, responsible to and financed by the Scottish Executive. Its aim is to create a climate in which arts of quality flourish and are enjoyed throughout Scotland.

The SAC's current priorities are education; Scotland's indigenous arts; encouraging international links and artistic innovation; creating greater access to the arts; and improving arts marketing. It distributes National Lottery money to the arts in Scotland.

The SAC funds 73 organisations on a continuing basis, including the four national companies – Scottish Opera, Royal Scottish National Orchestra, Scottish Chamber Orchestra and Scottish Ballet – art galleries, festivals, theatres, arts centres and touring companies. It also gives awards, bursaries and grants to writers and artists.

ARTS CENTRES

Listed is a selection of arts centres of special interest. A more comprehensive list can be obtained from the Scottish Arts Council.

CENTRE FOR CONTEMPORARY ARTS
350 Sauchiehall Street, Glasgow G2 3JD
0141-332 7521
Managing Director: Graham McKenzie
Hosts contemporary visual arts, performance, music and literary events. Has cafe/bar, bookshop and a number of cultural tenants.

CRAWFORD ARTS CENTRE
93 North Street, St. Andrews KY16 9AL
01334 474610
Gallery Director: Diana Sykes
Hosts temporary exhibitions of visual art and craft. Provides art classes for adults and children, artists' studio, and studio theatre.

DUNDEE CONTEMPORARY ARTS
152 Nethergate, Dundee DD1 4DY
01382 432000
Director: Andrew Nairne
Contains galleries, cinemas and extensive facilities for artists and designers.

AN LANNTAIR
Town Hall, South Beach, Stornoway, Isle of Lewis HS1 2BX
01851 703307
Director: Roddy Murray; *Chairman:* Dr John Smith
The main public arts facility in the Western Isles. Its roles include the provision of a forum for local, national and international arts.

LEMON TREE
5 West North Street, Aberdeen AB24 5AT
01224 647999
Director: Shona Powell; *Chair:* Mike Tuckwell
Arts centre, development agency, and community resource.

LYTH ARTS CENTRE
by Wick KW1 4UD
01955 641270
Director: William Wilson
Provides exhibitions of contemporary fine art, plus live performances by professional touring theatre, dance and music companies.

MACROBERT ARTS CENTRE
University of Stirling, Stirling FK9 4LA
01786 467159
Director: Liz Moran

PIER ARTS CENTRE
Victoria Street, Stromness, Orkney KW16 3AA
01856 850209
Director: Neil Firth; *Founder:* Margaret Gardiner
Permanent collection of 20th century British art, including works by Hepworth, Nicholson, Gabo, Frost, Heron, Paolozzi, Wallis. Programme of contemporary art exhibitions.

ATHLETICS

SCOTTISH ATHLETICS FEDERATION
Caledonia House, South Gyle, Edinburgh EH12 9DQ
0131-317 7320
Chief Executive: David Joy; *President:* Ron Morrison

BADMINTON

SCOTTISH BADMINTON UNION
Cockburn Centre, 40 Bogmoor Place,
Glasgow G51 4TQ
0141-445 1218
Chief Executive: Anne Smillie; *President:*
Ronald E Conway

BANKS
Listed are the Scottish head offices of non-Scottish banks as well as the major indigenous banks

ADAM & COMPANY GROUP
22 Charlotte Square, Edinburgh EH2
4DF
0131-225 8484
Managing Director: Raymond Entwistle;
Chairman: W M C Kennedy

BANK OF ENGLAND
Agency for Scotland, 19 St Vincent
Place, Glasgow G1 2DT
0141-221 7972
Agent for Scotland: Janet Bulloch
Reports to the Monetary Policy
Committee on business conditions in
Scotland, as well as representing the
Bank of England in Scotland.

BANK OF SCOTLAND
The Mound, Edinburgh EH1 1YZ
0131-442 7777
Group Chief Executive: Peter A Burt;
Governor: Sir John Shaw
Established by an Act of the Parliament
on 17 July 1695 "for the Carrying on and
Managing of a Public Bank". It is the
only bank ever to be founded by such an
Act and the only commercial institution
created by the Scots Parliament which is
still in existence. It is also unique in
being the oldest surviving UK clearing
bank founded specifically to make a
business of banking.
  The bank was set up primarily to
help develop Scotland's trade, mainly
with England and the Low Countries. It
was the first bank in Europe
successfully to issue paper currency,
redeemable for cash on demand. The
right to issue banknotes has been

maintained to the present day.
  It was not until 1774 that the first
branches were opened in Dumfries and
Kelso. Today the bank has more than
300 branches throughout Scotland, as
well as 24 in England.
  In the last 30 years there has been a
rapid expansion of its activities. It
played a central role in financing the
North Sea oil industry, and in 1959 it
became the first UK bank to instal a
computer to process its accounts
centrally.
  Bank of Wales was established as a
regional bank in 1986, and more recently
it acquired Bank of Western Australia
Ltd. Bank of Scotland Group now
employs 20,000 people in companies
and countries across the world.

BRITISH LINEN BANK LIMITED
4 Melville Street, Edinburgh EH3 7NX
0131-243 8386
Chief Executive: Professor J Robin
Browning
Merchant banking subsidiary of Bank of
Scotland, headquartered in Edinburgh.
A principal subsidiary within the group,
the British Linen Bank, celebrated in
1996 the 250th anniversary of the
granting of its royal charter.

CHASE MANHATTAN BANK
91 George Street, Edinburgh EH2 3ES
0131-225 7776
Managing Director (Scotland): Mark
Tennant

CITIBANK, NA
Capital House, 2 Festival Square,
Edinburgh EH3 9SU
0131-228 3000

CLYDESDALE BANK PLC
30 St Vincent Place, Glasgow G1 2HL
0141-248 7070
Chief Executive: John Wright
Founded in 1838. Operates 297 branches
in Scotland, England and the Isle of
Man.

MIDLAND BANK
76 Hanover Street, Edinburgh EH2 1HQ
0131-456 3257
Area Manager: David Mackay

NatWest
80 George Street, Edinburgh EH2 3DZ
0131-226 6181

The Royal Bank of Scotland plc
42 St Andrew Square, Edinburgh EH2 2YE
0131-556 8555
Group Chief Executive: Sir George Mathewson, CBE; *Chairman:* Rt Hon Viscount Younger of Leckie, KT, KCVO
Founded 1727, following the expiry of the Bank of Scotland's monopoly 11 years earlier. It merged in 1969 with the National Commercial Bank of Scotland. Royal Bank of Scotland International, launched in 1996, is now one of the world's largest offshore banks.

TSB Bank Scotland plc
Henry Duncan House, 120 George Street, Edinburgh EH2 4TS
0131-225 4555
Chief Executive: John A Spence; *Chairman:* Gordon A Anderson
Wholly owned subsidiary of Lloyds TSB Group plc.

Warburg Dillon Read
66 Hanover Street, Edinburgh EH2 1HH
0131-225 9186

BASKETBALL

Scottish Basketball Association
Caledonia House, South Gyle, Edinburgh EH12 9DQ
0131-317 7260
Director: Sadie F E Mason

BEREAVEMENT

CRUSE Bereavement Care (Scotland)
33 Boswall Parkway, Edinburgh EH5 2BR
0131-551 1511
Chief Officer: Ruth Hampton; *Chairman:* John Beaumont
Helps people who have been bereaved to go on with their lives in a positive way through counselling. Also trains those who work with the dying.

BLOOD TRANSFUSION

Scottish National Blood Transfusion Association
2 Otterburn Park, Edinburgh EH14 1JX
0131-443 7636
Secretary and Treasurer: William Mack; *Chairman:* Peter C Taylor
Promotes, encourages and maintains the principles of voluntary, non-remunerated blood donation, and safeguards and protects the interets of the voluntary donor.

Scottish National Blood Transfusion Service
Ellen's Glen Road, Edinburgh EH17 7QT
0131-536 5700
General Manager: Angus MacMillan Douglas
Provides a comprehensive range of blood components, blood products, clinical services and human tissue for patient care throughout Scotland. A thousand blood donors are needed every day in Scotland to supply hospitals throughout the country. Blood donor sessions – about 4,000 a year – take place in community centres, five regional blood donor centres, workplaces, and universities, colleges and schools.

BOOK PUBLISHERS
Listed is a selection of the larger publishers and a few others of special interest. A more comprehensive list is obtainable from the Scottish Publishers Association.

Acair Ltd
7 James Street, Stornoway, Isle of Lewis HS1 2QN
01851 703020

B&W Publishing Ltd
29 Inverleith Row, Edinburgh EH3 5QH
0131-552 5555

BUTTERWORTHS SCOTLAND
4 Hill Street, Edinburgh EH2 3JZ
0131-225 7828

CANONGATE BOOKS
14 High Street, Edinburgh EH1 1TE
0131-557 5111

CHAMBERS HARRAP
7 Hopetoun Crescent, Edinburgh EH7
4AY
0131-556 5929

EDINBURGH UNIVERSITY PRESS
22 George Square, Edinburgh EH8 9LF
0131-650 4218

W GREEN
21 Alva Street, Edinburgh EH2 4PS
0131-225 4879

HARCOURT BRACE & CO
Robert Stevenson House, 1-3 Baxter's
Place, Edinburgh EH1 3AF
0131-556 2424

HARPERCOLLINS
PUBLISHERS/HARPERCOLLINS
CARTOGRAPHIC
Westerhill Road, Bishopbriggs, Glasgow
G64 2QT
0141-772 3200

LOMOND BOOKS
36 West Shore Road, Granton,
Edinburgh EH5 1QD
0131-551 2261

MAINSTREAM PUBLISHING
7 Albany Street, Edinburgh EH1 3UG
0131-557 2959

MERCAT PRESS
James Thin Ltd, 53-59 South Bridge,
Edinburgh EH1 1YS
0131-556 6743

NEIL WILSON PUBLISHING LTD
Suite 303a, The Pentagon Centre, 36
Washington Street, Glasgow G3 8AZ
0141-221 1117

POLYGON
22 George Square, Edinburgh EH8 9LF
0131-650 8436

RAMSAY HEAD PRESS
15 Gloucester Place, Edinburgh EH3
6EE
0131-225 5646

SAINT ANDREW PRESS
121 George Street, Edinburgh EH2 4YN
0131-225 5722

**SCOTTISH CULTURAL PRESS AND
SCOTTISH CHILDREN'S PRESS**
Unit 13D, Newbattle Abbey Business
Annex, Newbattle Road, Dalkeith EH22
3LJ 0131-660 4757

BOWLING

SCOTTISH BOWLING ASSOCIATION
50 Wellington Street, Glasgow G2 6EF
0141-221 8999
Secretary: William S Forbes; *President:*
John Renwick

**SCOTTISH WOMEN'S BOWLING
ASSOCIATION**
3 Jamaica Street, Greenock PA15 1XX
01475 724676
Secretary: Mrs Eleanor Allan

BUILDING SOCIETIES

DUNFERMLINE BUILDING SOCIETY
Caledonia House, Carnegie Avenue,
Dunfermline KY11 5PJ
01383 627727
Chief Executive: David Smith, OBE;
Chairman: John Herd

SCOTTISH BUILDING SOCIETY
23 Manor Place, Edinburgh EH3 7XE
0131-220 1111
Chief Executive: Roderick Matheson;
Chairman: Peter C Brown

BUSINESS ORGANISATIONS

**CBI SCOTLAND (CONFEDERATION OF
BRITISH INDUSTRY)**
Beresford House, 5 Claremont Terrace,

Glasgow G3 7XT
0141-332 8661
Director: Iain M McMillan; *Chairman:* Andrew Dewar-Durie
Aims "to help create and sustain the conditions in which business in the UK can compete and prosper". Represents its members' views to the government and to other national and international administrations. Supplies advice, information and research services to members and provides a forum for the exchange and encouragement of best practice. The CBI claims to bring "business reality" to political debate, reacting to government proposals which it regards as unwelcome or ill-considered.

INSTITUTE OF DIRECTORS (SCOTLAND)
29 Abercrombie Place, Edinburgh EH3 6QE
0131-557 5488
Director: Tom Sunter

QUALITY SCOTLAND FOUNDATION
13 Abercromby Place, Edinburgh EH3 6LB
0131-556 2333
Chief Executive: David B Justice, MBE; *Chairman:* Andrew Cubie
Fourteen prominent Scottish-based organisations came together in 1991 with the mission of making commitment to quality "a recognised national characteristic". Non-profit-making and non-political, it aims to promote business excellence.

Launched in 1994, the Quality Scotland Award for Business Excellence includes four categories: manufacturing; service; smaller enterprise; and public sector. The awards are presented at an annual lunch following the Scottish Forum for Business Excellence.

SCOTTISH COUNCIL DEVELOPMENT AND INDUSTRY
23 Chester Street, Edinburgh EH3 7ET
0131-225 7911
Chief Executive: Alan Wilson; *Chairman:* Donald Turner; *President:* Dr Ian Preston, CBE
Established in 1946, an independent, broadly-based membership organisation (current membership: 2,200) which aims to influence and strengthen Scotland's economy through the formulation and promotion of innovative, non-partisan public policies and the delivery of market-driven services for members.

The Scottish Council Foundation, an independent think tank committed to developing longer-term public policy research, has been re-launched.

SCOTTISH FINANCIAL ENTERPRISE
91 George Street, Edinburgh EH2 3ES
0131-225 6990
Chief Executive: Ray Perman; *Chairman:* Mike Russell
Private sector initiative, established in 1986 to represent and promote the Scottish financial industry, SFE serves a membership of some 200 companies and individuals who are its principal funders, and operates in partnership with Scottish Enterprise and Highlands and Islands Enterprise. Its general aims are to strengthen Scotland's global financial role and to maintain the independence and cohesion of the industry.

SFE publishes a wide range of publications about facts, trends and issues, backed up by an intensive programme of briefings, seminars and conferences. It conducts regular surveys of its members, prepares research papers, represents the interests of its members to the government, regulatory bodies and the EC, arranges missions to or from countries which offer an actual or potential market, and helps with bids to attract new business to Scotland. It works with Scottish Enterprise to improve access to finance for small and medium-sized enterprises, aiming to develop a financial infrastructure not only for Scottish companies but for entrepreneurs from other parts of the EU interested in doing business in Scotland.

SFE was instrumental in founding the advanced management programme in Scotland, which aims to enhance the provision of business and management education.

BUSINESS ORGANISATIONS (YOUTH AND COMMUNITY)

COMMUNITY BUSINESS SCOTLAND
Society Place, West Calder EH55 8EA
01506 871370
Chief Executive: John Pearce

PRINCE'S SCOTTISH YOUTH BUSINESS TRUST
6th Floor, Mercantile Chambers, 53 Bothwell Street, Glasgow G2 6TS
0141-248 4999
Director: David Cooper
Provides seedcorn finance and professional support to young people in Scotland aged 18-25 to enable them to set up and run their own businesses. It has particular concern for the disadvantaged. The trust will identify and arrange training, help with the business plan, and suggest additional sources of support and finance. All applicants are formally interviewed. PSYBT works towards an annual target of 500 businesses a year.

RATHBONE COMMUNITY INDUSTRY SCOTLAND
CI Building, Scott Street, Motherwell ML1 1PN
01698 252326
Chief Executive: Anne Weinstock
Aims to ensure people with special educational or training needs realise their full potential and participate fully in the social and economic life of the community.

SCOTTISH BUSINESS IN THE COMMUNITY
30 Hanover Street, Edinburgh EH2 2DR
0131-220 3001
Chief Executive: Frank Pignatelli; *Chairman:* Sir Tom Farmer
Charity promoting business involvement with the community. SBC has developed business support groups to bring together business people and resources to help the disadvantaged residents of the large housing estates on the periphery of Scotland's cities. It is the main agency for arranging secondments from business to charitable, voluntary and community organisations.

SBC's aim is to make corporate community investment a natural part of good business practice. It is financed by the subscriptions of its members, who include most of Scotland's leading companies, and by the secondment of senior staff from private and public sector organisations.

Twelve business support groups work in schools and community groups giving practical assistance and advice as well as access to jobs and training opportunities. Action Scotland acts as a broker for people from industry, commerce and the public sector to use their business skills in the voluntary sector. The Scottish Corps of Retired Executives offers varied expertise to worthwhile causes, while the Professional Firms Group (accountants, solicitors, etc) provides its services free to community organisations.

YOUNG ENTERPRISE SCOTLAND
Graham Hills Building, 50 George Street, Glasgow G1 1BA
0141-548 4930
Chief Executive: Lynn Hendry
Scheme to encourage and develop enterprise and skills in older school students. Teams form companies which trade for about eight months.

CAMPING AND CARAVANNING

CAMPING AND CARAVANNING CLUB (SCOTTISH REGION)
20 The Oval, Clarkston, Glasgow G76 8LY
0141-637 5740
Secretary: Mrs P McIlraith; *Chairman:* D Batty

CARERS

CARERS NATIONAL ASSOCIATION
91 Mitchell Street, Glasgow G1 3LN
0141-221 9141

CROSSROADS (SCOTLAND) CARE ATTENDANT SCHEMES
24 George Square, Glasgow G2 1EG
0141-226 3793
Chief Executive: Jack Ryan; *Chairman:* W Douglas Allan
Provides respite care to carers in Scotland.

CHAMBERS OF COMMERCE

SCOTTISH CHAMBERS OF COMMERCE
Conference House, The Exchange, 152 Morrison Street, Edinburgh EH3 8EB
0131-477 8025
Director: Lex Gold; *Chairman:* Geoffrey Johnston
Chambers in Scotland represent 8,000 members ranging from the country's largest companies to the smallest retail and professional operations. Together they provide more than half the private sector jobs in Scotland. They vary in size from the chambers of Aberdeen, Dundee, Edinburgh and Glasgow, all with full-time professional staff, to small rural and island chambers serviced voluntarily.

Scottish Chambers of Commerce is the national body which promotes co-operation between chambers in the provision of services and represents their common interests. Policy is determined by a council on which all chambers have equal representation.

JUNIOR CHAMBER, SCOTLAND
24 Portland Road, Kilmarnock KA1 2BS
01563 572255
President: Graham McEwan

Local chambers:

ABERDEEN CHAMBER OF COMMERCE
27 Albyn Place, Aberdeen AB10 1DB
01224 252194
Chief Executive: Amanda Harvie

ALLANDER CHAMBER OF COMMERCE
2 Stewart Street, Milngavie, Glasgow G62 6BW
0141-956 4454
Secretary: Anne O'Hagan

ARBROATH CHAMBER OF COMMERCE
Business Shop Angus, 115 High Street, Arbroath DD11 1DP
01241 870563
Secretary: Laurie Smith

AYRSHIRE CHAMBER OF COMMERCE
Suite 1005, Glasgow Prestwick International Airport, Prestwick KA9 2PL 01292 678666
Executive Director: Robert H Leitch

CAITHNESS & SUTHERLAND CHAMBER OF COMMERCE
UKAEA, Dounreay, Thurso, Caithness
01847 802121
Secretary: Dr Bob Anderson

CENTRAL SCOTLAND CHAMBER OF COMMERCE
Haypark Business Centre, Marchmont Avenue, Polmont FK2 0NZ
01324 716868
Chief Executive: Andrew Fulton

CUMBERNAULD & DISTRICT CHAMBER OF COMMERCE
30 George Square, Glasgow G2 1EQ
0141-204 8347
Chairman and Secretary: Kevin Murphy

DUMFRIES & GALLOWAY CHAMBER OF TRADE AND COMMERCE
Dumfries Business Shop, 16 Buccleuch Street, Dumfries DG1 2AH
01387 266644
Secretary: Irene Porteous

DUNDEE & TAYSIDE CHAMBER OF COMMERCE
Chamber of Commerce Buildings, Panmure Street, Dundee DD1 1ED
01382 201122
Chief Executive: Harry Terrell

DUNOON CHAMBER OF COMMERCE
Ballochyle, Dunoon PA23 8RD
01369 704412
Secretary/Treasurer: Keith Lamanque

EAST KILBRIDE CHAMBER OF COMMERCE
PO Box 1, Scottish Enterprise Technology Park, East Kilbride G75 0NS
013552 38456
Secretary: Linda McDowall

EAST RENFREWSHIRE CHAMBER OF TRADE AND COMMERCE
49 Polmoon Street, Eaglesham G76 0BB
01355 303300
President: Margaret Robertson

EDINBURGH CHAMBER OF COMMERCE AND ENTERPRISE
Conference House, The Exchange, 152 Morrison Street, Edinburgh EH3 8EB
0131-477 7000
Chief Executive: Peter Stillwell

FIFE CHAMBER OF COMMERCE
Wemyssfield House, Wemyssfield, Kirkcaldy KY1 1XN
01592 201932
Chief Executive: Leon Wolk

FORT WILLIAM & DISTRICT CHAMBER OF COMMERCE
Scottish Crafts, 135-139 High Street, Fort William PH33 6EA
01397 704406
Chairman: Drew Purdon

GLASGOW CHAMBER OF COMMERCE
30 George Square, Glasgow G2 1EQ
0141-204 2121
Chief Executive: Peter Burdon; *President:* Subhash Joshi

GREENOCK CHAMBER OF COMMERCE
179A Dalrymple Street, Greenock PA15 1BX
01475 722233
Secretary: Elaine Brown

HAMILTON CHAMBER OF COMMERCE
Barncluith Business Centre, Townhead Street, Hamilton ML3 7DP
01698 426882
Secretary: Marion Currie

HELENSBURGH & LOMOND CHAMBER OF COMMERCE
81 James Street, Helensburgh G84 9LX
01436 676197
Chief Executive: John Wolfenden

INVERNESS & DISTRICT CHAMBER OF COMMERCE
PO Box 5512, Inverness IV2 3ZE
01463 718131
Director: Simon Cole-Hamilton

LEITH CHAMBER OF COMMERCE
Conference House, The Exchange, 152 Morrison Street, Edinburgh EH3 8EB
0131-477 7000
Secretary: Ann Baird

MID ARGYLL CHAMBER OF COMMERCE
Kilmory Industrial Estate, Lochgilphead, Argyll PA31 8RR
01546 606666
Secretary: Jane MacLeod

MIDLOTHIAN CHAMBER OF COMMERCE
29A Eskbank Road, Dalkeith EH22 1HJ
0131-654 1234
Chief Executive: Gregor Murray

MONTROSE CHAMBER OF COMMERCE
55 High Street, Montrose DD10 8LR
01674 671199
Secretary: Hamish Watt

MOTHERWELL AND DISTRICT CHAMBER OF COMMERCE
Town Hall Business Centre, 1–11 High Road, Motherwell ML1 3HU
01698 230200
Secretary: Ian Watson

MULL AND IONA CHAMBER OF COMMERCE
The Ferry Shop, Fionnphort, Isle of Mull PA66 6BL
01681 700470
President: Sandy Brunton

OBAN AND LORN CHAMBER OF COMMERCE
2/6 Stevenson Street, Oban PA34 5NB
01631 563158
Secretary: W Gordon Seaton

ORKNEY CHAMBER OF COMMERCE
PO Box 6202, Kirkwall, Orkney KW15 1YG
01856 872540
Secretary: Hazel Nicolson

PAISLEY & DISTRICT CHAMBER OF COMMERCE
Bute Court, St Andrews Drive, Glasgow Airport, Paisley PA3 2SW
0141-847 5450
Chief Executive: Elizabeth K Cameron

PEEBLESHIRE CHAMBER OF COMMERCE
Rosetta House, Rosetta Road, Peebles
EH45 8PG
01896 831483

PERTHSHIRE CHAMBER OF COMMERCE
The Atrium, 137 Glover Street, Perth
PH2 0JB
01738 637626
Secretary: Marilyn Wallace

**STRATHKELVIN CHAMBER OF COMMERCE
AND TRADE**
Bank of Scotland, 100 Cowgate,
Kirkintilloch, Glasgow G66 1JQ
0141-776 5599
Membership Secretary: Lex Gaston

WESTERN ISLES CHAMBER OF COMMERCE
MacKinnon Plant Hire, 18 Inaclete
Road, Stornoway, Isle of Lewis HS1 2RB
01851 702984
Chairman: Alastair MacKinnon

CHARITABLE TRUSTS

CARNEGIE HERO FUND TRUST
Abbey Park House, Dunfermline KY12
7PB
01383 723638
Secretary: William C Runciman;
Chairman: Dr A A H Lawson
Gives aid to a rescuer or to a rescuer's
family where a heroic act has brought
misfortune (concerned with cases which
have resulted in death or serious injury
only).

CARNEGIE UNITED KINGDOM TRUST
Comely Park House, Dunfermline KY12
7EJ
01383 721445
Secretary and Treasurer: John Naylor, OBE
Grant-making trust whose current
priorities are in arts, heritage and
community.

CHILDREN

BARNARDO'S SCOTLAND
235 Corstorphine Road, Edinburgh EH12
7AR
0131-334 9893
Director of Children's Services: Hugh
Mackintosh, OBE
Provides social welfare services for the
benefit of children and young people
most in need of them; promotes good
practice and developments; influences
social welfare policy; raises awareness
of and encourages good childcare.

THE BOYS' BRIGADE
Scottish HQ, Carronvale House,
Carronvale Road, Larbert FK5 3LH
01324 562008
Secretary: Ian McLaughlan; *Chairperson,
Scottish Committee:* Alistair F Marquis
National voluntary youth organisation
committed to the personal and social
development of children and young
people in Scotland. As part of the
community education provision,
promoting the concept of life-long
learning, it seeks to serve local churches
in most communities by offering a range
of informal educational programmes
which are led by voluntary youth
workers.

BOYS AND GIRLS CLUBS OF SCOTLAND
88 Giles Street, Edinburgh EH6 6BZ
0131-555 1729
Chief Adviser: Tom Leishman

**BRITISH AGENCIES FOR ADOPTION AND
FOSTERING**
40 Shandwick Place, Edinburgh EH2
4RT
0131-225 9285
Scottish Director: Barbara J Hudson
Concerned with supporting people
working to provide a high standard of
care for children.

CHILDLINE SCOTLAND
18 Albion Street, Glasgow G1 1LH
0141-552 1123
Director: Anne Houston
Provides free, confidential telephone
counselling for any child or young
person with any problem. The
organisation "speaks with the voice of
children" to influence policy and
practice in childcare services.

CHILDREN 1ST
41 Polwarth Terrace, Edinburgh EH11 1NU
0131-337 8539
Chief Executive: Margaret McKay
One of Scotland's leading childcare agencies. For 114 years the charity (formerly known as the Scottish Society for Prevention of Cruelty to Children) has protected children from harm and provided support and help to children and young people who have suffered violence, exploitation and all kinds of abuse and neglect.

CHILDREN IN SCOTLAND
Princes House, 5 Shandwick Place, Edinburgh EH2 4RG
0131-228 8484
Director: Bronwen Cohen; *Convener:* Rt Hon Bruce Millan
The central independent Scottish agency for over 300 voluntary, statutory and professional organisations and individuals working with children and families throughout Scotland. It aims to promote the exchange of information and the development of policies to improve children's quality of life, and services the Scottish All Party Parliamentary Group for Children.

CHILDREN'S HOSPICE ASSOCIATION SCOTLAND
18 Hanover Street, Edinburgh EH2 2EN
0131-226 4933
Chief Executive: Agnes Malone; *Chairman:* Professor Forrester Cockburn
Provides a hospice service to children and their families.

FAMILY MEDIATION SCOTLAND
127 Rose Street South Lane, Edinburgh EH2 4BB
0131-220 1610
Director: Elizabeth Foster; *Chair:* Hugh Donald
Supports 12 local mediation services throughout Scotland working to meet the needs of children of separating or divorced parents.

GIRLS' BRIGADE IN SCOTLAND
Boys' Brigade House, 168 Bath Street, Glasgow G2 4TQ
0141-332 1765
Secretary: Ann Webster; *National President:* Jean T Morrison
Part of an international, interdenominational, Christian, uniformed organisation for girls. Four specific areas are covered in its programme: spiritual, physical, education and service.

GUIDE ASSOCIATION SCOTLAND
16 Coates Crescent, Edinburgh EH3 7AH
0131-226 4511
Executive Director: Sally Pitches; *Scottish Chief Commissioner:* Mrs Sally McMath
Provides self-development opportunities to girls and young women through a programme of activities delivered by trained volunteer leaders.

NATIONAL FOSTER CARE ASSOCIATION
1 Melrose Street (off Queens Crescent), Glasgow G4 9BJ
0141-332 6655
Executive Director: Gerri McAndrew
Aims to ensure the highest standards of care for all children and young people who are fostered, by providing training, advice, support, information and consultancy.

ONE PARENT FAMILIES SCOTLAND
13 Gayfield Square, Edinburgh EH1 3NX
0131-556 3899
Director: Sue Robertson; *Convener:* Marilyn Jeffcoat
Helps lone parents achieve their full potential as individuals and as parents.

QUARRIERS – THE CARING COMMUNITIES
Quarriers Village, Bridge of Weir PA11 3SX
01505 612224

SAILORS' ORPHAN SOCIETY OF SCOTLAND
Cumbrae House, 15 Carlton Court, Glasgow G5 9JP
0141-429 2181
Secretary: Audrey Macnair
Provides financial support to orphans of sea-faring men throughout Scotland.

ST ANDREW'S CHILDREN'S SOCIETY
Gillis Centre, 113 Whitehouse Loan, Edinburgh EH9 1BB
0131-452 8248
Chairperson: Maureen McEvoy; *President:* Archbishop Keith O'Brien
Recruits, trains and approves adopting parents and foster carers. Works with everyone involved in adoption.

ST MARGARET OF SCOTLAND ADOPTION SOCIETY
274 Bath Street, Glasgow G2 4JR
0141-332 8371
Director: Margaret Campbell; *President:* His Eminence Cardinal Thomas J Winning
Voluntary adoption agency operating in the West of Scotland. Provides a range of pre- and post-adoption services.

SAVE THE CHILDREN FUND, SCOTLAND PROGRAMME OFFICE
7th Floor, Haymarket House, 8 Clifton Terrace, Edinburgh EH12 5DR
0131-527 8200
Director: Alison Davies
The organisation's work, based on the UN Convention on the Rights of the Child, has three aims: building a movement for children's rights in Scotland; promoting the interests of the most marginalised children; developing the role of children and young people as community activists. Aims to give children and young people the chance to take part in society by encouraging them to express their views, and to take part in research and in the development and running of initiatives addressing issues that concern them.

SCOTTISH ADOPTION ASSOCIATION
2 Commercial Street, Leith, Edinburgh EH6 6JA
0131-553 5060
Director: Ann Sutton
Aims to offer as comprehensive an adoption service as possible to all affected by adoption.

SCOTTISH CHILDMINDING ASSOCIATION
Room 7, Stirling Business Centre, Wellgreen, Stirling FK8 2DZ
01786 445377

Director: Anne McNellan, MBE; *Convener:* Kate Ramsey
Aims to raise the profile and quality of day-care by offering support, information and training.

SCOTTISH CHILDREN'S REPORTER ADMINISTRATION
Ochil House, Springkerse Business Park, Stirling FK7 7XE
01786 459500
Principal Reporter: Alan D Miller; *Chairman:* Sally Kuenssberg
As part of local government reorganisation in 1996, Children's Reporters and their support staff were united in one national organisation with a new professional framework and the status of a non-departmental public body funded directly by grant-in-aid. It is responsible for facilitating the work of Reporters, deploying and managing staff to carry out that work, and providing suitable accommodation for children's hearings.

A referral is a notification of concern about a child to the Reporter, as long as that concern can be related to one or more of the statutory grounds for intervention. For every referral received, the Reporter must make an appropriate investigation and reach a decision – a process which normally involves obtaining reports from agencies in contact with the child and family. Eight out of 10 children referred to children's hearings become subject to a supervision requirement.

SCOUT ASSOCIATION (SCOTTISH COUNCIL)
Fordell Firs, Hillend, Dunfermline KY11 7HQ
01383 419073
Chief Executive: James A Duffy; *Honorary President:* Rt Hon Earl of Airlie, KT, GCVO, PC, DL
Aims to promote the development of young people in achieving their full physical, intellectual, social and spiritual potential as individuals, as responsible citizens, and as members of their local, national and international communities.

STEPPING STONES IN SCOTLAND
55 Renfrew Street, Glasgow G2 3BD
0141-331 2828
Director: Isobel Lawson; *Chairperson:* Jane Macrae
National voluntary organisation working to empower families affected by disadvantage so that they can effectively seek to improve their own lives and the communities in which they live.

CHURCHES

ASSOCIATED PRESBYTERIAN CHURCHES
Drumalin, 16 Drummond Road, Inverness IV2 4NB
01463 223983
Clerk: Rev Dr M MacInnes

BAPTIST UNION OF SCOTLAND
14 Aytoun Road, Glasgow G41 5RT
0141-423 6169
General Secretary: Rev. Bill Slack; *President:* James Campbell
Among Oliver Cromwell's troops arriving in Scotland in the 17th century were many Baptist soldiers who used their influence to establish small churches in Leith, Perth, Cupar, Ayr and Aberdeen. When the army withdrew, these churches disappeared and for the next 100 years Baptist life in Scotland ceased to exist. It was revived in 1750 when a congregation was established in the village of Keiss, Caithness.

The Baptist Union of Scotland came into being in 1869. Strict practice gave way to greater freedom of worship and the introduction of hymns, choirs and organs. Rich Christian industrialists, including Coats of Paisley, Pullar of Perth and Quarrier of Bridge of Weir, gave financial support. Today, there are 170 churches in membership of the Baptist Union of Scotland, representing 15,000 members.

Baptists believe in the truths expressed in the historic creeds of the church, stressing the importance of personal faith in Christ as saviour and the importance of the Bible in guiding the conduct of individuals. A distinctive feature is their practice of Christian baptism – normally by total immersion in water – following the New Testament pattern of baptising those who have come to personal faith in Christ. Historically, Baptists have stood for the separation of church and state.

CHURCH OF SCOTLAND
121 George Street, Edinburgh EH2 4YN
0131-225 5722
Principal Clerk: Rev F A J Macdonald
Regards itself as a "national church" rather than an "established church". The third of the articles declaratory of the constitution in matters spiritual declares: "As a national church representative of the Christian faith of the Scottish people, (the church) acknowledges its distinctive call and duty to bring the ordinances of religion to the people in every parish in Scotland through a territorial ministry." The church enjoys spiritual freedom in that the state recognises "the separate and independent government and jurisdiction of the church in matters spiritual".

Since 1690, the settled government of the church has been presbyterian, the essential features of which are that ministers, elders and deacons participate on equal terms, that there is parity of ministers, and that there is a hierarchy of courts rather than of individuals. There are three courts: the kirk session (congregational); the presbytery (district or regional); and the General Assembly (national). The Assembly, which meets annually in May, does much of its business through standing committees. Its Moderator serves for one year and is styled Right Reverend.

Only 17% of Scotland's adult population are now members of the national church compared with an estimated 38% in 1960, when it celebrated the 400th anniversary of the Reformation.

CONGREGATIONAL UNION OF SCOTLAND
PO Box 189, Glasgow G1 2BX
0141-332 7667
General Secretary: Rev John Arthur; *Chairman:* Rev John W Dyce

FREE CHURCH OF SCOTLAND
The Mound, Edinburgh EH1 2LS
0131-226 4978
Principal Clerk: Rev Professor J L Mackay
In its worship and doctrine, the Free Church claims to adhere to the position adopted by the Church of Scotland at the Reformation. Its divergence dates from the disruption of 1843 when, under the leadership of Dr Thomas Chalmers, the evangelical party broke away from the Church of Scotland.

In the late 19th century, a movement to unite the splintered presbyterian churches was begun. A minority within the Free Church took the view that doctrines vital to the faith were being treated as open questions, and when the great majority entered the union of 1900 to form the United Free Church of Scotland (and, in 1929, to re-unite with the Church of Scotland), this minority elected to continue the Free Church of Scotland. The adherents of this "constitutionalist" party, as it was termed, were to be found mainly, though not exclusively, in the Highlands and islands.

Today the Free Church has 6,000 members in 120 congregations. Though much reduced in size, it maintains in continuity with the church of 1843 the post-Reformation system of doctrine and form of worship. The singing of the Scottish metrical psalms unaccompanied by instrumental music is a distinctive feature of its liturgy, but the chief emphasis of its worship is to be found in the centrality of the pulpit and the proclamation of a free and sovereign salvation.

The Free Church of Scotland College, which operates under the oversight of the General Assembly, prepares men for the ministry.

FREE PRESBYTERIAN CHURCH OF SCOTLAND
133 Woodlands Road, Glasgow G3 6LE
0141-332 9283
Principal Clerk: Rev John MacLeod
Pre-1900 breakaway from the Free Church. It has 3,000 adult members. There are 28 congregations in mainland Scotland, mainly in the Highlands, six on Lewis, three on Harris, one on North Uist, seven on Skye and Raasay, one in Northern Ireland and three in England.

The church maintains a wholehearted allegiance to the Westminster Confession of Faith. It holds that Christ is the sole head of the church; is opposed to the doctrine of universal redemption, believing that Christ died for the elect only; maintains that the Bible is the word of God from beginning to end; opposes the use of instrumental music (and hymns) in public worship; and exercises firm scriptural discipline.

ROMAN CATHOLIC CHURCH
General Secretariat, Bishops' Conference of Scotland, 64 Aitken Street, Airdrie ML6 6LT
01236 764061
General Secretary: Very Rev Mgr Henry Docherty; *President:* His Eminence Cardinal Thomas J Winning
By the end of the 12th century, there were clearly defined dioceses with territorial bishops in the (Roman Catholic) Church of Scotland. In 1560, following the purging of the Scottish church by John Knox, the ancient order collapsed, some RC bishops joining the reformed church.

The hierarchy formally ended with the death of James Beaton, Archbishop of Glasgow, in 1603, but long before then it was virtually impossible in many parts of the country to obtain a priest to carry out pastoral duties. An apostolic letter in March 1878 restored the hierarchy and divided Scotland into the province of St Andrews and Edinburgh with a metropolitan see and four suffragan sees of Aberdeen, Argyll and the Isles, Dunkeld, and Galloway; and the archdiocese of Glasgow directly subject to the Holy see. Apostolic constitutions in 1947 erected the archdiocese of Glasgow into a province, with a metropolitan see and two suffragan sees of Motherwell and Paisley.

By 1960, 400 years after the Reformation, the Roman Catholic Church had become the second most important church in Scotland with

530,000 adult members, 15% of the adult population, its revival having been brought about largely by the influx during the Industrial Revolution of Irish emigrants working in the new industries of the west of Scotland. Today, there is an estimated Catholic population of 725,000, which places its membership slightly ahead of that of the Church of Scotland.

SALVATION ARMY

30 Rutland Square, Edinburgh EH1 2BW
0131-221 9699
Scotland Secretary: Major Norman Armistead
Part of the universal Christian Church. Its purpose is to proclaim the Christian Gospel and serve the practical needs of humanity.

SCOTTISH EPISCOPAL CHURCH

21 Grosvenor Crescent, Edinburgh EH12 5EE
0131-225 6357
Secretary-General: John F Stuart; *Primus:* Most Rev Richard F Holloway
Called "Scottish" because it traces its history back to the earliest known Christian communities in Scotland; called "Episcopal" (from the word for bishops) because it has maintained that form of church order, of bishops, priests and deacons, which was in use from those early years until the late 1600s. Supported the Jacobite cause. A province of the worldwide Anglican communion, but financially self-supporting.

The church does not have archbishops. Instead one of its bishops is chosen as the primus (first among equals), thereby picking up a practice of the Scottish church prior to the 15th century. Describes its relationship with the Church of Scotland as cordial and is committed to unity.

The church is grouped into seven dioceses with a total membership of 53,000, more than half of whom live in Edinburgh and Glasgow.

SYNOD OF METHODIST CHURCH IN SCOTLAND

Central Hall, West Tollcross, Edinburgh EH3 9BP
0131-229 7937
Secretary: Rev David Cooper; *Chairperson:* Rev T Alan Anderson

UNITED FREE CHURCH OF SCOTLAND

11 Newton Place, Glasgow G3 7PR
0141-332 3435
Principal Clerk: Rev Joseph G McPhee; *General Secretary:* Rev John O Fulton
Founded in 1900 as a result of a union between the United Presbyterian Church and the Free Church (though those members of the Free Church who would not unite continued under that name). In 1929, a majority re-united with the Church of Scotland, leaving what constitutes today the United Free Church of Scotland.

The church is opposed to state establishment of religion and believes that any special state-church relationship is an implicit threat to spiritual autonomy. It further believes that the special recognition by the state of one denomination in Scotland places the churches on an unequal footing and is not in the best interests of inter-church relations.

CLANS

STANDING COUNCIL OF SCOTTISH CHIEFS

Hope Chambers, 52 Leith Walk, Edinburgh EH6 5HW
0131-554 6321
General Secretary: G A Way of Plean

COLLEGES OF FURTHER EDUCATION

ABERDEEN COLLEGE

Gallowgate, Aberdeen AB25 1BN
01224 612000
Principal: Rae Angus

ANGUS COLLEGE

Keptie Road, Arbroath DD11 3EA
01241 432600
Principal: John Burt

ANNIESLAND COLLEGE
Hatfield Drive, Glasgow G12 0YE
0141-357 3969
Principal: Linda McTavish

AYR COLLEGE
Dam Park, Ayr KA8 0EU
01292 265184
Principal: Frank Burns

BANFF AND BUCHAN COLLEGE OF FURTHER EDUCATION
Henderson Road, Fraserburgh AB43 9GA
01346 515777
Principal: Alex Gordon

BARONY COLLEGE
Parkgate, Dumfries DG1 3NE
01387 860251
Principal: David Rose

BELL COLLEGE OF TECHNOLOGY
Almada Street, Hamilton ML3 0JB
01698 283100
Principal: Dr Ken MacCallum

BORDERS COLLEGE
Thorniedean House, Melrose Road, Galashiels TD1 2AF
01896 757755
Principal: Dr Robert Murray

CARDONALD COLLEGE
690 Mosspark Drive, Glasgow G52 3AY
0141-272 3333
Principal: Ros Micklem

CENTRAL COLLEGE OF COMMERCE
300 Cathedral Street, Glasgow G1 2TA
0141-552 3941
Principal: Peter Duncan

CLACKMANNAN COLLEGE OF FURTHER EDUCATION
Branshill Road, Alloa FK10 3BT
01259 215121
Principal: John Taylor

CLYDEBANK COLLEGE
Kilbowie Road, Clydebank G81 2AA
0141-952 7771
Principal: Hugh Walker

COATBRIDGE COLLEGE
Kildonan Street, Coatbridge ML5 3LS
01236 422316
Principal: Dr Ian MacIver

CUMBERNAULD COLLEGE
Town Centre, Cumbernauld G67 1HU
01236 731811
Principal: Brian Lister

DUMFRIES AND GALLOWAY COLLEGE
Heathhall, Dumfries DG1 3QZ
01387 261261
Principal: James Neil

DUNDEE COLLEGE
Kingsway Campus, Old Galmis Road, Dundee DD3 8LE
01382 834834
Principal: Iain Ovens

EDINBURGH'S TELFORD COLLEGE
Crewe Toll, Edinburgh EH4 2NZ
0131-332 2491
Principal and Chief Executive: Fiona Baikie

ELMWOOD COLLEGE
Cupar KY15 4JB
01334 658800
Principal: Christina Potter

FALKIRK COLLEGE OF FURTHER AND HIGHER EDUCATION
Grangemouth Road, Falkirk FK2 9AD
01324 403000
Principal: Graham Clark

FIFE COLLEGE OF FURTHER AND HIGHER EDUCATION
St Brycedale Avenue, Kirkcaldy KY1 1EX
01592 268591
Principal: Joyce Johnston

GLASGOW COLLEGE OF BUILDING AND PRINTING
60 North Hanover Street, Glasgow G1 2BP
0141-332 9969
Principal: Thomas Wilson

GLASGOW COLLEGE OF FOOD TECHNOLOGY
230 Cathedral Street, Glasgow G1 2TG
0141-552 3751
Principal and Chief Executive: Donald H Leitch

GLASGOW COLLEGE OF NAUTICAL STUDIES
21 Thistle Street, Glasgow G5 9XB
0141-565 2500
Principal: Christopher Hunter

GLENROTHES COLLEGE
Stenton Road, Glenrothes KY6 2RA
01592 772233
Principal: T J Burness, OBE

INVERNESS COLLEGE
Longman Road, Inverness IV1 1SA
01463 236681
Principal: Gus MacKenzie

JAMES WATT COLLEGE OF FURTHER AND HIGHER EDUCATION
Finnart Street, Greenock PA16 8HF
01475 724433
Principal: Terry Davies

JEWEL AND ESK VALLEY COLLEGE
24 Milton Road East, Edinburgh EH15 2PP
0131-660 1010
Principal: John Lisgo

JOHN WHEATLEY COLLEGE
1346 Shettleston Road, Glasgow G32 9AT
0141-778 2426
Principal: Ian Graham

KILMARNOCK COLLEGE
Holehouse Road, Kilmarnock KA3 7AT
01563 523501
Principal: Michael Roebuck

LANGSIDE COLLEGE
50 Prospecthill Road, Glasgow G42 9LB
0141-649 4991
Principal: A Graeme Hyslop

LAUDER COLLEGE
Halbeath, Dunfermline KY11 8DY
01383 845000
Principal: Janet Lowe

LEWS CASTLE COLLEGE
Stornoway, Isle of Lewis HS2 0XR
01851 703311
Principal: David Green

MORAY COLLEGE
Moray Street, Elgin IV30 1JJ
01343 554321
Principal: Dr Robert Chalmers

MOTHERWELL COLLEGE
Dalzell Drive, Motherwell ML1 2DD
01698 232323
Principal: Richard Millham

NEWBATTLE ABBEY
Dalkeith EH22 3LL
0131-663 1921
Principal: William Conboy

NORTH GLASGOW COLLEGE
110 Flemington Street, Springburn, Glasgow G21 4BX
0141-558 9001
Principal: Ian Miller

OATRIDGE AGRICULTURAL COLLEGE
Ecclesmachan, Broxburn EH52 6NH
01506 854387
Principal: Christopher Nixon

ORKNEY COLLEGE
Kirkwall, Orkney KW15 1LX
01856 872839
Principal: Peter Scott

PERTH COLLEGE
Crieff Road, Perth PH1 2NX
01738 621171
Principal: Michael Webster

REID KERR COLLEGE
Renfrew Road, Paisley PA3 4DR
0141-581 2222
Principal: Matthew Aird

SABHAL MÒR OSTAIG
Teangue, Sleat, Isle of Skye IV44 8RQ
01471 844373
Director: Norman N Gillies

SHETLAND COLLEGE OF FURTHER EDUCATION
Gremista, Lerwick, Shetland ZE1 0PX
01595 695514
Principal: Gordon Dargie

SOUTH LANARKSHIRE COLLEGE
85 Hamilton Road, Glasgow G72 7NY
0141-641 6600
Principal: Susan Moore

STEVENSON COLLEGE
Bankhead Avenue, Edinburgh EH11
4DE
0131-535 4600
Principal: Michael Leech, OBE

STOW COLLEGE
43 Shamrock Street, Glasgow G4 9LD
0141-332 1786
Principal: David Snaith

THURSO COLLEGE
Ormlie Road, Thurso KW14 7EE
01847 896161
Principal: Raymond Murray

WEST LOTHIAN COLLEGE
Marjoribanks Street, Bathgate EH48 1QJ
01506 634300
Principal: Anthony Godden

COLLEGES OF HIGHER EDUCATION

EDINBURGH COLLEGE OF ART
Lauriston Place, Edinburgh EH3 9DF
0131-221 6000
Principal: Professor Alistair Rowan

GLASGOW SCHOOL OF ART
167 Renfrew Street, Glasgow G3 6RQ
0141-353 4500
Director: Professor Dugald Cameron

NORTHERN COLLEGE OF EDUCATION
Aberdeen Campus, Hilton Place,
Aberdeen AB24 4FA
01224 283500
Dundee Campus, Gardyne Road,
Dundee DD5 1NY
Tel: 01382 464000
Principal: David Adams

QUEEN MARGARET UNIVERSITY COLLEGE
Clerwood Terrace, Edinburgh EH12 8TS
0131-317 3000
Principal: Dr Joan Stringer

ROYAL SCOTTISH ACADEMY OF MUSIC
AND DRAMA
100 Renfrew Street, Glasgow G2 3DB
0141-332 4101
Principal: Philip Ledger

SAC (SCOTTISH AGRICULTURAL
COLLEGE)
West Mains Road, Edinburgh EH9 3JG
0131-535 4000
Principal: Professor Karl A Linklater

ST ANDREWS COLLEGE OF EDUCATION
Duntocher Road, Bearsden, Glasgow
G61 4QA
0141-943 1424
Principal: Professor B J McGettrick

COMMUNITY

ASSOCIATION OF SCOTTISH COMMUNITY
COUNCILS
21 Grosvenor Street, Edinburgh EH12
5ED
0131-225 4033
Secretary: Douglas Murray; *Chairperson:*
John MacKintosh
Aims to promote the role, effectiveness
and status of community councils in
Scotland; to encourage the exchange of
information; and to ascertain, co-
ordinate and express the views of
community councils.

SCOTTISH COMMUNITY DEVELOPMENT
CENTRE
329 Baltic Chambers, 50 Wellington
Street, Glasgow G2 6HJ
0141-248 1924
Directors: Stuart Hashagen/Alan Barr;
Committee Chairman: Professor R Trainor
Partnership between the University of
Glasgow and the Community
Development Foundation which aims to
promote best practice in community
development.

CONSERVATION

ANCIENT MONUMENTS BOARD FOR
SCOTLAND
Longmore House, Salisbury Place,

Edinburgh EH9 1SH
0131-668 8764
Secretary: Mr R Dalziel; *Chairman:* Professor M Lynch
Advises Scottish Ministers on the protection and preservation of monuments of national importance and the maintenance and preservation of monuments in his care. Encourages a close working relationship with other bodies and individuals concerned with Scotland's built heritage.

ARCHITECTURAL HERITAGE SOCIETY OF SCOTLAND
The Glasite Meeting House, 33 Barony Street, Edinburgh EH3 6NX
0131-557 0019
Director: Dr Seán O'Reilly; *Chair:* Adam Swan

ASSOCIATION FOR THE PROTECTION OF RURAL SCOTLAND
Gladstone's Land (3rd Floor), 483 Lawnmarket, Edinburgh EH1 2NT
0131-225 7012
Director: Joan Geddes; *Chairman:* Robin S Salvesen, DL; *President:* Rt Hon Lord Lang of Monkton
Charity, founded in 1926, which seeks to protect Scotland's countryside and to promote ideas for its care and improvement by means of constructive proposals, careful research and active involvement in the maintenance of landscape features. Its core work is involvement in land use matters, submitting comments on policies for structure and local plans, presenting precognitions at public inquiries and commenting on draft consultation papers.

CHARLES RENNIE MACKINTOSH SOCIETY
Queen's Cross, 870 Garscube Road, Glasgow G20 7EL
0141-946 6600
Director: David Mullane

COCKBURN ASSOCIATION (EDINBURGH CIVIC TRUST)
Trunk's Close, 55 High Street, Edinburgh EH1 1SR
0131-557 8686
Secretary: Terry Levinthal; *Chairman:*

Hon Lord Nimmo Smith
Maintains and enhances the amenity of the city of Edinburgh and its neighbourhood; protects and conserves its architectural, historical, and landscape heritage.

HISTORIC BUILDINGS COUNCIL FOR SCOTLAND
Longmore House, Salisbury Place, Edinburgh EH9 1SH
0131-668 8817
Secretary: Sheenagh Adams; *Chairman:* Sir Raymond Johnstone
Encourages the conservation and revitalisation of buildings of outstanding historic or architectural interest and promotes the preservation and enhancement of the character or appearance of outstanding conservation areas.

Established in 1953 under the Historic Buildings and Ancient Monuments Act, the council supports the government's policy that "no worthwhile building of architectural or historic merit is lost to our environment unless it is demonstrated beyond reasonable doubt that every effort has been exerted by all concerned to find practical ways of keeping it". Advises Scottish Ministers on applications for grants and loans towards repair or maintenance and co-operates closely with bodies and individuals who share its objective of keeping Scotland's built heritage alive and in use.

HISTORIC SCOTLAND
Longmore House, Salisbury Place, Edinburgh EH9 1SH
0131-668 8600
Chief Executive: Graeme Munro
Established as an executive agency in 1991 by the Secretary of State of Scotland. The agency is headed by the Director and Chief Executive, who is accountable to Scottish Ministers.

Historic Scotland's principal activities are to protect, present and promote Scotland's built heritage, which includes ancient monuments and archaeological sites, historic buildings, parks and gardens, and designed landscapes.

Historic Scotland is the largest operator of paid visitor attractions in Scotland. It safeguards the nation's built heritage by scheduling monuments of national importance, listing buildings of special architectural or historic interest and helping owners with maintenance and repair.

KEEP SCOTLAND BEAUTIFUL
7 Melville Terrace, Stirling FK8 2ND
01786 471333
Secretary: Avril Conlan

NATIONAL TRUST FOR SCOTLAND
5 Charlotte Square, Edinburgh EH2 4DU
0131-226 5922
Director: Trevor A Croft; *Chairman:* Professor J Cunningham, CBE
Exists "for the purposes of promoting the permanent preservation for the benefit of the nation of lands and buildings in Scotland of historic or national interest or natural beauty". It encourages the public to enjoy its 120 properties, which include castles and mansions, gardens, historic sites, islands, countryside, waterfalls, coastline and "little houses" (examples of Scotland's distinctive vernacular architecture).

Every year it welcomes two million visitors to those of its properties where numbers can be counted. It is estimated that as many again visit the countryside and open areas.

An independent charity founded in 1931, the trust is the largest voluntary conservation body in Scotland, dependent for its support on donations and legacies and the subscriptions of 228,000 members.

ROYAL COMMISSION ON THE ANCIENT AND HISTORICAL MONUMENTS OF SCOTLAND
John Sinclair House, 6 Bernard Terrace, Edinburgh EH8 9NX
0131-662 1456
Secretary and Curator, National Monuments Record of Scotland: R J Mercer; *Chairman:* Sir William Fraser
Independent non-departmental government body, established in 1908, financed by Parliament under the sponsorship of Historic Scotland. Its main objectives are to record and interpret the sites, monuments and buildings of Scotland's past, promoting a greater appreciation of their value through the maintenance of the National Monuments Record of Scotland (NMRS), and presenting them more directly by selective publications and exhibitions.

The birth of the commission reflected increasing concern about the destruction of the country's historical monuments and appreciation of the need for a nationwide assessment of surviving sites and structures. Every year the commission undertakes about 300 surveys of threatened buildings.

The National Archaeological Survey identifies and maps sites and monuments of all periods. The Thematic Architectural Survey deals strategically with classes of buildings of particular architectural or historical interest which are vulnerable to redundancy or other long-term threat. The National Monuments Record of Scotland, with its 117,000 site records, is the country's largest repository of information on ancient monuments and historic buildings.

SCOTTISH CHURCH ARCHITECTURAL HERITAGE TRUST
15 North Bank Street, Edinburgh EH1 2LP
0131-225 8644
Director: Florence MacKenzie, MBE; *Chairman:* Hon Lord Penrose
Awards grants for fabric repairs to Scottish churches of all denominations.

SCOTTISH CIVIC TRUST
Tobacco Merchant's House, 42 Miller Street, Glasgow G1 1DT
0141-221 1466
Director, Administration and Finance: John N P Ford; *Chairman:* Sir James Dunbar-Nasmith, CBE
Sees itself as both catalyst and guardian, aiming to encourage: well-informed public concern for the environment of both town and country; high quality in planning and in new architecture; the conservation and, where necessary,

adaptation for re-use of older buildings of distinction or historic interest; knowledgeable and therefore effective comment in planning matters; and the elimination of ugliness, whether resulting from social deprivation, bad design or neglect.

Founded in 1967, the trust is financed by donations, covenants and subscriptions, with help from local and central government.

SCOTTISH HISTORIC BUILDINGS TRUST
Saltcoats, Gullane, East Lothian EH31 2AG
01620 842757
Secretary: Gareth Jones; *Chairman:* George McNeill
Acquires, repairs, and identifies new uses for historic buildings which are at risk.

SCOTTISH INLAND WATERWAYS ASSOCIATION
1 Craiglockhart Crescent, Edinburgh WEH14 1EZ
0131-443 2533
Secretary: George A Hunter, OBE; *Chairman:* Donald MacKinnon
Membership consists of all canal societies in Scotland. Concerned with the protection of Scottish canals.

SCOTTISH NATURAL HERITAGE
12 Hope Terrace, Edinburgh EH9 2AS
0131-447 4784
Chief Executive: Roger Crofts; *Chairman:* John Markland
Established in 1992 from a merger of the Nature Conservancy Council for Scotland and the Countryside Commission for Scotland. A government agency which receives its funding of £36 million from the Scottish Executive.

It has two roles: to advise government and others about the management and use of natural heritage, and to carry out executive tasks on behalf of government. SNH's mission is "to work with Scotland's people to care for our natural heritage". Much of its conservation effort for species, habitats and landscapes focuses on parts of Scotland designated as SSSIs

(Sites of Special Scientific Interest), including Special Areas of Conservation, Special Protection Areas and National Nature Reserves, and National Scenic Areas.

SNH provides financial assistance to, and establishes special projects with, a wide range of bodies to replenish depleted areas in remote areas of the countryside and in and around towns and cities. It works through environmental education to increase the awareness and understanding of the natural heritage and encourages people to enjoy it by providing such facilities as footpaths and signposts, as well as grant-aiding the Scottish Countryside Ranger service.

The first UK government organisation to have a formal statutory responsibility for sustainability, SNH encourages the development of strategies and financial assistance schemes which recognise the importance of the natural heritage. Its priorities in the medium term are: to promote biodiversity; to manage special natural heritage sites, particularly the government's Natura 2000 programme to implement the EU's directives on habitats and birds; to facilitate the integrated management of the Cairngorms, and Loch Lomond and the Trossachs; to improve environmental education in Scotland; and to help land managers to care for the natural heritage and manage the public's enjoyment of it.

SCOTTISH RIGHTS OF WAY SOCIETY
24 Annandale Street, Edinburgh EH7 4AN
0131-558 1222
Secretary: Judith Lewis; *Chairman:* Dr Donald J Bennet
Safeguards rights of way throughout Scotland. Activities include putting up signposts and maintaining the National Catalogue of Rights of Way.

SCOTTISH SOCIETY FOR CONSERVATION & RESTORATION
The Glasite Meeting House, 33 Barony Street, Edinburgh EH3 6NX
0131-556 8417
Administrator: Eliane Martay; *Chair:* Jane

Hutchison
Independent organisation promoting the conservation and restoration of Scotland's historic, scientific and artistic materials. Provides a forum for people concerned with this, working in the public or independent sectors, or primarily interested in the conservation and restoration of objects and buildings.

WWF UK (WORLD WIDE FUND FOR NATURE)
8 The Square, Aberfeldy PH15 2DD
01887 820449
Head of WWF Scotland: Simon Pepper

CONSUMER ADVICE AND PROTECTION

CITIZENS ADVICE SCOTLAND
26 George Square, Edinburgh EH8 9LD
0131-667 0156
Chief Executive Officer: Kaliani Lyle;
Chair: John Crotch
Member bureaux of Citizens Advice Scotland (the Scottish Association of Citizens Advice Bureaux) give advice and information on problems brought by the public. There are 59 Citizens Advice Bureaux and 150 CAB service points in Scotland. The association's work is funded by the Department of Trade of Industry and from other sources. In addition to its information and advisory services, it lobbies policy-makers on social matters.

COMMISSIONER FOR LOCAL ADMINISTRATION IN SCOTLAND (LOCAL GOVERNMENT OMBUDSMAN)
23 Walker Street, Edinburgh EH3 7HX
0131-225 5300
Commissioner: Frederick C Marks, OBE;
Deputy Commissioner and Secretary: Janice H Renton
Free independent service for members of the public who have complaints of injustice arising from maladministration on the part of local government and related bodies. In addition to the 32 local authorities and their joint committees and boards, the ombudsman has jurisdiction over licensing boards, Scottish Homes (as landlord) and the Strathclyde Passenger Transport Authority.

Any individual or body can make a complaint, which requires to be in writing. A complaint form is available, but is not obligatory. Complaints must usually be made within 12 months of the problem arising and should first have been raised with the authority concerned. Emphasis is placed on facilitating the resolution of complaints. Of those taken up, about a third are satisfactorily resolved.

In cases where the ombudsman conducts a formal investigation, his findings are issued in a public report. He has no power to enforce his findings but, in practice, authorities generally comply with his recommendations which can include taking corrective action and paying financial compensation.

ELECTRICITY CONSUMERS' COMMITTEES
The Electricity Act 1989 established 14 Electricity Consumers' Committees to represent the interests of all electricity consumers. There are two in Scotland:
ELECTRICITY CONSUMERS' COMMITTEE FOR NORTH OF SCOTLAND
Regent Court, 70 West Regent Street, Glasgow G2 2QZ
0141-331 2552
ELECTRICITY CONSUMERS' COMMITTEE FOR SOUTHERN SCOTLAND
Regent Court, 70 West Regent Street, Glasgow G2 2QZ
0141-331 2552

ENERGY ACTION SCOTLAND
Suite 4a, Ingram House, 227 Ingram Street, Glasgow G1 1DA
0141-226 3064
Director: Ann Loughrey; *President:* David Marshall, MP
Assists fuel-poor homes by promoting affordable warmth through public and private sector investment in energy efficiency and energy conservation projects. Working with local authorities and housing providers, the organisation offers consultancy and training in energy advice and energy auditing, as well as information and a referral service.

GAS CONSUMERS COUNCIL SCOTLAND
86 George Street, Edinburgh EH2 3BU
0131-226 6523
Manager: Liz Futcher
Watchdog body set up by parliament in 1986. Its members are appointed by the President of the Board of Trade. The council takes up complaints when consumers feel they are getting nowhere; helps people with advice about any gas matter; and represents the consumers' point of view.

HEALTH SERVICE OMBUDSMAN FOR SCOTLAND
28 Thistle Street, Edinburgh EH2 1EN
0131-225 7465
Ombudsman: Michael Buckley
Investigates complaints about the National Health Service. The ombudsman may investigate complaints about hospitals or community health services which concern (a) poor service; (b) failure to purchase or provide a service which people are entitled to receive; (c) maladministration, such as avoidable delay, not following proper procedures, rudeness, etc. The ombudsman may also investigate complaints about the care and treatment provided by a doctor, nurse or other trained professional.

Before asking the ombudsman to look into a complaint, a patient must first take it up locally with his or her local hospital, clinic or surgery. If a complaint is found to be justified, the ombudsman will seek an apology or other remedy for the complainant. The ombudsman is completely independent of the NHS and the government. There is no charge for the service.

OFFICE OF GAS AND ELECTRICITY MARKETS (OFGEM)
Regent Court, 70 West Regent Street, Glasgow G2 2QZ
0141-331 2678

POST OFFICE USERS' COUNCIL FOR SCOTLAND
2 Greenside Lane, Edinburgh EH1 3AH
0131-244 5576
Completely independent of the Post Office. Set up as a statutory council in 1969 to represent the interests of users in Scotland. Its job is to make sure that users of postal services have a voice in matters affecting them, such as the standard or quality of a service and the price charged for it. Most of its work involves dealing with complaints and representations from residential and business customers who have tried to get satisfaction from the Post Office, but who are unhappy with the response. More generally, it keeps a close watch on Post Office performance as it affects Scotland.

RAIL USERS CONSULTATIVE COMMITTEE FOR SCOTLAND AND CALEDONIAN MACBRAYNE USERS CONSULTATIVE COMMITTEE
5th Floor, Corunna House, 29 Cadogan Street, Glasgow G2 7AB
0141-221 7760
Secretary: Bill Ure; *Chair:* Helen Millar, OBE
Statutory watchdogs protecting and promoting the interests of rail passengers, the Rail Users Consultative Committees (there are eight covering the UK) were set up under the Railways Act 1993 and are funded by the Rail Regulator. The train operating companies serving Scotland are: Great Northern Eastern Railway, ScotRail, and Virgin Trains; the committee for Scotland also has responsibility for dealing with matters concerning Caledonian MacBrayne shipping services.

The committee actively seeks the views of passengers, including those with special needs, and represents passengers' interests to the industry and to those who regulate or influence it. Locally it keeps watch on such matters as the punctuality and reliability of train services, timetable changes, safety and security, overcrowding, cleanliness, fares, the quality and design of trains, station facilities, provision of information at stations as well as on trains, and whether operators are meeting their franchise specifications.

Customers should first contact the company operating the service. If they are not satisfied with the response to their complaint, they should then contact the committee.

SCOTTISH ADVISORY COMMITTEE ON TELECOMMUNICATIONS
2 Greenside Lane, Edinburgh EH1 3AH
0131-244 5576
Established in 1984 to advise the Director General of the Office of Telecommunications (OFTEL) on regulatory policy and its effects on customers. Companies operating public telecommunications sytems are required by their licences to consider the committee's representations. Its secretariat handles customer complaints, but people who wish to complain should first give the supplier an opportunity to put things right.

SCOTTISH CONSUMER COUNCIL
Royal Exchange House, 100 Queen Street, Glasgow G1 3DN
0141-226 5261
Director: Martyn Evans; *Chairman:* Deirdre Hutton, CBE
Represents, promotes and safeguards the interests of consumers by providing advice, information and redress, identifying issues and problems, monitoring and reporting on services, influencing decision-making, responding to proposals and encouraging consumer representation in the public services and privatised utilities. It has a particular remit for those who face disadvantage in society.
The SCC does not deal with individual complaints or test consumer products. Established by the government in 1975, it is funded mainly through a grant from the Department of Trade and Industry.

SCOTTISH LEGAL SERVICES OMBUDSMAN
Mulberry House, 16 Picardy Place, Edinburgh EH1 3JT
0131-556 5574
Ombudsman: Garry S Watson
The ombudsman was appointed by the Secretary of State for Scotland as a consumer watchdog. He is not a legal practitioner and can therefore be objective in the conclusions he reaches.

The ombudsman investigates objections about the way in which a professional body has handled complaints against legal practitioners, makes recommendations where appropriate, and may take a case to the Scottish Solicitors Discipline Tribunal. The ombudsman is empowered to investigate complaints against members of the Law Society of Scotland, the Faculty of Advocates and the Scottish Conveyancing and Executry Services Board.
Consumers dissatisfied with a legal practitioner should contact the ombudsman only if they believe that neither the practitioner nor the professional body has responded satisfactorily to the complaint.
The ombudsman is entitled to recommend that a professional body pays compensation and costs to the complainer on account of loss, inconvenience or distress. The service is free.

SCOTTISH WATER AND SEWERAGE CUSTOMERS COUNCIL
Ochil House, Springkerse Business Park, Stirling FK7 7XE
01786 430200
Chairman: Bill Furness
Independent watchdog body established in 1996, at the same time as the three Scottish water authorities in the east, north and west. Approves the charges the water authorities make; approves and monitors their codes of practice; helps customers with complaints about the service provided by their water authority.
The Council was wound up on 31 October 1999, to be replaced on 1 November by a new Water Industry Commissioner for Scotland under the control of the Scottish Executive.

COUNSELLING

COSCA (CONFEDERATION OF SCOTTISH COUNSELLING AGENCIES)
18 Viewfield Street, Stirling FK8 1UA
01786 475140

Executive Director: Stewart Wilson; *Convenor:* Colin Kirkwood
Aims to support and develop all forms of counselling in Scotland.

COURTS AND TRIBUNALS

CHILD SUPPORT COMMISSIONERS
23 Melville Street, Edinburgh EH3 7PW
0131-225 2201

COUNCIL ON TRIBUNALS, SCOTTISH COMMITTEE
44 Palmerston Place, Edinburgh EH12 5BJ
0131-220 1236
Secretary: Marjorie MacRae; *Chairman:* R John Elliot, WS
The Scottish Committee exercises supervision of the operation of most tribunals and inquiries in Scotland. Established in 1958 by Act of Parliament. Keeps under review the working of some 40 tribunals in such fields as social security, education, taxation, employment and child care. The council regards openness, fairness and impartiality as the elements essential to the proper functioning of the tribunal and inquiry system. Its greatest concern is that lay men and women involved in any hearing system receive fair treatment and can obtain an unbiased decision on their case whatever the outcome.

The council has a statutory right to visit tribunals to observe their conduct at first hand. Visiting members take a close interest in such matters as the suitability of the premises, the working of the tribunal and its staffing, and the quality of any guidance literature. Shortcomings, if sufficiently serious, may be brought to the attention of the body responsible for the administration of the tribunal or inquiry concerned.

COURT OF THE LORD LYON
HM New Register House, Edinburgh EH1 3YT
0131-556 7255
Lord Lyon King of Arms: Sir Malcolm Innes of Edingight, KCVO
In Scotland, the use of armorial bearings is strictly controlled by statute and they may only be lawfully used and displayed if they have been granted by the Lord Lyon King of Arms and recorded in the Public Register of All Arms and Bearings in Scotland, a register established by Act of Parliament in 1672.

Armorial bearings are granted by the Lord Lyon King of Arms to private individuals, corporate bodies, schools, charities, etc, and once arms are granted they become the property and visual identity of the individual or organisation concerned. The Lord Lyon also considers petitions in a judicial capacity from those who wish to re-record the arms of an ancestor in the Public Register. Arms descend to the heir in each generation of the original grantee.

The Lord Lyon King of Arms, accompanied by three Heralds and three Pursuivants, appears on ceremonial occasions such as installation services of the Order of the Thistle and the opening of the General Assembly of the Church of Scotland. The Lord Lyon is appointed by the Crown, as is the Lyon Clerk and Keeper of the Records.

EMPLOYMENT TRIBUNALS IN SCOTLAND
Eagle Building, 215 Bothwell Street, Glasgow G2 7TS
0141-204 0730
Secretary: D Easton
Independent judicial bodies with jurisdiction to hear cases which relate to people's rights in the field of employment law. The issues it deals with include unfair dismissal, redundancy payments, and sex, race and disability discrimination, together with some health and safety matters.

The tribunal will always have a legally qualified chairman, who is appointed in Scotland by the Court of Session. Most cases are heard at permanent industrial tribunal offices. The tribunal will always send a written decision – and its reason for making that decision – to the parties or their representatives. Either party may apply for a review of the decision, or lodge an appeal against it within set time limits.

INDEPENDENT TRIBUNAL SERVICE
Scottish Regional Office, Wellington House, 134-136 Wellington Street, Glasgow G2 2XL
0141-353 1441
Regional Chairman: Mrs L T Parker
Independent, statutory body responsible for the running of Social Security, Medical, Vaccine Damage, Disability and Child Support appeal tribunals.

LANDS TRIBUNAL FOR SCOTLAND
1 Grosvenor Crescent, Edinburgh EH12 5ER
0131-225 7996
Clerk: Neil M Tainsh; *President*: Hon Lord McGhie
Independent judicial body constituted under the Lands Tribunal Act 1949, for the purpose of determining a wide range of questions relating to the valuation of land, compensation for the compulsory acquisition of land, allocation of feu duties, and the discharge or variation of restrictive land obligations. The Act also empowers the tribunal to accept the function of arbitration, under reference, by consent. Since 1970, the jurisdiction has been extended by numerous Acts of Parliament.

PENSIONS APPEAL TRIBUNALS FOR SCOTLAND
20 Walker Street, Edinburgh EH3 7HS
0131-220 1404
Secretary: Lesley E Young; *President*: Colin N McEachran, QC
Hears and decides on appeals against the rejection by the Department of Social Security of War Pension claims.

RENT ASSESSMENT PANEL FOR SCOTLAND
48 Manor Place, Edinburgh EH3 7EH
0131-226 1123
Secretary: Mrs N Eagle; *President*: John H Barton, WS
Provides chairmen and members for rent assessment committees. These committees determine rents for private sector housing.

SCOTTISH COURT SERVICE
Hayweight House, 23 Lauriston Street, Edinburgh EH3 9DQ
0131-229 9200
Chief Executive: Dr Michael Ewart
Provides and maintains court houses and supplies trained staff to meet the needs of the judiciary and court users.

SCOTTISH LAND COURT
1 Grosvenor Crescent, Edinburgh EH12 5ER
0131-225 3595
Principal Clerk: K H R Graham; *Chairman*: Hon Lord McGhie
Constituted by the Small Landholders (Scotland) Act 1911 and brought into being in 1912. The chairman was required to be an advocate of not fewer than 10 years' standing with the same rank and tenure as a judge of the Court of Session. The other members were to be appointed on the basis of their expert and practical knowledge of agriculture and the statute. One of the members had to be able to speak Gaelic.

The Act conferred on the court the jurisdictions which had been exercised by the original Crofters Commission in the seven crofting counties and extended the jurisdiction to landholders' holdings and statutory small tenancies throughout Scotland.

SCOTTISH SOLICITORS' DISCIPLINE TRIBUNAL
22 Rutland Square, Edinburgh EH1 2BB
0131-229 5860

SOCIAL SECURITY COMMISSIONERS
23 Melville Street, Edinburgh EH3 7PW
0131-225 2201
Secretary: Mrs M Watts
Commissioners are independent members of the judiciary. They exercise appellate jurisdiction on questions of law arising from appeal tribunals on matters under the governance of the Department of Social Security and on child support appeals.

CRICKET

SCOTTISH CRICKET UNION
Caledonia House, South Gyle,
Edinburgh EH12 9DQ
0131-317 7247
General Manager: Alex Ritchie; *Chairman:*
John Everett

CRIME

CRIMINAL INJURIES COMPENSATION
AUTHORITY
Tay House, 300 Bath Street, Glasgow G2
4JR
0141-331 2726
Chief Executive: Peter Spurgeon, CBE
Administers the government-funded
scheme to provide compensation for
innocent victims of violent crime.

CROWN OFFICE
25 Chambers Street, Edinburgh EH1
1LA
0131-226 2626
Crown Agent: Andrew Normand
Sole prosecuting authority in Scotland,
investigating sudden deaths, fires and
complaints of criminal conduct in
association with the Procurator Fiscal
Service.

VICTIM SUPPORT SCOTLAND
15/23 Hardwell Close, Edinburgh EH8
9RX
0131-668 4486
Director: Alison Paterson; *Honorary
President:* Sheriff Gordon Nicholson,
QC; *Chairperson:* James Brodie
National charity for crime victims.
Volunteers provide practical help and
emotional support to people affected by
crime. The service is free and
confidential.

CULTURE (SCOTTISH)

ROYAL CELTIC SOCIETY
23 Rutland Street, Edinburgh EH1 2RN
0131-228 6449
Secretary: J Gordon Cameron; *Chairman:*
A C Macpherson

Founded in 1820. Primary aims are to
maintain and promote interest in the
history, traditions, language and arts of
the Highlands and western isles.
Annual donations are made to cultural
bodies and events.

SALTIRE SOCIETY
9 Fountain Close, 22 High Street,
Edinburgh EH1 1TF
0131-556 1836
Director: Ian Scott; *President:* Paul H
Scott
Founded in 1936 by a group of people
who were anxious to see Scotland
restored to its proper position as a
cultural entity. The society aims to foster
and enrich the cultural heritage of
Scotland in all its aspects. It looks to the
future as well as to the past,
encouraging creativity as a living
element of European civilisation. It
encourages the study and appreciation
of arts and sciences and presents annual
awards for excellence in civil
engineering, planning, literature,
housing design, and science.

CURLING

ROYAL CALEDONIAN CURLING CLUB
Cairnie House, Ingliston Showground,
Newbridge EH28 2NB
0131-333 3003
Secretary: W J Duthie Thomson;
President: Ken Scott

CYCLING

CTC SCOTLAND
10 Woodhall Terrace, Edinburgh EH14
5BR
0131-453 3366
Secretary: Peter Hawkins; *Chairman:* Ron
Harrow
Voluntary national cycling association.
Represents cycling interests on national
bodies, campaigns for better cycling
facilities, produces an annual calendar
of events, and organises events
nationally and locally.

SCOTTISH CYCLISTS UNION
The Velodrome, Meadowbank Sports Centre, London Road, Edinburgh EH7 6AE
0131-652 0187
Executive Development Officer: Jim Riach

SUSTRANS SCOTLAND
3 Coates Place, Edinburgh EH3 7AA
0131-623 7600
Director: Bill Wright
"Sustrans" stands for sustainable transport. It works through practical projects to design and build routes for cyclists, walkers and wheelchair users.

DANCE

DANCE SCOTLAND
c/o The Big Hands Centre, 7 Water Row, Govan, Glasgow G51
0141-445 6000
Secretary: Maggie Singleton; *Chair:* Karen Woods
Supports all aspects of dance throughout Scotland. Publishes *Dance Network Directory* and *Dance News Scotland*.

ROYAL SCOTTISH COUNTRY DANCE SOCIETY
12 Coates Crescent, Edinburgh EH3 7AF
0131-225 3854
Director of Administration: Gill Parker; *Chairman:* Linda Gaul
Aims to promote Scottish country dancing and preserve its traditions by providing opportunities for members to learn dances and steps.

SCOTTISH BALLET
261 West Princes Street, Glasgow G4 9EE
0141-331 2931
General Manager: Norman L Quirk; *Chairman:* Peg Beveridge
Scotland's leading national and international touring classical ballet company. Formed by Peter Darrell as the Western Theatre Ballet in Bristol in 1957, it transferred to Glasgow in 1969 to become Scotland's national dance company.

In an average year the company gives 125 performances to a total audience of 115,000. Its work ranges from traditional classics using up to 50 dancers and an orchestra of 70 musicians to performances on the Edinburgh Fringe involving six dancers and a pianist.

The company has performed in a variety of spaces from the Festival Theatre in Edinburgh (the largest stage in Britain) to the village hall in Acharacle. Its programme of education and outreach has included a summer school for young people in Easterhouse, Glasgow, and work with visually and hearing-impaired adults.

SCOTTISH TRADITIONS OF DANCE TRUST
54 Blackfriars Street, Edinburgh EH1 1NE
0131-558 8737
Co-ordinator: Liam Paterson
The national organisation which exists to research, conserve, foster and promote all of Scotland's dance traditions.

DISABLED

BRITISH DEAF ASSOCIATION (SCOTLAND)
3rd Floor, Princes House, 5 Shandwick Place, Edinburgh EH2 4RG
0131-221 1137
Chief Executive: Jeff McWhinney; *Chairperson:* Austin Reeves
Supplies information to the deaf community about health issues, education, access to services, and the use of British sign language. Also supports young deaf people.

BRITISH LIMBLESS EX-SERVICEMEN'S ASSOCIATION
24 Dundas Street, Edinburgh EH3 6JN
0131-556 6828

CAPABILITY SCOTLAND
Central Office, 22 Corstorphine Road, Edinburgh EH12 6HP
0131-337 9876
Chief Executive: Alan Dickson

DISABILITY SCOTLAND
Princes House, 5 Shandwick Place, Edinburgh EH2 4RG
0131-229 8632
Director: Bob Benson; *Chairman:* Dr Graham Monteith
National body with over 220 disability organisations, and others, as members. Main focus is on information exchange, policy development and joint action.

DISABLEMENT INCOME GROUP – SCOTLAND
5 Quayside Street, Edinburgh EH6 6EJ
0131-555 2811
Chairman: Jack F McGregor, MBE
Free information, advice and advocacy on welfare benefits to disabled people all over Scotland.

ENABLE
6th Floor, 7 Buchanan Street, Glasgow G1 3HL
0141-226 4541
Director: Norman Dunning; *Chairperson:* David Barraclough; *President:* John Spence
Supports people with learning disabilities and their carers.

ERSKINE HOSPITAL
Bishopton, Renfrewshire PA7 5PU
0141-812 1100
Chief Executive: Colonel Martin Gibson, OBE; *Chairman:* Lt General Sir John Macmillan
Provides appropriate care (for example, nursing, residential, housing, supported employment, respite) to ex-Service men and women in Scotland.

GUIDE DOGS FOR THE BLIND ASSOCIATION
Princess Alexandra House, Dundee Road, Forfar DD8 1JA
01307 463531

PHAB SCOTLAND
5a Warriston Road, Edinburgh EH3 5LQ
0131-558 9912
Chief Executive: Fiona Hird

REHAB SCOTLAND
Melrose House, Cadogan Street, Glasgow
0141-204 5700
General Manager: Bertie Hunt; *Chairman:* Eric R Taylor
Charitable organisation providing vocational training and rehabilitation services to enable disabled and disadvantaged people to lead more rewarding lives through greater independence, equal opportunities and personal fulfilment.

RNIB SCOTLAND (ROYAL NATIONAL INSTITUTE FOR THE BLIND)
Dunedin House, 25 Ravelston Terrace, Edinburgh EH4 3TP
0131-311 8500
Director: Allan Murray

ROYAL NATIONAL INSTITUTE FOR DEAF PEOPLE
9 Clairmont Gardens, Glasgow G3 7LW
0141-332 0343
Director: Lilian Lawson
Aims to achieve a radically better quality of life for deaf and hard of hearing people. Campaigns, lobbies and raises awareness of deafness and hearing loss; provides services; carries out social, medical and technical research.

SCOTTISH EMPLOYMENT OPPORTUNITIES
Portcullis House, 21 India Street, Glasgow G2 4PZ
0141-226 4544
Director (Scotland): George Bond
Helps people with disabilities to find employment.

SCOTTISH DISABILITY SPORT
Fife Sports Institute, Viewfield Road, Glenrothes KY6 2RA
01592 415700
Administrator: Margaret MacPhee

SCOTTISH DISABLED SPORTS TRUST
7 Westerton of Mugdock, Milngavie G62 8LQ
0141-956 6415
Chairman of Trustees: A Mills

Charitable trust giving grants to appropriate sports organisations for disabled people.

SCOTTISH NATIONAL FEDERATION FOR THE WELFARE OF THE BLIND
PO Box 500, Gillespie Crescent, Edinburgh EH10 4HZ
0131-229 1456
Honorary Treasurer: Mr J B M Munro; *President:* Allan Murray
Charitable organisation concerned with blind and partially-sighted people in Scotland.

SCOTTISH NATIONAL INSTITUTION FOR THE WAR BLINDED
PO Box 500, Gillespie Crescent, Edinburgh EH10 4HZ
0131-229 1456
Secretary and Treasurer: Mr J B M Munro; *President:* Duke of Buccleuch and Queensberry, KT
Provides training, employment and aftercare to Scottish ex-Service, visually impaired men and women.

SCOTTISH SOCIETY FOR AUTISM
Hilton House, Alloa Business Park, Whins Road, Alloa FK10 3SA
01259 720044
Chief Executive: Donald J Liddell

SENSE SCOTLAND
45 Finnieston Street, Clydeway Centre, Glasgow G3 8JU
0141-564 2444
Director: Gillian Morbey, OBE; *Chairperson:* Roy Cox
Charitable company representing deafblind and multisensory impaired people. Provides a range of services including respite, residential and day care.

THISTLE FOUNDATION
Niddrie Mains Road, Edinburgh EH16 4EA
0131-661 9970
Director: Jayne Fisher

Promotes independence for physically disabled people by providing accommodation and support.

DISADVANTAGED

POVERTY ALLIANCE
162 Buchanan Street, Glasgow G1 2LL
0141-353 0440
Director: Damian Killeen

SCOTTISH LOW PAY UNIT
24 Sandyford Place, Glasgow G3 7NG
0141-221 4491
Director: Peter Hunter; *Chairperson:* Councillor Angus Graham
Informs low paid workers of pay and employment rights, carries out research, campaigns, provides training on rights and good employment practice.

WISE GROUP
72 Charlotte Street, Glasgow G1 5DW
0141-303 3131
Chief Executive: Alan Sinclair
Charitable organisation helping people into work.

DYSLEXIA

DYSLEXIA INSTITUTE
74 Victoria Crescent Road, Downanhill, Glasgow G12 9JN
0141-334 4549
Administrator: Elizabeth Robin; *Principal:* Elizabeth MacKenzie
Assesses and teaches dyslexic adults and children. Provides teacher training and short courses for parents and teachers.

SCOTTISH DYSLEXIA ASSOCIATION
Unit 3, Stirling Business Centre, Wellgreen, Stirling FK9 4UX
01786 446650
Chairman: Jean Traill; *President:* Gill Thomson
Aims to raise public awareness of dyslexia and its related difficulties.

Provides information, advice and support, workshops and speakers and acts as a resource centre.

EDUCATION

ASSOCIATION OF UNIVERSITY TEACHERS (SCOTLAND)
6 Castle Terrace, Edinburgh EH2 3AT
Regional Assistant General Secretary: David Bleiman; *President*: Angela Roger
Trade union and professional association for academic and related staff in Scottish higher education.

BRITISH COUNCIL SCOTLAND
3 Bruntsfield Crescent, Edinburgh EH10 4HD
0131-447 4716
Director Scotland: Eunice Crook
Promotes educational, cultural and technical co-operation between Britain and other countries, working to establish long-term worldwide partnerships and to improve international understanding. It has 228 offices in 109 countries.

Promotes those aspects of Scottish culture which are unique, in particular the arts, education, governance and law. Takes a leading role in encouraging Scottish participation in international initiatives in the arts and provides opportunities for the presentation of Scottish art and artists abroad. Provides support services to international students studying in Scotland. Its educational activities also include the Scottish international resource programme, a global network developing business links between companies and overseas middle and senior managers undertaking postgraduate work in Scotland.

The European young lawyers scheme provides a programme of academic study on the Scottish legal system and professional placement with Scottish solicitors and advocates for young lawyers from all over Europe.

CARNEGIE TRUST FOR THE UNIVERSITIES OF SCOTLAND
Cameron House, Abbey Park Place, Dunfermline KY12 7PZ
01383 622148
Secretary: Professor J T Coppock; *Chairman*: Sir Lewis Robertson, CBE
Assists the Scottish universities, facilitating research by their staff and graduates, and assists students of Scottish birth or extraction with the payment of fees for first degrees at Scottish universities.

COMMITTEE OF SCOTTISH HIGHER EDUCATION PRINCIPALS
St Andrew House, 141 West Nile Street, Glasgow G1 2RN
0141-353 1880
Secretary: Dr Ronald L. Crawford; *Convener*: Dr Ian Graham-Bryce
Representative body for higher education in Scotland.

COMMUNITY LEARNING SCOTLAND (FORMERLY SCOTTISH COMMUNITY EDUCATION COUNCIL)
Rosebery House, 9 Haymarket Terrace, Edinburgh EH12 5EZ
0131-313 2488
Chief Executive: Charlie McConnell; *Chairman*: Linda McTavish
Non-departmental public body, established in 1982 under its original title, which works to open up access to learning opportunities and overcome the barriers to learning. Recognising that many adults and young people are not attracted by the thought of returning to educational institutions, which are seen as neither relevant nor accessible, the council helps to enable them to develop their talents and skills in less formal settings.

Participation in community-based learning has doubled in the last 20 years, with a far higher proportion now coming from disadvantaged areas and groups. More than a million young people and adults across Scotland now regularly participate every week in subjects of their choice – acquiring job-seeking skills, setting up a business, engaging in the arts, taking part in health education groups, running a housing co-operative, improving numeracy and literacy, organising an environmental campaign or a youth group.

EDUCATIONAL BROADCASTING COUNCIL FOR SCOTLAND
Broadcasting House, 5 Queen Street, Edinburgh EH2 1JF
0131-248 4261
Secretary: John S. Russell, Secretary; *Chairman*: Ann Aucherlonie
Provides strategic policy and programming advice to BBC Scotland for schools programming and offers advice to BBC Network for schools and adult programming.

EDUCATIONAL INSTITUTE OF SCOTLAND
46 Moray Place, Edinburgh EH3 6BH
0131-225 6244
General Secretary: Ronald A Smith; *President*: Moira McCrossan
Founded in 1847 by royal charter, the EIS is the oldest teaching union in the world. The stated aim of the founding members was the "promotion of sound learning".

In addition to its professional role, the institute has developed through the years its function of seeking to improve and protect the pay and conditions of service of teachers and lecturers in Scotland. In recent years it has also played an important role in the campaign to protect the distinctive nature of Scottish education and the quality of education. The EIS has 50,000 members, representing 80% of teachers in Scotland.

GENERAL TEACHING COUNCIL FOR SCOTLAND
Clerwood House, 96 Clermiston Road, Edinburgh EH12 6UT
0131-314 6000
Registrar: David I M Sutherland; *Council Convener*: Mrs Norma Anne Watson
Established in 1955 in response to professional and public dissatisfaction with standards in Scottish schools in the 1950s and early 1960s, arising largely from the employment of unqualified people as "uncertificated teachers". The government set up a committee of enquiry under the chairmanship of Lord Wheatley, which recommended the establishment of a General Teaching Council for Scotland "in which, subject to appropriate safeguards, control of entry to the teaching profession would be vested".

The council has 49 members widely representative of the educational community. Every teacher registered to teach in Scotland is required to pay an annual registration fee (£10); the council is therefore self-financing and independent.

The council seeks to protect professional standards by maintaining a register of qualified teachers, advising on the supply of teachers, overseeing standards of entry to the profession, accrediting and reviewing the operation of all courses of initial teacher education, and exercising disciplinary powers. In a case of gross professional misconduct, the council has the power to remove the teacher's name from the register. It is illegal for an education authority to employ an unregistered teacher.

HEADTEACHERS' ASSOCIATION OF SCOTLAND
University of Strathclyde, Jordanhill Campus, Southbrae Drive, Glasgow G13 1PP
0141-950 3298
General Secretary: George Ross; *President*: Dr Nigel Lawrie
Promotes the highest standards of education in Scottish secondary schools and provides for the needs and interests of members (headteachers, depute and assistant headteachers).

LEAD SCOTLAND (LINKING EDUCATION AND DISABILITY)
Queen Margaret University College, Clerwood Terrace, Edinburgh EH12 8TS
0131-317 3439
Director: Rona Connolly
Provides guidance to physically disabled and/or sensory impaired adults enabling access to education, training and lifelong learning opportunities.

NAS/UWT (SCOTLAND)
69 Buchanan Street, Glasgow G1 3HL
0141-229 5790
Scottish Regional Official: Carol Fox

NATIONAL UNION OF STUDENTS SCOTLAND
26 Rutland Street, Edinburgh EH1 2AN
0131-221 1966
Director: Liam Jarnecki; *President*:
Richard Baker
Federation of student associations representing 80% of students in Scotland. Also provides welfare, training, developmental and commercial services to constituent members.

PROFESSIONAL ASSOCIATION OF TEACHERS IN SCOTLAND
4/6 Oak Lane, Edinburgh EH12 6XH
0131-317 8282
Secretary: Robert Christie

SCOTTISH CONSULTATIVE COUNCIL ON THE CURRICULUM
Gardyne Road, Broughty Ferry, Dundee DD5 1NY
01382 455053
Chief Executive: Mike Baughan; *Chairman*: Neil Galbraith
Independent, advisory organisation, the principal advisory body to Scottish Ministers on all curriculum matters relating to 3-18 year old pupils in Scottish schools. Believes that the school curriculum should foster young people who are highly motivated, enterprising and caring, confident and articulate, who value equally achievement and co-operation, and who have high aspirations for themselves and their community.

SCOTTISH COUNCIL OF INDEPENDENT SCHOOLS
21 Melville Streeet, Edinburgh EH3 7PE
0131-220 2106
Director: Judith Sischy; *Chairman*: Professor B J McGettrick
Communicates with government departments and other bodies on behalf of the independent sector, advises member schools on educational developments, develops in-service

training, and provides information for parents and the media. 73 member schools with 31,000 pupils.

SCOTTISH COUNCIL FOR EDUCATIONAL TECHNOLOGY
74 Victoria Crescent Road, Glasgow G12 7JN
0141-337 5000
Chief Executive: Nigel Paine; *Chairman*: Alistair Fleming
Aims to transform learning throughout life by harnessing the power of technology. Works with both school and post-school education to help them use technology effectively in the delivery of learning and teaching.

SCOTTISH COUNCIL FOR RESEARCH IN EDUCATION
15 St John Street, Edinburgh EH8 8JR
0131-557 2944
Director: Professor Wynne Harlen; *Chair*: R A Furness
Independent body, established in 1928 by a partnership of teaching unions, local authorities, universities and colleges. The council conducts research for the benefit of education and training in Scotland (and elsewhere) and is funded by contracts for specific projects, as well as by grants from local authorities and teacher unions. SCRE's work covers all phases of education, formal and informal, from pre-five to higher education, and includes overseas consultancies and collaborative projects with other institutions.

SCOTTISH FURTHER EDUCATION FUNDING COUNCIL
Donaldson House, 97 Haymarket Terrace, Edinburgh EH12 5HD
0131-313 6500
Chief Executive: Professor John Sizer, CBE; *Chairman*: Robert Beattie, MBE
Established in shadow form in January 1999 to secure the adequate and efficient provision of further education in Scotland. Since July 1999 it has been responsible for allocating funds to and monitoring the financial health of the further eduation sector.

SCOTTISH HIGHER EDUCATION FUNDING COUNCIL
Donaldson House, 97 Haymarket Terrace, Edinburgh EH12 5HD
0131-313 6500
Chief Executive: Professor John Sizer, CBE; *Chairman*: Dr Chris Masters
Provides financial support for Scottish higher education institutions. It distributes funds to support teaching and research; assesses the quality of higher education supported by the council; and provides the government with information and advice. Distributes more than £500 million each year, most of which is allocated through formula grants.

SCOTTISH JOINT COMMITTEE ON RELIGIOUS AND MORAL EDUCATION
46 Moray Place, Edinburgh EH3 6BH
0131-225 6244
Joint Secretaries: Fred Forrester, Rev. John Stevenson; *Convener*: Mrs Pamela Paterson
Concerned with an overview of religious and moral education in Scottish schools.

SCOTTISH OUT OF SCHOOL CARE NETWORK
Floor 9, Fleming House, 134 Renfrew Street, Glasgow G3 6ST
0141-331 1301
National Development Officer: Irene Audain; *Chair*: Sue Robertson
Scotland's lead representative body for school-aged childcare. Provides information, advice and membership services to individuals, organisations and local networks.

SCOTTISH PARENT TEACHER COUNCIL
63-65 Shandwick Place, Edinburgh EH2 4SD
0131-228 5320/1.
Convenor: Alison Kirby
National organisation for PAs/PTAs. Publishes a newsletter, gives advice to callers, responds to consultations, and operates an insurance scheme for members.

SCOTTISH PRE-SCHOOL PLAY ASSOCIATION
SPPA Centre, 14 Elliot Place, Glasgow G3 8EP
0141-221 4148
Chief Executive: Martha Simpson

SCOTTISH QUALIFICATIONS AUTHORITY
Hanover House, 24 Douglas Street, Glasgow G2 7NQ
0141-248 7900
Chief Executive: Ron Tuck; *Chairman*: David Miller, CBE
Scotland's national body for qualifications, since 1996 the successor to SCOTVEC and the Scottish Examination Board and now the only organisation responsible for the qualifications on offer in schools, colleges, training centres and workplaces.
The SQA, though self-financing, answers to government for the credibility, reliability and value of its qualifications. It upholds the quality of established qualifications and develops new ones.
Rationalising and unifying the qualifications system in Scotland was one of the aims behind the establishment of the new body. It is responsible for most types of qualification in Scotland except university degrees. These range from the standard grade, higher grade and national certificate modules taken by almost all school pupils to higher national certificates, higher national diplomas and Scottish vocational qualifications.

SCOTTISH SCHOOLS EQUIPMENT RESEARCH CENTRE (SSERC)
2nd Floor, St Mary's Building, 23 Holyrood Road, Edinburgh EH8 8AE
0131-558 8180
Director: J Richardson; *Chairperson*: Councillor David L. McGrouther, JP
Information, advisory and training service for Scottish science and technology education.

SCOTTISH SECONDARY TEACHERS' ASSOCIATION
15 Dundas Street, Edinburgh EH3 6QG
0131-556 5919
General Secretary: David Eaglesham

SEAD (SCOTTISH EDUCATION & ACTION FOR DEVELOPMENT)
23 Castle Street, Edinburgh EH2 3DN
0131-225 6550
Director: Fiona Sinclair; *Chair*: Martin Coyle
Membership organisation which challenges poverty and social injustice, working for development that puts communities at the heart of decision-making.

STUDENT AWARDS AGENCY FOR SCOTLAND
Gyleview House, 3 Redheughs Rigg, Edinburgh EH12 9HH
0131-476 8212
Chief Executive: K MacRae
Provides financial support and other related services for Scottish-domiciled students undertaking full-time courses of higher education throughout the UK. It administers the students' allowances scheme, the postgraduate students' allowances scheme, the Scottish studentship scheme and the nursing and midwifery bursary scheme. It makes resources available to the Student Loans Company and disburses access funds to eligible institutions in Scotland. It also advises the Scottish Ministers on student maintenance policy.

WORKERS' EDUCATIONAL ASSOCIATION
Riddles Court, 322 Lawnmarket, Edinburgh EH1 2PG
Scottish Secretary: Joyce Connon; *Convenor*: Esther Quinn
National democratic voluntary organisation providing adults with access to organised learning. Priority given to the most disadvantaged and excluded groups.

ELDERLY

ABBEYFIELD SOCIETY FOR SCOTLAND
15 West Maitland Street, Edinburgh EH12 5EA
0131-225 7801
General Secretary: Sue Jones; *Chairman*: Rev Dr J W S Clark
Provides lonely elderly people with their own home within family-sized homes run by groups of local volunteers.

AGE CONCERN SCOTLAND
113 Rose Street, Edinburgh EH2 3DT
0131-220 3345
Director: Maureen O'Neill
National voluntary organisation with the primary aim of improving the quality of life for older people in Scotland. Committed to working throughout Scotland to ensure that all older people have their rights upheld and their voices heard, and enjoy choice and control over all aspects of their lives. Provides a comprehensive information service on all issues affecting older people. Has more than 250 local groups providing practical services including day care, lunch clubs and information and advice, as well as social activities.

DISCOVERY AWARD
Ancrum Centre for the Environment, 10 Ancrum Road, Dundee DD2 2HZ
01382 641800
Director: Laurie M Young, MBE; *Chairperson*: Margaret Hutton
Achievement award offering challenges to individuals over the age of 50. Enables and encourages people to make choices about their own lives and to increase their contribution to life around them.

HELP THE AGED
Heriot House, Heriothill Terrace, Edinburgh EH7 4DY
0131-556 4666
Scottish Executive: Elizabeth Duncan

SCOTTISH PRE-RETIREMENT COUNCIL
Alexandra House, 204 Bath Street, Glasgow G2 4HL
0141-332 9427
Director: Archie McGown; *Chairman*: Ian B Smail
Promotes preparation and education for retirement.

ENERGY SUPPLIERS

BRITISH ENERGY PLC
10 Lochside Place, Edinburgh EH12 9DF
0131-527 2000
Chief Executive: Peter Hollins; *Chairman*:
John Robb
Operates eight nuclear stations and has
a market share of around 21% in the UK
and 50% in Scotland.

SCOTTISH AND SOUTHERN ENERGY PLC
10 Dunkeld Road, Perth PH1 5WA
01738 455040
Chief Executive: Jim Forbes
Formerly Scottish Hydro-Electric PLC.

SCOTTISHPOWER PLC
1 Atlantic Quay, Glasgow G2 8SP
0141-248 8200
Chief Executive: Ian Robinson
Serves around 5.5 million homes. The
company's activities span electricity,
gas, water, telecommunications and
retail. ScottishPower is one of the
biggest industrial groups in the UK with
a market capitalisation of almost £7bn.

ENTERPRISE COMPANIES

SCOTTISH ENTERPRISE
120 Bothwell Street, Glasgow G2 7JP
Tel.: 0141-248 2700
Chief Executive: Crawford W Beveridge,
CBE; *Chairman*: Sir Ian Wood
Serves the economic development and
skills needs of the people of Scotland.
Established in 1991 under the
Enterprise and New Towns (Scotland)
Act, it works in partnership with a wide
variety of organisations in the public
and private sectors – including a
network of 13 local enterprise
companies, business representative
organisations, local authorities,
education and training organisations,
companies and the wider community.
Scottish Enterprise covers all of
Scotland, except the Highlands and
Islands, and is funded by grant-in-aid
from the government.

HIGHLANDS AND ISLANDS ENTERPRISE
Bridge House, 20 Bridge Street,
Inverness IV1 1QR
01463 234171
Chief Executive: Iain Robertson, CBE;
Chairman: Dr James Hunter
Established in 1991 under the Enterprise
and New Towns (Scotland) Act for the
purpose of preparing, promoting,
assisting and undertaking measures for
the economic and social development of
the Highlands and Islands, maintaining
and enhancing skills, helping people to
establish themselves as self-employed
and improving the environment.
Financed mainly by government,
through the Scottish Executive
Enterprise and Lifelong Learning
Department.

Local enterprise companies:

ARGYLL AND THE ISLANDS ENTERPRISE
The Enterprise Centre, Kilmory
Industrial Estate, Lochgilphead PA31
8SH
01546 602281
Chief Executive: Ken Abernethy

CAITHNESS AND SUTHERLAND ENTERPRISE
Tollemache House, High Street, Thurso
KW14 8AZ
01847 896115
Chief Executive: Neil Money

DUMFRIES AND GALLOWAY ENTERPRISE
Solway House, Dumfries Enterprise
Park, Tinwald Downs Road, Heathhall,
Dumfries DG1 3SJ
01387 245000
Chief Executive: Irene Walker

DUNBARTONSHIRE ENTERPRISE
2nd Floor, Spectrum House, Clydebank
Business Park, Clydebank, Glasgow G81
2DR
0141-951 2121
Chief Executive: Dave Anderson

ENTERPRISE AYRSHIRE
17-19 Hill Street, Kilmarnock KA3 1HA
01563 526623
Chief Executive: Liz Connolly

FIFE ENTERPRISE
Kingdom House, Saltire Centre, Glenrothes KY6 2AQ
01592 623000
Chief Executive: David Waring

FORTH VALLEY ENTERPRISE
Laurel House, Laurelhill Business Park, Stirling FK7 9JQ
01786 451919
Chief Executive: Bill Morton

GLASGOW DEVELOPMENT AGENCY
Atrium Court, 50 Waterloo Street, Glasgow G2 6HQ
0141-204 1111
Chief Executive: Stuart Gulliver

GRAMPIAN ENTERPRISE
27 Albyn Place, Aberdeen AB10 1DB
01224 575100
Chief Executive: Ed Gillespie

INVERNESS AND NAIRN ENTERPRISE
The Greenhouse, Beechwood Business Park North, Inverness IV2 3BW
01463 713504
Chief Executive: Bill Sylvester

IOMAIRT NAN EILEAN SIAR (WESTERN ISLES ENTERPRISE)
James Square, 9 James Street, Stornoway, Isle of Lewis HS1 2NQ
01851 703703
Chief Executive: Donnie Macaulay

LANARKSHIRE DEVELOPMENT AGENCY
New Lanarkshire House, Strathclyde Business Park, Bellshill ML4 3AD
01698 745454
Chief Executive: Iain Carmichael

LOCHABER LIMITED
St Mary's House, Gordon Square, Fort William PH33 6DY
01397 704326
Chief Executive: Jackie Wright

LOTHIAN AND EDINBURGH ENTERPRISE LIMITED
Apex House, 99 Haymarket Terrace, Edinburgh EH12 5HD
0131-313 4000
Chief Executive: David Crichton

MORAY BADENOCH AND STRATHSPEY ENTERPRISE
Elgin Business Centre, Maisondieu Road, Elgin IV30 1RH
01343 550567
Chief Executive: Dick Ruane

ORKNEY ENTERPRISE
14 Queen Street, Kirkwall, Orkney KW15 1JE
01856 874638
Chief Executive: Ken Grant

RENFREWSHIRE ENTERPRISE
27 Causeyside Street, Paisley PA1 1UL
0141-848 0101
Chief Executive: Lorraine MacMillan

ROSS AND CROMARTY ENTERPRISE
69-71 High Street, Invergordon IV18 0AA
01349 853666
Chief Executive: Sandy Cumming

SCOTTISH BORDERS ENTERPRISE
Bridge Street, Galashiels TD1 1SW
01896 758991
Chief Executive: Jim McFarlane

SCOTTISH ENTERPRISE TAYSIDE
45 North Lindsay Street, Dundee DD1 1HT
01382 223100
Chief Executive: Graham McKee

SHETLAND ENTERPRISE
Toll Clock Shopping Centre, 26 North Road, Lerwick, Shetland ZE1 0DE
01595 693177
Chief Executive: David Finch

SKYE & LOCHALSH ENTERPRISE
King's House, The Green, Portree, Isle of Skye IV51 9BS
01478 612841
Chief Executive: Robert D. Muir

ENTERPRISE TRUSTS

BUSINESS ENTERPRISE SCOTLAND (NATIONAL ASSOCIATION OF ENTERPRISE TRUSTS)
18 Forth Street, Edinburgh EH1 3LH

0131-550 3839
Chief Executive: Robin Miller
Founded in 1996 by the Scottish enterprise trusts to answer the requirement for a lead body to guide, shape, promote and represent their network. BES represents the trusts to the Scottish Executive, Scottish Enterprise, local authorities and others.

It provides training, organises members' meetings and runs a service quality programme. Individual enterprise trusts provide start-up advice to people wishing to go into business for themselves, as well as marketing and business planning advice to existing businesses.

Local enterprise trusts:

ABERDEEN ENTERPRISE TRUST
27 Albyn Place, Aberdeen AB10 1DB
01224 575100
Chief Executive: Bill Ferguson

AYR LOCALITY ENTERPRISE RESOURCES TRUST
Ayr Business Centre, 16 Smith Street, Ayr KA7 1TD
01292 264181
Chief Executive: Bill Dunn

CLYDEBANK ECONOMIC DEVELOPMENT COMPANY LIMITED
Phoenix House, South Avenue, Clydebank Business Park, Clydebank G81 2LG
0141-951 1131
Chief Executive: Alastair Muir

CLYDESDALE DEVELOPMENT COMPANY LIMITED
129 Hyndford Road, Lanark ML11 9AU
01555 665064
General Manager: Chris Parkin

CUMBERNAULD AREA ENTERPRISE
100 Telford Road, Lenzie Mill, Cumbernauld G67 2NJ
01236 611600
Director: Jim Telford

DEVELOPING NORTH AYRSHIRE
Sovereign House, Academy Road, Irvine KA12 8RL
01294 315120
General Manager: John R. Logan

EAST AYRSHIRE BUSINESS PARTNERSHIP
16 Glaisnock Street, Cumnock KA18 1DA
01290 421159
Chief Executive: Sheila White

EAST DUNBARTONSHIRE ENTERPRISE TRUST
Enterprise House, Southbank Business Park, Kirkintilloch G66 1XQ
0141-777 7171
Chief Executive: Andrew Thomson

EDINBURGH BUSINESS DEVELOPMENT
Conference House, The Exchange, 152 Morrison Street, Edinburgh EH3 8EB
0131-477 8000
Divisional Director: Grahame Cunningham

ENTERPRISE NORTH EAST LIMITED
Business Centre, Glebefield, 21 Links Terrace, Peterhead AB42 2XA
01779 472224
Chief Executive: Ian Moir

FALKIRK ENTERPRISE ACTION TRUST
Falkirk & District Business Park, Newhouse Road, Grangemouth FK3 8LL
01324 665500
Director: Sandy Riddell

FIFE BUSINESS SHOP
Enterprise Centre, Mitchelston Drive, Mitchelston Industrial Estate, Kirkcaldy KY1 3NF
01592 655339
Manager: Linda Fitzsimmons

GLASGOW OPPORTUNITIES
7 West George Street, Glasgow G2 1EQ
0141-221 0955
Executive Director: Agnes Samuel

GORDON ENTERPRISE TRUST
Business Development Centre, Thainstone Business Centre, Thainstone, Inverurie AB51 5TB
01467 621166
Director: Jackie Hall

HAMILTON ENTERPRISE DEVELOPMENT COMPANY
Barncluith Business Centre, Townhead Street, Hamilton ML3 7DP
01698 429425
Director: Ronnie Smith

HIGHLAND OPPORTUNITY LIMITED
Planning and Development Department, Highland Council, Glenurquhart Road, Inverness IV3 5NX
01463 702000
Company Secretary: Frank Allan

INVERCLYDE ENTERPRISE TRUST
5 East Blackhall Street, Greenock PA15 1HD
01475 892191
Manager: Tony Sinclair

KINCARDINE AND DEESIDE ENTERPRISE TRUST
Aboyne Business Centre, Unit 1, Huntly Road, Aboyne AB34 5HE
013398 87222
Chief Executive: Chris Travis

LOMOND ENTERPRISE PARTNERS
2/2 Vale of Leven Industrial Estate, Dumbarton G82 3PD
01389 750005
Chief Executive: Graham Keith

MIDLOTHIAN ENTERPRISE TRUST
29A Eskbank Road, Dalkeith EH22 1HJ
0131-654 1234
Director: Gregor Murray

STIRLING ENTERPRISE
John Player Building, Stirling FK7 7RP
01783 463416
Executive Director: Derek Gavin

WEST LOTHIAN ECONOMIC DEVELOPMENT
The Business Centre, Almondvale Boulevard, Livingtson EH51 6QP
01506 777400
Business Development Manager: Alistair Shaw

ENVIRONMENT

FRIENDS OF THE EARTH SCOTLAND (FOE SCOTLAND)
72 Newhaven Road, Edinburgh EH6 5QG
0131-554 9977
Director: Kevin Dunion, OBE; *Chairman*: Dr Mark Huxham
Campaigns for environmental justice, our right to live in a better environment, and our responsibility to share the world's resources fairly.

HABITAT SCOTLAND
Hazelmount, Heron Place, Portree, Isle of Skye IV51 9EU
01478 612898
Director: Graeme Robertson; *Chairman*: William McGhee
Independent environmental research charity.

JOHN MUIR TRUST
41 Commercial Street, Leith EH6 6JD
0131-554 0114
Director: Nigel Hawkins; *Chairman*: Andrew Thin
Owns areas of wild land and manages them for conservation benefits, taking into account the needs of the local community.

LIVING WATER CHARITABLE TRUST
5 Holyrood Road, Edinburgh EH8 8AE
0131-558 3313
Environmental education; community outreach; ecological water and waste management and treatment.

SCOTTISH ENVIRONMENT PROTECTION AGENCY
Erskine Court, Castle Business Park, Stirling FK9 4TR
01786 457700
Chief Executive: Alasdair Paton; *Chairman*: Professor W A Turmeau
Established under the Environment Act

1995 as a non-departmental public body. SEPA took on the responsibilities of HM Industrial Pollution Inspectorate, seven river purification boards and their counterparts in the three islands councils, as well as the functions of 56 district and islands councils, thus creating for the first time a single agency responsible for the control of pollution of the air, land, sea and water.

SEPA's mission is "to provide an efficient and integrated environmental protection system for Scotland which will both improve the environment and contribute to the government's goal of sustainable development".

Accountable to the Scottish Parliament, SEPA is responsible for preserving and improving the quality of rivers and lochs, estuaries and coastal waters, dealing with 40,000 consents a year relating to the discharge of materials. It also regulates 1,200 of Scotland's most complex industrial processes, including oil refineries, paper and chemical works, the disposal and treatment of 13 million tonnes of controlled waste, involving 800 managed sites and 6,500 carriers, and oversees programmes to restore land damaged by contamination.

SEPA registers organisations handling radioactive materials, controls the discharges of radioactive waste from Scottish nuclear installations (which supply about 50% of our electricity requirements) and monitors radioactivity in Scotland.

SCOTTISH ENVIRONMENTAL EDUCATION COUNCIL
University of Stirling, Stirling FK9 4LA
01786 467867
Chief Executive: Betsy King; *President*: Professor John C Smith
Promotes, supports and helps to develop education for environmentally sustainable living.

SCOTTISH FIELD STUDIES ASSOCIATION
Kindrogan Field Centre, Enochdhu, Blairgowrie, PH10 7PG
01250 881286

Director: Neil Morgan; *Chairman*: Alan Pike
Assists in the popularisation of field studies in Scotland, provides facilities for every kind of field study, and provides a means of contact among societies engaged in field study.

SCOTTISH WILD LAND GROUP
8 Hartington Place, Edinburgh EH10 4LE
0131-229 2094
Co-ordinator: Alistair Cant
Campaigns to conserve and enhance wild land in Scotland and protects it against intrusive developments. Supports local communities in conserving wild land.

EQUAL OPPORTUNITIES

EQUAL OPPORTUNITIES COMMISSION SCOTLAND
Stock Exchange House, 7 Nelson Mandela Place, Glasgow G2 1QW
Tel.: 0141-248 5833
Director Scotland: Morag Alexander; *Commissioner for Scotland*: Dr Joan Stringer
Public body set up under the Sex Discrimination Act 1975, working to remove unlawful discrimination on grounds of sex or marriage, and to promote equal opportunities for women and men. These commitments often involve the commission in legal cases to uphold the basic principle of equal rights. Sometimes the desired end can be achieved by giving information and advice, but in situations where people refuse to act in accordance with the sex discrimination laws, the EOC, as a law enforcement body, has powers to take legal action.

The Scottish office delivers the commission's services throughout Scotland. It runs training sessions for lay advisers and lawyers, publishes guides to good practice for a specifically Scottish readership, and offers free advice based on practical experience.

EUROPE

EUROPEAN COMMISSION REPRESENTATION
IN SCOTLAND
9 Alva Street, Edinburgh EH2 4PH
0131-225 2058
Head of Representation: Elizabeth Holt

EXHIBITION AND CONFERENCE CENTRES

EDINBURGH INTERNATIONAL CONFERENCE
CENTRE
The Exchange, Morrison Street,
Edinburgh EH3 8EE
0131-300 3000
Chief Executive: Hans Rissmann;
Chairman: Donald Anderson

SCOTTISH EXHIBITION AND CONFERENCE
CENTRE
Exhibition Way, Glasgow G3 8YW
0141-248 3000
Chief Executive: Michael Closier

FAMILY PLANNING

FAMILY PLANNING ASSOCIATION,
SCOTLAND
Unit 10, Firhill Business Centre, 76
Firhill Road, Glasgow G20 7BA
0141-576 5088
Chief Executive: Anne Weyman;
Chairperson: Dr D Robertson
Works to advance the sexual health and
reproductive rights and choices of all
people throughout the country.

FENCING

SCOTTISH FENCING
The Cockburn Centre, 40 Bogmoor
Place, Glasgow G51 4TQ
0141-445 1602
Administrator: Colin Grahamslaw

FESTIVALS
Listed is a selection of festivals of special
interest. A more comprehensive list can be
obtained from the Scottish Arts Council.

CELTIC CONNECTIONS
Glasgow Royal Concert Hall, 2
Sauchiehall Street, Glasgow G2 3NY
0141-332 6633
Festival Administrator: Colin Hynd

CELTIC FILM AND TELEVISION FESTIVAL
249 West George Street, Glasgow G2
4QE
0141-302 1737
Chief Executive: Frances Hendron

DUMFRIES AND GALLOWAY ARTS FESTIVAL
Gracefield Arts Centre, 28 Edinburgh
Road, Dumfries DG1 1NW
01387 260447
Hon Secretary: Ruth Bell; Chairman: Beryl
Jago, MBE

EDINBURGH FESTIVAL FRINGE
180 High Street, Edinburgh EH1 1QS
0131-226 5257
Director: Hilary Strong; Chairperson:
Baroness Smith of Gilmorehill
Cited by the Guinness Book of Records
as the largest arts festival in the world,
playing host every August to 10,000
performers of every art form and
entertainment imaginable.

The fringe originated informally at
the first Edinburgh International
Festival in 1947, when six Scottish
companies and two English decided to
turn up uninvited. They were referred to
originally as "festival adjuncts", but this
name was quickly dropped and the
phrase "fringe" came into being in
August 1948 when Robert Kemp wrote
describing a production in Dunfermline
Abbey as being "on the fringes of the
festival".

The Festival Fringe Society was
formed in 1958 to publish a
comprehensive programme, sell tickets
centrally, and offer advice to future
performers. It was agreed that there
would never be any form of artistic
vetting – a policy maintained to the
present day.

EDINBURGH INTERNATIONAL FESTIVAL
The Hubb, Castlehill, Royal Mile,
Edinburgh EH1 2NE
0131-473 2099
Festival Director and Chief Executive:
Brian McMaster, CBE
Lasts for three weeks from the middle of August to early September. Its founders in 1947 believed that the programme should be of the highest possible artistic standard; that the festival should enliven and enrich the cultural life of Europe, Britain and Scotland; and that it should provide a period of flowering of the human spirit.

Using all the major concert and theatre venues in the city, the festival brings to Edinburgh some of the best in international theatre, music, dance and opera. The audience is 60% Scottish-based, but the festival also attracts many visitors to the city, with 25% coming from the rest of the UK and 15% from overseas.

EDINBURGH MILITARY TATTOO
Tattoo Office, 32 Market Street, Edinburgh EH1 1QB
0131-225 1188
Chief Executive and Producer: Brigadier Melville Jameson

HIGHLAND FESTIVAL
40 Huntly Street, Inverness IV3 5HR
01463 719000

ST MAGNUS FESTIVAL
Strandal, Nicolson Street, Kirkwall KW15 1ED
01856 872669

SCOTTISH INTERNATIONAL CHILDREN'S FESTIVAL
45a George Street, Edinburgh EH2 2HT
0131-225 8050
Director: Tony Reekie

SCOTTISH INTERNATIONAL STORYTELLING FESTIVAL
The Netherbow Arts Centre, 43-45 High Street, Edinburgh EH1 1SR
0131-557 5724
Director: Joanna Bremner

FILM

BAFTA SCOTLAND (BRITISH ACADEMY OF FILM AND TELEVISION ARTS)
74 Victoria Crescent Road, Glasgow G12 9JN
0141-357 4317
Director: Alison Forsyth; *Committee Chair*: Blair Jenkins
Rewards Scottish industry and talent in film and television.

SCOTTISH SCREEN
249 West George Street, Glasgow G2 4RB
0141-302 1700
Chief Executive: John Archer; *Chairman*: James Lee
Unified organisation which came into existence in 1997 from the merger of the Scottish Film Council, Scottish Film Production Fund, Scottish Broadcast and Film Training, and Scottish Screen Locations.

A film and television agency funded by the government, charged with promoting film both as an industry and as a moving image culture, it brings together education, training, script development, production finance, locations, marketing, exhibitions and archives in a one-stop shop. It is part of Scottish Screen's role to stimulate debate on film and television matters and to represent the interests of the industry to government.

The agency's locations department aims to attract production companies to film in Scotland. Scottish Screen Training provides courses and events to encourage technical and creative talent. Scottish Screen Development considers 350 film projects a year, of which about 20 will be given development finance. Scottish Screen Production advises on production finance available from the Glasgow Film Fund and administers four short film schemes. The Scottish National Film and Video Archive, established in 1976, locates and preserves the indigenous film heritage. Scottish Screen Exhibition promotes public screenings. The agency also acts as a distributor.

FISHING

FISHERIES RESEARCH SERVICES
Marine Laboratory, PO Box 101, Victoria Road, Aberdeen AB11 9DB
01224 876544
Chief Executive: Professor A D Hawkins
Marine Laboratory provides expert scientific and technical advice on marine and freshwater fisheries, aquaculture, and the protection of the aquatic environment and its wildlife. The laboratory monitors the state of the fish and shellfish stocks exploited by Scottish fishermen, investigates fishing methods and ways of promoting the conservation of fish stocks through technical measures, monitors the state of the seas, and carries out the statutory inspection of fish and shellfish farms.
Freshwater Fisheries Laboratory is the only government research laboratory in Britain wholly devoted to freshwater fisheries. Monitors the reported annual catches of salmon and sea trout, and provides scientific advice to government.

FISHING CO-OPERATIVES (UK)
20 Elgin Street Industrial Estate, Dunfermline KY12 7SN
01383 738830

SCOTTISH FISHERIES PROTECTION AGENCY
Pentland House, 47 Robb's Loan, Edinburgh EH14 1TY
0131-244 6059
Chief Executive: P E Du Vivier
Britain's sea fisheries have been protected and controlled by authority of parliament for nearly 200 years. The 19th-century "Commissioners of the British White Herring Fishery" used naval vessels to superintend the fisheries. In 1882 responsibility for protecting sea fisheries in Scottish waters was given to the Fishery Board for Scotland, and in 1939 its functions were transferred to the Secretary of State for Scotland. The present agency is responsible to the Scottish Executive Rural Affairs Department.

It enforces fisheries legislation and regulations in the 185,000 square miles of sea around Scotland and in Scottish ports, with the aim of conserving fish stocks. Aims to deter and detect illegal fishing. Among its resources are two surveillance aircraft based at Prestwick, five offshore patrol vessels based at Leith and Greenock, two inshore patrol vessels and a fast launch, and fishery offices at 19 of the main fishing ports in Scotland.

SCOTTISH FISHERMEN'S FEDERATION
14 Regent Quay, Aberdeen AB11 5AE
01224 582583
Chief Executive: Hamish Morrison, OBE;
President: Alexander Smith
Represents the political interests of Scotland's seven main fishing associations to the UK government and European institutions.

SCOTTISH FISHERMEN'S ORGANISATION
Braehead, 601 Queensferry Road, Edinburgh EH4 6EA
0131-339 7972
Chief Executive: I M MacSween

SCOTTISH SALMON FARMERS' MARKETING BOARD
Drummond House, Scott Street, Perth PH1 5EJ
01738 635973
Marketing Manager: Michael A. Lloyd;
Chairman: Dr Marshall Halliday
Marketing arm of the Scottish salmon industry. Manages the marketing and promotion of Tartan Quality-Mark Salmon in the UK and Label Rouge Salmon in France, on behalf of fresh and smoked salmon companies.

SCOTTISH SALMON GROWERS ASSOCIATION
Drummond House, Scott Street, Perth PH1 5EJ
01738 635420
Chief Executive: Julian J J Crowe;
Chairman: Earl of Lindsay
Trade association representing the interests of Scotland's salmon fisheries.

SCOTTISH WHITE FISH PRODUCERS' ASSOCIATION LTD
40 Broad Street, Fraserburgh AB43 9AH
01346 514545

Secretary: George MacRae; *Chairman*: Michael Park
Develops the interests of commercial seagoing fishermen.

SEA FISH INDUSTRY AUTHORITY
18 Logie Mill, Logie Green Road, Edinburgh EH7 4HG
0131-558 3331
Chief Executive: Alasdair C Fairbairn; *Chairman*: Eric Davey
Replaced the White Fish Authority and the Herring Industry Board in 1981. Works with the industry to meet consumer demands, raise standards, improve efficiency, and secure a prosperous future. Undertakes research and development; provides or helps with training; promotes the marketing and consumption of sea fish; gives financial assistance to co-operatives.

FITNESS

FITNESS SCOTLAND
Caledonia House, South Gyle, Edinburgh EH12 9DQ
0131-317 7243
Manager: Jennifer Small

FOOD

TASTE OF SCOTLAND
33 Melville Street, Edinburgh EH3 7JF
0131-220 1900
Chief Executive: Amanda Clark
Publishes annual guide to good eating places in Scotland through a stringent quality assurance programme.

FOOTBALL

SCOTTISH FOOTBALL ASSOCIATION
6 Park Gardens, Glasgow G3 7YF
0141-332 6372
Chief Executive: David Taylor; *President*: Jack McGinn
Governing body for football in Scotland.

SCOTTISH FOOTBALL LEAGUE
188 West Regent Street, Glasgow G2 4RY
0141-248 3844
Secretary: Peter Donald
Promotes and extends association football and provides League Championship and League Cup competitions for the clubs. Concludes commercial contracts on their behalf.

FREEMASONRY

GRAND LODGE OF ANTIENT FREE AND ACCEPTED MASONS OF SCOTLAND
Freemasons' Hall, 96 George Street, Edinburgh EH2 3DH
0131-225 5304
Grand Secretary: C Martin McGibbon
Governing body for freemasonry in Scotland.

GAELIC

COMHAIRLE NAN LEABHRAICHEAN (THE GAELIC BOOKS COUNCIL)
22 Mansfield Street, Glasgow G11 5QP
0141-337 6211
Director: Ian MacDonald; *Chairperson*: A G Boyd Robertson
Assists publishers with grants for books, commissions authors, and provides an editorial service. It has its own bookshop and publishes a catalogue of all Gaelic and Gaelic-related books in print.

COMHAIRLE NAN SGOILTEAN ARAICH
53 Church Street, Inverness IV1 1DR
01463 225469
Concerned with pre-school education.

AN COMUNN GAIDHEALACH
109 Church Street, Inverness IV1 1EY
01463 231226
Chief Executive: Donald John MacSween; *President*: Ann Draper
Works for the preservation and development of the Gaelic language. Organises and stages the annual National Mod and produces the Gaelic

newspaper *An Gaidheal Ur.* There are branches of the association throughout the world and thousands of members, many of whom work voluntarily on behalf of the language.

COMUNN NA GAIDHLIG
5 Mitchell's Lane, Inverness IV2 3HQ
Tel.: 01463 234138
Chief Executive: Allan Campbell; *Chairperson:* Mairi Bremner
Gaelic language development agency, established in 1984 to co-ordinate the revival of Gaelic at all levels and sectors in Scotland.

FEISEAN NAN GAIDHEAL
Nicolson House, Somerled Square, Portree, Isle of Skye IV51 9EJ
01478 613355
Secretary: Rita Hunter; *Chairman:* John Macdonald
Independent umbrella organisation promoting and supporting the tuition of traditional Gaelic music, song and dance.

GARDENS

SCOTLAND'S GARDENS SCHEME
31 Castle Terrace, Edinburgh EH1 2EL
0131-229 1870
Director: R St Clair-Ford
Opens mainly private gardens all over Scotland for charity.

GAY RIGHTS

OUTRIGHT SCOTLAND
Lesbian, Gay and Bisexual Centre, 58a Broughton Street, Edinburgh EH1 3SA
0131-228 6147
Secretary: Alec Deary; *President:* Janey Buchan
Scotland's only national membership-based organisation promoting the interests and rights of lesbian, gay, bisexual and transgendered people.

GENEALOGY

SCOTS ANCESTRY RESEARCH SOCIETY
134 Thornhill Road, Falkirk FK2 7AZ
Hon Secretary: Lorna Walker
Undertakes genealogical research in Scottish records for people of Scottish descent all over the world.

SCOTTISH GENEALOGY SOCIETY
15 Victoria Terrace, Edinburgh EH1 2JL
0131-220 3677
Hon Secretary: Miss J P S Ferguson
Promotes research into Scottish family history; collects, exchanges and publishes information and material relating to Scottish genealogy by means of meetings, lectures, etc.

GOLF

LADIES GOLF UNION
The Scores, St Andrews KY16 9AT
01334 475811
Administrator: Julie Hall; *President:* Miss B A B Jackson
Governing body of ladies' amateur golf.

ROYAL AND ANCIENT GOLF CLUB
The Links, St Andrews KY16 9JD
01334 472112
Secretary: Peter Dawson; *Chairman, General Committee:* Ian Webb
Governing body for rules of golf for all countries of the world (except USA). Organisers of Open Golf Championship.

SCOTTISH GOLF UNION
Scottish National Golf Centre, Drumoig, Leuchars, St Andrews KY16 0DW
01382 549500
Secretary: Hamish Grey

SCOTTISH LADIES GOLFING ASSOCIATION
Scottish National Golf Centre, Drumoig, Leuchars, St Andrews KY16 0DW
01382 549502
Secretary: Susan Simpson

GOVERNMENT

See pages 22-27 for detailed information about the new Scottish Executive. Some public bodies are listed under subject category.

ACCOUNTS COMMISSION FOR SCOTLAND
18 George Street, Edinburgh EH2 2QU
0131-477 1234
Controller of Audit: Robert Black;
Chairman: Professor Ian Percy
Established in 1975 as a statutory, independent body which through the audit process helps local authorities and the health service in Scotland to achieve the highest standards of financial stewardship. It oversees the external audit of 47 NHS trusts, 15 health boards, five other health service bodies, 32 councils and 27 joint boards. Half of the audits are conducted by private accountancy firms and the others by the commission's staff.

If auditors believe that there is something seriously wrong (such as a financial loss due to illegality, negligence or misconduct), they must report this immediately to the audited body and to the controller of audit. In the case of the health service, the controller may conduct his own investigation and make a report to the commission. In the case of local authorities, the commission may hold a public hearing and may then make its own report and recommendations.

BENEFITS AGENCY
Central Support Unit Scotland, Argyle House, 3 Lady Lawson Street, Edinburgh EH3 9SH
Tel.: 0131-229 4311
Area Director: A Roy, OBE

COMPANIES HOUSE
37 Castle Terrace, Edinburgh EH1 3EB
0131-535 5855
Registrar of Companies: Jim Henderson
Executive agency of the Department of Trade and Industry, responsible for: the incorporation and striking off of companies and the registration of documents required to be delivered under companies, insolvency and related legislation; and the provision of company information to the public.

THE CROWN ESTATE
Crown Estate Office, 10 Charlotte Square, Edinburgh EH2 4DR
0131-226 7241
Head of Scottish Estates: Michael Cunliffe;
Scottish Commissioner: Ian Grant
Manages property held "in right of the Crown". In Scotland, this includes commercial property, agricultural land, about half the foreshore, and almost all the seabed. All profit is paid to the Treasury.

COMMON SERVICES AGENCY FOR THE NATIONAL HEALTH SERVICE
Trinity Park House, South Trinity Road, Edinburgh EH5 3SE
0131-552 6255
General Manager: F F Gibb, CBE;
Chairman: Graeme Millar
Provides and co-ordinates for the NHS in Scotland: national data processing and information services, health surveillance, blood transfusion and laboratory requests, specialist legal, technical, and purchasing services, commissioning specialist care.

EMPLOYMENT SERVICE – OFFICE FOR SCOTLAND
Argyle House, 3 Lady Lawson Street, Edinburgh EH3 9SD
0131-221 4000
Director: A R Brown
Runs the Job Centre network in Scotland.

HEALTH AND SAFETY EXECUTIVE
Belford House, 59 Belford Road, Edinburgh EH4 3UE
0131-247 2000
Field Operations Director (Scotland): Linda Williams
Responsible for the control of risks to people's health and safety from work activities and the enforcement of health and safety legislation.

INLAND REVENUE SCOTLAND
Clarendon House, 114-116 George Street, Edinburgh EH2 4LH
0131-473 4000
Director: Ian Gerrie

LOCAL GOVERNMENT BOUNDARY COMMISSION FOR SCOTLAND
3 Drumsheugh Gardens, Edinburgh EH3 7QZ
0131-538 7510
Secretary: R Smith; *Chairman*: Hon Lord Osborne
Permanent body appointed under the Local Government (Scotland) Act 1973 to keep under review local government boundaries and electoral areas.

PARLIAMENTARY BOUNDARY COMMISSION FOR SCOTLAND
3 Drumsheugh Gardens, Edinburgh EH3 7JQ
0131-538 7513
Secretary: Bob Smith
Keeps under review the boundaries of the Parliamentary constituencies in Scotland.

SCOTLAND COLLECTION (HM CUSTOMS AND EXCISE)
44 York Place, Edinburgh EH1 3JW
Tel.: 0131-469 2000
Collector: Ian Mackay
Executive unit within the Customs and Excise department. Formed in 1995, it collects and manages VAT, insurance premium tax, landfill tax, excise duties (including air passenger duty); collects EU duties and levies; enforces import and export prohibitions.

SCOTTISH INDUSTRIAL DEVELOPMENT ADVISORY BOARD
Meridian Court, 5 Cadogan Street, Glasgow G2 6AT
0141-242 5676
Chairman: J J G Good, CBE

SCOTTISH TRAFFIC AREA OFFICE
J Floor, Argyle House, 3 Lady Lawson Street, Edinburgh EH3 9SE
0131-529 8501
Administrative Director: John Bannister
Responsible for HGV and PSV operator licensing.

VALUATION OFFICE AGENCY
58 Frederick Street, Edinburgh EH2 1NG
0131-225 9602
Chief Valuer (Scotland): Allan Ainslie

Provides valuation and property-related advice for all classes of property to the public sector, including government departments, local authorities, the NHS and non-departmental public bodies.

HEALTH BOARDS

ARGYLL AND CLYDE HEALTH BOARD
Ross House, Hawkhead Road, Paisley PA2 7BN
0141-842 7200
General Manager: N A McConachie; *Chairman*: Malcolm Jones

AYRSHIRE AND ARRAN HEALTH BOARD
Boswell House, 10 Arthur Street, Ayr KA7 1QJ
01292 611040
General Manager: Mrs Wia-yin Hatton; *Chairman*: John Morrow

BORDERS HEALTH BOARD
Newstead, Melrose TD6 9DB
01896 825500
General Manager: Dr Lindsay Burley; *Chairman*: David A G Kilshaw

DUMFRIES AND GALLOWAY HEALTH BOARD
Grierson House, The Crichton, Bankend Road, Dumfries DG1 4ZH
01387 272700
General Manager: N M Campbell; *Chairman*: J A Ross, CBE

FIFE HEALTH BOARD
Springfield House, Cupar KY15 5UP
01334 656200
General Manager: Patricia Frost; *Chairman*: Charlotte Stenhouse, JP

FORTH VALLEY HEALTH BOARD
33 Spittal Street, Stirling FK8 1DX
01786 463031
General Manager: David Hird; *Chairman*: Euan Bell-Scott

GRAMPIAN HEALTH BOARD
Summerfield House, 2 Eday Road, Aberdeen AB15 6RE

01224 663456
General Manager: Frank Hartnett; *Chair*:
Dr Calum MacLeod, CBE

GREATER GLASGOW HEALTH BOARD
Dalian House, 350 St Vincent Street,
Glasgow G3 8YZ
0141-201 4444
Chief Executive: Chris Spry; *Chairman*:
Professor David L Hamblen

HIGHLAND HEALTH BOARD
Beechwood Park, Inverness IV2 3HG
01463 704800
Acting General Manager: Dr Eric Baijal;
Chairman: Caroline Thomson

LANARKSHIRE HEALTH BOARD
14 Beckford Street, Hamilton ML3 0TA
01698 281313
General Manager: T A Divers; *Chairman:*
Ian Livingstone

LOTHIAN HEALTH
Deaconess House, 148 Pleasance,
Edinburgh EH8 9RS
0131-536 9000
General Manager: Trevor Jones; *Chairman*:
Margaret Ford

ORKNEY HEALTH BOARD
Garden House, New Scapa Road,
Kirkwall KW15 1BQ
01856 885400
General Manager: Judi Wellden;
Chairman: Eoin Leslie

SHETLAND HEALTH BOARD
Brevik House, South Road, Lerwick ZE1
0RB
01595 696767
General Manager: Brian Atherton;
Chairman: John Telford

TAYSIDE HEALTH BOARD
Gateway House, Luna Place, Dundee
DD2 1TP
01382 561818
General Manager: Tim Brett; *Chairman*:
Frances Havenga

WESTERN ISLES HEALTH BOARD
37 South Beach Street, Stornoway, Isle of
Lewis HS1 2BN

01851 702997
Chief Executive: Murdo MacLennan;
Chair: Alexander Matheson

HEALTH ORGANISATIONS

ASH SCOTLAND (ACTION ON SMOKING AND HEALTH)
8 Frederick Street, Edinburgh EH2 2HB
0131-225 4725
Director: Maureen Moore; *Chair*:
Professor Keith Fox
Campaigns for effective tobacco control
policies; provides support services for
those addicted to nicotine.

HEALTH EDUCATION BOARD FOR SCOTLAND
Woodburn House, Canaan Lane,
Edinburgh EH10 4SG
0131-536 5500
Chief Executive: Professor Andrew
Tannahill; *Chairman*: David R Campbell
Public body established in 1991 and
funded by the Scottish Executive which
aims to promote good health by: helping
to ensure that people have adequate
information about health and factors
which influence it; helping people to
acquire the motivation and skills which
enable them to adopt and maintain
healthy lifestyles; influencing health-
related attitudes throughout society and
stimulating environments conducive to
good health.

NETWORK SCOTLAND
The Mews, 57 Ruthven Lane, Glasgow
G12 9JQ
0141-357 1774
Director: David McNiven; *Chairman*:
Fiona Ballantyne
Health and public sector telephone
information service.

SCOTTISH ASSOCIATION OF HEALTH COUNCILS
24a Palmerston Place, Edinburgh EH12
5AL
0131-220 4101
Director: Patricia Dawson; *Convener*:
Andrew Gardiner

Seeks to be the national voice of the public in health matters.

HIGHLAND DANCING

SCOTTISH OFFICIAL BOARD OF HIGHLAND DANCING
32 Grange Loan, Edinburgh EH9 2NR
0131-668 3965
Secretary: Marjory Rowan; Chairman: Miss S Russell
Governing body for Highland dancing.

HIGHLAND GAMES

SCOTTISH GAMES ASSOCIATION
24 Florence Place, Perth PH1 5BH
01738 627782
Secretary: Andrew Rettie; President: Alan Sim

HISTORY

GENERAL REGISTER OFFICE FOR SCOTLAND
New Register House, Edinburgh EH1 3YT
0131-334 0380
Ladywell House, Edinburgh EH12 7TF
Tel.: 0131-314 4243
Registrar General : J Randall
Government department established by Act of Parliament in 1854 and headed by the Registrar General for Scotland, who is appointed by Scottish Ministers. The office administers civil registration of "vital events" – births, deaths, marriages, divorces and adoptions – and the statutes relating to the formalities of marriage. It arranges periodic censuses of Scotland's population and maintains the NHS central register of patients. New Register House, one of the most advanced ancestral research facilities in the world, is the prime source of genealogical records in Scotland, giving the serious searcher access to unique records and a source of reference books.

Before the introduction of compulsory civil registration in 1855, the registers of births, deaths, marriages, etc, were kept by parish ministers or session clerks. These old parish registers, numbering 3,500, are far from complete and for some parishes there are no registers at all. Even where pre-1855 records do exist, they contain relatively little information.

The branch of the department based at Ladywell House publishes a wide range of reports and tables on vital statistics, population statistics and census statistics.

Every year, the department oversees the local registration of 170,000 "vital events"; undertakes up to 25,000 searches on behalf of personal callers and postal customers; issues up to 30,000 copies of entries in statutory registers; maintains 100 search places for members of the public themselves to access the open records, allowing 450,000 such accesses each year; deals with 7,000 requests for statistical information; processes 500,000 changes to the NHS central register; and handles up to 50,000 transactions in connection with medical research projects. It is also preparing for the next census (in 2001) involving two million households.

Three years ago, the department introduced central electronic recording of all births, deaths and marriages from information obtained by local registration offices.

NATIONAL ARCHIVES OF SCOTLAND
HM General Register House, 2 Princes Street, Edinburgh EH1 3YY
Tel.: 0131-535 1314
Keeper of the Records of Scotland: Patrick M Cadell
As the repository for the public and legal records of Scotland, the National Archives of Scotland (formerly known as the Scottish Record Office) is responsible for maintaining the national archives. In addition, it accepts many local and private archives.

The records cover the period from the 12th century to the present day, ranging from medieval parchments to modern microfiche, from the formal records of government and the law courts to personal letters and diaries. The holdings include family papers and estate records, thousands of hand-drawn and engraved maps and plans which illustrate the changing face of urban and rural Scotland, the Scottish railway archives, and the records of a number of firms, charities and public bodies.

The office provides personal access to the records through its search rooms and answers postal inquiries from all over the world.

REGISTERS OF SCOTLAND
Meadowbank House, 153 London Road, Edinburgh EH8 7AU
0131-659 6111
Keeper of the Registers: Alan Ramage
Information about property and property transactions is available to the general public at either the Registers of Scotland or the Scottish Record Office, and can be obtained by paying a fee. The main registers are the Sasine Register, established in 1617, and the Land Register, introduced into Scotland by the 1979 Land Registration Scotland Act. Both deal with the registration of property and interests in property. Unlike the Sasine Register (which is being replaced), the Land Register does not provide historical information on past owners of properties. It is an up to date statement of the ownership and details of each registered title, which can be easily found by reference to the Ordnance Survey map.

Land registration is a modern system allowing for the simple transfer of registered property. By dispensing with the need to examine legal documents spanning a long period to ensure that the title to a property is sound, it helps make conveyancing transactions simpler. Staff deal with half a million transactions every year.

SCOTTISH HISTORY SOCIETY
Department of Scottish History, University of Edinburgh, 17 Buccleuch Place, Edinburgh EH8 9LN
0131-650 4030
Hon Secretary: Dr S Boardman

SCOTTISH RECORDS ASSOCIATION
National Archives of Scotland, HM General Register House, 2 Princes Street, Edinburgh EH1 3YY
0131-535 1314
Honorary Secretary: Dr T Clarke; Chairman: Dr Athol L Murray
For all those interested in the preservation and use of Scotland's historical records. Publishes journal, *Scottish Archives*.

1745 ASSOCIATION
Ferry Cottage, Corran, Ardgour, Fort William PH33 7AA
01855 841306
Secretary: Miss C Aikman; *President*: David Lumsden of Cushnie
Studies the period of Jacobite history (1688-1788), marks sites of Jacobite interest, publishes a journal three times a year, organises annual gathering, visits to houses and annual dinner.

HOCKEY

SCOTTISH HOCKEY UNION
34 Cramond Road North, Edinburgh EH4 6JD
0131-312 8870

HORSES

SCOTTISH EQUESTRIAN ASSOCIATION
Boreland, Fearnan, Aberfeldy PH15 2PG
01887 830 274
Secretary: Iain Menzies; *Chairperson*: Lorna Clarke
New governing body in Scotland for all equestrian activities. Launched February 1999.

TREKKING AND RIDING SOCIETY OF SCOTLAND
Boreland, Fearnan, Aberfeldy PH15 2PG
01887 830274
Secretary: Liz Menzies
Recreational and holiday riding.

HOUSING

SCOTTISH COUNCIL FOR SINGLE
HOMELESS
5th Floor, Wellgate House, 200 Cowgate,
Edinburgh EH1 1NQ
0131-226 4382
Director: Robert Aldridge; *Convener*:
Alice Ann Jackson
National charity promoting the interests
of single homeless people.

SCOTTISH FEDERATION OF HOUSING
ASSOCIATIONS
38 York Place, Edinburgh EH1 3HU
0131-556 5777
Director: David Orr
Voice of housing associations and co-
operatives, representing them in
negotiations on housing policy with
government and other bodies, as well as
campaigning on their behalf. A
membership organisation, it promotes,
encourages and assists the formation of
housing associations and provides
training, advice and support to help
them operate.

SCOTTISH HOMES
Thistle House, 91 Haymarket Terrace,
Edinburgh EH12 5HE
0131-313 0044
Chief Executive: Peter McKinlay;
Chairman: John Ward
National housing agency for Scotland.
Established in 1989, it helps to provide
good housing and contributes to the
regeneration of local communities. It
works in partnership with local
authorities, housing associations, the
voluntary sector, private developers,
economic development agencies,
financial institutions and local
authorities to tackle Scotland's housing
problems. Funded through an annual
grant from the government, rental
income and receipts from the sale of its
own houses.

SHELTER – SCOTTISH CAMPAIGN FOR
HOMELESS PEOPLE
4th Floor, Scotiabank House, 6 South
Charlotte Street, Edinburgh EH2 4AW
0131-473 7170

Director: Liz Nicholson; *Chairman,
Scottish Supporters' Council*: Peter
Robson

TENANT PARTICIPATION ADVISORY
SERVICE
74-78 Saltmarket, Glasgow G1 5LD
0141-552 3633
Director: Lesley Baird

HUMAN RELATIONS

SCOTTISH INSTITUTE OF HUMAN
RELATIONS
56 Albany Street, Edinburgh EH1 3QR
0131-556 0924
Director: Alan Harrow

HUMAN RIGHTS

AMNESTY INTERNATIONAL
11 Jeffrey Street, Edinburgh EH1 1DR
0131-557 2957
Scottish Development Officer: Rosemary
Burnett; *Chair*: Andrew McEntee
Works worldwide for the release of
prisoners of conscience, fair trials for
political prisoners, and an end to
torture, extra-judicial killings,
"disappearances", and the death penalty.

SCOTTISH HUMAN RIGHTS CENTRE
146 Holland Street, Glasgow G2 4NG
0141-332 5960
Director: Professor Alan Miller; *Chair*:
John Scott
Promotes human rights in Scotland
through public education and advice;
research; scrutiny of legislation;
monitoring of human rights treaties.

ICE HOCKEY

SCOTTISH ICE HOCKEY ASSOCIATION
Glenburn House, 21 Braeburn Drive,
Currie EH14 6AQ
0131-449 3163
Secretary: Aileen Robertson; *Chairman*:
Jim Anderson

ICE SKATING

SCOTTISH ICE SKATING ASSOCIATION
The Ice Sports Centre, Riversdale Crescent, Edinburgh EH12 5XN
0131-337 3976
Administrator: John Macdonald

IMMIGRATION

IMMIGRATION APPELLATE AUTHORITY – SCOTLAND
5th Floor, Portcullis House, 21 India Street, Glasgow G2 4PZ
0141-221 3489
Regional Adjudicator: Mungo E Deans
Independent tribunal which considers appeals against decisions made by the Home Secretary or an Entry Clearance Officer to refuse entry to the UK and extension of visa. It also deals with political asylum appeals.

SCOTTISH REFUGEE COUNCIL
43 Broughton Street, Edinburgh EH1 3JU
0131-557 8083
Chief Executive: Sally Daghlian; *Chair*: Councillor Margaret McGregor
Provides advice, information, legal representation and practical assistance to asylum seekers and refugees in Scotland and campaigns on issues which affect them.

INSURANCE COMPANIES AND PERSONAL FINANCE

ABBEY NATIONAL FINANCIAL AND INVESTMENT SERVICES plc
Abbey National House, 301 St Vincent Street, Glasgow G2 5HN
0141-248 6321
Managing Director: Graham Pottinger; *Chairman*: Sir William Fraser

CGU INSURANCE
Pitheavlis, Perth PH2 0NH
01738 621202
Managing Director: Cees Schrauwers

SCOTTISH AMICABLE LIFE ASSURANCE SOCIETY
PO Box 25, Craigforth, Stirling FK9 4UE
01786 448844
Managing Director: Roy Nicolson; *Chairman:* Sir Peter Davis

SCOTTISH EQUITABLE PLC
Edinburgh Park, Edinburgh EH12 9SE
0131-339 9191
Managing Director: Graham Dumble; *Chairman:* David Henderson

SCOTTISH LIFE ASSURANCE COMPANY
19 St Andrew Square, Edinburgh EH2 1YE
0131-456 7777
Group Chief Executive: Brian Duffin

SCOTTISH MUTUAL ASSURANCE PLC
Abbey National House, 301 St Vincent Street, Glasgow G2 5HN
0141-248 6321
Managing Director: Graham Pottinger

SCOTTISH PROVIDENT INSTITUTION
7-11 Melville Street, Edinburgh EH3 7YZ
0131-527 1100
Group Managing Director: David Woods; *Chairman*: John Foden

SCOTTISH WIDOWS' FUND AND LIFE ASSURANCE SOCIETY
15 Dalkeith Road, Edinburgh EH16 5BU
0131-655 6000
Group Chief Executive: M D Ross; *Chairman*: Lawrence M Urquhart

STANDARD LIFE ASSURANCE CO
Standard Life House, 30 Lothian Road, Edinburgh EH1 2DH
0131-225 2552
Managing Director: Scott Bell

INTERNATIONAL

BRITISH RED CROSS – HEAD OFFICE (SCOTLAND)
Alexandra House, 204 Bath Street, Glasgow G2 4HL
0141-332 9591

Director: David Whyte; *Chairman, Scottish Council*: Rosalind Birchall
Gives skilled and impartial care to people in crisis everywhere, meeting the needs of vulnerable people in times of emergency. Twelve Scottish branches.

CONCERN WORLDWIDE
40 St. Enoch Square, Glasgow G1 4DH
0141-221 3610
Director: David Welch

FEED THE MINDS
41 George IV Bridge, Edinburgh EH1 1EL
0131-226 5254
Scottish Secretary: Alan C Ross
Works inter-denominationally to help Christian literature and communication projects around the world.

INSTITUT FRANÇAIS D'ECOSSE
13 Randolph Crescent, Edinburgh EH3 7TT
0131-225 5366
Director: Jean-Marc Terrasse
Promotion of French language and culture.

INTERNATIONAL VOLUNTARY SERVICE
7 Upper Bow, Edinburgh EH1 2JN
0131-226 6722
Director: Neil Harrower

OXFAM IN SCOTLAND
Floor 5, Fleming House, 134 Renfrew Street, Glasgow G3 6ST
0141-331 2724
Head of Scotland: Marie Hearle

SCOTTISH CAMPAIGN FOR NUCLEAR DISARMAMENT (CND)
15 Barrland Street, Glasgow G41
0141-423 1222
Administrator: John Ainslie; *Chair*: Neil Cruickshank
Campaigns for the elimination of nuclear weapons.

JUDO

SCOTTISH JUDO FEDERATION
Caledonia House, South Gyle, Edinburgh EH12 9DQ

Chief Executive: Colin McIver; *Chairperson*: Richard Kenney

LACROSSE

SCOTTISH LACROSSE ASSOCIATION
St Leonards School, St Andrews
01334 475149
Secretary: June Caithness; *President*: Elspeth Semple

LANGUAGE

ENGLISH SPEAKING UNION – SCOTLAND
23 Atholl Crescent, Edinburgh EH3 8HQ
0131-229 1528
Chairman: J Grant Carson

SCOTS LANGUAGE SOCIETY
Scots Language Resource Centre, AK Bell Library, York Place, Perth PH2 8EP
01738 440199
Preses: Rod Lovie
Tae forder an uphaud the Scots leid in leiterature, poetrie, drama, sang an ballant.

SCOTTISH ESPERANTO ASSOCIATION
47 Airbles Crescent, Motherwell ML1 3AP
01698 263199
Hon Secretary: David W Bisset; *President*: Ed Robertson
Promotion of Esperanto: improving proficiency in the language; encouraging dissemination of Scottish culture by means of Esperanto.

SCOTTISH GAELIC TEXTS SOCIETY
Department of Celtic, Taylor Building, University of Aberdeen AB24 3UB
Hon Secretary: Dr Richard A V Cox; *President*: Rev Dr R MacLeod
Promotes the publication of texts in the Scottish Gaelic language.

LAW

See also: Courts and Tribunals

ABERDEEN BAR ASSOCIATION
23 Adelphi, Aberdeen AB11 5BL
01224 588599
Secretary: Lynn Bentley; *President*: Peter Shepherd

EDINBURGH BAR ASSOCIATION
Messrs McCourts, 53 George IV Bridge, Edinburgh EH1 1EJ
0131-225 6555

FACULTY OF ADVOCATES
Advocates' Library, Parliament House, Edinburgh EH1 1RF
0131-226 5071
Dean of Faculty: G N H Emslie, QC
Part of the College of Justice, which was founded in 1532. A self-governing organisation consisting of those admitted to practise before the Court of Session, the faculty is located within its own library in Parliament House, where the Supreme Courts are also to be found. The library, founded in 1682, is the only copyright law library in Scotland and is open 24 hours a day, 365 days a year.

The faculty is headed by an elected dean and has 375 practising members, of whom 75 are women. Candidates for admission to the office of advocate are called intrants. There are no restrictions to entry provided an intrant satisfies the relevant standards in law and experience and has undertaken a period of pupillage.

FAMILY LAW ASSOCIATION
c/o Sheridan McDermott & Company, 166 Buchanan Street, Glasgow
Secretary: Lynne V Di Biasio; *Chair*: Elizabeth McFarlane
Brings together solicitors with an interest predominantly in family law. Represents family law interests relating to new legislation, court practice, legal aid, etc.

GLASGOW BAR ASSOCIATION
Gallacher & Co., 106 Cowgate, Kirkintilloch G66 1JU
0141-776 1111
Secretary: Martin Hughes

LAW SOCIETY OF SCOTLAND
26 Drumsheugh Gardens, Edinburgh EH3 7YR
0131-226 7411
Chief Executive: Douglas R Mill; *President*: Philip J S Dry
Governing body of the Scottish legal profession. Promotes the interests of both practising solicitors and the public. Regulates its members and provides services which include: continuing legal education; advice on professional practice, European law, mediation, changes in the law, and marketing; a solicitor referral service for the public; and Dial-A-Law, a telephone information service for the public. It also promotes law reforms and undertakes legal research.

There are around 9,000 solicitors in Scotland, most in private practice, although 20% work in central and local government, industry and commerce. The society has a council of 50 members of the profession.

LEGAL DEFENCE UNION
Kidsons Impey, 274 Sauchiehall Street, Glasgow G2 3EH
0141-307 5000

ROYAL FACULTY OF PROCURATORS IN GLASGOW
12 Nelson Mandela Place, Glasgow G2 1BT
0141-331 0533
Clerk and Treasurer: Alastair James Campbell; *Dean*: Walter Semple
Seeks to provide a centre for the legal profession in Glasgow, including library services, auditing, and education and training. The Faculty Hall is also available to other organisations as a conference venue.

SCOTTISH ASSOCIATION OF LAW CENTRES
65 George Street, Paisley PA1 2JY
0141-561 7266
Secretary: Lynn Welsh; *Chair*: Bob Lennie
Promotes and supports Scottish law centres.

SCOTTISH CHARITIES OFFICE
Crown Office, 25 Chambers Street, Edinburgh EH1 1LA
0131-226 2626
Division of the Crown Office operating under the authority of the Lord Advocate. The law gives to the Lord Advocate the power to investigate misconduct or mismanagement in the administration of charitable organisations. The investigations are carried out by the Scottish Charities Office, which has a multi-disciplinary legal, accountancy and investigative staff.

SCOTTISH CHILD LAW CENTRE
Cranston House, 108 Argyle Street, Glasgow G2 8BH
0141-226 3434
Director: Deirdre Watson; *Convenor*: Ross Macfarlane
Charitable legal advice line for Scots law as it applies to under 25s.

SCOTTISH COUNCIL OF LAW REPORTING
Law Society's Hall, 26 Drumsheugh Gardens, Edinburgh EH3 7YR
0131-226 7411
Deputy Secretary: David Cullen; *Chairman*: Angus Stewart, QC
Publisher of Session Cases and the Faculty Digest.

SCOTTISH LAW AGENTS SOCIETY
SSC Library, 11 Parliament Square, Edinburgh EH1 1RF
0131-225 5061
Secretary: Janice H Webster, WS; *President*: David P H MacLennan, WS
Voluntary organisation of Scottish solicitors, founded in 1884. Operates specialist committees; publishes *Scottish Law Gazette* and *Memorandum Book*; represents the interests of its members; administers a Benevolent Fund.

SCOTTISH LAW COMMISSION
140 Causewayside, Edinburgh EH9 1PR
0131-668 2131
Secretary: J G S MacLean; *Chairman*: Hon Lord Gill
Established in 1965 under the Law Commissions Act for the purpose of promoting the reform of the law of Scotland.

SCOTTISH LEGAL AID BOARD
44 Drumsheugh Gardens, Edinburgh EH3 7SW
0131-226 7061
Chief Executive: Lindsay Montgomery; *Chairman*: Jean Couper
Responsible for the administration of civil and criminal legal aid, as well as advice and assistance. In Scotland it determines eligibility for legal aid (other than for solemn criminal cases, where it is determined by the courts) and controls payments from the Legal Aid Fund in respect of legal aid and advice and assistance.

Non-departmental public body sponsored by the Scottish Executive Justice Department, established in 1987, which manages legal aid in Scotland. It derives its general powers and functions from the Legal Aid (Scotland) Act 1986. The board's main tasks are: to assess and where appropriate grant applications for legal aid; to scrutinise and pay legal aid accounts submitted by solicitors and advocates; and to advise the Secretary of State for Scotland on legal aid matters.

SHERIFFS' ASSOCIATION
PO Box 23, 1 Carlton Place, Glasgow G5 9DA
0141-429 8888
Hon Secretary: Sheriff Brian A Lockhart; *President*: Sheriff Alexander B Wilkinson
Promotion of the interests of the sheriffs of Scotland. Considers all subjects connected with the law and administration of justice.

SIGNET OFFICE
2 Parliament Square, Edinburgh EH1 1RQ
0131-225 2595

SOCIETY OF ADVOCATES IN ABERDEEN
Advocates' Hall, Concert Court, Aberdeen AB10 1BS
01224 640079

SOCIETY OF PROCURATORS AND SOLICITORS IN THE CITY AND COUNTY OF PERTH
Ridley Seath & Co, 40 St John Street, Perth PH1 5SP
01738 630737

SOCIETY OF WRITERS TO HM SIGNET
Signet Library, Parliament Square, Edinburgh EH1 1RF
0131-225 4923
General Manager: J R C Foster; *Deputy Keeper of the Signet*: R John Elliot
Body of solicitors based primarily in Edinburgh. Maintains and improves the standards of professional knowledge, practice and competence of its members through the provision of library, educational and other facilities. Provides a forum for discussion of legislation and other matters affecting the law and its practice in Scotland. Promotes social activity. Acts as guardian of the Signet Library and of the works of scholarly and historical importance contained within it.

SSC SOCIETY
SSC Library, 11 Parliament Square, Edinburgh EH1 1RF
0131-225 6268
Keeper of the Library: C A Wilcox; *Secretary*: Dr Ian L S Balfour; *President*: Francis M McConnell
Legal society formed in 1784 by royal charter to maintain standards in the solicitor profession, to uphold Scots law, and to encourage solicitors in public service.

STAIR SOCIETY
Saltire Court, 20 Castle Terrace, Edinburgh EH1 2ET
0131-228 9900
Secretary and Treasurer: Thomas H Drysdale; *President*: Rt Hon Lord Hope of Craighead
Encourages and advances the knowledge of the history of Scots law.

LAWN TENNIS

SCOTTISH LAWN TENNIS ASSOCIATION
177 Colinton Road, Edinburgh EH14 1BZ
0131-444 1984
Secretary and Treasurer: Gloria Grosset; *President*: Alan G Christie

LIBRARIES

NATIONAL LIBRARY OF SCOTLAND
George IV Bridge, Edinburgh EH1 1EW
0131-226 4531
Librarian and Secretary to Board of Trustees: Ian D McGowan
Scotland's largest library, serving both as a general research library of international importance and as the world's leading repository for the written record of Scotland's history and culture.

Direct descendant of the Advocates' Library (the library of the Scottish Bar), which was founded in 1689, the National Library since 1710 has had the privilege of legal deposit (the right to claim a copy of every book published in the UK and Ireland), and is currently one of five libraries in the UK to enjoy this privilege and the only one north of Cambridge. Created by Act of Parliament in 1925, when the Advocates' Library (by then a national library in all but name) gifted all but its legal collections to the nation.

The library holds Scotland's largest collection of books and manuscripts: 6.5 million printed items and pamphlets, 100,000 volumes of manuscripts, 20,000 current newspapers and periodicals, on 85 miles of shelves. Among the library's treasures are the last letter of Mary Queen of Scots, the Gutenberg Bible, Earl Haig's war diaries, and the world's most significant collection of Sir Walter Scott's manuscripts.

Access is restricted to those carrying out research or reference work requiring material not easily available in other libraries.

SCOTTISH LIBRARY ASSOCIATION
Scottish Centre for Information and
Library Services, 1 John Street, Hamilton
ML3 7EU
01698 458888
Director: Robert Craig

SCOTTISH LIBRARY AND INFORMATION
COUNCIL
Scottish Centre for Information and
Library Services, 1 John Street, Hamilton
ML3 7EU
01698 458888
Director: Robert Craig
Advises government on library and
information matters, promotes and
monitors standards, provides grant-aid
for projects.

LIGHTHOUSES

NORTHERN LIGHTHOUSE BOARD
(COMMISSIONERS OF NORTHERN
LIGHTHOUSES)
84 George Street, Edinburgh EH2 3DA
0131-226 7051
Chief Executive: Captain J B Taylor
Created by Act of Parliament in 1786,
authorising the construction of four
lighthouses in Scotland and the
establishment of a commission for their
administration. Responsible now for a
network of 200 lights, 144 lit buoys, 38
unlit buoys, 41 unlit beacons, 27 racons
and nine radio beacons. For the delivery
of stores and supplies, the board has
two ships, MV Pharos based at Oban
and MV Fingal based at Stromness.

The area covered reaches from
Muckle Flugga in Shetland to the Calf of
Man. From Edinburgh headquarters, 66
automated major lighthouses are
monitored by land-line and radio link
and by satellite, night and day
throughout the year. Running costs are
met from a general lighthouse fund,
financed by the collection of light dues
paid by ships loading or discharging
cargoes at British and Irish ports and by
fishing vessels over 10 metres in length.
A programme to automate all major
lighthouses was completed in March
1998. The Board's motto is "In Salutem
Omnium" (For the Safety of All).

LITERATURE

ASSOCIATION FOR SCOTTISH LITERARY
STUDIES
Department of Scottish History, 9
University Gardens, University of
Glasgow, Glasgow G12 8QH
0141-330 5309
Secretary: Jim Alison; *President*: Dorothy
McMillan
Educational charity promoting and
publishing the languages and literature
of Scotland.

EDINBURGH BIBLIOGRAPHICAL SOCIETY
Department of Antiquarian Books,
National Library of Scotland, George IV
Bridge, Edinburgh EH1 1EW
0131-226 4531
Honorary Secretary: Richard Ovenden;
President: Brenda E Moon
Promotion and study of bibliography
and the history of the book.

EDINBURGH INTERNATIONAL BOOK
FESTIVAL
Scottish Book Centre, 137 Dundee
Street, Foutainbridge, Edinburgh EH11
1BG
0131-228 5444
Director: Faith Liddell; *Chairman*: Fred
Johnston
Celebrates and promotes books and the
written word.

INTERNATIONAL PEN SCOTTISH CENTRE
26 East Clyde Street, Helensburgh G84
7PG
01436 672010
President: Robin Lloyd-Jones
Writers' association with centres
worldwide, which aims to foster
friendly co-operation between writers
and to defend freedom of expression.

SCOTTISH BOOK SOURCE
137 Dundee Street, Edinburgh EH11
1BG
0131-229 6800
Manager: Lavinia Drew
Offers distribution services to Scottish
publishers. Owned by the Scottish
Publishers Association and a number of
individual publishers.

SCOTTISH BOOK TRUST
Scottish Book Centre, 137 Dundee Street, Edinburgh EH11 1BG
0131-229 3663
Executive Director: Lindsey Fraser; *Chairman*: Professor Rory Watson
Promotes the role of books and literature in the enrichment and enjoyment of life.

SCOTTISH PUBLISHERS ASSOCIATION
Scottish Book Centre, 137 Dundee Street, Edinburgh EH11 1BG
0131-228 6866
Director: Lorraine Fannin; *Chairman*: Peter Mackenzie
Aims to help publishing concerns in Scotland to conduct their book publishing businesses in a professional manner, and to market their output to the widest possible readership. Encourages the development of a literary culture in Scotland.

SCOTTISH TEXT SOCIETY
27 George Square, Edinburgh EH8 9LD
Secretary: Lorna Pike; *President*: Professor R J Lyall
Furthers the study and teaching of Scottish literature, its language and history, in particular by publishing editions of original texts.

LOCAL GOVERNMENT

COSLA
Rosebery House, 9 Haymarket Terrace, Edinburgh EH12 5XZ
0131-474 9200
Chief Executive: Douglas Sinclair; *President*: Keith Geddes
Representative voice of Scottish local government. Aims to provide national leadership to help councils strengthen local democracy and community support for local goverment; to increase the role and influence of local government; to increase the control which local government has over its affairs; to establish effective relationships with government, European institutions and partner organisations.

COSLA acts as the employers' association on behalf of its member councils, negotiating salaries, wages and conditions of service for local government employees in Scotland. It also has a responsibility to develop, encourage and promote best practice for local government in partnership with its member councils.

Local authorities:

ABERDEEN CITY COUNCIL
Town House, Broad Street, Aberdeen AB10 1FY
01224 522000
Chief Executive: Douglas Paterson

ABERDEENSHIRE COUNCIL
Woodhill House, Westburn Road, Aberdeen AB16 5GB
01467 620981
Chief Executive: A G Campbell

ANGUS COUNCIL
7 The Cross, Forfar DD8 1BX
01307 461460
Chief Executive: A B Watson

ARGYLL AND BUTE COUNCIL
Kilmory, Lochgilphead PA31 8RT
01546 602127
Chief Executive: J McLellan

CLACKMANNANSHIRE COUNCIL
Greenfield, Alloa FK10 2AD
01259 450000
Chief Executive: Bob Allan

DUMFRIES AND GALLOWAY COUNCIL
Council Offices, English Street, Dumfries DG1 2DD
01387 260000
Chief Executive: P N Jones

DUNDEE CITY COUNCIL
City Chambers, 21 City Square, Dundee DD1 3BY
01382 434000
Chief Executive: A Stephen

EAST AYRSHIRE COUNCIL
Council Headquarters, London Road, Kilmarnock KA3 7BU
01563 576000
Chief Executive: D Montgomery

EAST DUNBARTONSHIRE COUNCIL
PO Box 4, Tom Johnston House, Civic Way, Kirkintilloch G66 4TJ
0141-578 8000
Chief Executive: C Mallon

EAST LOTHIAN COUNCIL
Council Buildings, Haddington EH41 3HA
01620 827827
Chief Executive: J Lindsay

EAST RENFREWSHIRE COUNCIL
Council Headquarters, Eastwood Park, Rouken Glen Road, Giffnock, East Renfrewshire G46 6UG
0141-577 3000
Chief Executive: P Daniels

CITY OF EDINBURGH COUNCIL
Wellington Court, 10 Waterloo Place, Edinburgh EH1 3EG
0131-469 3002
Chief Executive: T N Aitchison

FALKIRK COUNCIL
Municipal Buildings, Falkirk FK1 5RS
01324 506070
Chief Executive: Mary Pitcaithly

FIFE COUNCIL
Fife House, North Street, Glenrothes KY7 5LT
01592 414141
Chief Executive: Douglas Sinclair

GLASGOW CITY COUNCIL
City Chambers, George Square, Glasgow G2 1DU
0141-287 2000
Acting Chief Executive: J Andrew

HIGHLAND COUNCIL
Council Buildings, Glenurquhart Road, Inverness IV3 5NX
01463 702000
Chief Executive: A D McCourt

INVERCLYDE COUNCIL
Municipal Buildings, Clyde Square, Greenock PA15 1LY
01475 717171
Chief Executive: R Cleary

MIDLOTHIAN COUNCIL
Midlothian House, Buccleuch Street, Dalkeith EH22 1DN
0131-270 7500
Chief Executive: T Muir

MORAY COUNCIL
Council Offices, High Street, Elgin IV30 1BX
01343 543451
Chief Executive: Brian Stewart

NORTH AYRSHIRE COUNCIL
Cunninghame House, Irvine KA12 8EE
01294 324100
Chief Executive: Bernard Devine

NORTH LANARKSHIRE COUNCIL
PO Box 14, Civic Centre, Motherwell ML1 1TW
01698 302222
Chief Executive: A Cowe

ORKNEY ISLANDS COUNCIL
Council Offices, Kirkwall KW15 1NY
01856 873535
Chief Executive: A Buchan

PERTH AND KINROSS COUNCIL
PO Box 77, 2 High Street, Perth PH1 5PH
01738 475000
Chief Executive: H Robertson

RENFREWSHIRE COUNCIL
North Building, Cotton Street, Paisley PA1 1WB
0141-842 5000
Chief Executive: T Scholes

SCOTTISH BORDERS COUNCIL
Newtown St Boswells, Melrose TD6 0SA
01835 824000
Chief Executive: A M Croall

SHETLAND ISLANDS COUNCIL
Town Hall, Lerwick ZE1 0HB
01595 693535
Chief Executive: vacant

SOUTH AYRSHIRE COUNCIL
County Buildings, Wellington Square, Ayr KA7 1DR
01292 612000
Chief Executive: G W F Thorley

SOUTH LANARKSHIRE COUNCIL
Council Offices, Almada Street, Hamilton ML3 0AA
01698 454444
Chief Executive: M Docherty

STIRLING COUNCIL
Viewforth, Stirling FK8 2ET
01786 443322
Chief Executive: K Yates

WEST DUNBARTONSHIRE COUNCIL
Garshake Road, Dumbarton G82 3PU
01389 737000
Acting Chief Executive: T Huntingford

WEST LOTHIAN COUNCIL
West Lothian House, Almondvale Boulevard, Livingston EH54 6QG
01506 777000
Chief Executive: A M Linkston

WESTERN ISLES COUNCIL (COMHAIRLE NAN EILEAN SIAR)
Council Offices, Sandwick Road, Stornoway HS1 2BW
01851 703773
Chief Executive: N Galbraith

MAGAZINES
Listed are periodicals of special interest. For a more comprehensive list, consult Benn's Media Directory.

ACCOUNTANTS MAGAZINE
27 Queen Street, Edinburgh EH2 1LA
0131-225 5673
Editor: Rob Outram

CHAPMAN
4 Broughton Place, Edinburgh EH1 3RX
0131-557 2207
Editor: Joy Hendry

LIFE AND WORK
121 George Street, Edinburgh EH2 4YN
0131-225 5722
Editor: vacant

THE LIST
14 High Street, Edinburgh EH1 1TE
0131-558 1191
Editor: Alan Morrison

SCOTS LAW TIMES
W Green & Son Ltd, 21 Alva Street, Edinburgh EH2 4PS
0131-225 4879
Editor: Peter Nicholson

THE SCOTS MAGAZINE
2 Albert Square, Dundee DD1 9QJ
01382 223131
Editor: John Methven

SCOTTISH BANKER
43 Queensferry Street Lane, Edinburgh EH2 2AB
0131-535 5555
Editor: Mark Meredith

SCOTTISH BUSINESS INSIDER
43 Queensferry Street Lane, Edinburgh EH2 4PF
0131-535 5555
Editor: Bill Millar

SCOTTISH CATHOLIC OBSERVER
19 Waterloo Street, Glasgow G2 6BT
0141-221 4956
Editor: Eddie Barnes

SCOTTISH EDUCATIONAL JOURNAL
Educational Institute of Scotland, 46 Moray Place, Edinburgh EH3 6BH
0131-225 6244
Editor: Simon Macaulay

THE SCOTTISH FARMER
6th Floor, 195 Albion Street, Glasgow G1 1QQ
0141-302 7700
Editor: Alasdair Fletcher

SCOTTISH FIELD
Royston House, Caroline Park, Edinburgh EH5 1QJ
0131-551 2942
Editor: Archie Mackenzie

SCOTTISH REVIEW
Carrick Media, 1/4 Galt House, 31 Bank Street, Irvine KA12 0LL
01294 311322
Editor: Kenneth Roy

TIMES EDUCATIONAL SUPPLEMENT SCOTLAND
Scott House, 10 South St Andrew Street, Edinburgh EH2 2AZ
0131-557 1133
Editor: Willis Pickard

MARRIAGE AND RELATIONSHIPS

COUPLE COUNSELLING SCOTLAND
40 N Castle Street, Edinburgh EH2 3BN
0131-225 5006
Director: Frances Love; *Chairperson*: Lady Caplan
Exists to promote, co-ordinate and develop a confidential counselling service to those in marriage and other intimate personal relationships throughout Scotland.

SCOTTISH MARRIAGE CARE
50 Greenock Road, Paisley PA3 2LE
0141-889 6972
Chief Executive: Mary Toner; *Chairperson*: Veronica Mullen
Supports marriage and relationships with preparation for marriage courses, counselling, and training.

MEDICAL CHARITIES
Listed is a selection of the larger charities and some others of special interest. A more comprehensive list can be obtained from the Scottish Council for Voluntary Organisations.

ALZHEIMER SCOTLAND – ACTION ON DEMENTIA
22 Drumsheugh Gardens, Edinburgh EH3 7RN
0131-243 1453
Director: Jim Jackson

ARTHRITIS RESEARCH CAMPAIGN
140 High Street, Lochee, Dundee DD2 3BZ
01382 400911

BACUP SCOTLAND (BRITISH ASSOCIATION OF CANCER UNITED PATIENTS)
30 Bell Street, Glasgow G1 1LG
0141-553 1553
Chief Executive: Jean Mossman; *Chairman*: Maurice Slevin

BRITISH DIABETIC ASSOCIATION SCOTLAND
34 West George Street (4th Floor), Glasgow G2 1DA
0141-332 2700
Regional Manager: Delia Henry

BRITISH HEART FOUNDATION
45a Moray Place, Edinburgh EH3 6BQ
0131-226 3705
Director: John Prosser

CANCER RESEARCH CAMPAIGN SCOTLAND
226 Queensferry Road, Edinburgh EH4 2BP
0131-343 1344
Regional Director: W McKinlay

CHEST, HEART AND STROKE SCOTLAND
65 North Castle Street, Edinburgh EH2 3LT
0131-225 6963
Chief Executive: David Clark

CRUSAID SCOTLAND
24a Ainslie Place, Edinburgh EH3 6AJ
0131-225 8918
Executive Director: W David Wilson; *Chairman*: John Steer
Provides HIV/AIDS education, prevention and care. Operates an individual hardship fund.

EPILEPSY ASSOCIATION OF SCOTLAND
48 Govan Road, Glasgow G51 1JL
0141-427 4911
Chief Executive: Hilary Mounfield; *Chairman*: Peter Guest

MACMILLAN CANCER RELIEF
9 Castle Terrace, Edinburgh EH1 2DP
0131-229 3276
Chief Executive: N Young

MARIE CURIE CANCER CARE
21 Rutland Street, Edinburgh EH1 2AH
0131-229 8332
Secretary (Scotland): Sarah Gootrian

ME FOUNDATION (SCOTLAND)
8 Inverleith Gardens, Edinburgh EH3
5PU
0131-478 7879
Secretary: George Smart; *Chairperson:*
Helen Armstrong

MULTIPLE SCLEROSIS SOCIETY IN
SCOTLAND
2a North Charlotte Street, Edinburgh
EH2 4HR
0131-225 3600
General Secretary: T J Hope Thomson

MUSCULAR DYSTROPHY CAMPAIGN
3rd Floor, Princes House, 5 Shandwick
Place, Edinburgh EH2 4RG
0131-221 0066
Director: Ken Brown

NATIONAL ASTHMA CAMPAIGN
SCOTLAND
21 Coates Crescent, Edinburgh EH3 7AF
0131-226 2544
Director: Marjory O'Donnell

PAIN ASSOCIATION SCOTLAND
Cramond House, Cramond Glebe Road,
Edinburgh EH4 6NS
0131-312 7955
National Organiser: David Falconer

SCOTTISH COT DEATH TRUST
Royal Hospital for Sick Children,
Yorkhill, Glasgow G3 8SJ
0141-357 3946
Director: Hazel Brooke, MBE; *Chairman:*
Dr Angus Gibson

SCOTTISH DOWN'S SYNDROME
ASSOCIATION
158 Balgreen Road, Edinburgh EH11
3AU
0131-313 4225
Director: Karen Watchman; *Chairperson:*
Ivy Blair

SCOTTISH SPINA BIFIDA ASSOCIATION
190 Queensferry Road, Edinburgh EH4
2BW
0131-332 0743
Chief Executive: Andrew H D Wynd;
President: Professor D G Young

SARGENT CANCER FUND FOR CHILDREN
(SCOTLAND)
158 South Street, St Andrews KY16 9EG
01334 470044
Scottish Co-ordinator: Morag McIntosh;
President: Countess of Ancram

TENOVUS - SCOTLAND
234 St Vincent Street, Glasgow G2 5RJ
0141-221 6268
General Secretary: E R Read; *Chairman:*
Sir Malcolm Macnaughton
Supports medical/dental research
projects across the full spectrum of the
sciences.

MENTAL HEALTH

MENTAL HEALTH FOUNDATION SCOTLAND
24 George Square, Glasgow G2 1EG
0141-572 0125
Acting Director: Tim Pickles

MENTAL WELFARE COMMISSION FOR
SCOTLAND
Argyle House, K Floor, 3 Lady Lawson
Street, Edinburgh EH3 9SH
0131-222 6111
Director: Dr James A T Dyer; *Chair:* Sir
William K Reid, KCB
A Crown-appointed statutory body
with a remit to protect the welfare and
rights of people vulnerable through
mental disorder. Independent body,
separate from the government and the
medical, legal and social work
professions, which safeguards the
welfare and rights of people with
mental illness or with mental handicap
whether they are in hospital, living in
their own homes, or in other
accommodation.
    The commission has existed in
various forms since 1859. Those who
serve on it are appointed by the Queen.
It considers complaints, reports on
individual situations, and requests for
discharge from people who are detained
in hospital, liable to detention or on
guardianship under the Mental Health
(Scotland) Act 1984. The Mental Health

(Patients in the Community) Act 1995 introduced community care orders in Scotland.

NATIONAL SCHIZOPHRENIA FELLOWSHIP (SCOTLAND)
Claremont House, 130 East Claremont Street, Edinburgh EH7 4LB
0131-557 8969
Chief Executive: Mary Weir; *Chairman*: Susan Kirkwood

RICHMOND FELLOWSHIP SCOTLAND
26 Park Circus, Glasgow G3 6AP
0141-353 4050
Director and Secretary: Peter Millar
Supported living, day services, community advocacy, and counselling.

SCOTTISH ASSOCIATION FOR MENTAL HEALTH
Cumbrae House, 15 Carlton Court, Glasgow G5 9JP
0141-429 4800
Chief Executive: Ms S M Barcus; *Chair*: Lady Marion Fraser
Campaigns on mental health issues, providing an information service. 66 projects across Scotland.

STATE HOSPITAL
Carstairs Junction, by Lanark ML11 8RP
01555 840293
General Manager: Dick Manson; *Chairman*: Nicky James
Responsible for providing high-quality high-security mental health services to patients from Scotland and Northern Ireland whose behaviour may lead them to pose a significant threat to others.

MOTOR SPORT

ROYAL SCOTTISH AUTOMOBILE CLUB
11 Blythswood Square, Glasgow G2 4AG
0141-204 4999
Secretary: Jonathan C Lord; *Chairman*: I B M Lyle
Promotion and development of motor sport in Scotland.

MOUNTAINEERING AND HILL-WALKING

MOUNTAINEERING COUNCIL OF SCOTLAND
4a St Catherines Road, Perth PH1 5SE
01738 638227
National Officer: Kevin Howett; *President*: John Donohoe
Representative body for mountaineers, including those on ski, climbers and hill-walkers. Aims to protect the mountain environment, safeguard and secure access to hill and crag, and initiate and encourage safe practice in the mountains.

RAMBLERS' ASSOCIATION (SCOTLAND)
Kingfisher House, Auld Mart Business Park, Milnathort, Kinross KY13 9DA
01577 861222
Scottish Officer: Dave Morris; *Chairman, Scottish Council*: Kate Walsham
Promotes health benefits of walking, campaigns for more freedom of access to countryside and on other environmental issues.

SCOTTISH MOUNTAIN LEADER TRAINING BOARD
Glenmore Lodge, Aviemore PH22 1QU
01479 861248
Secretary: Allen Fyffe; *Chair*: John Newman-Carter
Develops and operates schemes for training and assessing those engaged in leading others on the mountains and moorlands of the UK.

MUSEUMS AND GALLERIES
Listed is a selection of the larger museums and galleries and visual arts organisations .

EDINBURGH CITY MUSEUMS AND ART GALLERIES
City Art Centre, 2 Market Street, Edinburgh EH1 1DE
0131-529 3993
Acting Head of Heritage and Arts: Derek Janes
Consists of: Huntly House Museum, Museum of Childhood, Writers'

Museum, City Art Centre, Brass Rubbing Centre, The People's Story Museum, Scott Monument, Nelson Monument, Lauriston Castle, Queensferry Museum, Newhaven Heritage Museum.

GLASGOW MUSEUMS AND GALLERIES
Kelvingrove, Glasgow G3 8AG
0141-357 3929
Head of Service: Mark O'Neill
The oldest of the city's galleries, Kelvingrove, was opened in 1893 on a surplus of income from the 1888 Exhibition. It is now part of a group of civic-controlled galleries including the People's Palace, St Mungo Museum of Religious Life and Art, Provand's Lordship and Pollok House, which together house collections ranging from armour and ancient artefacts to religious art and displays of working-class Glaswegian life.

The Burrell Collection, housed in a purpose-built gallery, contains the collection of a Glasgow entrepreneur, Sir William Burrell, who travelled the world collecting treasures. In 1996 Glasgow opened a Gallery of Modern Art in the city centre, which features paintings and sculptures by living artists.

NATIONAL GALLERIES OF SCOTLAND
The Mound, Edinburgh EH2 2EL
0131-624 6200
Director: Timothy Clifford; *Keeper*: Michael Clarke; *Chairman*: Rt Hon Countess of Airlie, DCVO
The National Galleries of Scotland are housed in three separate and distinctive buildings in Edinburgh, but share a common aim: to exhibit, acquire and conserve the finest and most significant works of art for the enjoyment and benefit of the public. The galleries are governed by a board of trustees and funds for running them and purchasing works of art are provided by the government, though the galleries also benefit from private benefaction.

The **National Gallery of Scotland**, founded in 1859, contains one of the finest collections of paintings, prints and drawings in Europe. Its master pieces – from pre-Renaissance to post-Impressionism – include works by Raphael, Velasquez, Rembrandt, Turner, Degas and Van Gogh. It is also the home of the world's finest collection of Scottish painting from Ramsay to Raeburn and McTaggart. The gallery covers European painting, drawing and sculpture from the medieval period until about 1900.

The **Scottish National Portrait Gallery** contains portraits of famous Scots from the 16th century to the present day, ranging from Mary Queen of Scots and Bonnie Prince Charlie to Hugh MacDiarmid and Sir Alexander Gibson. It also houses the Scottish Photography Archive.

The **Scottish National Gallery of Modern Art** covers international painting, drawing and sculpture from about 1900 to the present day, and houses examples of the best of Scottish modern art from Bellany, Peploe, Paolozzi, and Joan Eardley.

NATIONAL MUSEUMS OF SCOTLAND
Royal Museum, Chambers Street, Edinburgh EH1 1JF
0131-225 7534
Director: Mark Jones
Sets out to provide Scotland with a national museum service of international standing which preserves and enhances the collections in its care and promotes research on them so that they can be used to communicate and increase knowledge, understanding and enjoyment of human and natural history.

The **Museum of Scotland**, opened in 1998, displays national collections built up over two centuries, and includes a 20th-century gallery displaying objects chosen by the people of Scotland.

The **Royal Museum** houses international collections in a magnificent Victorian building whose main hall is one of the most impressive public spaces in the country. The objects on display range from the endangered giant panda to working scale models of British steam engines.

Shambellie House Museum of Costume at New Abbey, near Dumfries, presents period clothes in appropriate settings. Other museums in the group include the **Scottish Agricultural Museum** and the **Museum of Flight**, both at Ingliston.

A new **Scottish United Services Museum** at Edinburgh Castle will open in 2000, and a **Museum of Scottish Country Life** at Kittochside, near East Kilbride, will open in 2001.

ROYAL GLASGOW INSTITUTE OF THE FINE ARTS
Second Floor, 5 Oswald Street, Glasgow G1 4QR
0141-248 7411
Secretary: Gordon C McAllister; *President*: Dr Kenneth G Chrystie
Promotes art by open exhibitions and lectures and with a small gallery to encourage solo or group exhibitions.

ROYAL SCOTTISH ACADEMY
The Mound, Edinburgh EH2 2EL
0131-225 6671
Administrative Secretary: Bruce Laidlaw; *President*: Dr Ian McKenzie Smith, OBE
Founded in 1826 when 11 artists met in Edinburgh with the object of improving conditions for artists and art exhibitions in Scotland. Based loosely on the Royal Academy in London, it consisted of academicians and associates in the fields of painting, sculpture and architecture.

The first annual exhibition was held in premises in Waterloo Place, Edinburgh, in 1827 and has continued without a break (the 173rd in 1999), although the venue has changed.

Designed in 1822 by William Henry Playfair, who also designed the National Gallery, the Royal Scottish Academy building was first occupied by the Royal Institution for the Encouragement of the Fine Arts in Scotland and was known then as "The Royal Institution". The building is owned by the government and administered by the National Galleries of Scotland. There are on average 40 full members of the academy and 50 associate members, elected from the disciplines of painting, sculpture, architecture and printmaking.

ROYAL SCOTTISH SOCIETY OF PAINTERS IN WATERCOLOURS
29 Waterloo Street, Glasgow G2 6BZ
01355 233725
Secretary: Roger Frame
The declared aim of the founders in 1878 was "to do for Scotland what has been done for England and to give the watercolour art the position it deserves and which is at present not the case". Offers encouragement to artists of all ages by financial awards. Its annual exhibition in January is held at the Royal Scottish Academy galleries.

SCOTTISH MUSEUMS COUNCIL
County House, 20-22 Torphichen Street, Edinburgh EH3 8JB
0131-229 7465
Director: Jane Ryder; *Chair*: Professor Malcolm McLeod
National agency for central government support to Scotland's local museums. Founded in 1964, SMC is an independent company with charitable status. The 200-strong membership cares for some 330 museums and galleries.

The Council aims to improve the quality of museums and gallery provision in Scotland by providing a range of advice, services and financial support to its membership and by working to promote recognition of the essential role played by museums in the cultural, social and economic vitality of Scotland.

MUSIC

ASSEMBLY DIRECT
89 Giles Street, Edinburgh EH6 6BZ
0131-553 4000
Directors: Fiona Alexander/Roger Spence

BBC SCOTTISH SYMPHONY ORCHESTRA
BBC Scotland, Queen Margaret Drive, Glasgow G12 8DG
0141-338 2606
Director: Hugh Macdonald
Founded in 1935 with Ian Whyte as its conductor, the SSO worked initially as a

studio orchestra. After the Second World War, it was invited to participate in the Edinburgh Festival and thus established its policy of giving public concerts. Contemporary music, especially music by Scottish composers, has always been central to its work. Since 1996, it has increasingly focused on special projects such as the Glasgow Beethoven series, a Sibelius cycle and a Nielsen cycle. Most of its concerts and studio recordings are broadcast on BBC Radio 3.

BT SCOTTISH ENSEMBLE
5 Newton Terrace Lane, Glasgow G3 7PB
0141-221 2222
General Manager: Heather Duncan

CAPPELLA NOVA
1/R, 172 Hyndland Road, Glasgow G12 9HZ
0141-552 0634
Manager: Rebecca Tavener; *Chairperson:* Lord Balfour of Burleigh
Professional vocal ensemble, prominent in Scottish early and contemporary vocal music.

COUNCIL FOR MUSIC IN HOSPITALS
10 Forth Street, Edinburgh EH1 3LD
0131-556 5848
Director: Alison Frazer; *Chairperson:* John Riley
Provides concerts by professional musicians for people in hospitals, hospices, nursing and residential homes, and day centres for people with disabilities.

LIVE MUSIC NOW! (SCOTLAND)
14 Lennox Street, Edinburgh EH4 1QA
0131-332 6356
Director: Carol Main; *Chairman:* Hon Mrs Elizabeth Fairbairn
Aims to bring live music of high standard to all in the community, especially those who are disadvantaged, while giving outstanding young musicians performance opportunities.

NATIONAL YOUTH ORCHESTRA OF SCOTLAND
13 Somerset Place, Glasgow G3 7JT
0141-332 8311
Director: Richard Chester; *Chairman:* Iain Harrison
Provides orchestral and jazz training for young musicians resident in Scotland.

PARAGON ENSEMBLE LTD
1 Bowmont Gardens, Glasgow G12 9LR
0141-342 4242
General Manager: Andrew Logan

PIOBAIREACHD SOCIETY
16-24 Otago Street, Glasgow G12 8JH
0141-334 3587
Secretary: Dugald MacNeil; *President:* Andrew Wright
Encourages the study and playing of piobaireachd on the Highland bagpipe.

ROYAL SCOTTISH NATIONAL ORCHESTRA
73 Claremont Street, Glasgow G3 7JB
0141-226 3868
Chief Executive: Simon Crookall
Founded in 1890. An 89-member orchestra, it is a major provider of symphonic music, gives about 100 concerts each year in Edinburgh, Aberdeen, Dundee, Perth and other venues, and makes regular tours overseas. Its work also includes recordings and performances for radio and television.

ROYAL SCOTTISH PIPE BAND ASSOCIATION
45 Washington Street, Glasgow G3 8AZ
0141-221 5414
Executive Officer: I M White; *Chairman:* M Connell
Promotes and encourages the culture and advancement of pipe band music internationally. Organises and operates the World, European, British, Scottish and Cowal Championships.

SCOTTISH AMATEUR MUSIC ASSOCIATION
18 Craigton Crescent, Alva FK12 5DS
01259 760249
Hon Secretary: Margaret Simpson; *Chairperson, Executive Committee:* E J B Catto
Encourages and stimulates amateur music-making throughout Scotland by organising and running residential courses.

SCOTTISH CHAMBER ORCHESTRA
4 Royal Terrace, Edinburgh EH7 5AB
0131-557 6800
Managing Director: Roy McEwan;
Chairman: Donald Macdonald
Promotion of orchestral music throughout Scotland and abroad. Since it was formed in 1974, the SCO has visited the USA four times and tours regularly throughout Europe. It has commissioned more than 50 new works and enjoys close relationships with several leading composers. The SCO Chorus was formed in 1991 to provide the orchestra with a resident choir.

SCOTTISH EARLY MUSIC ASSOCIATION AND EARLY MUSIC CONSORT
2 Port Dundas Place, Glasgow G2 3LD
0141-333 1178

SCOTTISH MUSIC INFORMATION CENTRE
1 Bowmont Gardens, Glasgow G12 9LR
0141-334 6393
Director: Morag Brooksbank;
Chairperson: Louise Mitchell
Independent organisation which documents, preserves and promotes Scottish music of all types and of all periods.

SCOTTISH NATIONAL JAZZ ORCHESTRA
Smythe Music, PO Box 3743, Lanark ML11 9WD
Director: Tommy Smith

SCOTTISH OPERA
39 Elmbank Crescent, Glasgow G2 4PT
0141-248 4567
General Director: Adrian Trickey
Scotland's national opera company and the largest performing arts organisation in Scotland. Founded in 1962 by Sir Alexander Gibson, it staged its first production, *Madama Butterfly*, at the King's Theatre, Glasgow, and set up a permanent home at the Theatre Royal, Glasgow, in 1974. In its early years, under the guidance of Sir Alexander Gibson, it established a considerable reputation with such productions as *The Trojans*, *The Ring Cycle*, *Der Rosenkavalier*, *Turn of the Screw* and *Die Meistersinger*.

Scottish Opera is committed to bringing the widest range of opera, performed to the highest standard, to the maximum audience throughout Scotland and the rest of Britain. As owners of the Theatre Royal, it is also responsible for the administration and development of one of Scotland's principal theatres. It employs 200 people, including a full-time chorus and full-size orchestra.

In a typical season it gives some 90 main-scale performances. In addition, Scottish Opera Go Round and Essential Scottish Opera visit smaller venues not always served by other professional opera companies. The company's educational unit, Scottish Opera For All, works extensively in the community.

SCOTTISH SOCIETY OF COMPOSERS
4 Glen Road, Lennoxtown G65 7JX
01360 313217
Secretary: Derek Ball; *Chairperson*: Neil Butterworth
Promotes wider knowledge of contemporary music in Scotland through international and local liaison, annual awards to musicians, distribution of catalogues, sponsorship of new music recording.

TRADITIONAL MUSIC AND SONG ASSOCIATION OF SCOTLAND
95-97 St Leonards Street, Edinburgh EH8 9QY
0131-667 5587
National Organiser: Elspeth Cowie;
Convener: Citty Finlayson

NETBALL

SCOTTISH NETBALL ASSOCIATION
Ainslie Road, Hillington Business Park, Glasgow G52 4RU
0141-570 4016
Administrator: David McLaughlan;
Chairperson: Dr Irene O'Brien

NEWSPAPERS

DAILY RECORD
Anderston Quay, Glasgow G3 8DA
0141-248 7000
Editor: Martin Clarke

DUNDEE COURIER
80 Kingsway East, Dundee DD4 8SL
01382 223131
Editor: Adrian Arthur

EDINBURGH EVENING NEWS
20 North Bridge, Edinburgh EH1 1YT
0131-225 2468
Editor: John McLellan

EVENING EXPRESS
Lang Stracht, Mastrick, Aberdeen
AB9 8AF
01224 690222
Editor: Donald Martin

EVENING TELEGRAPH
80 Kingsway East, Dundee DD4 8SL
01382 223131
Editor: Alan Proctor

EVENING TIMES
195 Albion Street, Glasgow G1 1QP
0141-552 6255
Editor: Charles McGhee

GREENOCK TELEGRAPH
2 Crawfurd Street, Greenock PA15 1LH
01475 726511
Editor: Ian Wilson

THE HERALD
195 Albion Street, Glasgow G1 1PQ
0141-552 6255
Editor: Harry Reid

PRESS AND JOURNAL
Lang Stracht, Mastrick, Aberdeen
AB9 8AF
01224 690222
Editor: Derek Tucker

SCOTLAND ON SUNDAY
20 North Bridge, Edinburgh EH1 1YT
0131-225 2468
Editor: John McGurk

THE SCOTSMAN
20 North Bridge, Edinburgh EH1 1YT
0131-225 2468
Editor: Alan Ruddock

SUNDAY HERALD
195 Albion Street, Glasgow G1 1PQ
0141-302 7800
Editor: Andrew Jaspan

SUNDAY MAIL
Anderston Quay, Glasgow G3 8DA
0141-248 7000
Editor: Jim Cassidy

SUNDAY POST
2 Albert Square, Courier Buildings,
Dundee DD1 9QJ
01382 223131
Editor: Russell Reid

PLANNING AND DESIGN

PLANNING AID FOR SCOTLAND
Bonnington Mill, 72 Newhaven Road,
Edinburgh EH6 5QG
0131-555 1565
Director: Hazel Sears

PLANNING EXCHANGE
Tontine House, 8 Gordon Street,
Glasgow G1 3PL
0141-248 8541
Managing Director: Anthony Burton,
OBE; *Chairman*: Rt Hon Bruce Millan
Provides information and expertise in
the fields of economic, environmental
and social development.

**ROYAL FINE ART COMMISSION FOR
SCOTLAND**
Bakehouse Close, 146 Canongate,
Edinburgh EH8 8DD
0131-556 6699
Secretary: Charles Prosser; *Chairman*: Rt
Hon Lord Cameron of Lochbroom
Advisory body operating outside the
machinery of government, whose terms
of reference are set by royal warrant.
Established to provide an independent
view on matters of general
environmental, planning and design
criteria.

In considering whether to call in planning applications for new developments, the Scottish Ministers take particular account of the commission's views. Planning authorities are advised to seek its advice on a development proposal which is likely to have a strong visual impact or to be of exceptional environmental significance, such as a prominent proposal within a conservation area.

SCOTTISH DESIGN
120 Bothwell Street, Glasgow G2 7JP
0141-221 6121
Chief Executive: Andy Travers
Offers consultancy services for businesses in all aspects of design and product development, operating in partnership with the Scottish Enterprise network, industrial and educational organisations, and the Scottish design industry. It aims to improve the competitiveness and performance of business.

POETRY

THE BURNS FEDERATION
Dick Institute, Elmbank Avenue, Kilmarnock.
01563 572469
Chief Executive: Shirley Bell; *President*: Robert Dalziel
Stimulates the development of Scottish literature, art, and music and encourages and arranges competitions for school children. Helps and encourages Burns Clubs and kindred societies.

POETRY ASSOCIATION OF SCOTLAND
The Orchard, Muirton, Auchterarder PH3 1ND
01764 662211

SCOTTISH POETRY LIBRARY
5 Crichton's Close, Edinburgh EH8 8DT
0131-557 2876
Director: Tessa Ransford
Stocks Scottish and international poetry for free browsing and borrowing. Travelling van service, postal lendings, branches, catalogues, indexes. Newsletter and reading room for members.

POLICE FORCES

CENTRAL SCOTLAND POLICE
Randolphfield, Stirling FK8 2HD
01786 456000
Chief Constable: William M Wilson

DUMFRIES AND GALLOWAY CONSTABULARY
Cornwall Mount, Dumfries DG1 1PZ
01387 252112
Chief Constable: William Rae

FIFE POLICE
Detroit Road, Glenrothes KY6 2RJ
01592 418888
Chief Constable: J P Hamilton, QPM

GRAMPIAN POLICE
Queen Street, Aberdeen AB10 1ZA
01224 386000
Chief Constable: Andrew Brown

LOTHIAN AND BORDERS POLICE
Fettes Avenue, Edinburgh EH4 1RB
0131-311 3131
Chief Constable: Roy Cameron

NORTHERN CONSTABULARY
Perth Road, Inverness IV2 3SY
01463 715555
Chief Constable: W A Robertson

STRATHCLYDE POLICE
173 Pitt Street, Glasgow G2 4JS
0141-532 2000
Chief Constable: John Orr OBE, QPM

TAYSIDE POLICE
PO Box 59, West Bell Street, Dundee DD1 9JU
01382 223200
Chief Constable: William A Spence

POLICE ORGANISATIONS

SCOTTISH POLICE COLLEGE
Tulliallan Castle, Kincardine, Alloa FK10 4BE

01259 732000
Director: D Garbutt, QPM
Provision of central police training for the Scottish police service.

SCOTTISH POLICE FEDERATION
5 Woodside Place, Glasgow G3 7QF
0141-332 5234
General Secretary: Douglas J Keil, QPM; *Chairman*: James Fraser, QPM
Representative body of constables, sergeants, inspectors and chief inspectors in the Scottish police service. Considers and brings to the notice of the authorities and the Secretary of State for Scotland matters affecting welfare and efficiency.

POLITICAL PARTIES AND ORGANISATIONS

SCOTTISH CONSERVATIVE AND UNIONIST PARTY
Suite 1/1, 14 Links Place, Leith, Edinburgh EH6 7EZ
0131-555 2900
Director: Roger Pratt, CBE; *Head of Campaigns and Operations*: David Canzini; *Chairman*: Raymond Robertson
Has operated in various forms and under various formal titles since the late 17th century. In 1955 the party polled just over 50% of the Scottish votes in the general election and won 36 of the 71 seats compared with Labour's 34. Since this high point the party's fortunes have declined steadily. In the 1997 general election its share of the poll fell to 17.5%, and the party lost all 11 of its seats.

SCOTTISH GREEN PARTY
PO Box 14080, Edinburgh EH10 6YG
0141-571 0086
Principal Spokespersons: Robin Harper and Marian Coyne

SCOTTISH LABOUR PARTY
Keir Hardie Campaign Office, 4th Floor, Delta House, 50 West Nile Street, Glasgow G1 2NA

0141-572 6900
Acting Scottish General Secretary: Lesley Quinn
Party most widely supported by the electorate since the Second World War. In the general election of 1997, it received 45.6% of the votes cast, and won 56 of the 72 seats, an increase of seven compared with the 1992 election. The party is governed by an executive committee which brings together representatives of local party organisations, trade unions, and specific sections including women's, socialist societies, the Scottish Co-operative Party, youth and local government.

SCOTTISH LIBERAL DEMOCRATS
4 Clifton Terrace, Edinburgh EH12 5DR
0131-337 2314
Chief Executive: Willie Rennie; *Party Administrator*: Rae Grant; *President*: Roy Thomson

SCOTTISH NATIONAL PARTY
6 North Charlotte Street, Edinburgh EH2 4JH
0131-226 3661
Director of Headquarters and Organisation: Allison Hunter
Has its origins in the formation of the National Party of Scotland in 1928. Six years later, it merged with the Scottish Party to found the Scottish National Party, which in its early years occasionally endorsed Labour or Liberal candidates pledged to an agreed scheme of self-government, but more often ran its own candidates. In 1945, at the Motherwell by-election, Dr Robert McIntyre became the first Scottish nationalist to be elected exclusively on that ticket.

The party reconstituted itself in 1948 to exclude members of other parties and set out to secure a majority of the 71 Scottish seats before negotiating with the UK government for the establishment of a Scottish parliament. In the 1997 general election the SNP was Scotland's second party with 22.1% of the poll, winning six seats. It describes itself as a moderate left-of-centre party.

PORT AUTHORITIES

ABERDEEN HARBOUR BOARD
Harbour Office, 16 Regent Quay, Aberdeen AB11 5SS
01224 597000
General Manager: R B Braithwaite; *Chairman*: D R Paton

CLYDEPORT
16 Robertson Street, Glasgow G2 8DS
0141-221 8733
Chief Executive: Tom Allison

FORTH PORTS
Tower Place, Leith, Edinburgh EH6 7DB
0131-555 8750
Chief Executive: Alistair Fleming

POSTAL SERVICES

SCOTTISH POST OFFICE BOARD
102 West Port, Edinburgh EH3 9HS
0131-228 7300
Service Delivery Director: Alexander Gibb; *Chairman*: John M Ward, CBE
Represents The Post Office in Scotland and advises the main board in London on Scottish opinions of Post Office policy as well as on a wide range of social, economic and political issues. The Post Office is a public sector group required by government to operate its services commercially. It also has a long tradition of strong social commitment, particularly to rural areas.

PRISONS AND PRISONERS

APEX SCOTLAND
9 Great Stuart Street, Edinburgh EH3 7TP
0131-220 0130
Director: Jeane Freeman; *Chairman*: John Carruthers, MBE
Aims to create equality of access to employment and employment opportunities for individuals with a criminal record.

HOWARD LEAGUE SCOTLAND
17 Warriston Crescent, Edinburgh EH3 5LB
0131-556 1687
Director: Drummond Hunter

PAROLE BOARD FOR SCOTLAND
Saughton House, Broomhouse Drive, Edinburgh EH11 3XD
0131-244 8755
Secretary: H P Boyle; *Chairman*: Ian McNee
Directs and advises Scottish Ministers on the release on licence and recall from licence of persons serving sentences of imprisonment or detention whose cases have been referred to the board, and the conditions of such licences. Under a law introduced in 1993, prisoners serving less than four years are released automatically after serving half of their sentence. Only those prisoners serving four years or more and who have served half their sentences are now eligible for consideration by the board.

SACRO
31 Palmerston Place, Edinburgh EH12 5AP
0131-226 4222
Chief Executive: Susan Matheson; *Chair*: Dr David Colvin, CBE
Increases community safety by providing a range of services to reduce offending and by being an advisor and advocate of criminal and social policy.

SCOTTISH PRISON COMPLAINTS COMMISSION
Government Buildings, Broomhouse Drive, Edinburgh EH11 3XA
0131-244 8423
Commissioner: Dr Jim McManus
Investigation of complaints from prisoners who have not obtained satisfaction from the prison internal complaints system.

SCOTTISH PRISON SERVICE
Calton House, 5 Redheughs Rigg, Edinburgh EH12 9HW
0131-556 8400
Chief Executive: Tony Cameron
Established in 1993 as an executive

agency of the Scottish Office. Manages the following establishments: Aberdeen Prison; Barlinnie Prison, Glasgow; Castle Huntly Prison, near Dundee; Cornton Vale Prison and Young Offenders Institution, Stirling; Dumfries Prison and Young Offenders Institution; Dungavel Prison, near Strathaven; Edinburgh Prison; Friarton Prison, Perth; Glenochil Prison and Young Offenders Institution, Tullibody; Greenock Prison; Inverness Prison; Longriggend Prison, near Airdrie; Low Moss Prison, Bishopbriggs; Noranside Prison, near Forfar; Penninghame Prison, Newton Stewart; Perth Prison; Peterhead Prison; Polmont Young Offenders Institution, near Falkirk; Shotts Prison.

PROFESSIONAL BODIES AND LEARNED SOCIETIES

ASSOCIATION OF CHARTERED CERTIFIED ACCOUNTANTS
1 Woodside Place, Glasgow G3 7QF
0141-309 4097
Head of ACCA Scotland: Wylie Cunningham

BRITISH ASSOCIATION OF SOCIAL WORKERS – SCOTLAND
28 North Bridge, Edinburgh EH1 1QG
0131-225 4549
Scottish Secretary: Ian Johnston; *Scottish Convener*: Liz Timms

BRITISH MEDICAL ASSOCIATION
3 Hill Place, Edinburgh EH3 9NB
0131-662 4820
Scottish Secretary: Dr Brian T Potter; *Chairman*: Arthur Morris, FRCS
Regarded as the voice of the medical profession. A voluntary professional association, independent trade union, scientific and educational body and publishing house, it represents doctors from all branches of medicine in the UK. Founded in 1832, it has a UK membership of 111,000, of whom 12,000 are in Scotland.

CHARTERED INSTITUTE OF BANKERS IN SCOTLAND
38 Drumsheugh Gardens, Edinburgh EH3 7SW
0131-473 7777
Chief Executive: Charles Munn; *President*: Fred Goodwin
Oldest professional body of its kind in the world, founded in 1875, the institute offers a platform for the exchange and development of ideas about financial services, helps its 12,500 members to improve their knowledge and expertise, and provides a framework for lifelong learning.
ACIBS (for students who pass the associateship programme), MCIBS (primarily a management programme) and FCIBS (the highest level, attained by many years' experience and by nomination) are the letters denoting membership. The institute is committed to continuing professional development of its members through education programmes.

CHARTERED INSTITUTE OF PUBLIC FINANCE AND ACCOUNTANCY
8 North West Circus Place, Edinburgh EH3 6ST
0131-220 4316
Scottish Director: Ian Doig

COMMITTEE OF SCOTTISH CLEARING BANKERS
38 Drumsheugh Gardens, Edinburgh EH3 7SW
0131-473 7770
Secretary: Gordon P Fenton
"Trade association" for four Scottish clearing banks.

DAVID HUME INSTITUTE
21 George Square, Edinburgh EH8 9LD
0131-650 4633
Director: Professor Hector MacQueen
Promotes discourse and research on economic and legal aspects of public policy quelstions by arranging seminars, lectures and conferences and by publication of monographs.

FACULTY OF ACTUARIES
Maclaurin House, 18 Dublin Street, Edinburgh EH1 3PP
0131-240 1300
Secretary: W W Mair; *President*: C W F Low
Professional body for actuaries in Scotland, although it also has members based overseas. One of its main objects is to train young men and women for qualification as actuaries.

HARVEIAN SOCIETY OF EDINBURGH
Respiratory Medicine Unit, Department of Medicine, Royal Infirmary, Edinburgh EH3 9YW
Joint Secretaries: A B MacGregor, Professor N J Douglas
Promotes the scientific and medical discoveries of William Harvey through an annual festival.

INSTITUTE OF CHARTERED ACCOUNTANTS OF SCOTLAND
27 Queen Street, Edinburgh EH2 1LA
0131-225 5673
Chief Executive and Secretary: Peter Johnston; *President*: David L Spence
Oldest accountancy body in the world with a membership of 14,000 in around 100 countries. The institute educates its students as well as examining them. The professional designatory letters CA are exclusive in the British Isles to members of the institute.

NATIONAL BOARD FOR NURSING, MIDWIFERY AND HEALTH VISITING FOR SCOTLAND
22 Queen Street, Edinburgh EH2 1NT
0131-226 7371
Chief Executive: David Benton; *Chairman*: Isobel Mackinlay
Ensuring standards of professional education for nurses, midwives and health visitors in Scotland.

QUEEN'S NURSING INSTITUTE SCOTLAND
31 Castle Terrace, Edinburgh EH1 2EL
0131-229 2333
Director and Treasurer: George D C Preston; *Chairman of Council*: Lady Prosser
Welfare of retired Queen's nurses; professional development of community nurses; funding of community nursing projects.

ROYAL COLLEGE OF GENERAL PRACTITIONERS – SCOTTISH COUNCIL
25 Queen Street, Edinburgh EH2 1JX
0131-260 6800
Honorary Secretary: Dr. G.S. Dyker; *Chairman, Scottish Council*: Dr Colin M Hunter
Academic professional body for general practitioners.

ROYAL COLLEGE OF MIDWIVES, SCOTTISH BOARD
37 Frederick Street, Edinburgh EH2 1EP
0131-225 1633
Director: Patricia Purton
Exists to promote the art and science of midwifery and to protect and advance the interests of midwives and the midwifery profession. The Scottish Board acts as a forum for discussion and to promote continuing education for midwives.

ROYAL COLLEGE OF NURSING, SCOTTISH BOARD
42 South Oswald Road, Edinburgh EH9 2HH
0131-662 1010
Acting Board Secretary: Margaret Pullin

ROYAL COLLEGE OF PHYSICIANS OF EDINBURGH
9 Queen Street, Edinburgh EH2 1JQ
0131-225 7324
Secretary: A C Parker; *President*: Professor J C Petrie
Founded in 1681. Concerned with promoting and maintaining specialist standards among physicians. It has 2,000 fellows in the UK and about the same number overseas. The college disseminates knowledge by meetings and publications.

ROYAL COLLEGE OF PHYSICIANS AND SURGEONS OF GLASGOW
232-242 St Vincent Street, Glasgow G2 5RJ
0141-221 6072
Registrar: Robert K Littlejohn; *President*: Colin MacKay

Founded in 1599. The college has 4,500 members and fellows in many countries. It sets examinations and maintains standards of practice in all medical specialties.

ROYAL COLLEGE OF SURGEONS OF EDINBURGH
Nicolson Street, Edinburgh EH8 9DW
0131-527 1600
Secretary: A S Campbell; *President*: Professor A G D Maran
Founded in 1505. Concerned with education and training for medical and surgical practice and for the maintenance of high standards of professional competence and conduct. It is the college's policy to invest in education and training for surgeons at all stages.

ROYAL ENVIRONMENTAL HEALTH INSTITUTE OF SCOTLAND
3 Manor Place, Edinburgh EH3 7DH
0131-225 6999
Chief Executive: John Frater

ROYAL INCORPORATION OF ARCHITECTS IN SCOTLAND
15 Rutland Square, Edinburgh EH1 2BE
0131-229 7205
Secretary and Treasurer: Sebastian Tombs; *President*: Iain Dickson
Professional body for chartered architects in Scotland, founded in 1840, with a current membership of 3,000. It publishes books and journals, organises exhibitions and events, helps to co-ordinate architectural competitions, and keeps members up to date with the latest developments in the profession.

Potential clients can obtain help in finding an architect for their project, as well as general guidance on design, from the RIAS client advisory service. Its bookshops stock specialist architecture and design titles, including books published by the RIAS's own Rutland Press.

ROYAL INSTITUTION OF CHARTERED SURVEYORS IN SCOTLAND
9 Manor Place, Edinburgh EH3 7DN
0131-225 7078
Director: Eileen Masterman; *Hon*

Secretary: J Ronald Dawson
Established in 1868, it is now one of the largest professional institutions in the world with a current membership in Scotland of 8,000. The RICS defines and maintains the educational standards and competence required for qualification as a chartered surveyor, lays down standards of professional conduct, and is active in advising government on measures needed for the proper planning, development and management of property.

ROYAL PHILOSOPHICAL SOCIETY OF GLASGOW
Philosophy Department, West Quadrangle, University of Glasgow, Glasgow G12 8QQ
0141-334 4144
Secretary and Treasurer: E. Borowski; *President*: George Gorman
Organises public lectures on topics of general interest in the arts and sciences.

ROYAL SCOTTISH GEOGRAPHICAL SOCIETY
Graham Hills Building, 40 George Street, Glasgow G1 1QE
0141-552 3330
Director: Dr D M Munro; *Chairman of Council*: Professor George Gordon
Founded as an educational trust in 1884. Foremost independent body in Scotland promoting the understanding of the relationships between people, places and the environment through geographical research, education, debate, travel and exploration. Stimulates research into the nature and causes of change in human and physical environments on earth, disseminates knowledge of these changes and their possible consequences, and evaluates current environmental issues.

Each year from September to March, the RSGS presents more than 100 illustrated talks at its centres throughout the country. The society helps with the funding of Scottish-based expeditions to many parts of the world, many of the expeditions returning with new scientific discoveries. Its medals and fellowships are among the world's most prestigious awards for outstanding contributions to geography and exploration.

ROYAL SOCIETY OF EDINBURGH
22-24 George Street, Edinburgh
EH2 2PQ
0131-240 5000
Executive Secretary: Dr William Duncan;
President: Professor M A Jeeves
Established in 1783 under a Royal Charter granted by George III for the "Advancement of Learning and Useful Knowledge". In recent years the society has recaptured the spirit of the original Charter and represents all branches of learning. It is a wholly independent body with charitable status, governed by a council elected from among its 1,200-strong fellowship. The fellowship includes distinguished individuals drawn from science, arts, letters, technology, the professions, industry and commerce.

Although the society was founded and is based in Edinburgh, from the earliest days the fellows have been drawn from all parts of Scotland and beyond. In seeking to achieve the "Advancement of Learning and Useful Knowledge", the society undertakes a wide range of activities, including the organisation of meetings and symposia aimed both at the specialist and the general public; the publication of learned journals; the award of research fellowships, scholarships and prizes; and the organisation of activities aimed at young people throughout Scotland.

The society provides an important neutral forum for informed consideration of topics concerning the well-being of Scotland. As well as regularly providing advice to parliament and government, it undertakes specific projects, such as those in support of the Technology Ventures Strategy and the Foresight Initiative.

ROYAL TOWN PLANNING INSTITUTE IN SCOTLAND
57 Melville Street, Edinburgh EH3 7HL
0131-226 1909
Director: W Graham U'ren

Charitable organisation with a royal charter, advancing the art and science of town planning. The Edinburgh office acts as a first point of contact in Scotland for all RTPI services, including professional standards, public affairs and conferences.

RELIGIOUS ORGANISATIONS
See also: Churches

ACTION OF CHURCHES TOGETHER IN SCOTLAND
Scottish Churches House, Dunblane FK15 0AJ
01786 823588
General Secretary: Rev Dr Kevin Franz

APOSTLESHIP OF THE SEA (SCOTLAND)
937 Dumbarton Road, Glasgow G14 9UF
0141-339 6657
National Director: Leo Gilbert
Welfare and provision of facilities for seafarers – including Stella Maris Club and accommodation.

CHRISTIAN AID SCOTLAND
41 George IV Bridge, Edinburgh EH1 1EL
0131-220 1254
National Secretary: Rev John N Wylie;
Chairperson: Margaret Macintosh
Aid and development in more than 60 countries worldwide, as well as education and campaigning in the UK on the causes of poverty.

IONA COMMUNITY
Pearce Institute, 840 Govan Road, Glasgow G51 3UU
0141-445 4561
Leader: Rev Norman Shanks
Ecumenical Christian community founded in 1938 by the late George MacLeod (Lord MacLeod of Fuinary). Gathered around the rebuilding of the ancient monastic buildings of Iona Abbey, the community has sought ever since the "rebuilding of the common life", bringing together work and

worship, prayer and politics, the sacred and the secular.

The members – from many backgrounds, countries and denominations – are committed to a rule of daily prayer and Bible study, sharing and accounting for their use of time and money, to regular meeting, and to action for justice and peace. The community maintains three centres on Iona and Mull, and a base in Glasgow. In 1997 many people travelled to Iona to commemorate the 1400th anniversary of the death of St Columba.

LEPROSY MISSION
89 Barnton Street, Stirling FK8 1HJ
01786 449266

NATIONAL BIBLE SOCIETY OF SCOTLAND
7 Hampton Terrace, Edinburgh
EH12 5XU
0131-337 9701
Executive Director: Rev Dr Graham Houston

SCIAF (SCOTTISH CATHOLIC INTERNATIONAL AID FUND)
5 Oswald Street, Glasgow G1 4QR
0141-221 4447
Director: Paul Chitnis; *President*: Rt Rev John Mone

SCOTTISH CATHOLIC ARCHIVES
Columba House, 16 Drummond Place, Edinburgh EH3 6PL
0131-556 3661
Keeper of the Archives: Dr Christine Johnson

SCOTTISH CATHOLIC TRIBUNAL
22 Woodrow Road, Glasgow G41 5PN
0141-427 3036
President: Rev James G Nicol
First instance court of the Catholic Church in Scotland, dealing with nullity of marriage, separation of spouses, privileges of faith, and other canonical matters.

SCOTTISH CHURCH HISTORY SOCIETY
39 Southside Road, Inverness IV2 4XA
01463 231140

Hon Secretary: Rev Dr P H Donald; *President*: Professor S J Brown
Encourages the study of all aspects of Scottish church history.

SCOTTISH CHURCHES WORLD EXCHANGE
23 Inverleith Terrace, Edinburgh EH3 5NS
0131-315 4444
Director: Rev Robert Anderson
Draws on the churches' extensive network of international contacts to provide opportunities for people of all ages and skills to live and work overseas for a year.

SCOTTISH COUNCIL OF JEWISH COMMUNITIES
222 Fenwick Road, Glasgow G46 6UE
0141-577 8208
Convener: E J Borowski
Represents the Jewish community of Scotland in its relations with government and others.

SCOTTISH CRUSADERS
Challenge House, 29 Canal Street, Glasgow G4 0AD
0141-331 2400
Director: Kevin Simpson; *Chairman*: Dr Norris Thompson
Christian-based youth organisation working with young people aged 8-18 years.

SCOTTISH REFORMATION SOCIETY
The Society, The Magdalen Chapel, 41 Cowgate, Edinburgh EH1 1JR
0131-220 1450
Secretary: Rev. Sinclair Horne; *Chairman*: Rev E H Sawer
Religious organisation founded in 1851 to promote a witness to the heritage of the Reformation – its history, theology and principles, and their application to the present day.

SCOTTISH SUNDAY SCHOOL UNION FOR CHRISTIAN EDUCATION
236 Stonelaw Road, Burnside, Glasgow G73 3SA
0141-613 1787
General Secretary: Lynne Collingham

SCRIPTURE UNION SCOTLAND
9 Canal Street, Glasgow G4 0AB
0141-332 1162
General Director: Rev David Clark;
Chairperson: Moira L McCarrell
Seeks first to encourage young people in
Scotland to consider embracing the
Christian faith and second to encourage
Bible reading among those of all ages.

SOCIETY FOR THE PROTECTION OF
UNBORN CHILDREN
5 St Vincent Place, Glasgow G1 2DH
0141-221 2094
Manager: John F Crabbe; *Chairperson*:
Agnes Girvan
Seeks to protect with love human life
from the moment of conception until
natural death.

SOCIETY OF ST VINCENT DE PAUL
546 Sauchiehall Street, Glasgow G2 3NG
0141-332 7752
National Secretary: K Gorman; *National
President*: John J Murphy
Aims to relieve all forms of poverty by
person to person contact, regardless of
race or creed.

SOCIETY IN SCOTLAND FOR PROPAGATING
CHRISTIAN KNOWLEDGE
Tods, Murray WS, 66 Queen Street,
Edinburgh EH2 4NE
0131-226 4771

RESCUE ORGANISATIONS

MOUNTAIN RESCUE COMMITTEE OF
SCOTLAND
31 Craigfern Drive, Blanefield, Glasgow
G63 9DP
01360 770431
Secretary: Dr Bob Sharp; *Chairman*: Dave
Whalley, BEM

ROYAL NATIONAL LIFEBOAT INSTITUTION
Belleview House, Hopetoun Street,
Edinburgh EH7 4ND
0131-557 9171
National Organiser Scotland: Maren
Fitzgerald

RUGBY

SCOTTISH RUGBY UNION
Murrayfield, Edinburgh EH12 5PJ
0131-346 5000
Secretary: I A L Hogg

SAFETY

MARITIME AND COASTGUARD AGENCY
Scotland and Northern Ireland Region,
Marine House, Blaikies Quay, Aberdeen
AB11 5EZ
01224 574122
Regional Manager: Michael Comerford

RoSPA (ROYAL SOCIETY FOR THE
PREVENTION OF ACCIDENTS)
Slateford House, 53 Lanark Road,
Edinburgh EH14 1TL
0131-455 7457
Head, Training Division: Dr Karen
McDonnell; *Heads, Safety Policy Division*:
Mary Reilly, Michael A McDonnell

SCOTTISH ACCIDENT PREVENTION
COUNCIL
Slateford House, 53 Lanark Road,
Edinburgh EH14 1TL
0131-455 7457
Secretary: Michael A McDonnell

SAILING

ROYAL YACHTING ASSOCIATION,
SCOTLAND
Caledonia House, South Gyle,
Edinburgh EH12 9DQ
0131-317 7388
Honorary Secretary: Stewart Boyd

SCIENCE

BOTANICAL SOCIETY OF SCOTLAND
Royal Botanic Garden, Inverleith Row,
Edinburgh EH3 5LR
0131-552 7171
Hon Secretary: Robert Galt; *President*:

Professor Elizabeth Cutter
Founded in 1836 as the Botanical Society of Edinburgh, the society exists to promote the study of plants and to exchange information among members. It publishes a scientific journal, holds lectures and arranges symposia to discuss botanical issues.

DUNSTAFFNAGE MARINE LABORATORY
PO Box 3, Oban PA34 4AD
01631 562244
Director: Dr G B Shimmield
Centre for coastal and marine sciences, sponsored by Natural Environment Research Council.

EDINBURGH INTERNATIONAL SCIENCE FESTIVAL
149 Rose Street, Edinburgh EH2 4LS
0131-220 3977
Director: Dr Simon Gage; *Chairman*: Councillor Donald Anderson
World's first and largest public celebration of science and technology.

HANNAH RESEARCH INSTITUTE
Ayr KA6 5HL
01292 674000
Director: Professor Malcolm Peaker
International centre for biological research in lactation, reproduction and metabolism, ranging from the whole animal through organs, tissues and cells to molecular biology, milk and the science and technology of dairy foods.

MACAULAY LAND USE RESEARCH INSTITUTE
Craigiebuckler, Aberdeen AB15 8QH
01224 318611
Director: Professor T J Maxwell; *Chairman*: Professor Janet I Sprent
Established by the Scottish Office in 1987 from the merger of the Macaulay Institute for Soil Research and the Hill Farming Research Organisation, in response to the need for agriculture to take account of other land uses and the developing environmental policy objectives of the EC and UK. Undertakes research that contributes to the creation of opportunities for rural development and viable rural communities, while at the same time protecting the environment.

MOREDUN RESEARCH INSTITUTE
408 Gilmerton Road, Edinburgh EH17 7JH
0131-664 3262
Director: Professor Q A McKellar; *Chairman*: John Izat
Promotes multidisciplinary study of selected animal pathogens, the diseases they cause and the response to the infected host. Its activities contribute new knowledge to biological science, comparative medicine, environmental protection and public health.

ROSLIN INSTITUTE
Roslin, Midlothian EH25 9PS
0131-527 4200
Chief Executive: Professor Grahame Bulfield
Works to understand and improve the productivity, breeding and welfare of farm animals. Created in 1993 from the Edinburgh Research Station of the Insitute of Animal Physiology and Genetics Research, which in turn was the result of the amalgamation in 1986 of the Poultry Research Centre and the Animal Breeding Research Organisation.

The institute is the UK's major centre for research on molecular and quantitative genetics of farm animals and poultry science and has important programmes of rersearch on transgenic technology, development, growth, reproduction and animal welfare. In 1997 it succeeded in producing live lambs by nuclear transfer from a variety of differentiated cultured cells. One, "Dolly", was created from an adult mammary cell – a breakthrough which attracted intense interest internationally.

ROWETT RESEARCH INSTITUTE
Greenburn Road, Bucksburn, Aberdeen AB21 9SB
01224 712751
Chief Executive Officer: Professor Ian Bremner; *Chairman*: Dr James Stewart
Founded in 1913 under the direction of Dr John Boyd Orr to carry out research

on nutrition related to farm animals, the institute swiftly expanded its remit to cover humans also. Boyd Orr was the first to demonstrate the link between poverty, a poor diet and ill-health and was recognised as the father of modern food and health policies. The institute boasts three Nobel Laureates, including Boyd Orr, among the scientists it has employed.

In recent years, as consumers have become more aware of the positive value of good nutrition and more demanding in their choice of food, the insitute has emphasised its lead role in highlighting the importance of diet. Human and animal studies are undertaken together to improve the welfare and health of humans, to enhance food quality and safety, and to improve animal welfare through the efficient husbandry of milk- and meat-producing animals.

ROYAL BOTANIC GARDEN EDINBURGH

20a Inverleith Row, Edinburgh EH3 5LR
0131-552 7171
Regius Keeper: Professor Stephen Blackmore

In 1670, a physic garden for the cultivation of medicinal and other plants for medical students was established on a plot of ground near Holyrood Abbey. There were two subsequent moves before the present garden, covering 30 hectares, was established at Inverleith in 1823. In 1986 it acquired the status of a non-departmental public body.

The national botanic garden of Scotland aims to explore and explain the diversity of plants and fungi on earth, and their importance to mankind. It is first and foremost an international scientific institution, conducting major research in plant science. In addition, it curates its living and preserved collections as a basis for research and education and for the training of professional botanists and horticulturists. Finally, it encourages the public to enjoy the collections.

Its three specialist gardens provide a range of climatic and soil conditions: Younger Botanic Garden, near Dunoon;

Logan Botanic Garden, near Stranraer; and Dawyck Botanic Garden, near Stobo, Peeblesshire. The Pringle Chinese collection – the most significant horticultural development at Inverleith since 1914 – was opened by the Princess Royal in 1997. Consisting mostly of taxa from recent expeditions, it represents an internationally significant collection of Chinese plants of known wild origin.

SCOTTISH ASSOCIATION FOR MARINE SCIENCE

PO Box 3, Oban PA34 4AD
01631 562244
Director: Dr Graham B Shimmield; *Secretary*: Professor J B L Matthews, FRSE

SCOTTISH CROP RESEARCH INSTITUTE

Invergowrie, Dundee DD2 5DA
01382 562731
Director: Professor J R Hillman

Aims to increase knowledge in the basic biological sciences, to improve crop quality and utilisation, and to develop environmentally benign methods of protecting crops from depredations by pests, pathogens and weeds. A non-departmental public body, it was formed in 1981 from the merger of the Scottish Plant Breeding Station and the Scottish Horticultural Research Institute.

Varieties bred by SCRI (and its predecessor organisations) are widely released throughout the world. The "Glen" series of raspberries accounts for 95% of Scottish and 70% of UK certified stocks, while a fifth of the UK main-crop potato area is planted to SCRI varieties. SCRI is the UK's lead centre for research on potatoes, barley, brassicas and soft fruit crops and carries out additional research on a range of temperate, sub-tropical and tropical crops.

UK ASTRONOMY TECHNOLOGY CENTRE

Royal Observatory Edinburgh, Blackford Hill, Edinburgh EH9 3HJ
0131-668 8100
Director: Dr Adrian Russell

Granted the title Royal Observatory by George IV in 1822, having begun its existence in 1811 as the Astronomical Institution of Edinburgh. The original observatory was opened in 1818 on Calton Hill, on the site of an earlier observatory which had been run primarily as a scientific novelty. ROE moved away from the smoke of the town centre to its present site on Blackford Hill in 1896.

In 1957 the Astronomer Royal for Scotland, Hermann Bruck, diverted much of the observatory's effort to the development of new instrumentation, which led to an increasing involvement with modern technology, including (in 1959) pioneering use of one of the few computers in Britain. A foreign observing site was established with the installation of a Schmidt telescope in Italy and a space research team began to develop instruments for observing the ultraviolet from rockets. In 1965 responsibility for the observatory passed from the Scottish Office to the Science Research Council. It is now an establishment of the Particle Physics and Astronomy Research Council (PPARC), a government-funded research organisation whose astronomy programme is directed towards the study of the origin, content and evolution of the universe.

In 1997 PPARC announced that the case for continuing two UK observatories (at Greenwich and Edinburgh) was not sustainable and that there should be a single UK astronomy technology centre based at Edinburgh. It claimed that the move would free £2.4 million a year for re-investment in astronomy. Research interests include cosmology, star formation, studies of the Milky Way and astronomical biology (search for signs of life on other planets).

SHINTY

CAMANACHD ASSOCIATION
Algarve, Badabrie, Banavie, Fort William PH33 7LX
01397 772772
Executive Officer: Alastair MacIntyre

SHOOTING

BRITISH ASSOCIATION FOR SHOOTING AND CONSERVATION
Scottish Centre, Trochry, Dunkeld PH8 0DY
01350 723226
Director: Dr Colin Shedden
Represents and safeguards the interests of all those who enjoy shooting sports.

SKIING

SNOWSPORT SCOTLAND
Caledonia House, South Gyle, Edinburgh EH12 9DQ
0131-317 7280
Chief Executive: Bruce Crawford
Fosters and develops skiing and snowboarding in Scotland.

SPORT AND RECREATION

See also entries for individual sports' governing bodies under the name of the sport

NATIONAL PLAYING FIELDS ASSOCIATION (SCOTLAND)
20 Queen Street, Edinburgh EH2 1JX
0131-225 4307
Secretary/Treasurer: Stephen Barr; *Chairman*: David Reynolds

SCOTTISH SPORTS COUNCIL
Caledonia House, South Gyle, Edinburgh EH12 9DQ
0131-317 7200
Chief Executive: Allan Alstead; *Chairman*: Graeme Simmers
Established in 1972, the council leads the development of sport and physical recreation in Scotland, with the aim of increasing participation and improving standards of performance. Focuses its resources on investing in high quality sporting opportunities for young people; and a comprehensive programme for aspiring and top performers which will improve standards of performance. Distributes more than £20 million a year to develop

the infrastructure of Scottish sport through the Lottery sports fund.

The council's national sports centres develop the skills of instructors, coaches and leaders, and provide a training ground for Scotland's national squads. The centres also offer courses and tuition for individuals, clubs and schools.

Glenmore Lodge All-year-round outdoor activities, including skiing, rock climbing, mountaineering, kayaking and open Canadian canoeing. Concerned with mountain safety. Offers accommodation and amenities.

Cumbrae Coaching at every level in a range of water sports, including dinghy sailing, cruising, board sailing, canoeing, sub aqua driving. Works with colleges to develop vocational training in sport.

Inverclyde Facilities for 30 team and individual indoor and outdoor sports. 24 governing bodies of sport use the facilities to train national squads and the centre is a regular venue for national and international championships. Runs a sports sciences programme.

SQUASH

SCOTTISH SQUASH
Caledonia House, South Gyle, Edinburgh EH12 9DQ
0131-317 7343
Administration Manager: F N Brydon

STOCK EXCHANGE

LONDON STOCK EXCHANGE
69 Buchanan Street, Glasgow G1 3HL
0141-221 7060
Senior Manager: Stephen Robertson

SURVEYS

BRITISH GEOLOGICAL SURVEY
Murchison House, West Mains Road, Edinburgh EH9 3LA

0131-667 1000
Head of Station: Dr Chris Browitt
Provides nation-wide surveys and monitoring and develops and disseminates expertise and information in the earth sciences for government, industry and the public. Covers geology, environmental geochemistry, groundwater, earthquakes, offshore oil.

ORDNANCE SURVEY
Grayfield House, 5 Bankhead Avenue, Edinburgh EH11 4AE
0131-442 3985
Britain's national mapping agency, for business, leisure, educational and administrative use. Creates paper maps and computer data products which are internationally renowned.

SWIMMING

SCOTTISH AMATEUR SWIMMING ASSOCIATION
Holmhills Farm, Greenlees Road, Cambuslang G72 8DT
0141-641 8818
Chief Executive: Paul Bush

TARTANS

SCOTTISH TARTANS SOCIETY
Port-na-Craig Road, Pitlochry
PH16 5NQ
01796 474079
Hon Secretary: John Montgomery; *President*: Duncan W Paisley of Westerlea
Register of all publicly known tartans worldwide. Archive; library; research; museums in Edinburgh, Franklin (USA).

TELEVISION AND RADIO

BBC SCOTLAND
Broadcasting House, Queen Margaret Drive, Glasgow G12 8DG
0141-339 8844

Controller: John McCormick; *National Governor and Chairman, Broadcasting Council for Scotland*: Sir Robert Smith
The only broadcasting organisation serving the whole of Scotland. As a public service broadcaster, it aims to cater for Scotland's distinctive audience needs in such programming areas as education and religion, as well as providing high-profile drama, entertainment, news and sport.

INDEPENDENT TELEVISION COMMISSION
123 Blythswood Street, Glasgow
G2 4AN
0141-226 4436
Head of ITC Scotland: Brian Marjoribanks
Public body responsible for licensing and regulating all non-BBC television services operating in or for the UK. These include ITV, Channel 4, Channel 5, digital services, and a range of cable, satellite, text and data services. The National Office in Scotland has a particular responsibility to liaise with the licensees in Scotland and to promote awareness and understanding of the ITC's functions.

MORAY FIRTH RADIO
PO Box 271, Inverness IV3 8UJ
01463 224433
Managing Director: Thomas Prag

NORTH SOUND RADIO
45 Kings Gate, Aberdeen AB15 4EL
01224 337000
Managing Director: Rod Webster

RADIO BORDERS
Tweedside Park, Galashiels TD1 3TD
01896 759444
Managing Director: Danny Gallagher

RADIO CLYDE
Clydebank Business Park, Glasgow
G81 2RX
0141-306 2200
Managing Director: Alex Dickson, OBE

RADIO FORTH
Forth House, Forth Street, Edinburgh
EH1 3LF
0131-556 9255
Managing Director: Tom Steele

SCOT FM
Albert Quay, Leith EH6 7DN
0131-554 6677
Managing Director: Mike Bawden

SCOTTISH MEDIA GROUP
Chief Executive: Andrew Flanagan
Brings together several prominent broadcasting organisations, as well as newspaper titles, following the merger of Scottish Television and Grampian Television and the acquisition of the *Herald* and *Evening Times*.

SCOTTISH TELEVISION
Cowcaddens, Glasgow G2 3PR
0141-300 3000
Controller: R Scott Ferguson
ITV licensee for central Scotland since commercial television began in 1957. Produces 1,000 hours of regional programmes each year, broadcasting to 3.8 million viewers in its transmission area.

GRAMPIAN TELEVISION
Queen's Cross, Aberdeen AB15 4XJ
01224 846846
Controller: Derrick Thomson
ITV licensee for the north of Scotland, the ITV network's largest geographic transmission area. Produces 400 hours of regional programmes each year, broadcasting to 1.1 million viewers in its transmission area.

TAY FM AND RADIO TAY AM
P O Box 123, 6 North Isla Street, Dundee
DD1 9UF
01382 200800
Managing Director: Alex Wilkie

WEST SOUND
54a Holmston Road, Ayr KA7 3BE
01292 283662
Managing Director: Paul Cooney

THEATRE (AMATEUR)

SCOTTISH COMMUNITY DRAMA ASSOCIATION
5 York Place, Edinburgh EH1 3EB
0131-557 5552
Administrative Assistant: Richard Kay;
Chairperson: Morna Barron

Development of amateur drama in Scotland. Binds together amateur societies throughout the country and offers them advice, encouragement and practical help.

SCOTTISH YOUTH THEATRE
6th Floor, Gordon Chambers, 90 Mitchell Street, Glasgow G1 3NQ
0141-221 5127
Director: Mary McCluskey; *Chair of Board*: Bryan Beattie
Enables, stimulates and directly provides a quality theatre arts experience to young people in Scotland.

THEATRE (PROFESSIONAL)

Listed is a selection of the larger professional theatre companies.
See also: Theatres and Concert Halls

ARCHES THEATRE COMPANY
Arches Theatre, 30 Midland Street, Glasgow G1 4PR
0141-221 9736
Artistic Director: Andy Arnold; *Chair, Board of Directors*: Lesley Thomson

BORDERLINE THEATRE COMPANY
North Harbour Street, Ayr KA8 8AA
01292 281010
Chief Executive: Eddie Jackson; *Artistic Director*: Leslie Finlay
One of Scotland's leading touring theatre companies.

BRUNTON THEATRE COMPANY
High Street, Musselburgh EH21 6AA
0131-665 9900
Artistic Director: Mark Thomson; *General Manager*: Lesley Smith

BYRE THEATRE
36 South Street, St Andrews KY16 9JT
01334 476288.
Artistic Director: Ken Alexander
A completely new Byre Theatre is being built on the site of the old theatre and will open on the site of the old theatre in the summer of 2000. It will present a programme of its own productions supported by professional touring companies and local amateur societies.

CITIZENS THEATRE
Gorbals, Glasgow G5 9DS
0141-429 5561
Director: Giles Havergal; *Chair*: Professor Jan McDonald
Founded in 1943 by James Bridie, who intended it to be a home of the Scottish theatre with a policy of positive encouragement for native dramatists and actors, although he believed that it should also draw on English theatrical resources. The company was set up in a 19th-century music hall in Glasgow Gorbals, where it remains to the present day.

The present company was formed in 1970 under the direction of Giles Havergal and bases its repertoire on British and foreign classics. Since 1992 the company has operated in three theatres: the 600-seat main theatre and two smaller studio theatres. The company has toured extensively abroad and has been widely acclaimed for its innovative work as well as for important translations of modern and classical European drama.

COMMUNICADO THEATRE COMPANY
2 Hill Street, Edinburgh EH2 3JZ
0131-624 4040
Artistic Director: Helena Kaut-Howson
Touring theatre to venues all over Scotland and beyond.

DUNDEE REP
Tay Square, Dundee DD1 1PB
01382 227684
Artistic Director: Hamish Glen
Established in 1939 and moved to a new purpose-built theatre in 1983. Operating as a producing house, it stages an average of six of its own productions every season. As a receiving house, it hosts work from visiting companies. The theatre increases access to performing arts through an extensive community drama programme. It is also the home of Scottish Dance Theatre, founded in 1986, a contemporary dance company with a national remit.

MULL THEATRE
Dervaig, Isle of Mull, Argyll PA75 6QW
01688 400377
Artistic Director: Alasdair McCrone

PERTH THEATRE
185 High Street, Perth PH1 5UW
01738 472700
Artistic Director: Michael Winter
Repertory theatre founded in 1935 by
David Steuart and Marjorie Dence. In
1939 the first Scottish Theatre Festival
was launched there. In 1946 the theatre
became a non-profit-making organisation with financial support from the
Arts Council, and after Marjorie Dence's
death in 1966 it was bought by the local
authority. Iain Cuthbertson, its director
in the 1967-68 season, mounted an
ambitious programme of Scottish plays.
Since then, the company has favoured a
more orthodox play policy.

PITLOCHRY FESTIVAL THEATRE
Port-na-Craig, Pitlochry PH16 5DR
01796 484600
Festival Director: Clive Perry; *Chairman of
Board*: Gordon Halliwell
The inspiration of John Stewart, who
conceived the idea of a "theatre in the
hills" for the presentation of a festival of
plays in repertory. In May 1951 the
theatre opened in a marquee housing a
fan-shaped auditorium and an
unusually large stage.
    The early Pitlochry seasons
presented six plays running from the
spring to the early autumn, typically
including one Scottish play, a work by a
foreign author, a classic or near classic, a
new play and one or two pot-boilers. In
a modified fashion this pattern has been
maintained to the present day, with the
addition of concerts, art exhibitions and
lectures.
    In 1981, the company moved to a
purpose-built theatre on the outskirts of
the small Highland town where it is
based. An unusually high proportion of
its turnover (70%) is generated through
ticket sales.

PORTRONA
41 Crossbost, Lochs, Isle of Lewis
01851 860461

ROYAL LYCEUM THEATRE COMPANY
Grindlay Street, Edinburgh EH3 9AX
0131-248 4800
Artistic Director: Kenny Ireland;
Chairman: Dr Michael Shea
Launched in 1965 as the Edinburgh
Civic Theatre Company at the Royal
Lyceum, under the artistic direction of
Tom Fleming. Bill Bryden, while
associate director of the company
between 1971 and 1975, presented new
work by Scottish writers, including
himself. Each year the present company
produces between 10 and 12 plays
representative of both contemporary
and classical theatre, and runs an
education programme.

7:84 THEATRE COMPANY
333 Woodlands Road, Glasgow G3 6NG
0141-334 6686
Artistic Director: Iain Reekie; *Chair of
Board*: Bill Speirs
Touring theatre company with a 25-year
history of presenting challenging theatre
that explores current social, cultural and
political issues.

TAG THEATRE COMPANY
18 Albion Street, Glasgow G1 1LH
0141-552 4949
Artistic Director: James Brining;
Chairperson: Professor Jan McDonald
Scotland's national theatre for young
people, with a vision to allow every
young person in Scotland the
opportunity to see and participate in the
excitement of live theatre.

THEATRE WORKSHOP
34 Hamilton Place, Edinburgh
EH3 5AX
0131-225 7942
Artistic Director: Robert Rae

TOSG THEATRE COMPANY
Sabhal Mor Ostaig, Teangue, Sleat, Isle
of Skye IV44 8RQ
01471 844443

TRAMWAY
25 Albert Drive, Pollokshields, Glasgow
G41 2PE
0141-422 2023

TRAVERSE THEATRE
10 Cambridge Street, Edinburgh
EH1 2ED
0131-228 3223
Artistic Director: Philip Howard; *Chair*:
John Scott Moncrieff
Established in 1963 as a private club in a
former lodging house in Edinburgh. Its
first auditorium held 60 spectators on
either side of the acting area. It has
moved premises twice. From the start, it
has championed the cause of new and
experimental work, including plays by
Scottish writers.

TRON THEATRE
63 Trongate, Glasgow G1 5HB
0141-552 3748
Artistic Director: Irina Brown; *Chairman*:
Michael Russell
Produces and presents a varied
programme of contemporary and
classical drama, comedy, music and
dance from Scotland and abroad.

WILDCAT STAGE PRODUCTIONS
69 Buchanan Street, Glasgow G1 3HL
0141-314 3732

THEATRES AND CONCERT HALLS
*Listed is a selection of the larger theatres and
a few others of special interest*

CUMBERNAULD THEATRE
Braehead Road, Kildrum, Cumbernauld
G67 2BN
01236 737235

EDEN COURT THEATRE
Bishop Road, Inverness IV3 5SA
01463 239841
Theatre Director: Colin Marr

EDINBURGH FESTIVAL THEATRE
13/29 Nicolson Street, Edinburgh EH8
9FT
0131-662 1112
General Manager and Chief Executive:
Stephen Barry

EDINBURGH PLAYHOUSE
18/22 Greenside Place, Edinburgh EH1
3AA
0131-557 2692
General Manager: Andrew Lyst

GLASGOW ROYAL CONCERT HALL
2 Sauchiehall Street, Glasgow G2
0141-332 6633
Director: Louise Mitchell

HIS MAJESTY'S THEATRE
Rosemount Viaduct, Aberdeen
AB25 1GL
01224 637788

KING'S THEATRE (EDINBURGH)
Administration Offices: 13/29 Nicolson
Street, Edinburgh EH8 9FT
0131-662 1112
Chief Executive and General Manager:
Stephen Barry

KING'S THEATRE (GLASGOW)
294 Bath Street, Glasgow G2 4JN
0141-248 5153

MITCHELL THEATRE
3 Granville Street, Glasgow G3 7DR
0141-287 4855

PAVILION THEATRE
121 Renfield Street, Glasgow G2 3AX
0141-332 1846

QUEEN'S HALL
Clerk Street, Edinburgh EH8 9JG
0131-668 3456
General Manager: Paul Gudgin

THEATRE ROYAL (GLASGOW)
282 Hope Street, Glasgow G2 3QA
0141-332 3321

TOURIST BOARDS

SCOTTISH TOURIST BOARD
23 Ravelston Terrace, Edinburgh
EH4 3EU
0131-332 2433
Chief Executive: Tom Buncle; *Chairman*:
Lord Gordon of Strathblane

Established under the Development of Tourism Act 1969 to attract visitors to Scotland and encourage them to travel widely within Scotland. Its mission is the generation of jobs and wealth. It aims to promote the highest standards of service and hospitality. Financed by government, through the Scottish Executive.

Local tourist boards:

ABERDEEN AND GRAMPIAN TOURIST BOARD
27 Albyn Place, Aberdeen AB10 1YL
01224 288800
Chief Executive: Alan Clarke

ANGUS & CITY OF DUNDEE TOURIST BOARD
21 Castle Street, Dundee DD1 3AA
01382 527527
Chief Executive: Dr Colin Smith

ARGYLL, THE ISLES, LOCH LOMOND, STIRLING, TROSSACHS TOURIST BOARD
Old Town Jail, St John Street, Stirling FK8 1EA
01786 445222
Chief Executive: James Fraser

AYRSHIRE & ARRAN TOURIST BOARD
Burns House, Burns Statue Square, Ayr KA7 1UP
01292 262555
Interim Chief Executive: Ian Robertson

DUMFRIES AND GALLOWAY TOURIST BOARD
64 Whitesands, Dumfries DG1 2RS
01387 245550
Chief Executive: Norma Hart

EDINBURGH & LOTHIANS TOURIST BOARD
4 Rothesay Terrace, Edinburgh EH3 7RY
0131-473 3600
Chief Executive: Jack Munro

GREATER GLASGOW & CLYDE VALLEY TOURIST BOARD
11 George Square, Glasgow G2 1DY
0141-204 4480
Chief Executive: Eddie Friel

HIGHLANDS OF SCOTLAND TOURIST BOARD
Peffery House, Strathpeffer IV14 9HA
01997 421160
Chief Executive: David Noble

KINGDOM OF FIFE TOURIST BOARD
Haig House, Haig Business Park, Balgonie Road, Markinch KY7 6AQ
01592 750066
Chief Executive: Patrick Laughlin

ORKNEY TOURIST BOARD
6 Broad Street, Kirkwall, Orkney KW15 1NX
01856 872856
Chief Executive: Gareth Crichton

PERTHSHIRE TOURIST BOARD
Lower City Mills, West Mill Street, Perth PH1 5QP
01738 627958
Chief Executive: John L Grainger, MBE

SCOTTISH BORDERS TOURIST BOARD
Shepherds Mills, Whinfield Road, Selkirk TD7 5DT
01750 20555
Chief Executive: Riddell Graham

SHETLAND ISLANDS TOURISM
Market Cross, Lerwick, Shetland ZE1 0LU
01595 693434
Chief Executive: Maurice Mullay

WESTERN ISLES TOURIST BOARD
4 South Beach, Stornoway, Isle of Lewis HS1 2XY
01851 701818
Chief Executive: Angus MacMillan

TRADE ORGANISATIONS

HARRIS TWEED AUTHORITY
6 Garden Road, Stornoway HS1 2QJ
01851 702269
Chief Executive: Ian A Mackenzie

SCOTCH MALT WHISKY SOCIETY
The Vaults, 87 Giles Street, Edinburgh EH6 6BZ
0131-554 3451

SCOTCH WHISKY ASSOCIATION
20 Atholl Crescent, Edinburgh EH3 8HF
0131-222 9200
Director General: Hugh Morison; *Chairman*: John McGrath

SCOTTISH ASSOCIATION OF MASTER BAKERS
4 Torphichen Street, Edinburgh EH3 8JQ
0131-229 1401
Chief Executive: Ian Hay

SCOTTISH BUILDING EMPLOYERS' FEDERATION
Carron Grange, Carron Grange Avenue, Stenhousemuir FK5 3BQ
01324 555550
Chief Executive: S C Patten; *President*: J C Scott

SCOTTISH DAILY NEWSPAPER SOCIETY
48 Palmerston Place, Edinburgh EH12 5DE
0131-220 4353
Director: Jim Raeburn; *President*: Michael Jones

SCOTTISH DECORATORS' FEDERATION
Federation House, 222 Queensferry Road, Edinburgh EH4 2BN
0131-343 3300
National Director: Ian H Rogers; *President*: G Nicolson

SCOTTISH ENGINEERING
105 West George Street, Glasgow G2 1QL
0141-221 3181

SCOTTISH FOOD TRADE ASSOCIATION
GCFT Business Enterprises, 230 Cathedral Street, Glasgow G1 2TG
0141-552 1655

SCOTTISH GROCERS' FEDERATION
Federation House, 222 Queensferry Road, Edinburgh EH4 2BN
0131-343 3300
Chief Executive: Lawrie Dewar; *President*: Eddie Thompson

SCOTTISH LICENSED TRADE ASSOCIATION
10 Walker Street, Edinburgh EH3 7LA
0131-225 5169
Secretary: Colin A Wilkinson; *President*: Paul D C Waterson

SCOTTISH MOTOR TRADE ASSOCIATION
3 Palmerston Place, Edinburgh EH12 5AF
0131-225 3643
Chief Executive: Alister Dow; *President*: George MacDonald

SCOTTISH NEWSPAPER PUBLISHERS' ASSOCIATION
48 Palmerston Place, Edinburgh EH12 5DE
0131-220 4353
Director: Jim Raeburn; *President*: Alex Lumsden

SCOTTISH AND NORTHERN IRELAND PLUMBING EMPLOYERS' FEDERATION
2 Walker Street, Edinburgh EH3 7LB
0131-225 2255

SCOTTISH PHARMACEUTICAL FEDERATION
135 Wellington Street, Glasgow G2 2XD
0141-221 1235
Secretary/Treasurer: F E J McCrossin; *Chairman*: G E Allan

SCOTTISH PRINT EMPLOYERS' FEDERATION
48 Palmerston Place, Edinburgh EH12 5DE
0131-220 4353
Director: Jim Raeburn; *President*: John Crerar

TRANSPORT OPERATORS

CALEDONIAN MACBRAYNE
The Pier, Gourock PA19 1QP
01475 650100
Managing Director: Captain John Simkins; *Chairman*: Rear-Admiral N E Rankin
Passenger and vehicle ferry services to Clyde and Western Isles islands.

RAILTRACK PLC
Buchanan House, 58 Port Dundas Road, Glasgow G4 0LQ

0141-332 9811
Director Scotland Zone: Janette Anderson
Owners of Britain's tracks, signals, and stations, maintaining the infrastructure of the railway.

SCOTRAIL

Caledonian Chambers, 87 Union Street, Glasgow G1 3TA
0141-332 9811
Managing Director: Alastair McPherson
Scotland's national rail operator, providing 95% of passenger train services north of the border. Runs suburban, inter-urban and rural services in Scotland and the Caledonian sleeper service to and from London. In March 1997 the National Express Group began a seven-year franchise for the operation of ScotRail.

SCOTTISH AIRPORTS LTD

St Andrew's Drive, Glasgow Airport, Paisley PA3 2SW
0141-848 4050
Managing Director: Donal Dowds
Owns and operates Scotland's three principal airports at Aberdeen, Edinburgh and Glasgow, providing core services to the individual operating companies. Although Scottish Airports Ltd is part of BAA plc, it is a devolved company with a registered head office at Paisley. Major investment initiatives are planned and developed in Scotland, and agreed by BAA. Almost 9% of BAA shares (92 million) are beneficially owned by companies based in Scotland. SAL and the three operating companies together employ 1,100 staff, and a further 9,000 people work at the airports.

Aberdeen provides air transport links with Orkney and Shetland and daily scheduled services to London and other UK destinations. It is also Scotland's gateway to Scandinavia. Edinburgh has frequent daily scheduled services to London and other airports in the UK, as well as flights to several destinations in continental Europe. Among Glasgow's services are 70 flights each weekday to and from London.

STAGECOACH HOLDINGS plc

Charlotte House, 20 Charlotte Street, Perth PH1 5LL
01738 442111
Chief Executive: Mike Kinski; *Chairman*: Brian Souter
International bus, rail and airports operator

STRATHCLYDE PASSENGER TRANSPORT AUTHORITY

12 West George Street, Glasgow G2 1HN
0141-333 3100
Director General: Dr Malcolm Reed
Finances and specifies passenger rail services in Strathclyde. Also operates Glasgow Underground, Renfrew ferry, major bus stations, and a network of travel centres. Subsidises socially necessary bus services.

TRANSPORT ORGANISATIONS

SCOTTISH ASSOCIATION FOR PUBLIC TRANSPORT

5 St Vincent Place, Glasgow G1 2HT
0141-639 3697
Hon Secretary: Alastair Reid; *Chair*: Dr John McCormick
Campaigns for integrated transport in, to, and from Scotland, improvements in public passenger transport, and shifts from roads to rail and water-borne freight.

SCOTTISH RAILWAY PRESERVATION SOCIETY

The Station, Union Street, Bo'ness EH51 9AQ
01506 822298
General Secretary: Dr Neil Gilmour; *Chairman*: W Peddie
Aims to establish a working Scottish railway museum. Volunteer members operate the Bo'ness and Kinneil Railway, SRPS Railtours and the Scottish Railway Exhibition.

SCOTTISH TRAMWAY AND TRANSPORT SOCIETY

PO Box 78, Glasgow G3 6ER
General Secretary: Stuart Little

Publication of books and videos on Scottish tramway history and support for preservation schemes.

UNIONS

SCOTTISH TRADES UNION CONGRESS
333 Woodlands Road, Glasgow G3 6NG
0141-337 8100
General Secretary: Bill Speirs; *Chairperson*: Anne Middleton
First convened in Glasgow in 1897. Initially 30 of the 45 affiliated unions were small independent Scottish unions which then existed in such industries as textiles and engineering (although a number, like the railwaymen, were always nationally organised). Over the years, the number of separate Scottish unions declined through successive amalgamations, until today there are only six out of an affiliate membership of 52. The number of members rose from 76,000 in 1898 to 1,050,000 in 1978, from which peak it has declined to 800,000.

Congress meets annually for a week in April, the venue varying from year to year. It is completely independent (not a Scottish regional organisation of the TUC) and is financed from the subscriptions of affiliated unions. Hours and conditions of work have remained a central preoccupation, but the STUC has played a wider role by campaigning for new industry and from time to time has organised mass demonstrations against unemployment, closures, and cuts in public expenditure.

Listed is a selection of the largest unions and a few others of special interest

AMALGAMATED ENGINEERING & ELECTRICAL UNION
145/165 West Regent Street, Glasgow G2 4RZ
0141-248 7131

BRITISH ACTORS' EQUITY ASSOCIATION
114 Union Street, Glasgow G1 3QQ
0141-248 2472

BROADCASTING, ENTERTAINMENT, CINEMATOGRAPH AND THEATRE UNION
114 Union Street, Glasgow G2 3QQ
0141-248 9558

FIRE BRIGADES UNION
4th Floor, 52 St Enoch Square, Glasgow G1 4AA
0141 221 2309

GMB
Fountain House, 1/3 Woodside Crescent, Glasgow G3 7UJ
0141-332 8641

GRAPHICAL, PAPER AND MEDIA UNION
Graphical House, 222 Clyde Street, Glasgow G1 4JT
0141-221 7730

INSTITUTION OF PROFESSIONALS, MANAGERS AND SPECIALISTS
18 Melville Terrace, Stirling FK8 2NQ
01786 465999
National Officer: Alan Denney

MANUFACTURING, SCIENCE AND FINANCE
1 Woodlands Terrace, Glasgow G3 6DD
0141-331 1216
National Secretary Scotland: John Wall

MUSICIANS' UNION
11 Sandyford Place, Sauchiehall Street, Glasgow G3 7NB
0141-248 3723

NATIONAL UNION OF JOURNALISTS
114 Union Street, Glasgow G1 3QQ
0141-248 7748
Scottish Organiser: Paul Holleran

NATIONAL UNION OF RAIL, MARITIME AND TRANSPORT WORKERS
180 Hope Street, Glasgow G2 2UE
0141-332 1117

PUBLIC AND COMMERCIAL SERVICES UNION
6 Hillside Crescent, Edinburgh EH7 5DY
0131-556 0407
Scottish Secretary: Eddie Reilly

SCOTTISH PRISON OFFICERS' ASSOCIATION
21 Calder Road, Edinburgh EH11 3PF
0131-443 8105
General Secretary: Derek Turner

TRANSPORT AND GENERAL WORKERS' UNION
290 Bath Street, Glasgow G2 4LD
0141-332 7321

UNIFI
146 Argyle Street, Glasgow G2 8BL
0141-221 6475

UNION OF CONSTRUCTION, ALLIED TRADES AND TECHNICIANS
6 Fitzroy Place, Glasgow G3 7RL
0141-221 4893
Scottish Secretary: A S Ritchie

UNION OF SHOP, DISTRIBUTIVE AND ALLIED WORKERS
Muirfield, 342 Albert Drive, Glasgow G41 5PG
0141-427 6561

UNISON
14 West Campbell Street, Glasgow G2 6RX
0141-332 0006
Scottish Secretary: Matt Smith

UNIVERSITIES

UNIVERSITY OF ABERDEEN
Aberdeen AB24 3FX
01224 272000
Principal and Vice-Chancellor: Professor C Duncan Rice
History: Founded in 1495 as King's College. A second university, Marischal College, was founded in 1593. They merged in 1860. *Faculties*: Arts and Divinity; Medicine and Medical Sciences; Social Sciences and Law; Science and Engineering. *Number of students*: 11,000. *Main undergraduate awards*: MA, BSc, BD, BTh, LTh, LLB, BLE, MB, ChB, BMedBiol, BEng, MEng, BScEng. *Key features*: New Institute of Medical Sciences. 49% of first degree students in university accommodation.

UNIVERSITY OF ABERTAY, DUNDEE
Bell Street, Dundee DD1 1HG
01382 308000
Principal and Vice-Chancellor: Professor B King
History: Established as a university in 1994, with origins in the foundation of Dundee Technical College in 1888. *Schools*: Accounting and Law; Construction and Environment; Engineering; Health and Nursing; Informatics; Management; Molecular and Life Sciences; Social Sciences. *Number of students*: 4,000. *Main undergraduate awards*: BA, BSc, BEng. *Key features*: Smallest university in Britain. 20% of all students in university accommodation.

UNIVERSITY OF DUNDEE
Dundee DD1 4HN
01382 223181
Principal and Vice-Chancellor: Dr I J Graham-Bryce
History: Founded in 1967, the successor to University College, Dundee, which had been part of the University of St Andrews since 1881. *Faculties*: Medicine and Dentistry; Science and Engineering; Law and Accounting; Arts and Social Sciences; Architecture and Art and Design. *Number of students*: 8,500. *Main undergraduate awards*: BA, BAcc, BArch, BDes, BDS, BEng, BFin, BMSc, BSc, LLB, MA, MB, ChB. *Key features*: Duncan of Jordanstone College, formerly an independent institution, now the Faculty of Architecture and Art and Design – with 1,600 students, the university's largest faculty. 30% of all students in university accommodation.

UNIVERSITY OF EDINBURGH
Old College, South Bridge, Edinburgh EH8 9YL
0131-650 1000
Principal and Vice-Chancellor: Professor Stewart Sutherland
History: Granted a charter by James VI

in 1582, the Town Council providing the necessary finances. *Faculties:* Divinity; Law; Medicine; Arts; Science and Engineering; Music; Social Sciences; Veterinary Medicine. *Number of students:* 17,500. *Main undergraduate awards:* BA, BCom, BD, BEng, BMus, BSc, BV&MS, LLB, MA, MB, ChB, MEng, MChem, MChemPhys, MPhys. *Key features:* 29% of all students in university accommodation. Alumni include David Hume, Walter Scott, J M Barrie, R L Stevenson.

UNIVERSITY OF GLASGOW
Glasgow G12 8QQ
0141-339 8855
Principal and Vice-Chancellor: Professor Sir Graeme Davies
History: Founded in 1451. Moved in 1871 from the city centre to the present campus in the West End. *Faculties:* Arts; Science; Medicine; Law and Financial Studies; Divinity; Engineering; Veterinary Medicine; Social Sciences. *Number of students:* 18,100. *Main undergraduate awards:* BA, BAcc, BArch, BD, BDS, BEd, BMus, BN, BSc, BEng, MEng, LLB, MA, MB, ChB, MSci, BVMS, BTechEd, BTheol, BTechnol. *Key features:* 40% of first degree students live at home.

GLASGOW CALEDONIAN UNIVERSITY
Cowcaddens Road, Glasgow G4 0BA
0141-331 3000
Principal: Dr Ian Johnston, CB
History: Founded in 1993 from the merger of the former Glasgow Polytechnic and the Queen's College, Glasgow. *Faculties:* Business; Health; Science and Technology. *Number of students:* 13,000. *Main undergraduate awards:* BA, BSc, BEng. *Key features:* Three campuses. Only 5% of all students in university accommodation.

HERIOT-WATT UNIVERSITY
Riccarton, Edinburgh EH14 4AS
0131-449 5111
Principal and Vice-Chancellor: Professor

John S Archer
History: Founded in 1966, but tracing its origins to the foundation of Edinburgh School of Arts in 1821. *Faculties:* Science; Engineering; Economics and Social Studies; Environmental Studies; Art and Design; Textiles. *Number of students:* 5,500. *Main undergraduate awards:* BA, BArch, BEd, BEng, BSc, MEng. *Key features:* Faculties of Environmental Studies and Art and Design are operated jointly with Edinburgh College of Art; Faculty of Textiles with Scottish College of Textiles. 40% of all students in university accommodation.

NAPIER UNIVERSITY
219 Colinton Road, Edinburgh EH14 1DJ
0131-444 2266
Principal: Professor John Mavor
History: Opened in 1964 as Napier College of Science and Technology, acquiring full degree-awarding powers in 1992. *Faculties:* Arts and Social Sciences; Engineering and Computing; Science; Napier Business School; Health Studies. *Number of students:* 11,500. *Main undergraduate awards:* BA, BEng, BSc. *Key features:* 10 sites throughout Edinburgh (and beyond). 21% of all students in university accommodation.

OPEN UNIVERSITY IN SCOTLAND
10 Drumsheugh Gardens, Edinburgh EH3 7QJ
0131-226 3851
Director: Peter Syme
History: Established by royal charter in 1969. *Faculties:* Arts, Education, Health and Social Welfare, Law, Management, Maths and Computing, Modern Languages, Science, Social Sciences, Technology. *Number of students:* 12,000 in Scotland, 200,000 in the UK as a whole. *Main undergraduate awards:* BA, BSc. *Key features:* part-time open learning with extensive tutor support and opportunities for regular contact with fellow students. No qualifications required to study at undergraduate

level. Courses taught using a variety of multi-media course materials, from written texts to videos and computer software.

UNIVERSITY OF PAISLEY
High Street, Paisley PA1 2BE
0141-848 3000
Principal and Vice-Chancellor: Professor Richard W Shaw
History: Founded in 1897 as Paisley Technical College and School of Art. Given university status in 1992. Merged with Craigie College of Education in 1993. *Faculties:* Education; Engineering; Science and Technology; Business; Health and Social Sciences. *Number of students:* 9,000. *Main undergraduate awards:* BA, BAcc, BEd, BEng, BSc, BEng. *Key features:* Main campus, Paisley. Craigie campus in Ayr specialises in education, business, media, nursing. 20% of all students in university accommodation.

ROBERT GORDON UNIVERSITY
Schoolhill, Aberdeen AB10 1FR
01224 262000
Principal and Vice-Chancellor: Professor William Stevely
History: Started as Robert Gordon's College in 1881. Acquired central institution status in 1903, awarded university title in 1992. *Faculties:* Science and Technology; Health and Food; Design; Management. *Number of students:* 6,000. *Main undergraduate awards:* BA, BSc, BEng. *Key features:* Semester system. 25% of all students in university accommodation.

UNIVERSITY OF ST ANDREWS
College Gate, St Andrews KY16 9AJ
01334 476161
Principal and Vice-Chancellor: Professor Struther Arnott
History: Founded in 1411, Scotland's oldest university and third oldest in UK.

Faculties: Arts; Divinity; Science. *Number of students:* 5,500. *Main undergraduate awards:* BD, MA, BSc, MChem, MSc, MTheol. *Key features:* Tradition of red gowns. 41% of students are English, 13% from overseas. 66% of all students in university accommodation.

UNIVERSITY OF STIRLING
Stirling FK9 4LA
01786 473171
Principal and Vice-Chancellor: Professor A Miller, CBE
History: Founded in 1967. *Faculties:* Arts; Human Sciences; Management; Natural Sciences. *Number of students:* 7,500. *Main undergraduate awards:* BA, BSc, BAcc. *Key features:* Two semesters, each of 15 weeks. 60% of all students in university accommodation.

UNIVERSITY OF STRATHCLYDE
16 Richmond Street, Glasgow G1 1XQ
0141-552 4400
Principal and Vice-Chancellor: Professor Sir John P Arbuthnott
History: Formed as Anderson's Institution in 1796, became Royal Technical College in 1912, Royal College of Science and Technology in 1956. Full university status was granted in 1964. *Faculties:* Science; Engineering; Arts and Social Studies; Strathclyde Business School (incorporating the Graduate Business School); Education. *Number of students:* 14,000. *Main undergraduate awards:* BA, BArch, BSc, BEng, MEng, BEd, LLB. *Key features:* 19% of all students in university accommodation. 57% first degree students live at home.

VOLLEYBALL

SCOTTISH VOLLEYBALL ASSOCIATION
48 The Pleasance, Edinburgh EH8 9TJ
0131-556 4633
Director: Nick Moody

VOLUNTEERING

CSV SCOTLAND (COMMUNITY SERVICE VOLUNTEERS SCOTLAND)
Wellgate House, 200 Cowgate, Edinburgh EH1 1NQ
0131-622 7766
Director Scotland: Claire Stevens; *Chairperson*: John Pulford
Promotes active citizenship through a nationwide programme of volunteering, training and community action opportunities.

EDINBURGH VOLUNTARY ORGANISATIONS COUNCIL
Ainslie House, 11 St. Colme Street, Edinburgh EH3 6AG
0131-539 1087
Director: Shulah Allan; *Chairperson*: Maureen O'Neill
Umbrella body for the voluntary sector in Edinburgh.

GLASGOW COUNCIL FOR THE VOLUNTARY SECTOR
11 Queens Crescent, Glasgow G4 9AS
0141-332 2444
Director: Helen Macneil
Umbrella body for the voluntary sector in Glasgow.

SCOTTISH COUNCIL FOR VOLUNTARY ORGANISATIONS
19 Claremont Crescent, Edinburgh EH7 4QD
0131-556 3882
Director: Martin Sime; *Convener*: Neil McIntosh
Established in 1936 as an umbrella body for voluntary organisations in Scotland, of which almost 1,000 are members. Works to promote and advocate the interests of the voluntary sector, publishing a weekly newspaper, handling 3,500 inquiries a year, maintaining a database of potential sources of charitable funding, running training courses, conferences and seminars, and undertaking specialist analysis of public policy as it affects voluntary bodies.
Its European unit is the first point of contact for charities wishing to gain access to European funds.

VOLUNTEER DEVELOPMENT SCOTLAND
72 Murray Place, Stirling FK8 2BX
01786 479593
Director: Liz Burns, OBE; *Chair*: Rea Roulston
National centre for volunteering.

WATER

EAST OF SCOTLAND WATER
Pentland Gait, 597 Calder Road, Edinburgh EH11 4HJ
0131-453 7500
Chief Executive: Rod Rennet; *Chairperson*: Councillor Robert Cairns

NORTH OF SCOTLAND WATER
Cairngorm House, Beechwood Park North, Inverness IV2 3ED
01463 245400
Chief Executive: Alastair D F Findlay

WEST OF SCOTLAND WATER
419 Balmore Road, Glasgow G22 6NU
0141-355 5333
Chief Executive: Ernie Chambers

WOMEN

CHURCH OF SCOTLAND GUILD
121 George Street, Edinburgh EH2 4YN
0131-225 5722
General Secretary: Alison M Twaddle; *National Convener*: Helen Longmuir
Invites women to commit their lives to Christ and enables them to express their faith in worship, prayer and action through various projects.

ROYAL SOCIETY FOR THE RELIEF OF INDIGENT GENTLEWOMEN OF SCOTLAND
14 Rutland Square, Edinburgh

EH1 2BD
0131-229 2308
Secretary and Cashier: George F Goddard;
Chairman: D H Galbraith
Offers financial assistance to ladies of Scottish birth or background with professional or business backgrounds.

Scottish Women's Aid
Norton Park, 57 Albion Road, Edinburgh EH7 5QY
0131-475 2372

Scottish Women's Rural Institutes
42 Heriot Row, Edinburgh EH3 6ES
0131-225 1724
General Secretary: Anne Peacock; *National Chairman*: Shirley Wallace
Educational and social opportunities for women – handcrafts, cookery, sport, drama, etc.

Women's Royal Voluntary Service
Scottish Divisional Office, 44 Albany Street, Edinburgh EH1 3QR
0131-558 8028
Director: Anne Boyd
Provides services for those in need in the community through 20,000 volunteers.

YOUTH

Duke of Edinburgh's Award
69 Dublin Street, Edinburgh EH3 6NS
0131-556 9097
Secretary for Scotland: Janet Shepherd
Young people aged 14-25 undertake a challenging programme of leisure pursuits involving community service, skills, physical recreation and expeditions. Three levels of award – Bronze, Silver and Gold. Non-competitive and available to all.

Fairbridge in Scotland
57 Albion Road, Edinburgh EH7 5QY
0131-475 2303
Director: Tom Watson

Scottish Youth Hostels Association
7 Glebe Crescent, Stirling FK8 2JA
01786 891400
General Secretary: W B Forsyth; *Chairman*: J P Lawson
To help all, but especially young people of limited means to know, use and appreciate the Scottish countryside and places of historic and cultural interest in Scotland, particularly by providing simple hostel accommodation for them on their travels.

YMCA Scotland
James Love House, 11 Rutland Street, Edinburgh EH1 2AE
0131-228 1464
National General Secretary: John Knox; *President*: Lord Hogg of Cumbernauld
Provides quality educational, training, support and recreational programmes aimed at physical, social, mental and spiritual development, especially for young people.

Youth Clubs Scotland
Balfour House, 19 Bonnington Grove, Edinburgh EH6 4BL
0131-554 2561
Chief Executive: Carol Downie

Youthlink Scotland
Central Halls, West Tollcross, Edinburgh EH3 9BP
0131-229 0339
Chief Executive: George Johnston; *President*: Jim Stretton
Exists to support and promote the work and collective aspirations of voluntary youth organisations.

YWCA
7 Randolph Crescent, Edinburgh EH3 7TH
0131-225 7592
Scottish Director: Isabel A Carr
Worldwide charity which improves the quality of life for young women, by providing opportunities for personal and spiritual development and by campaigning on issues of concern, such as poverty and violence against women.

The Way We Live

The Vital Statistics

Unless otherwise stated for purposes of comparison, figures are for most recent year available

Population

Population
5,120 million

Population 25 years ago
5,233 million

Number of men
2,484 million

Number of women
2,635 million

Number of men aged 75+
117,017

Number of women aged 75+
225,285

Number of single men aged 16+
671,085

Number of single women aged 16+
571,074

Number of widowed men
76,496

Number of widowed women
285,586

Number of widowed women aged 16-24
29

Birth and Death

Number of births
57,319

Number of births 25 years ago
74,392

Number of boys born
29,496

Number of girls born
27,823

Percentage of births to mothers aged 30+
44

Percentage of births to mothers aged 30+ 10 years ago
14

Number of babies born to girls between 13 and 15
433

Number of abortions performed
12,307

Number of abortions performed on teenagers
2,742

Number of abortions performed on single women
8,702

Number of abortions performed at 20 weeks and over
110

Percentage of babies born to unmarried parents
38.9

Percentage of babies born to unmarried parents 25 years ago
8.8

Percentage of babies born to unmarried parents with different parental addresses
16.1

Number of births where both father and mother were born in the Indian sub-continent
384

Number of sets of triplets
19

Number of pairs of twins
810

Number of stillbirths
351

Number of stillbirths 25 years ago
873

Number of infant deaths
320

Number of infant deaths 25 years ago
1,412

Number of deaths
59,164

Number of deaths 25 years ago
64,545

*Number of deaths from falling on or
from ladders or scaffolding*
1

Number of deaths from falling into a hole
3

Number of deaths from CJD
6

*Number of deaths from accidental
drowning*
16

Number of deaths from excessive cold
19

Number of deaths from tuberculosis
46

Number of deaths from AIDS
80

*Number of deaths from motor vehicle
traffic accidents*
382

*Number of deaths from suicide and self-
inflicted injury*
649

Number of deaths from mental disorders
1,725

*Number of deaths from malignant
neoplasms*
14,752

Number of deaths from heart disease
16,634

Life expectancy for men
72.6

Life expectancy for men 100 years ago
43.9

Life expectancy for women
78.1

*Life expectancy for women
100 years ago*
46.3

Marriage and Divorce

Number of marriages
29,668

Number of marriages 25 years ago
42,018

Average age of men marrying
33.8

*Average age of men marrying
10 years ago*
29.6

Average age for first marriage, men
29.8

Average age of women marrying
31.4

*Average age of women marrying
10 years ago*
27.3

Average age for first mariage, women
27.9

*Percentage of marriages celebrated in
Church of Scotland*
34.9

*Percentage of marriages celebrated in
Roman Catholic Church*
8

*Percentage of marriages celebrated in
other churches*
13.6

Percentage of civil marriages
43.5

Number of irregular marriages
6

Number of divorces
12,384

Number of divorces 25 years ago
7,135

Number of divorced men
133,274

Number of divorced women
161,757

Number of divorced women aged 16-19
18

Number of divorces after four years of marriage or less
1,766

Number of divorces after between 10 and 14 years of marriage
2,456

Number of divorces after 30 years of marriage or more
680

Average duration of marriage in divorce cases
12

Percentage of men and women divorcing who had been divorced previously
14

Percentage of divorces in which one or both of the partners had been under 21 at the time of marriage
36

Percentage of divorces on ground of adultery
6.7

Percentage of divorces on ground of adultery 10 years ago
11.4

Percentage of divorces on ground of non-cohabitation
68.7

Percentage of divorces on ground of non-cohabitation 10 years ago
56.7

Average age of divorced men re-marrying
41.9

Average age of divorced women re-marrying
39.0

Health

Number of beds in NHS hospitals
40,783

Number of inpatient discharges from NHS hospitals
973,325

Number of inpatient discharges from NHS hospitals five years ago
941,740

Average number of days spent in NHS hospital
11

Average inpatient waiting list
47,081

Average inpatient waiting list five years ago
59,225

Number of operations performed in Scottish hospitals
827,950

Number of operations performed in Scottish hospitals five years ago
612,530

Number of heart bypass operations
4,390

Number of cervical smear tests
480,600

*Number of cancers detected by cervical
screening*
247

Number of nurses and midwives
61,950

Number of family doctors
3,650

Average GP list size
1,468

Average cost of prescription
£10.02

*Average contribution by patient to cost
of prescription*
£0.62

*Number of women registered with a GP
for contraceptive services*
323,000

Number of dentists
1,798

Number of fillings
3,164,000

Number of extractions
577,000

Average cost of dental course
£36

*Percentage of births by
Caesarean method*
17.6

*Average number of days in maternity
unit for birth of baby*
4

*Percentage of ambulance calls not
answered within target time of 21
minutes in sparsely populated areas*
8

*Percentage of ambulance calls not
answered within target time of 21
minutes in Shetland*
22

*Percentage of ambulance calls not
answered within target time of 21
minutes in Western Isles*
13

*Number of residents aged 65 and over in
Greater Glasgow nursing homes
suffering from HIV or AIDS*
25

*Percentage of residents aged 65 and over
in Scottish nursing homes
suffering from dementia*
33.1

Number of blood donor attendances
303,848

*Number of blood donor attendances
five years ago*
347,648

Number of cases of chickenpox
33,413

Number of cases of mumps
282

Number of cases of malaria
57

Number of cases of food poisoning
10,144

*Percentage of adults aged 16+
smoking cigarettes*
30

*Percentage of secondary school children
who are regular smokers*
14

*Percentage of 12-year-old children
who are regular smokers*
4

Welfare

Number of recipients of Income Support
408,000

*Average weekly award of
Income Support*
£52.76

*Number of recipients of Income Support
for two years or more*
281,000

*Number of recipients of
Family Credit*
70,000

*Average weekly award of
Family Credit*
£56.69

*Number of recipients of
Housing Benefit*
533,000

*Average weekly amount of
Housing Benefit*
£34.40

Number of Cold Weather Payments
462

*Average award of Cold Weather
Payment*
£9

Number of Crisis Loans
149,043

Average award of Crisis Loan
£56

Number of Funeral Payments
6,884

Average award of Funeral Payment
£787

*Number of claimants for Sickness and
Invalidity Benefit*
399,300

*Number of children referred to
Children's Reporters*
26,862

*Number of children referred to
Children's Reporters 10 years ago*
21,865

*Percentage of boys referred for non-
attendance at school*
24

*Percentage of girls referred for non-
attendance at school*
19

Number of children held in secure units
88

Number of home helps
11,266

Number of people receiving home helps
92,754

*Number of people receiving home helps
10 years ago*
71,780

Housing

Number of dwellings
2,246,000

*Percentage of dwellings
owner-occupied*
59.2

*Percentage of dwellings
owner-occupied 10 years ago*
43.1

*Percentage of dwellings rented from
public autorities*
29.7

*Percentage of dwellings rented from
public authorities 10 years ago*
46.9

Number of new dwellings completed
20,686

*Number of new dwellings completed by
public authorities*
241

*Percentage of housing stock below
tolerable standard*
4

*Number of households containing
one person*
2,136,000

*Number of households containing
two or more people*
1,496,000

Average household size
2.4

*Number of sales of
public authority dwellings*
21,656

*Number of sales of public authority
dwellings 10 years ago*
14,275

*Average weekly rent charged by
local authority*
£33.60

*Average weekly rent charged in
Edinburgh*
£45.35

Average weekly rent charged in Angus
£25.14

*Number of homeless people assessed by
local authorities*
41,000

*Number of homeless people assessed by
local authorities 10 years ago*
26,200

Education

Number of publicly-funded schools
3,869

Number of independent schools
114

*Number of pupils in
publicly-funded schools*
816,826

*Number of pupils in
independent schools*
32,782

*Percentage of school pupils taking
school meals*
44.5

*Percentage of pupils entitled to
free school meals*
19.7

Number of primary teachers
22,187

*Percentage of primary teachers
who are women*
91

Number of secondary teachers
23,875

Percentage of pupils staying on to S5
76.5

Percentage of pupils staying on to S6
42.2

Number of school leavers
65,988

*Percentage of school leavers leaving
without SCE qualifications*
6.5

*Percentage of school leavers leaving
without SCE qualifications 10 years ago*
19.3

*Percentage of people of working age with
some kind of qualification*
82

*Percentage of school leavers leaving with
5 or more Higher Grades at A-C*
17.5

*Number of students on
further education courses*
287,098

*Number of students on
full-time higher education courses*
156,997

*Number of students on full-time higher
education courses 10 years ago*
81,640

Getting and spending

Number of working men
1,230,000

Number of working women
1,047,000

Number of people working in manufacturing industries
317,000

Number of people working in hotels and restaurants
129,500

Percentage of workforce who are women
45.9

Number of self-employed men
168,000

Number of self-employed women
63,000

Number of part-time male workers
100,000

Number of part-time female workers
441,000

Percentage of male jobs which are part-time
8.1

Percentage of female jobs which are part-time
42.1

Number of men working in coal mining and peat-extraction
2,300

Number of women working in coal mining and peat-extraction
100

Number of people employed by the Inland Revenue
5,690

Number of people employed by local authority social services
37,241

Number of days lost because of industrial stoppages
52,000

Number of days lost because of industrial stoppages two years ago
71,000

Number of claimants in receipt of unemployment-related benefits for more than two years
16,294

Average gross weekly earnings of full-time male employees
£378

Average gross weekly earnings of full-time female employees
£272

Percentage of full-time male employees earning under £200 a week
11.7

Percentage of full-time female employees earning under £200 a week
31.4

Percentage of male employees earning over £800 a week
3.8

Percentage of households with weekly gross income of under £75
8.3

Percentage of households with weekly gross income of £600 and over
16.6

Average weekly income per household
£367.40

Average weekly household spend on food
£56.08

Average weekly household spend on housing
£39.28

Average weekly household spend on alcohol
£12.28

Average weekly household spend on tobacco
£7.84

Average weekly household spend on fruit and vegetables
£5.59

Crime

Number of crimes and offences
907,525

Number of crimes and offences 10 years ago
843,536

Percentage of crimes cleared up
39

Percentage of housebreaking crimes cleared up
18

Number of non-sexual crimes of violence
19,164

Number of crimes of indecency
7,147

Number of crimes of dishonesty
267,207

Number of drunk driving offences
11,208

Number of speeding offences
91,922

Number of crimes recorded per 10,000 population
821

Number of crimes recorded per 10,000 population five years ago
1,105

Number of homicides
118

Number of homicides 10 years ago
79

Number of crimes and offences in which a firearm was alleged to have been used
1,185·

Number of crimes and offences in which a firearm was alleged to have been used five years ago
1,959

Number of policemen and women
15,050

Number of policemen and women 10 years ago
13,476

Number of drug seizures
13,826

Number of drug seizures 10 years ago
3,414

Number of drivers disqualified
23,205

Number of crimes and offences committed by under-16s
161

Number of people sent to prison
12,134

Number of people sent to prison 10 years ago
9,859

Average daily population in penal establishments
5,862

Average daily population in penal establishments 10 years ago
5,446

Number of adults serving life or indeterminate sentences
443

Number of young offenders serving life or indeterminate sentences
27

The Quality of Life

The quality of life in Scotland is far from uniform. We decided to put broadly perceived regional variations to a specific test by examining how Council areas perform in four key categories.

First, as an index of PROSPERITY (or the lack of it) we looked at the percentage of pupils eligible for free school meals. The Council areas are listed in descending order of economic well-being.

Pupils entitled to free school meals by education authority

Percentage

Scottish average	**19.7**
Aberdeenshire	5.6
Scottish Borders	6.6
Shetland Islands	7.7
Perth and Kinross	8.1
Orkney Islands	8.4
Moray	9.4
East Dunbartonshire	10.0
East Renfrewshire	10.2
Angus	10.4
Dumfries & Galloway	12.0
Western Isles	12.5
Highland	12.9
East Lothian	13.3
Aberdeen City	13.3
Argyll & Bute	13.4
South Ayrshire	15.5
Stirling	16.0
Midlothian	16.5
Fife	17.4
Falkirk	18.1
West Lothian	18.5
Clackmannanshire	20.0
South Lanarkshire	20.4
East Ayrshire	20.5
Dundee City	21.5
Renfrewshire	21.6
Inverclyde	23.9
City of Edinburgh	24.6
North Lanarkshire	24.7
North Ayrshire	25.4
West Dunbartonshire	28.8
Glasgow City	41.4

Next, we researched attitudes to LAW AND ORDER by aggregating the figures for (a) crimes of domestic housebreaking; (b) vandalism; (c) petty assault; (d) breach of the peace. The Council areas are listed in descending order of lawful behaviour.

Selected crimes recorded by the police

Rate per 10,000 population

Scottish average	**463**
Orkney Islands	173
Western Isles	245
Shetland Islands	266
East Renfrewshire	270
Scottish Borders	276
East Dunbartonshire	285
East Lothian	300
Perth and Kinross	325
Stirling	339
Argyll and Bute	341
Aberdeenshire	353
Dumfries and Galloway	368
Midlothian	373
Highland	375
Angus	392
South Lanarkshire	395
Falkirk	398
Clackmannanshire	408
Fife	417
North Ayrshire	417
West Lothian	427
South Ayrshire	437
North Lanarkshire	438
East Ayrshire	440
City of Edinburgh	470
Renfrewshire	522
Inverclyde	530
Moray	531
West Dunbartonshire	567
Dundee City	631
Aberdeen City	632
Glasgow City	747

How to judge the SOCIAL STABILITY of Scottish society? One way is by logging the number of births to unmarried parents registered with different parental addresses (as distinct from the much larger number of unmarried parents registered at the same address and denoting a non-marital permanent relationship).

Live births to unmarried parents registered with different parental addresses

Percentage

Scottish average	**16.1**
Shetland Islands	5.7
Aberdeenshire	6.4
East Renfrewshire	8.2
Moray	8.5
Scottish Borders	9.2
Perth and Kinross	9.7
East Dunbartonshire	9.8
Orkney Islands	9.8
Angus	11.3
Argyll and Bute	11.5
East Lothian	11.5
Highland	11.9
Midlothian	12.0
Western Isles	12.4
Dumfries & Galloway	13.2
West Lothian	13.7
City of Edinburgh	14.0
Aberdeen City	14.3
Fife	14.6
South Lanarkshire	15.3
Stirling	15.6
Falkirk	15.7
Renfrewshire	17.6
East Ayrshire	19.0
North Lanarkshire	19.7
South Ayrshire	19.7
Clackmannanshire	20.1
North Ayrshire	22.3
West Dunbartonshire	23.3
Dundee City	24.4
Inverclyde	24.7
Glasgow City	25.0

Finally, the HEALTH of the nation measured by the number of deaths from heart disease in each Council area.

Deaths from heart disease

Standardised mortality rate

Scottish average	**100**
Scottish Borders	74
East Renfrewshire	76
East Dunbartonshire	77
Stirling	77
Perth and Kinross	82
Aberdeenshire	85
City of Edinburgh	86
Clackmannanshire	87
Moray	89
Western Isles	90

Dundee City	91
South Ayrshire	91
East Lothian	93
Highland	93
Angus	94
Argyll and Bute	95
Shetland	96
Dumfries and Galloway	98
Falkirk	98
Fife	100
Aberdeen City	101
North Ayrshire	101
Renfrewshire	107
Midlothian	111
East Ayrshire	114
West Lothian	114
South Lanarkshire	117
West Dunbartonshire	117
North Lanarkshire	118
Glasgow City	119
Orkney	119
Inverclyde	128

So – where is the most desirable place to live? Averaging results from the four categories produced the following overall result:

1 Scottish Borders
2 East Renfrewshire
3 Aberdeenshire
4 Perth and Kinross
5 East Dunbartonshire
  Shetland
7 Western Isles
8 Orkney
9 East Lothian
10 Moray
11 Angus
12 Argyll and Bute
  Highland
14 Dumfries and Galloway
15 Midlothian
16 Stirling
17 Clackmannanshire
  South Ayrshire
19 Edinburgh
20 Falkirk
  Fife
22 West Lothian
23 Aberdeen City
24 South Lanarkshire
25 Dundee City
26 East Ayrshire
27 Renfrewshire
28 North Ayrshire
29 North Lanarkshire
30 West Dunbartonshire
31 Inverclyde
32 Glasgow City

The Annual Report

*Excerpts from the annual reports of more than 50
prominent Scottish organisations*

Agriculture

**Crofters
Commission**

[1]
More than 30% of respondents to our discussion document referred to the need for employment opportunities in crofting areas. Crofting and agriculture have strong links and crofts provide a base for setting up new innovative businesses. Crofters and their families need part-time flexible jobs to complement income from croft work.

[2]
Some people enter crofting principally to access housing grants, preventing others from a crofting start. This could be averted through finance enabling non-crofters to establish homes in rural communities. A balance must be struck between the need to decroft for housing and other development and the maintenance of a pool of croftland. Crofters should retain the right to decroft their house site and garden ground but the rules should be tightened to allow decrofting only in the local interest.

[3]
Young people are important to crofting. They help retain local services, safeguard traditional croft skills, fuel community activity and bring into use land which has fallen into disrepair. The Croft Entrant Schemes (CES) introduce young people to areas with fragile population structures by encouraging inactive crofters to release crofts. Demand for crofts remains high. More than 200 people are seeking crofts through the scheme but are frustrated by the lack of available crofts.

Annual Report 1998-99

Animals

**Royal
Zoological
Society of
Scotland**

[1]
One of the major achievements this year [at Edinburgh Zoo] was to bring a pair of highly endangered Alaotran gentle lemurs into the collection [of Primates] from the Jersey Wildlife Preservation Trust. They have settled into

their very well designed enclosure, which mimics their natural reed bed habitat. They leap across from vertical position to vertical position, as they do normally in the wild and as we had hoped they would in their new home. The pair has been seen mating by vistitors, so we now wait to see if there will be any offspring in the near future.

[2]
The gorillas have not shown any interest in adding to their group and this may be related to the dour mâle's behaviour.

[3]
The young male ostrich reached maturity this summer and vigorous displays to attract the reluctant female and to repel the keepers have kept all concerned on the move to avoid him.

[4]
The ever-curious penguins have had serious problems with items that they have swallowed. Two died as a result of ice cream sticks swallowed and we have had a change in the type of ice cream offered in the park as a result.

Annual Report 1998

Scottish Society for the Prevention of Cruelty to Animals

[1]
Prosecution of animal abusers by the Inspectors is always the final step in a progressive system aimed at preventing cruelty. In 1998, 89 cases were lodged with Procurators Fiscal with a view to prosecution, and the courts dealt with 113 cases. Farm animal cases and domestic animal cases ran neck-and-neck, with 28 farming prosecutions and 29 domestic. As farm cases almost always involve large numbers of animals, this is a worrying trend. Another serious concern is the long list of cases waiting to be heard in court. Increasingly, however, courts are recognising the seriousness of animal cases and sentencing reflects this. Five people were sent to prison, and 15 were banned, for varying periods, from keeping animals.

[2]
Accidents and environmental problems can take a heavy toll of Scotland's animals, particularly wild animals and birds. Winter storms at sea, just after the start of the grey seal pupping season, brought dozens of seals into Middlebank Wildlife Centre around the New Year. A rare honey buzzard came ashore by fishing boat at Aberdeen,

after becoming exhausted on its migratory route, and was escorted to Gibraltar – courtesy of British Airways and GB Airways – by a Scottish SPCA Inspector.

Annual Report 1998

Arts

Scottish Arts Council

[1]
The Council found itself under attack following a series of difficult, sometimes painful, decisions involving ballet, theatre and film. We took them because we thought they were right, because in circumstances where funding is limited, we do not believe in 'equal misery for all'. Rather, we know that we can only back those organisations and enterprises where there is evidence of excellence, where new audiences are being created, and where the arts engage with the public.

[2]
In the late sixties our predecessors dreamt of a concert hall in Glasgow and a theatre which could show opera during the Edinburgh International Festival. In the late nineties we see these dreams realised, and more: An Tobar on Mull, An Tuireann on Skye and An Lanntair on Lewis, Dundee Contemporary Arts, art.tm and the Eden Court Theatre in Inverness. But, you might say, these are just buildings and the arts are about people. Thirty years ago, no-one thought to ask Scots what they thought about the arts. This year a System 3 survey found that 96% of us believe they give widespread pleasure.

[3]
We are convinced that the arts in general, and music in particular, are in danger of being given less prominence in the school curriculum. Financial pressures and the widespread misperception that the arts are of less importance than other subjects, can lead to them being under threat within hard-pressed local authorities. By working with councils, government, teachers and parents we hope that we can return the arts to their central role in the education of our children. All our research, and there is much of it, shows that an early introduction to the arts has a dramatic effect on the learning ability of young people. It encourages their involvement in learning, it stimulates interest, and it encourages the creative impulse.

Annual Report 1997-98

National Museums of Scotland

The Museum of Scotland opened on St Andrew's Day 1998 to overwhelming popular and critical acclaim. At the royal opening Her Majesty The Queen and His Royal Highness The Duke of Edinburgh were greeted by a fanfare, Musis Aurora Benigna, composed for the occasion by Sir Peter Maxwell Davies and performed by the Scottish Chamber Orchestra Brass Ensemble. The reading of a specially commissioned Gaelic poem by Aonghas Macneacail followed and John Kenny played a replica of NMS's 2,000 year old carnyx (battle trumpet). In her speech the Queen described the Museum as 'a fitting home for all the magnificent objects around us; a home in which to tell their story for our benefit and for the benefit and enjoyment of those who come after us'.

Annual Report 1998-99

National Galleries of Scotland

[1]
After extended public debate, the Trustees of the National Galleries of Scotland settled on converting the old Post Office Building in George Square, Glasgow, into a National Gallery of Scottish Art and Design, in which it was intended to house Scottish painting, sculpture, drawings, prints, architecture, design, photography, and philately. The Post Office Board co-operated closely with us on this venture, and agreed to transfer their own museum from London to form part of the complex. The building was also intended to provide two excellent restaurants, a good shop, and ample temporary exhibition space. The debate was sharply polarised, with general enthusiasm and support for the scheme in Glasgow and the west but widespread hostility in Edinburgh and the east. However, the Heritage Lottery Fund turned down this exciting and ambitious scheme which, had it been on the banks of the Thames, may have had more chance of success.

Next, the Trustees decided on a more modest scheme at half the price. This was in the Old Sheriff Court, off Ingram Street, Glasgow, and on a smaller scale. After more public debate, this was also rejected by the Heritage Lottery Fund. So, after a great deal of staff time and considerable expenditure by the Glasgow Development Agency, some 70% of our Scottish collections are now condemned to remain in store for the foreseeable future and, regrettably, Glasgow still remains a city neglected by the National Galleries of Scotland.

[2]
Because Edinburgh (and indeed Scotland) has such a

small population, it is not easy to attract substantial sponsorship and major exhibitions. Indeed, until Scotland has greatly-improved communications and boasts a real international airport, it will continue to be difficult to persuade the art world to venture north – other than for the annual Edinburgh International Festival. Outwith the realms of Scottish art, portraiture, and photography, our collections are still significantly smaller and less comprehensive than the much more generously Government-supported national institutions south of the border. We are very fortunate to have had on loan since 1945 a magnificent group of pictures from the Duke of Sutherland's collection for, without them, the National Galleries of Scotland would have no paintings by Raphael or Titian. For fourteenth and fifteenth-century European pictures, the National Gallery, Trafalgar Square, boasts the *entire* Sainsbury Wing, but we have only one small gallery. No painting by Durer or Stubbs is in Edinburgh. Nothing by Michelangelo exists in Scotland. If Edinburgh, or indeed Scotland, is to become more self-sufficient artistically, it must surely be argued that greater resources should be made available to us in order to acquire masterpieces that will stimulate our population. If, with current-day prices, this is politically difficult to achieve, then at least many more items could be distributed to us in Scotland making use of 'in lieu' tax procedures.

From Director's Report in Review 1994-97

Edinburgh International Festival

The decision by the Festival Fringe to move its dates a week earlier than the International Festival in 1998 caused a great deal of controversy and debate. We greatly regret this split and believe that it is damaging to the long term health of the Festival City, as it dilutes the impact of the combined events, which is unique in the world. It is not possible for the Edinburgh International Festival to follow suit. We plan and contract artists up to three or four years ahead, which means that we are unable to make any move in the short term. In the longer term, moving our dates earlier would make it impossible for us to present many of the best international companies and orchestras. European holidays for many leading companies, coupled with the schedules of other major festivals such as Saltzburg, mean that these organisations are often not available to us until late August or early September.

Annual Report 1998

Business

Scottish Enterprise

[1]

We have always been clear that sustainable prosperity in Scotland needs successful Scottish companies. This is particularly important in the small- and medium-sized sectors which form the most powerful centre for growth. During the year, the Government set a target of creating 100,000 new Scottish companies over the next 10 years and in the last year we have made solid progress towards that goal.

[2]

Clusters development depends on a number of different players working together on a common programme of new and creative activities. Each player encourages excellence in the others, and each plays a part in creating the result. For example, an economic cluster will bring together manufacturing, research and development, education, services, infrastructure provision and distribution. It will also include the private, public and third sectors, all working competitively towards the same goal. The Alba Centre in Livingston is Scotland's leading centre towards the next generation of microprocessor technology. By combining up-to-date technology and research, infrastructure and services, it is the perfect example of the clusters approach.

Annual Report 1998-99

Highlands and Islands Enterprise

[1]

This is not the desperately impoverished region that it once was. But it remains a place where wages are, on average, lower than they should be; where poor housing still has to be eradicated; where by no means everyone is able to realise their potential in the way we should like.

We have to cope constructively with short-term threats of the kind arising from the problems and uncertainties affecting agriculture, the fishing industry, salmon farming and our fabrication yards – yards which, incidentally, have provided some of the best paid employment to be found in the Highlands and Islands. We have to build on our growing portfolios of modern technological and knowledge-based industries in sectors including biochemical, pharmaceutical, software development and information and communication technology.

More fundamentally, we have to ensure – not least by means of Iomairt aig an Oir or Initiative at the Edge – that expanding economies and rising populations become the rule right across our area. What has been achieved in localities like Skye, I believe, can be achieved in localities like Kintyre, the Western Isles and south-east Sutherland as well. Difficulties whose origins lie deep in our past will not be eradicated overnight, however. Indeed they will not be eradicated at all unless all of us in the Highlands and Islands work together for the Highlands and Islands' betterment.

Chairman's Foreword, Annual Report, 1998-99

Scottish Financial Enterprise

Financial services in Scotland had an exceptionally vibrant year in 1998. The profitability of the banks, for example, and their acknowledged excellence and record of innovation has been recognised as amongst the best in the world and was achieved at a time when many other banking systems were plainly struggling. The same was true of the life sector, which featured not only excellent conventional growth but an unprecedented number of novel ventures. Likewise, the performance of the independent investment management sector was in aggregate excellent, earning accolades and spinning off yet more new ventures and products. Employment growth has been powerful in almost all areas of the industry, pushing it even further towards the front as one of Scotland's core industries.

Annual Report 1998

Scottish Council Development and Industry

[1]
As we review the last year, major factors have emerged: the strength of sterling, allied to persistently high interest rates, has caused profound problems for our manufacturers and exporters. Preparation for the introduction of the Euro has become an increasingly urgent issue and low oil prices have disturbed many economies. Volatile market conditions in a world of instantly mobile capital have revealed the fragility of reliance on inward investments. This last year has been difficult and the next will probably be more so. Scotland will continue to be confronted with questions over its ability to compete in a world economy and to create the wealth that it requires to fund its many aspirations.
[2]
Scotland remains inhibited by skills shortages in some of our most important industries. The eclipse of traditional apprenticeships has been lamented and members report widespread recruitment difficulties. The skills of our

workforce in adapting to ever challenging circumstances in production processes, technology and know-how are crucial to our future.

Annual Report 1997-98

Scottish Tourist Board

[1]
The drop [in total visitor spend] is disappointing...The effect of a strong pound had already slowed down the rate of growth in the previous year and played some part this year not only in deterring visitors from some European countries whose currency had weakened dramatically against the pound, but more significantly in making the cost of holidays abroad more attractive in cost terms to the English and Scots themselves.

[2]
It is almost axiomatic that visitors from abroad do not come to Scotland for the weather and do not regard it as a deterrent. Native Scots however can quite understandably get a bit fed up of dreich days and the prospect of guaranteed sunshine abroad can prove more attractive when there is a continuous spell of bad weather at home. Nonetheless we must redouble our efforts to convince the Scots themselves of the pleasures of finding out more about their own country.

Annual Report 1998-99

Children

Scottish Children's Reporter Administration

[1]
The incidence of children being brought to the Reporter's notice continues to increase. Nevertheless, there is evidence that while more children were referred due to concerns about their care or protection, the overall level of offending by children and young people was stable, in comparison to previous years.

[2]
The reduction in the number of child protection orders granted, as compared to the number of place of safety orders granted under the previous legislation, is far from surprising since a major element of the new provisions [of the 1995 Children (Scotland) Act] was the introduction of a higher threshold test for granting of an order...It is less easy to account for the increased number of children detained, either in custody or in a place of safety, after

being charged with committing a crime or offence...Finally, there remains as much scope for concern about some children who are not referred to the Reporter, as about those who are. The 1995 Act introduced one wholly new ground for referral of a child to the Reporter: that he or she has misused alcohol or any drug. But persistent indications of increased drug misuse among children and young people do not yet appear to be reflected in the pattern of reporting under this new provision. The answer may lie partly in the time required for all referring agencies to become familiar with the new ground for referral, and partly in the low availability at present of drug treatment services dedicated to under-16 age groups.

Annual Report 1997-98

Children 1st (Royal Scottish Society for Prevention of Cruelty to Children)

[1]
Of the thousand or so children we supported last year, many had been harmed by physical, sexual and emotional abuse. Considerable sums are spent investigating abuse and prosecuting perpetrators, but little is invested in victims and their needs. There is an urgent requirement for more services for the treatment and recovery of abused children. The opening of our Aberdeen centre in November 1998, in conjunction with the City Council, will help, but there is still far too little provision of this kind of sevice.
[2]
Society is more aware these days of the extent of domestic violence, but attention tends to focus on the abused partner. Children are the forgotten victims. They see and hear what is going on, they may live in fear or be traumatised. This may show itself in bed-wetting, aggressive behaviour, or withdrawal.

Annual Review 1998

Conservation and Environment

Historic Scotland

[1]
Not all of our monuments are prehistoric or medieval. The project to review the state of military structures erected around our shores during the two World Wars – the 20th century equivalent of earlier fortifications – is nearing completion and work is now progressing on the best way to preserve these fragile structures for future generations.

[2]

A key element to recording our built heritage is the listing of historic buildings. During the year the review of Scotland's buildings continued with the completion of burghs such as Montrose and Kirkwall, and the larger part of Ayr.

[3]

Historic Scotland is often required to deal with treasures from our past with particular sensitivity. This was the case in June when we returned the casket believed to contain the heart of Robert the Bruce to Melrose Abbey on the anniversary of the Battle of Bannockburn.

Annual Report 1998-99

National Trust for Scotland

...in the countryside three very important developments took place during the past year. First, after a three-year study by a specially appointed crofting working group, the Trust has developed a policy framework for the overall management of crofting activity on its six crofting estates of Balmacara, Canna, Fair Isle, Iona, Kintail and Torridon. Secondly, the Trust has supported proposals for the establishments of National Parks for Loch Lomond and the Trossachs and for the Cairngorms which contain, respectively, the Trust properties of Ben Lomond and the Mar Lodge Estate. It has also supported the establishment of working parties to consider other potential National Trust areas. Thirdly, after three years of field work under Trust supervision, an important conservation handbook on grazing in upland areas was published, funded by the European Union Life Programme. The handbook is expected to assist land managers across Europe in managing their mountain and upland habitats.

Annual Report 1997-98

Royal Fine Art Commission for Scotland

[1]

It is implicit in the policy of each planning authority that everyone should benefit from a high standard of amenity. To achieve this in a balanced and creative way the new [planning] authorities must be discriminating in the work of persuading developers and deciding planning applications. All sites where industrial development is encouraged, and not just those of the utmost significance, require the character as well as the quality of any intervention to be right. To ensure that great damage is not done to places of outstanding architectural or landscape quality, they need to be planned recognising their special importance. We therefore see standardisation of systems and the application of routine practices as threats to the successful planning, design, development, maintenance and improvement of our surroundings.

[2]

Good planning requires understanding of the settings of the historic buildings for which Scotland is especially renowned, its relics of past enmities in the form of castles and forts; its celebration of peaceful times, its Churches, public buildings and country houses; and its mills, docks and other industrial developments.

The ends of conservation can be given a substantial boost by the new authorities but there must always be developments which provide opportunities for ambitious new architecture and the reorganisation and integration of private motor traffic and public transport. Our special plea is that planning authorities and their officials should recognise the constant need for design quality; not merely as a desirable "add on" (for who could argue against that?) but as the means of upgrading areas, prolonging the life expectation of developments, ensuring that owners sustain their properties, and generally enhancing life for those in their part of Scotland.

Report for 1996

Scottish Civic Trust

Retail developments figured particularly strongly in the annual load of casework. Government planning policy has at last altered to discourage further development of out-of-town supermarkets and other large stores, with the result that developers have begun to concentrate on sites close to or within town centres. These happen regularly to border or impinge on Conservation Areas, listed buildings and their settings. Such projects invariably seek large areas of dedicated car parking, and frequently a petrol filling station, altogether occupying much more space than the supermarket building itself. The Trust commented on schemes of this kind at Forfar, Lanark, Greenock and most notably at Kelso. Here a developer, faced with competition from rivals seeking other sites, even proposed to take and rebuild a large early 19th-century B-listed villa to make way for his project. The Trust strongly opposed this application, recommending other sites as more suitable.

The rush to build more shopping space has also been intense in the cities. In central Glasgow, Buchanan Street and its neighbourhood has seen demand probably unprecedented since Edwardian times. The Trust made comment on a number of costly schemes for retail use of landmark listed buildings such as the General Post Office, Lanarkshire House, the Stock Exchange and the Athenaeum Theatre, in addition to prominent banks and former hotels. Many of these involved the loss of some original internal quality, balanced to varying degrees by a commitment to restore the external fabric to a high standard.

The trend was less to be seen in Edinburgh, except for the most ambitious project of all – to create an underground shopping mall beneath the whole western section of Princes Street. Together with other independent commentators, the Trust considered it unwise to approve the scheme in principle without first considering its likely effect on the amenity of the adjacent Gardens, the means of servicing it and evidence of the design quality of links to the outside world. In the capital, the conspicuous current boom is rather in hotels.

Annual Report 1997-98

Association for the Protection of Rural Scotland

[1]
Advertisements and their prominence in the countryside has long been of concern to APRS, and it was one of the major achievements of the post-war planning system to recognise these concerns in the 1961 regulations. Recently, advertising hoardings and a proliferation of roadside signs, and intrusively located and lighted motorway gantry signs, have given rise to concern over the effectiveness of current controls.

[2]
APRS maintained its objection to the construction of a wind power station at Craigenlee Fell near Portpatrick on the grounds of visual impact and loss of amenity. The Association considers individual wind farm applications each on their own merit, with particular regard to landscape impact. APRS encourages the use of renewable energy and favours wind farms which are sited appropriately.

Annual Report 1998

Consumers

Citizens Advice Scotland

[1]
Only a few weeks ago I visited a bureau in the Borders. Using devil advocates through Citizens Advice Scotland Free Representation Unit, the bureau was able to

represent seven clients with appeals against unfair selection for redundancy. The hearing lasted twelve days. Although the bureau had yet to hear the tribunal's decision, win or lose these clients had been given the opportunity to state their case at a hearing. The CAB was the only organisation who would take on this representation in the area, as the clients had been turned down by other solicitors.

[2]

Consumer debt continued to be the largest single problem bureaux dealt with...This upward trend in debt problems is also reflected in the ever-increasing number of clients using CAB money advice services. There is no single reason for these increases, but factors include the rapidly expanding consumer credit sector's new products and marketing techniques encouraging the consumer to borrow ever more. Low income clients face difficulties obtaining credit at reasonable rates of interest, and are more likely to receive unreasonable demands from creditors.

Annual Report 1998-99

North of Scotland Electricity Consumers' Committee

The severe storms which started on Boxing Day and continued through to the New Year affected over 80,000 Scottish Hydro-Electric customers. The company decided that it would not make compensation payments to all customers who had been without supply for more than 24 hours, and was the only company affected by the storms to take such a decision...Customers in Scottish Hydro-Electric's area have consumption which is 1/3 above the United Kingdom average and have the poorest availability of supply, and yet individual compensation payments are hardly ever made. The Committee believe that this falls short of how a customer-oriented company should be acting and will be continuing discussions with the company to introduce a much-improved level of compensation payments for customers off supply for lengthy periods.

Annual Report 1998-99

Southern Scotland Electricity Consumers' Committee

Last year the big story was quality of supply when the worst storms ever recorded paralysed ScottishPower's supply network leaving thousands of consumers in the Borders off supply for extended periods. That situation highlighted a problem area where the Committee felt that the company could do better and with Committee pressure it did. So much so that by the end of the year the company had new emergency procedures in place, confirmed more capital would be put into the network and made compensation payments to more than 3,300 customers. The Committee was, of course, pleased that the company had shown an immediate willingness to improve its services and commended the move to pay compensation. However the event opened up a whole new debate involving quality of supply, guaranteed standards payments and severe weather exemptions.

Annual Report 1997-98

Rail Users' Consultative Committee for Scotland

[1]
Readers of newspapers and television viewers can be forgiven for believing that rail services are going from bad to worse. All we seem to hear about is cancelled or late trains, overcrowded trains, safety problems and escalating complaints statistics. In short, a picture of an extremely poor service, and, of course, some of this is true, but it is emphatically not the case with internal Scottish rail services. ScotRail is top of the class, the best performing rail company in the country. Scotland's rail travellers must be the envy of passengers in other parts of the country.

[2]
The Committee found it difficult to understand why Railtrack, with a guaranteed and substantial income stream from the Train Operating Companies (chiefly ScotRail), in the form of Track Access Charges, was unable to commit the company to definite projects where there is a clear need for replacement and enhancement of existing facilities, e.g. the route btween Aberdeen and Inverness.

[3]
[Comfort] has been an area of concern to the Committee, which has been increasingly aware of the improved levels of comfort offered not only in private cars but in coaches and buses over the last 10 years, whereas rail vehicle interiors have not significantly changed.

From Annual Report 1997-98

Education

Scottish Community Education Council

By May 1997 participation rates in lifelong learning in Scotland had become amongst the lowest in the European Union. Social exclusion and educational inequality had widened, 600,000 adult Scots had functional literacy problems, yet only 1% now received adult basic education support. The democratic deficit in relation to Westminster, Brussels and corporate/media power and the poor turnout in local elections by the young and within deprived communities was a growing cause for concern.

Annual Report 1997-98

Scottish Qualifications Authority

[1]
The formation of the Scottish Qualifications Authority on 1 April 1997, by merging the functions of SCOTVEC and the Scottish Examination Board, was a significant event in the history of Scottish education. It was the first step towards the realisation of many long-term goals: closing the gap between academic and vocational qualifications, the creation of a simple and flexible qualifications framework, and a system of credit transfer which will increase access and make progression easier.

[2]
In the course of this first year, we have become clearer about what we want to achieve as an organisation. Our mission statement refers to our role in enhancing lifelong learning – we have a major contribution to make to the lifelong learning agenda by developing a qualifications system which is flexible enough to provide opportunities for all kinds of learners in a wide range of settings. Because we have responsibility for all types of qualification (except degrees) we also have a wonderful opportunity to build a national qualifications framework which is coherent, with qualifications liked in clear progression pathways, and simple – and therefore well understood by the Scottish public. The most important characteristic of our qualifications – all our qualifications – is that they must be based on rigorous standards. The commitment to clear and consistent standards is at the heart of everything we do.

Annual Report 1997-98

Scottish Higher Education Funding Council

Between 1985 and 1995 the percentage of the population aged 25-59 who gained a higher education qualification moved from 11% to 20%. Whilst this growth is impressive, the Council believes that a higher education qualification target for this age group of 50% by 2010 is required if Scotland is to remain internationally competitive.

Annual Report 1997-98

Environment

Scottish Natural Heritage

[1]
During the year we were able to demonstrate the importance of the natural heritage and its better use and management in a wide variety of ways. We identified the substantial number of jobs created directly and indirectly as a result of Scotland's heritage of wildlife and landscape. We were able to demonstrate many new practices. For instance, in arable farming our manual on Targeted Inputs for a Better Rural Environment advised on new techniques which could benefit both farmers' livelihoods and the natural heritage of these areas. Our 'Plants for Wildlife' initiative demonstrated how everyone with access to a window-box or garden could contribute to wildlife diversity on their own doorstep. The collaborative research with other partners, particularly at Langholm, demonstrated how objective scientific endeavour could inform how to improve the management of grouse moors and at the same time secure the continuing protection of wild birds.

[2]
The European beaver has been extinct in the British Isles since at least the 16th century. We have now conducted studies which suggest that we could bring the beaver back to Scotland, without any habitat restoration, and that Scotland could eventually support a population of up to 1,000 animals in the wild.

[3]
Since 1957 the island of Rum has been in public ownership and managed as a National Nature Reserve (NNR). Our vision for Rum is that it should not only be biologically more diverse and productive, but that it should also have the potential to sustain a larger human community than can be accommodated today, without compromising the island's natural environment. Before 1957, Rum was known as the 'forbidden island'. Since then it has welcomed tens of thousands of visitors. It is our intention that Rum will continue to play a vital role in the local economy.

[4]
Fishermen and environmentalists are often perceived to be at loggerheads over marine issues, but this year a major breakthrough was made in the search for a common understanding. A new agreement was forged with Shetland's sandeel fishermen, which aims to secure sustainable economic development while protecting

internationally important seabird colonies...[the agreement] allows fishermen to catch up to 7,000 tonnes of sandeels a year, more than twice the previous Total Allowable Catch, and prevents fishing from 1 June to 31 July when the demand for sandeels from seabirds is at its highest.

[5]

We worked with two communities and two local authorities on either side of the Clyde to develop two very different Local Nature Reserves. Coves Community Park on the south shore of the Clyde is a gentle mixture of grasslands and open water situated high above the towns of Gourock and Greenock. Looking across the water you might just spot Duchess Wood rising behind Helensburgh. Duchess Wood has an altogether different mood; here the open vistas of Coves Community Park are replaced with enclosing gorge walls and soaring trees. The two reserves are, however, linked by more than the Clyde. They testify to the determination of the local communities to secure the protection of well-loved natural areas.

[6]

Scottish Natural Heritage, the Millennium Forest Scotland Trust (MFST) and the Central Scotland Countryside Trust funded a project which seeks to consolidate and expand the surviving native woodland resource in the Central Belt by extending existing woodland through the planting of native trees. This Native Woodlands Initiative will provide a substantial proportion of eventual forest. A project report is in preparation; it is expected to recommend greater community involvement with native woodlands and, where MFST is already involved, to provide better links with communities. This reflects the increasing interest of communities in non-commercial woodlands for recreation and for the enjoyment of their landscapes.

Annual Report 1997-98

Scottish Environment Protection Agency

[1]

...the trend of progressive improvement in river quality may have slowed down, and even been reversed in some areas.

[2]

Overall there was a modest improvement in the conditions of coastal waters around Scotland with 16.7km of unsatisfactory and seriously polluted waters eliminated. Significant improvements occurred along the

Fife coastline of the Firth of Forth and west of North Berwick, as a result of new sewage treatment schemes commissioned by East of Scotland Water, with smaller improvements also recorded on the Ayrshire coast...However, unsatisfactory continuous and intermittent sewage discharges are still the primary cause of poor quality and caused deteriorations at Kinghorn, Burntisland, Cramond, Portobello and along 11.3km of the coastline in North Region.

[3]
In the 1997 bathing season, 18 out of Scotland's 23 identified bathing waters complied with the mandatory standards...This compares with 21 sites which complied in the 1996 bathing season. SEPA is jointly funding an investigation with the West of Scotland Water Authority to identify the reasons for failure of the standards at the five bathing waters which do not comply with the Directive's requirements.

[4]
Following advice from SEPA to the Scottish Office, an Order under the Food and Environment Protection Act was placed prohibiting the harvesting of all seafoods in an area of sea adjacent to Dounreay. This followed the discovery of an area of the sea-bed contaminated with fragments of spent nuclear fuel. During the year, SEPA in conjunction with the National Radiological Protection Board began a detailed study into the likelihood of encounter and the consequences these fragments might have on human health and the environment.

From Annual Report 1997-98

Government

Scottish Trades Union Congress

Working according to the principles of the Constitutional Steering Group, it [the Scottish Parliament] will be a Parliament of a new type – elected by a fairer voting system, transparent in its operations and open to the needs and demands of Scottish civil society, including the Trade Union Movement. It will disappointingly have very few – perhaps no – black faces, a failure that must be remedied in the second set of elections: but it will almost certainly have a higher percentage of women than any other legislature in the world, and that advance owes a great, great deal to the work of the STUC Women's Committee.

General Council Annual Report 1999

Accounts Commission for Scotland

[1]
...Councils made considerable efforts to improve the inspection of residential care homes and food hygiene inspections. However, much remains to be done in reducing the level of tenants' rent arrears and increasing the amount of household waste recycled. Generally, small improvements have been made in some functions but there has been no marked reduction in the gap between good and poor performers. There was an early warning signal that the performance of fire brigades in responding to fires in major town centres and built-up areas might be slipping.

[2]
Our study found wide variations in the proportions of council tax collected within the year by local authorities. Some of the factors affecting collection levels (deprivation, population density) are beyond councils' control but the audit revealed wide variations due to differences in collection and debt recovery practices.

[3]
Two separate cases were reported where former employees [of local authorities] continued to be paid and accept salaries after the date of termination of their employment. In each case the amount involved was about £25,000.

Annual Report 1998

Convention of Scottish Local Authorities (COSLA)

[1]
A visitor to Scotland trying to find out about local government in 1998-99 might have gained the impression from some parts of the media that Scottish local government was awash with sleaze and incompetence in its Direct Labour Organisations. The role of the media in exposing shortcomings in any public service is invaluable and healthy; the public have a right to expect both the highest standards of conduct and of performance. But sometimes the facts are not allowed to get in the way of a 'good story' and the failings in one or two councils can all too quickly be translated as the shortcomings of local government as a whole.

[2]
We need to remember that local government was in the vanguard in the argument for a Scottish Parliament. We must be realistic, not defensive, about the Parliament, open as much to its opportunities for the joint better government of Scotland as to the danger of us becoming

over-defensive and introspective in our relationship with it. Our legitimacy lies in our own hands, in the quality of our own performance and the depth of our support in our own communities.

Annual Report 1998-99

Local Government Ombudsman

It is worthy of note that, while complaints to my office in the last year have risen only marginally, complaints about planning issues have increased by more than 25%. It is abundantly clear that, in relation to planning matters, the public not only wish to be consulted but also expect Councils to pay heed to what they say. The other area which has caused me concern during the year is the arrangements which are in place for dealing with complaints against senior police officers. It does not seem to me that the current system, whereby such complaints are dealt with by police authorities themselves, can realistically be expected to inspire public confidence.

Annual Report 1998-99

Council on Tribunals, Scottish Committee

We acknowledge the arguments for the speedy suspension of a councillor facing serious allegations of misconduct, but we strongly advocate that this provision should only be exercised very sparingly, after the most careful consideration and only where the allegations are sufficient to justify that action. [Comment on powers of proposed Standards Commission.]

Annual Report 1997-98

Health

Health Education Board for Scotland

Without concerted action across all sectors to counter those life circumstances which generate ill-health, such as poverty, unemployment, social exclusion, poor housing and dispiriting community environments, we can but scrape at the surface of Scotland's preventable ills, and we cannot put right the injustice of health inequalities. At the same time as tackling disadvantaged circumstances which predispose to ill-health, we as a nation and communities must do what we can to identify and nurture those sorts of life circumstances that create good health. In so doing we should acknowledge that good health is not just 'not being ill'. It also has to do with physical, mental and social well-being, fitness, quality of life, self-confidence, a sense of purpose and worth, and the development of individuals, families, communities and society as a whole.

Annual Report 1997-98

Mental Welfare Commission for Scotland

[1]
...The Commission has been pleased to note many significant changes in a positive therapeutic direction over the last few years [at the State Hospital, Carstairs], while security has also been strengthened. Patient facilities have been significantly upgraded with new building and refurbishment and are now all situated on what was the west site. The bleak East Wing has now been demolished and replaced by a ploughed field. There have been welcome developments in Psychology and Occupational Therapy staffing. Recorded use of seclusion (supervised confinement in a locked room for protection of the patient and others in psychiatric emergencies) has declined to a very low level.

[2]
Both the Commission and the State Hospital remain very concerned about the welfare and rights of patients who remain in the State Hospital long after it has been agreed by all concerned that they no longer require high security, because of delays in their being able to move to a suitable facility in a local hospital – sometimes because no such facility exists. This is wrong and unacceptable...In the last year, the Commission has very strongly taken up the cases of three men with learning disabilities who were considered fit to leave the State Hospital in 1995 and are still there. Their local base would be Merchiston Hospital but it lacks forensic facilities and has been considered unsuitable.

[3]
Although the Mental Health Act regulates intervention with mail, it is silent about staff in relation to patients' telephone calls. While security sometimes requires intervention, the Commission was concerned to note in June 1997 that the hospital's written policy was that *all* patient phone calls would be monitored by staff. Despite being assured that practice differed from this policy, the Commission took an interest in the revision of the policy and is now satisfied that privacy in phone calls is decided on an individual basis.

Annual Report 1997-98

Scottish Ambulance Service

While paramedics have been trained in sophisticated cardiac monitoring techniques for many years, our decision to introduce automated defibrillators into each of our front line accident and emergency ambulances allowed our staff to provide improved patient care. It also met our objective of bringing more hospital services closer to patients. This drive was further strengthened last year by the consolidation of Emergency Telephone Instruction (EMTI) which allows specially trained staff in our operations rooms to advise those people making emergency calls on the treatment they might appropriately give until our specially trained people arrive.

Annual Report 1998-99

Housing

Scottish Homes

Tackling the causes of homelessness is a major plank in the Government's social inclusion strategy and the past twelve months saw Scottish Homes make a significant contribution in helping homeless people find a house of their own...Projects such as the £2.4 million Aberdeen Foyer which provides housing for up to 27 vulnerable young people is an example of our commitment to make an effective contribution to the reduction of homelessness. Across Scotland, funding by the agency helped provide permanent accommodation for 2,300 homeless people during the year.

Annual Report 1998-99

Scottish Federation of Housing Associations

New Housing Partnerships represent both a threat and an opportunity to tenants. The threat is that large local authorities will take the apparently easy option of taking their housing departments and placing them lock, stock and barrel into the private sector. The opportunity is that, after careful consultation with tenants, councils will involve existing housing associations and help create new bodies which will provide their tenants with the homes they want at rents they can afford...We are determined that tenants should be involved in shaping the proposals for their communities; and that any changes should be first and foremost for their benefit.

Annual Report 1998-99

Law

Scottish Legal Services Ombudsman

[1]
In my Report last year I expressed my concern with the leniency of a number of the sanctions imposed by the [Scottish Solicitors' Discipline] Tribunal. Subsequently I had a valuable meeting with its Chairman and the Clerk to the Tribunal. The Chairman was firmly of the view that it was not within my remit to be critical of the Tribunal's decisions. I agreed that my remit was silent on the subject, but as I noted in my Report, the Tribunal's findings represent the end result of a disciplinary process which often starts within the Law Society. It would therefore be illogical of me to criticise the Law Society's handling of complaints and not make myself familiar with and comment on those cases which the Law Society prosecutes before the Tribunal. At a more recent meeting with the Chairman, we discussed cases dealt with in the course of 1998. Again, I was disturbed by the level of understanding shown towards a number of solicitors who were found guilty of professional misconduct and who had had their practising certificates restricted as opposed to being struck off, despite having demonstrated either dishonesty or a total disregard for their clients' affairs. In one case the solicitor had been found guilty of misappropriation, but the Tribunal 'held back from imposing the ultimate sanction' because he was under pressure and did not have the maturity to recognise his duty to follow established procedures. The solicitor was 33 years of age, some 10 years older than Mr Pitt the Younger when he became Prime Minister. To my mind that is not looking after the interests of the public, and at a time when certain sections of the press are baying for an end to self-regulation, I believe that the independent Tribunal should recognise that a solicitor who misappropriates or consistently fails clients should lose the right to practise within the profession.

[2]
Important changes have been implemented by the Law Society as regards the way in which it deals with complaints...but I suggest that the Society has been its own worst enemy when it comes to putting forward the case for self-regulation, as I believe it has failed to add to the informed debate by getting its message across to the public, a message about the changes that have taken place and its plans for dealing with complaints.

Annual Report 1998

Scottish Consumer Council

Following concerns raised by various sources on the effectiveness of the Law Society of Scotland's complaints procedure, the SCC carried out, with the co-operation of the Law Society, a major survey of the experiences of complainants. The research provided considerable evidence of consumer dissatisfaction with the way in which complaints about solicitors are handled in Scotland both by solicitors and the Law Society. The SCC believes that there is an urgent need for both to adopt a more client-centred approach to dealing with complaints. The report suggests a number of ways in which the present system could be improved in the interests of consumers. However, such changes would not go far enough. It is essential that complaints are dealt with by a body which is seen to be independent and impartial. The fundamental root of the problem from the consumer's point of view is that the Law Society is seen as being on the side of the solicitor. The only effective solution to the problem is the establishment of an independent review body to deal with complaints about solicitors in Scotland...

Annual Report 1998-99

Law Society of Scotland

I have, on a number of occasions, nailed my colours to the mast in relation to self-regulation. I think we do it very well, although there is always room for improvement.

Presidential Foreword to Annual Report 1998

Scottish Legal Aid Board

The coming year will see the new registration system for criminal legal aid practitioners come into effect and the Public Defence Solicitors' Office opening its doors in Edinburgh. We will be heavily involved in ensuring that registered solicitors comply with the Code of Practice and will be closely monitoring the PDSO pilot.

Annual Report 1997-98

Scottish Law Commission

Long leasehold tenure has many of the characteristics of ownership. Leases for periods of 999 years, or leases subject to indefinite rights of renewal, are in practice if not in law equivalent to perpetual feus. They were recognised as such by some landlords. Many were granted because of restrictions on the power to feu. The problems caused by these leases are well documented. Tenants, on expiry of their leases, lose possession of their homes which, in some cases, they or members of their family have built. They may be entitled to no compensation or to inadequate compensation. They may have to pay large sums to their landlord to buy back property which they regard as their own. Under our Fifth Programme of Law Reform we set ourselves the objective of examining leasehold tenure, in particular long leases of residential subjects, as a long-term project.

We have not yet started work on the project and are unlikely to do so until after we have completed our projects on feudal tenure and real burdens. However, our work on leasehold casualties has highlighted the wider problem as to the future of ultra-long leasehold tenure...There is a strong argument that the interest of the tenant under a lease for several hundred years should be converted into outright ownership on payment of compensation to the landlord. Several respondents to our discussion paper on leasehold casualties advocated this solution to the problem of leasehold casualties. While we were not persuaded by these arguments, the abolition of leasehold casualties will make it easier to deal with the problems of ultra-long leasehold tenure.

Annual Report 1997-98

Scottish Court Service

As a whole, the mix of Sheriff Court criminal business has moved upwards in terms of seriousness, with less serious criminal offences being taken in the District Courts and through alternative disposals. New solemn criminal cases in the Sheriff Court have increased by 11% since 1995. High Court business continues to grow. It is anticipated that the overall trend of increasing seriousness will continue. The proportion of cases which proceed to trial or proof is one of the most significant variables for SCS. This proportion continues to grow.

Annual Report 1998-99

Scottish Prison Complaints Commission

[1]
Appeals against verdicts and punishments imposed in orderly rooms, where governors adjudicate on allegations of breaches of discipline within the prison by prisoners, continue to constitute the subject matter of the most common applications to the Commission. While the Commission remains concerned about the way in which many orderly rooms are conducted, it is perhaps not surprising that they form such a large part of the Commission's business. Not only is the very existence of an appeals mechanism comparatively recent, but the

procedures are also relatively familiar to prisoners so that any sense of grievance is much more likely to be followed up by use of the appeals mechanism than in areas where prisoners have less familiarity. Security categories are the second biggest class of cases coming to the Commission, partly again because of the increased openness in making these decisions and issuing the reasons for them under the 1994 Rules. Prisoners also see a reduction in their security category as a milestone in progressing through their sentence and are naturally concerned if they fail to meet targets which they set for themselves. Equally, an increase in security category represents a significant backward step and may thus cause a sense of grievance. Visits are crucially important to many prisoners and most of the complaints referred to the Commission relate to prisoners having been placed on 'closed visit' conditions, where there is no possibility of physical contact with visitors, as a result of a decision by the governor that ordinary visit conditions may be abused, usually for the introduction of illicit items to the prison.

[2]
The applicant [in a case before the Commission] complained that the governor of the prison in which he was detained had intercepted the applicant's correspondence, copied some of it and sent these copies to the police. The governor-in-charge accepted in his response that 'Since April we have passed copies of six letters to the police at their request'. The governor had provided this response to the prisoner in a purely descriptive fashion. The Commission sought from the governor a justification for this action. We had expected either that there was a warrant from the police for this to be done or that the letters had contained information relating to the commission of a crime. We were informed that neither of these circumstances applied. It thus appeared to the Commission that there had been a clear breach of the prisoner's rights in relation to his correspondence and we recommended that this should be brought to the attention of the governor, and a formal apology should be issued to the prisoner and that compensation should be paid to the prisoner. The Chief Executive [of the Scottish Prison Service] accepted these recommendations, though there was further discussion on the precise nature of the compensation to be paid to the prisoner before agreement was reached.

Annual Report 1998

Media

BBC Scotland The development of digital technology is revolutionising broadcasting and telecommunications. It is affecting everything we do: from the way we make programmes through to the range and type of services we can deliver. The year under review saw a major step forward with the successful launch of the first digital service specifically for audiences in Scotland: BBC Choice Scotland which provides two hours of programmes every weekday night between 10pm and midnight, aimed, generally, at a younger audience.

Annual Report 1998-99

Scottish Media Group 1998 was a frustrating year for Scottish Television Enterprises (STE), our network programme and distribution arm, and our performance was below expectations...1998's performance indicated that we were not developing new programme ideas sufficiently in tune with the direction of our major customer, ITV...We have therefore decided to refocus on our relationship with ITV and redirect our development spend.

Annual Report 1998

Scottish Screen The board and management have had to grapple with a number of fundamental issues. For example, is public intervention best directed at helping to build strong, viable production companies, or to helping individual projects to get made? ... On this issue, the board has decided to place a higher priority on growing successful independent production companies with the capability to produce both feature films and television drama.

Annual Report 1998-99

Science

Roslin Institute [1]
The public and media interest in cloning showed little signs of waning over the past 12 months and Institute staff continued to be in great demand as speakers at meetings on science and ethics all over the world. A sweater knitted from Dolly's first fleece has been donated to the Science Museum in London by the Cystic Fibrosis Trust and has already been to Japan as part of a travelling exhibition on modern biotechnology. The Science

Museum also bought the electric pulse generator that 'sparked' the reconstructed egg that became Dolly into life. It joins Watson and Crick's model of the double helix and the first gas chromatograph in the museum's unique collection of original equipment involved in major scientific breakthroughs. Dolly herself has been promised to the National Museum of Scotland in Edinburgh when she dies. Sheep can live to 12 or 13 years of age, so the taxidermist-in-waiting will need to be patient.

[2]

Dolly was mated with a Welsh Mountain ram in late November and her pregnancy was confirmed by ultrasound a couple of months later. The pregnancy progressed normally and Dolly delivered her first lamb, Bonnie, in the early hours of Easter Monday morning...The birth was not just an opportunity for positive publicity. Commercial success of nuclear transfer demands that cloned animals should be able to breed normally. There was no particular reason for suspecting Dolly would have any problems in conceiving or successfully carrying a pregnancy to term, but it was still satisfying for all concerned when everything went to plan.

Annual Report 1997-98

Rowett Research Institute

Boyd Orr, the first Director of the Rowett, demonstrated in the 1930s the value of animal protein to promote the growth of stunted children and the fundamental link between poverty, a poor diet and impaired health. These concepts established priorities for meat and milk production, with agriculture departments throughout the world developing a huge range of strategies to ensure that even the poor were properly fed. Now we are in the throes of a second revolution where we will still recognise the need for animal protein – especially meat – for children and young women especially but add new dimensions in terms of total fat and dietary density, n-3 fatty acids, selenium, folate, zinc, and perhaps copper requirements with novel approaches to limiting the transfer of infections and boosting the immunity of animals and man. It is indeed an exciting time for the Rowett.

Annual Report 1997-98

Royal Botanic Garden Edinburgh

There is an urgent need to raise the public profile of the Garden, and to explain more clearly to the general public that it is not just an outstanding public amenity, but a scientific and horticultural institution of international status – indeed, one of the top five botanic gardens in the world. The only justification for maintaining the living collections of plants that the public enjoy is to provide the basic material for the Garden's scientific research and that of other similar research institutions world-wide with which material is shared. Without the high-quality science to justify the extensive and outstanding living collections, which represent something like 7% of the world's flora, the Garden would be no more than an Edinburgh park with a good but severely restricted range of plants; there are many examples of such gardens in the UK.

Annual Report 1998-99

Sport

Scottish Sports Council

[1]
We must ensure that sport is readily available to everybody. For our young people this means securing a minimum provision of physical education in primary schools and increasing the range and frequency of participation...we must significantly increase opportunities for Scotland's disadvantaged groups to participate in sport.

[2]
Over 50 secondary schools throughout Scotland are now involved in the School Sport Co-ordinator pilot scheme. Each school has appointed a part-time co-ordinator whose role is five-fold: to manage and develop sport programmes; to introduce teacher/coach development and support programmes; to create primary/secondary links; to build club and community links; and to monitor and evaluate the programmes. The scheme will become nationally available during the 1998-99 school year thanks to an initial £1 million of support from the Lottery Sports Fund. By 2003 every secondary school in Scotland should have a school sport co-ordinator.

[3]
We must increase our direct support for Scotland's top athletes to allow them to reach even greater heights: a Scottish Institute of Sport will be the ideal way to do this. We need to create a culture of support for sport in Scotland and we must ensure that our sports have clear performance plans.

Annual Report 1997-98

People

The Queen's Household in Scotland

Hereditary Lord High Constable: Earl of Erroll; *Hereditary Master of the Household:* Duke of Argyll; *Lord Lyon King of Arms:* Sir Malcolm Innes of Edingight, KCVO; *Hereditary Bearer of the Royal Banner of Scotland:* Earl of Dundee; *Hereditary Bearer of the Scottish National Flag:* Earl of Lauderdale; *Hereditary Keepers: Palace of Holyroodhouse:* Duke of Hamilton and Brandon; *Falkland Palace:* N Crichton-Stuart; *Stirling Castle:* Earl of Mar and Kellie; *Dunstaffnage Castle:* Duke of Argyll; *Dunconnel Castle:* Sir Charles Maclean, Bt; *Hereditary Carver:* Major Sir Ralph Anstruther, Bt, GCVO, MC; *Keeper of Dumbarton Castle:* Brigadier D Hardie, TD; *Governor of Edinburgh Castle:* Major-General J Hall, OBE; *Historiographer:* Professor T C Smout, CBE; *Botanist:* Professor D Henderson, CBE; *Sculptor in Ordinary:* Professor Sir Eduardo Paolozzi, CBE; *Astronomer:* Professor J Brown; *Heralds: Albany:* J A Spens, RD; *Rothesay:* Sir Crispin Agnew of Lochnaw, Bt, QC; *Ross:* C J Burnett; *Pursuivants: Kintyre:* J C G George; *Unicorn:* Alastair Campbell of Airds; *Carrick:* Mrs C G W Roads, MVO

ECCLESIASTICAL HOUSEHOLD

Dean of the Chapel Royal: Very Rev J Harkness, CB, OBE; *Dean of the Order of the Thistle:* Very Rev G I Macmillan; *Chaplains in Ordinary:* Very Rev J Harkness, CB, OBE; Very Rev G I Macmillan; Rev M D Craig; Very Rev J L Weatherhead; Rev C Robertson; Very Rev J A Simpson; Rev N W Drummond; Rev J Paterson; Rev A Symington; Rev J B Cairns; *Extra Chaplains:* Very Rev W R Sanderson; Rev T J T Nicol, LVO, MBE, MC, TD; Very Rev Prof J McIntyre, CVO; Rev C Forrester-Paton; Rev H W M Cant; Very Rev R A S Barbour, KCVO, MC; Rev K MacVicar, MBE, DFC, TD; Very Rev W B Johnston; Rev A J C Macfarlane; Rev M I Levison; Rev J K Angus, LVO, TD; Rev J McLeod; Very Rev W J Morris, KCVO; Rev A S Todd; Very Rev W B R Macmillan; *Domestic Chaplain, Balmoral:* Rev R P Sloan

MEDICAL HOUSEHOLD

Physicians in Scotland: P Brunt, OBE, MD; A Toft, CBE; *Surgeon in Scotland:* J Engeset; *Apothecary to the Household at Balmoral:* D J A Glass; *Apothecary to the Household at the Palace of Holyroodhouse:* Dr J Cormack

THE QUEEN'S BODY GUARD FOR SCOTLAND (ROYAL COMPANY OF ARCHERS)

Captain-General and Gold Stick for Scotland: Major Sir Hew Hamilton-Dalrymple, Bt, KCVO; *Captains:* Duke of Buccleuch and Queensberry, KT, VRD; Earl of Airlie, KT, GCVO; Captain Sir Iain Tennant, KT; Marquess of Lothian, KCVO; *Lieutenants:* Cdre Sir John Clerk of Penicuik, Bt, CBE, VRD; Earl of Elgin and Kincardine, KT; Col G R Simpson, DSO, LVO, TD; Major Sir David Butter, KCVO, MC; *Ensigns:* Earl of Minto, OBE; Major-General Sir John Swinton, KCVO, OBE; General Sir Michael Gow, GCB; Hon Lord Elliott, MC; *Brigadiers:* Major Hon Sir Lachlan Maclean, Bt; Viscount Younger of Leckie, KT, KCVO, TD, PC; Captain G Burnet, LVO; Duke of Montrose; Lt-Gen Sir Norman Arthur, KCB; Hon Sir William Macpherson of Cluny, TD; Lord Nickson, KBE; Major Lord Glenarthur; Earl of Dalkeith; Major R Y Henderson, TD; Col H F O Bewsher, LVO, OBE; Lord Ramsay; Brigadier C D M Ritchie, CBE; *Adjutant:* Major Hon Sir Lachlan Maclean, Bt; *Surgeon:* Dr P A P Mackenzie, TD; *Chaplain:* Very Rev W J Morris, KCVO; *President of the Council and Silver Stick for Scotland:* Duke of Buccleuch and Queensberry, KT, VRD; *Vice-President:* Captain Sir Iain Tennant, KT; *Secretary:* Captain J D B Younger; *Treasurer:* J M Haldane of Gleneagles

Order of The Thistle

Order of chivalry consisting of the sovereign and 16 knights. May have existed under James V. Disappeared at the time of the Reformation. Revived by James VII in 1687.

Knights

1966	Earl of Wemyss and March
1971	Earl of Dalhousie
1973	Sir Donald Cameron of Lochiel
1978	Duke of Buccleuch and Queensberry
1981	Earl of Elgin and Kincardine
1981	Lord Thomson of Monifieth
1983	Lord MacLehose of Beoch
1985	Earl of Airlie
1986	Captain Sir Iain Tennant
1995	Viscount Younger of Leckie
1996	Viscount Arbuthnot
1996	Earl of Crawford and Balcarres
1996	Lady Fraser
1996	Lord Macfarlane of Bearsden
1997	Lord Mackay of Clashfern

Lords Lieutenant

Aberdeenshire Captain C A Farquharson
Angus Earl of Airlie, KT, GCVO, PC
Argyll and Bute Duke of Argyll
Ayrshire and Arran Major R Y Henderson, TD
Banffshire J A S McPherson, CBE
Berwickshire Major-General Sir John Swinton, KCVO, OBE
Caithness Major G T Dunnett, TD
Clackmannan Lt-Col R C Stewart, CBE, TD
Dumfries Captain R C Cunningham-Jardine
Dunbartonshire Brigadier D D G Hardie, TD
East Lothian Sir Hew Hamilton-Dalrymple, Bt, KCVO
Fife Earl of Elgin and Kincardine, KT
Inverness Lord Gray of Contin, PC
Kincardineshire Viscount of Arbuthnott, CBE, DSC, FRSE
Lanarkshire H B Sneddon, CBE
Midlothian Captain G W Burnet, LVO
Moray Air Vice-Marshal G A Chesworth, CB, OBE, DFC
Nairn Earl of Leven and Melville
Orkney G R Marwick
Perth and Kinross Sir David Montgomery, Bt
Renfrewshire C H Parker, OBE
Ross and Cromarty Captain R W K Stirling of Fairburn, TD
Roxburgh, Ettrick and Lauderdale Dr June Paterson-Brown
Shetland J H Scott
Stirling and Falkirk Lt-Col J Stirling of Garden, CBE, TD
Sutherland Major-General D Houston, CBE
Stewartry of Kirkcudbright Lt-Gen Sir Norman Arthur, KCB
Tweeddale Captain J D B Younger

West Lothian Earl of Morton
Western Isles Viscount Dunrossil, CMG
Wigtown Major E S Orr-Ewing
The Lord Provosts of the four cities are Lords Lieutenant for those cities ex officio.

Privy Council

Scottish Members

1984	Earl of Airlie
1996	Michael Ancram
1996	Gordon Brown
1990	Earl of Caithness
1984	Lord Cameron of Lochbroom
1970	Lord Campbell of Croy
1997	Thomas Clarke
1996	Lord Clyde
1996	Robin Cook
1972	Earl of Crawford and Balcarres
1997	Hon Lord Cullen
1997	Alistair Darling
1996	Donald Dewar
1996	Lord James Douglas-Hamilton
1972	Lord Emslie
1995	Sir Michael Forsyth
1989	Lord Fraser of Carmyllie
1982	Lord Gray of Contin
1997	Lord Hardie of Blackford
1989	Lord Hope of Craighead
1970	Lord Hughes
1997	Lord Irvine of Lairg
1988	Lord Jauncey of Tullichettle
1976	Lord Keith of Kinkel
1990	Ian Lang
1964	Marquess of Lansdowne
1977	Dickson Mabon
1996	Lord Mackay of Ardbrecknish
1979	Lord Mackay of Clashfern
1996	Lord Mackay of Drumadoon
1975	Bruce Millan
1995	Sir Hector Monro
1974	Hon Lord Murray
1957	Earl of Perth
1986	Sir Malcolm Rifkind
1997	George Robertson
1992	Lord Rodger of Earlsferry
1985	Hon Lord Ross
1977	Lord Steel of Aikwood
1974	Lord Stodart of Leaston
1964	Lord Stott
1977	Gavin Strang
1995	Lord Strathclyde
1966	Lord Thomson of Monifieth
1970	Hon Lord Wylie
1979	Viscount Younger of Leckie

Lord High Commissioners

1995	Lady Marion Fraser
1996	HRH Princess Royal
1997	Rt Hon Lord Macfarlane of Bearsden
1998	Lord Hogg of Cumbernauld
1999	Lord Hogg of Cumbernauld

The Peerage

* denotes title designated as Scottish (pre-Union of the Parliaments)

Dukes

1701   *Argyll (12th), Ian Campbell; b 1937; s 1973

1703   *Atholl (11th), John Murray; b 1929; s 1996

1663   *Buccleuch (9th) and Queensberry (11th), Walter Francis John Montagu Douglas Scott, KT, VRD; b 1923; s 1973

1900   Fife (3rd), James George Alexander Bannerman Carnegie; b 1929; s 1959

1643   *Hamilton (15th) and Brandon (12th), Angus Alan Douglas Douglas-Hamilton; b 1938; s 1973 *Premier Peer of Scotland*

1707   *Montrose (8th), James Graham; b 1935; s 1992

1707   *Roxburghe (10th), Guy David Innes-Ker; b 1954; s 1974 *Premier Baronet of Scotland*

Marquesses

1831   Ailsa (8th), Archibald Angus Charles Kennedy; b 1956; s 1994

1796   Bute (7th), John Colum Crichton-Stuart; b 1958; s 1993

1599   *Huntly (13th), Granville Charles Gomer Gordon; b 1944; s 1987 *Premier Marquess of Scotland*

1784   Lansdowne (8th), George John Charles Mercer Nairne Petty-Fitzmaurice, PC; b 1912; s 1944

1902   Linlithgow (4th), Adrian John Charles Hope; b 1946; s 1987

1701   *Lothian (12th), Peter Francis Walter Kerr, KCVO; b 1922; s 1940

1682   *Queensberry (12th), David Harrington Angus Douglas; b 1929; s 1954

1694   *Tweeddale (13th), Edward Douglas John Hay; b 1947; s 1979

Earls

1639   Airlie (13th), David George Coke Patrick Ogilvy, KT, GCVO, PC; b 1926; s 1968

1662   *Annandale and Hartfell (11th), Patrick Andrew Wentworth Hope Johnstone; b 1941; claim established 1985

1922   Balfour (4th), Gerald Arthur James Balfour; b 1925; s 1968

1677   *Breadalbane and Holland (10th), John Romer Boreland Campbell; b 1919; s 1959

1469   *Buchan (17th), Malcolm Harry Erskine; b 1930; s 1984

1455   *Caithness (20th), Malcolm Ian Sinclair; b 1948; s 1965

1827   Cawdor (7th), Colin Robert Vaughan Campbell; b 1962; s 1993

1398   *Crawford (29th) and Balcarres (12th), Robert Alexander Lindsay, KT PC; b 1927; s 1975

1861   Cromartie (5th), John Ruaridh Blunt Grant Mackenzie; b 1948; s 1989

1633   *Dalhousie (16th), Simon Ramsay, KT, GCVO, GBE, MC; b 1914; s 1950

1660   *Dundee (12th), Alexander Henry Scrymgeour; b 1949; s 1983

1669   *Dundonald (15th), Iain Alexander Douglas Blair Cochrane; b 1961; s 1986

1686   *Dunmore (12th), Malcolm Kenneth Murray; b 1946; s 1995

1507   *Eglinton (18th) and Winton (9th), Archibald George Montgomerie; b 1939; s 1966

1633   *Elgin (11th) and Kincardine (15th), Andrew Douglas Alexander Thomas Bruce, KT; b 1924; s 1968

1452   *Erroll (24th), Merlin Sereld Victor Gilbert Hay; b 1948; s 1978 *Hereditary Lord High Constable and Knight Marischal of Scotland*

1623	*Galloway (13th), Randolph Keith Reginald Stewart; b 1928; s 1978
1703	*Glasgow (10th), Patrick Robin Archibald Boyle; b 1939; s 1984
1619	*Haddington (13th), John George Baillie-Hamilton; b 1941; s 1986
1919	Haig (2nd), George Alexander Eugene Douglas Haig, OBE; b 1918; s 1928
1605	*Home (15th), David Alexander Cospatrick Douglas-Home, CVO; b 1943; s 1995
1633	*Kinnoull (15th), Arthur William George Patrick Hay; b 1935; s 1938
1677	*Kintore (13th), Michael Canning William John Keith; b 1939; s 1989
1624	*Lauderdale (17th), Patrick Francis Maitland; b 1911; s 1968
1641	*Leven (14th) and Melville (13th), Alexander Robert Leslie Melville; b 1924; s 1947
1633	*Lindsay (16th), James Randolph Lindesay-Bethune; b 1955; s 1989
1838	Lovelace (5th), Peter Axel William Locke King; b 1951; s 1964
1776 and 1792	Mansfield and Mansfield (8th), William David Mungo James Murray; b 1930; s 1971
1565	*Mar (14th) and Kellie (16th), James Thorne Erskine; b 1949; s 1994
1813	Minto (6th), Gilbert Edward George Lariston Elliot-Murray-Kynynmound, OBE; b 1928; s 1975
1562	*Moray (20th), Douglas John Moray Stuart; b 1928; s 1974
1458	*Morton (22nd), John Charles Sholto Douglas; b 1927; s 1976
1660	*Newburgh (12th), Don Filippo Giambattista Camillo Francesco Aldo Maria Rospigliosi; b 1942; s 1986
1647	*Northesk (14th), David John MacRae Carnegie; b 1954; s 1994
1696	*Orkney (9th), (Oliver) Peter St John; b 1938; s 1998
1605	*Perth (17th), John David Drummond, PC; b 1907; s 1951
1703	*Rosebery (7th), Neil Archibald Primrose; b 1929; s 1974
1457	*Rothes (21st), Ian Lionel Malcolm Leslie; b 1932; s 1975
1701	*Seafield (13th), Ian Derek Francis Ogilvie-Grant; b 1939; s 1969
1646	*Selkirk. Disclaimed for life, 1994, by Rt Hon Lord James Douglas-Hamilton; b 1942
1703	*Stair (14th), John David James Dalrymple; b 1961; s 1996
1606	*Strathmore and Kinghorne (18th), Michael Fergus Bowes Lyon; b 1957; s 1987
1633	*Wemyss (12th) and March (8th), Francis David Charteris, KT; b 1912; s 1937

Countesses in their own right

1643	*Dysart (11th in line), Rosamund Agnes Greaves, b 1914; s 1975
1633	*Loudoun (13th in line), Barbara Huddleston Abney-Hastings; b 1919; s 1960
1115c	*Mar (31st in line), Margaret of Mar; b 1940; s 1975
1235c	*Sutherland (24th in line), Elizabeth Millicent Sutherland; b 1921; s 1963

Viscounts

1642	*of Arbuthnott (16th), John Campbell Arbuthnott, KT, CBE, DSC; b 1924; s 1966
1902	Colville of Culross (4th), John Mark Alexander Colville, QC; b 1933; s 1945
1620	*Falkland (15th), Lucius Edward William Plantagenet Cary; b 1935; s 1984. *Premier Scottish Viscount on the Roll*
1651	*of Oxfuird (13th), George Hubbard Makgill, CBE; b 1934; s 1986
1959	Stuart of Findhorn (2nd), David Randolph Moray Stuart; b 1924; s 1971
1952	Thurso (3rd), John Archibald Sinclair; b 1953; s 1995

1938	Weir (3rd), William Kenneth James Weir; b 1933; s 1975
1923	Younger of Leckie (4th), George Kenneth Hotson Younger, KT, KCVO, TD, PC; b 1931; s 1997

Barons/Lords

1607	*Balfour of Burleigh (8th), Robert Bruce; b 1927; s 1967
1647	*Belhaven and Stenton (13th), Robert Anthony Carmichael Hamilton; b 1927; s 1961
1903	Biddulph (5th), (Anthony) Nicholas Colin Maitland Biddulph; b 1959; s 1988
1452	*Borthwick (24th), John Hugh Borthwick; b 1940; s 1997
1942	Bruntisfield (2nd), John Robert Warrender, OBE, MC, TD; b 1921; s 1993
1948	Clydesmuir (3rd), David Ronald Colville; b 1949; s 1996
1919	Cochrane of Cults (4th), (Ralph Henry) Vere Cochrane; b 1926; s 1990
1509	*Elphinstone (19th), Alexander Mountstuart Elphinstone; b 1980; s 1994
1627	*Fairfax of Cameron (14th), Nicholas John Albert Fairfax; b 1956; s 1964
1445	*Forbes (22nd), Nigel Ivan Forbes, KBE; b 1918; s 1953 *Premier Lord of Scotland*
1917	Forteviot (4th), John James Evelyn Dewar; b 1938; s 1993
1918	Glenarthur (4th), Simon Mark Arthur; b 1944; s 1976
1445	*Gray (22nd), Angus Diarmid Ian Campbell-Gray; b 1931; s 1946
1902	Kinross (5th), Christopher Patrick Balfour; b 1949; s 1985
1458	*Lovat (16th), Simon Fraser; b 1977; s 1995
1914	Lyell (3rd), Charles Lyell; b 1939; s 1943
1776	Macdonald (8th), Godfrey James Macdonald of Macdonald; b 1947; s 1970
1951	Macpherson of Drumochter (2nd), (James) Gordon Macpherson; b 1924; s 1965
1873	Moncreiff (5th), Harry Robert Wellwood Moncreiff; b 1915; s 1942
1627	*Napier (14th) and Ettrick (5th), Francis Nigel Napier, KCVO; b 1930; s 1954
1690	*Polwarth (10th), Henry Alexander Hepburne-Scott, TD; b 1916; s 1944
1932	Rankeillour (4th), Peter St Thomas More Henry Hope; b 1935; s 1967
1628	*Reay (14th), Hugh William Mackay; b 1937; s 1963
1651	*Rollo (14th), David Eric Howard Rollo; b 1943; s 1997
1911	Rowallan (4th), John Polson Cameron Corbett; b 1947; s 1993
1489	*Sempill (21st), James William Stuart Whitemore Sempill; b 1949; s 1995
1449	*Sinclair (17th), Charles Murray Kennedy St Clair, CVO; b 1914; s 1957
1955	Strathclyde (2nd), Thomas Galloway Dunlop du Roy de Blicquy Galbraith, PC; b 1960; s 1985
1564	*Torphichen (15th), James Andrew Douglas Sandilands; b 1946; s 1975

Baronesses/Ladies in their own right

1490	*Herries of Terregles (14th in line), Anne Elizabeth Fitzalan-Howard; b 1938; s 1975
1602	*Kinloss (12th in line), Beatrice Mary Grenville Freeman-Grenville; b 1922; s 1944
1445	*Saltoun (20th in line), Flora Marjory Fraser; b 1930; s 1979
1628	Strange (16th in line), (Jean) Cherry Drummond of Megginch; b 1928; title called out of abeyance, 1986

Life Peers

1974	Balniel, Earl of Crawford and Balcarres. *See Earls.*

1977	Cameron of Lochbroom, Kenneth John Cameron, PC; b 1931
1981	Campbell of Alloway, Alan Robertson Campbell, QC; b 1917
1974	Campbell of Croy, Gordon Thomas Calthrop Campbell, MC, PC; b 1921
1983	Carmichael of Kelvingrove, Neil George Carmichael; b 1921
1996	Clyde, James John Clyde, b 1932
1980	Emslie, George Carlyle Emslie, MBE, PC; b 1919
1992	Ewing of Kirkford, Harry Ewing; b 1931
1989	Fraser of Carmyllie, Peter Lovat Fraser, PC, QC; b 1945
1997	Gordon of Strathblane, James Stuart Gordon, CBE; b 1936
1983	Gray of Contin, James (Hamish) Hector Northey Gray, PC; b 1927
1997	Hardie, Andrew Rutherford Hardie, QC, PC; b 1946
1997	Hogg of Cumbernauld, Norman Hogg; b 1938
1995	Hope of Craighead (James Arthur) David Hope, PC; b 1938
1997	Hughes of Woodside, Robert Hughes; b 1932
1961	Hughes, William Hughes, CBE, PC; b 1911
1987	Irvine of Lairg, Alexander Andrew Mackay Irvine, PC, QC; b 1940
1988	Jauncey of Tullichettle, Charles Eliot Jauncey, PC; b 1925
1975	Kirkhill, John Farquharson Smith; b 1930
1977	Keith of Kinkel, Henry Shanks Keith, GBE, PC; b. 1922
1991	Laing of Dunphail, Hector Laing; b 1923
1997	Lang of Monkton, Ian Bruce Lang, PC; b 1940
1984	Macaulay of Bragar, Donald Macaulay, QC; b 1933
1976	McCluskey, John Herbert McCluskey; b 1929
1991	Macfarlane of Bearsden, Norman Somerville Macfarlane, KT; b 1926
1991	Mackay of Ardbrecknish, John Jackson Mackay, PC; b 1938
1979	Mackay of Clashfern, James Peter Hymers Mackay, PC; b 1927
1995	Mackay of Drumadoon, Donald Sage Mackay, b 1946
1988	Mackenzie-Stuart, Alexander John Mackenzie Stuart; b 1924
1974	Mackie of Benshie, George Yull Mackie, CBE, DSO, DFC; b 1919
1982	MacLehose of Beoch, (Crawford) Murray MacLehose, KT, GBE, KCMG, KCVO; b 1917
1997	Monro of Langholm, Hector Monro; b 1922
1994	Nickson, David Wigley Nickson, KBE; b 1929
1990	Pearson of Rannoch, Malcolm Everard MacLaren Pearson; b 1942
1992	Rodger of Earlsferry, Alan Ferguson Rodger, PC, QC; b 1944
1997	Russell-Johnston, (David) Russell-Johnston; b 1932
1985	Sanderson of Bowden, Charles Russell Sanderson; b 1933
1997	Selkirk of Douglas, James Alexander Douglas-Hamilton; b 1942
1997	Steel of Aikwood, David Martin Scott Steel, KBE, PC; b 1938
1981	Stodart of Leaston, James Anthony Stodart, PC; b 1916
1968	Taylor of Gryfe, Thomas Johnston Taylor; b 1912
1977	Thomson of Monifieth, George Morgan Thomson, KT, PC, b 1921
1974	Wallace of Campsie, George Wallace; b 1915
1997	Watson of Invergowrie, Michael Goodall Watson; b 1949
1992	Wilson of Tillyorn, David Clive Wilson, GCMG; b 1934
1992	Younger of Prestwick. See Viscounts.

Baronesses

1982	Carnegy of Lour, Elizabeth Patricia Carnegy of Lour; b 1925.
1971	Macleod of Borve, Evelyn Hester MacLeod; b 1915
1995	Smith of Gilmorehill, Elizabeth Margaret Smith; b 1940
1997	Linklater of Butterstone, Veronica Linklater; b 1943

The Judiciary

Judges of Court of Session

Lord President and Lord Justice General
Rt Hon Lord Rodger of Earlsferry (Adam Ferguson Rodger), b 1944
Lords of Session
First Division, Inner House
Hon Lord Sutherland (Ranald Sutherland), b 1932
Hon Lord Prosser (William Prosser), b 1934
Hon Lord Caplan (Philip Caplan), b 1929
Lords of Session
Second Division, Inner House
Rt Hon Lord Cullen (William Cullen), *Lord Justice Clerk*, b 1935
Rt Hon Lord McCluskey (John McCluskey), b 1929
Hon Lord Kirkwood (Ian Kirkwood), b 1932
Hon Lord Coulsfield (John Cameron), b 1934
Lords of Session
Outer House
Hon Lord Milligan (James Milligan), b 1934
Rt Hon Lord Cameron of Lochbroom (Kenneth John Cameron), b 1931
Hon Lord Marnoch (Michael Bruce), b 1938
Hon Lord MacLean (Ranald MacLean), b 1938
Hon Lord Penrose (George Penrose), b 1938
Hon Lord Osborne (Kenneth Osborne), b 1937
Hon Lord Abernethy (Alistair Cameron), b 1938
Hon Lord Johnston (Alan Johnston), b 1942
Hon Lord Gill (Brian Gill), b 1942
Hon Lord Hamilton (Arthur Hamilton), b 1942
Hon Lord Dawson (Thomas Dawson), b 1948
Hon Lord Macfadyen (Donald Macfadyen), b 1945
Hon Lady Cosgrove (Hazel Aronson), b 1946
Hon Lord Nimmo Smith (William Nimmo Smith), b 1942
Hon Lord Philip (Alexander Philip), b 1942
Hon Lord Kingarth (Derek Emslie), b 1949

Hon Lord Bonomy (Iain Bonomy), b 1946
Hon Lord Eassie (Ronald Mackay), b 1945

Sheriffs

Grampian, Highlands and Islands
D J Risk, *Sheriff Principal*, b 1941
Aberdeen and Stonehaven
D Kelbie, b 1945
A S Jessop, b 1943
A Pollock, b 1944
Mrs A M Cowan
C J Harris, QC
Peterhead and Banff
K A McLernan, b 1941
Elgin
N McPartlin, b 1939
Inverness, Lochmaddy, Portree, Stornoway, Dingwall, Tain, Wick and Dornoch
W J Fulton
D Booker-Milburn, b 1940
J O A Fraser, b 1937
I A Cameron, b 1938
G K Buchanan
Kirkwall and Lerwick
C S Mackenzie, b 1938
Fort William
C G McKay, b 1942 (also *Oban*)

Tayside, Central and Fife
J J Maguire, QC, *Sheriff Principal*, b 1934
Arbroath and Forfar
K A Veal, b 1946
C N R Stein, b 1948
Dundee
R A Davidson, b 1947
A L Stewart, QC, b 1938
J P Scott
G J Evans, b 1944 (also *Cupar*)
Falkirk
A V Sheehan, b 1936
A J Murphy, b 1946
Perth
J F Wheatley, QC, b 1941
J C McInnes, QC, b 1938
Mrs P M M Bowman, b 1944
Stirling
Hon R E G Younger, b 1940
Alloa
W M Reid, b 1938
Cupar
G J Evans, b 1944 (also Dundee)
Dunfermline
J S Forbes, b 1936
C W Palmer, b 1945
Kirkcaldy

F J Keane, b 1936
Mrs L G Patrick, b 1941
I D Dunbar

Lothian and Borders
C G B Nicholson, QC, *Sheriff Principal,* b 1935
Edinburgh
R G Craik, QC, b 1940 (also *Peebles*)
Miss I A Poole, b 1941
R J D Scott, b 1939 (also *Peebles*)
A M Bell, b 1940
J M S Horsburgh, QC, b 1938
G W S Presslie (also *Haddington*)
J A Farrell, b 1943
A Lothian
I D MacPhail, QC, b 1938
C N Stoddart, b 1948
A B Wilkinson, QC, b 1932
Mrs D J B Robertson, b 1937
N M P Morrison, QC, b 1948
Miss M M Stephen
Mrs M L E Jarvie, QC
Peebles
R G Craik, QC (also *Edinburgh*)
R J D Scott, b 1939 (also *Edinburgh*)
Linlithgow
H R MacLean, b 1931
G R Fleming, b 1949
K A Ross, b 1949
Haddington
G W S Presslie (also *Edinburgh*)
Jedburgh, Duns, Selkirk
J V Paterson, b 1928

North Strathclyde
R C Hay, CBE, *Sheriff Principal,* b 1933
Oban
C G McKay, b 1942 (also *Fort William*)
Dumbarton
J T Fitzsimons
T Scott
S W H Fraser, b 1951
Paisley
R G Smith, b 1933
J Spy, b 1952
C K Higgins, b 1945
N Douglas
D J Pender, b 1949
W Dunlop, b 1944 (also *Campbeltown*)
Greenock
J P Herald, b 1946 (also *Rothesay*)
Sir Stephen Young, b 1947
Kilmarnock
T M Croan, b 1932
D B Smith, b 1936
T F Russell, b 1931
Dunoon
A W Noble, b 1954
Campbeltown
W Dunlop, b 1944 (also *Paisley*)

Rothesay
J P Herald, b 1946 (also *Greenock*)

Glasgow and Strathkelvin
E F Bowen, QC, *Sheriff Principal,* b 1945
Glasgow
B Kearney, b 1935
G H Gordon, CBE, QC, b 1929
B A Lockhart, b 1942
I G Pirie, b 1933
Mrs A L A Duncan, b 1947
A C Henry
J K Mitchell
A G Johnston, b 1944
J P Murphy, b 1932
Miss S A O Raeburn, QC, b 1954
D Convery
J McGowan, b 1944
B A Kerr, QC
Mrs C M A F Gimblett, b 1939
I A S Peebles, QC
C W McFarlane, QC
K M Maciver
H Matthews, QC
J D Lowe, CB, b 1948
J A Baird
Miss R E A Rae, QC, b 1950
T A K Drummond, QC, b 1943

South Strathclyde, Dumfries and Galloway
G L Cox, QC, *Sheriff Principal,* b 1933
Hamilton
L Cameron, b 1935
A C Macpherson, b 1939
W F Lunny, b 1938
D C Russell, b 1939
V J Canavan, b 1944 (also Airdrie)
W E Gibson, b 1934
H Stirling, b 1938
J H Stewart, b 1944
H S Neilson
Lanark
J D Allan, b 1941
Ayr
N Gow, QC, b 1932
R G McEwan, QC, b 1943
C B Miller, b 1946
Stranraer and Kirkcudbright
J R Smith
Dumfries
K G Barr, b 1941
M J Fletcher, b 1945
J R Smith (also *Stranraer* and *Kirkcudbright*)
Airdrie
V J Canavan, b 1944 (also Hamilton)
J C Morris, QC
R H Dickson, b 1945
I C Simpson, b 1949

The Churches

Church of Scotland
Moderator 1998: Rev Professor Alan Main, b 1936
Moderator 1999: Rev John B Cairns, b 1942

Free Church of Scotland
Moderator 1998: Rev Donald K Macleod, b 1928
Moderator 1999: Rev Kenneth Macleod, b 1933

United Free Church of Scotland
Moderator 1998: Rev J C Allan, b 1938
Moderator 1999: Rev Douglas Scrimgeour, b 1930

Free Presbyterian Church of Scotland
Moderator 1998: Rev Donald Ross, b 1937
Moderator 1999: Rev George G Hutton, b 1948

Roman Catholic Church
Archbishops
St Andrews and Edinburgh Most Rev Keith Patrick O'Brien, b 1938
Glasgow His Eminence Cardinal Thomas Joseph Winning, b 1925

Bishops
Aberdeen Rt Rev Mario Conti, b 1934
Argyll and the Isles post vacant
Dunkeld Rt Rev Vincent Logan, b 1941
Galloway Rt Rev Maurice Taylor, b 1926
Motherwell Rt Rev Joseph Devine, b 1937
Paisley Rt Rev John A Mone, b 1929

Scottish Episcopal Church
Bishops
Edinburgh Most Rev Richard Frederick Holloway, b 1933
Aberdeen and Orkney Rt Rev Andrew Bruce Cameron, b 1941
Argyll and the Isles Rt Rev Douglas MacLean Cameron, b 1935
Brechin Rt Rev Neville Chamberlain, b 1939
Glasgow and Galloway Rt Rev Dr Idris Jones, b 1943
Moray, Ross and Caithness Rt Rev John Michael Crook, b 1940
St Andrews, Dunkeld and Dunblane Rt Rev Michael Harry George Henley, b 1938

Chiefs of Clans & Names

denotes living outside Scotland
Agnew Sir Crispin Agnew of Lochnaw, Bt, QC
Anstruther Sir Ralph Anstruther of that Ilk, Bt, GCVO, MC
Arbuthnott Viscount of Arbuthnott, KT, CBE, DSC
Barclay *Peter C Barclay of Towie Barclay and of that Ilk
Borthwick Lord Borthwick
Boyd *Lord Kilmarnock
Boyle Earl of Glasgow
Brodie Ninian Brodie of Brodie
Bruce Earl of Elgin and Kincardine, KT
Buchan David S Buchan
Burnett J C A Burnett of Leys
Cameron Sir Donald Cameron of Lochiel, KT, CVO, TD
Campbell Duke of Argyll
Carmichael Richard J Carmichael of Carmichael
Carnegie Duke of Fife
Cathcart *Maj-Gen Earl Cathcart, CB, DSO, MC
Charteris Earl of Wemyss and March, KT

Clan Chattan *M K Mackintosh of Clan Chattan
Chisholm *Hamish Chisholm of Chisholm (The Chisholm)
Cochrane Earl of Dundonald
Colquhoun Sir Ivar Colquhoun of Luss
Cranstoun David A S Cranstoun of that Ilk
Crichton vacant
Cumming Sir William Cumming of Altyre, Bt
Darroch *Captain Duncan Darroch of Gourock
Davidson *Alister G Davidson of Davidston
Dewar *Kenneth Dewar of that Ilk and Vogrie
Drummond Earl of Perth, PC
Dunbar *Sir James Dunbar of Mochrum, Bt
Dundas *David D Dundas of Dundas
Durie *Raymond V D Durie of Durie
Elliott Mrs Margaret Eliott of Redheugh
Erskine Earl of Mar and Kellie
Farquharson Captain A Farquharson of Invercauld, MC
Fergusson Sir Charles Fergusson of Kilkerran, Bt
Forbes Lord Forbes, KBE
Forsyth Alistair Forsyth of that Ilk

Fraser Lady Saltoun
Fraser (of Lovat) Lord Lovat
Gayre R Gayre of Gayre and Nigg
Gordon Marquess of Huntly
Graham Duke of Montrose
Grant Lord Strathspey
Grierson *Sir Michael Grierson of Lag, Bt
Haig Earl Haig, OBE
Haldane Martin Haldane of Gleneagles
Hannay Ramsey Hannay of Kirkdale and of that Ilk
Hay *Earl of Erroll
Henderson *John Henderson of Fordell
Hunter *Pauline Hunter of Hunterston
Irvine of Drum *David C Irvine of Drum
Jardine *Sir Alexander Jardine of Applegirth, Bt
Johnstone Earl of Annandale and Hartfell
Keith Earl of Kintore
Kennedy Marquess of Ailsa
Kerr Marquess of Lothian, KCVO
Kincaid *Mrs Heather V Kincaid of Kincaid
Lamont *Peter N Lamont of that Ilk
Leask *Madam Leask of Leask
Lennox *Edward J H Lennox of that Ilk
Leslie *Earl of Rothes
Lindsay Earl of Crawford and Balcarres, KT, PC
Lockhart Angus H Lockhart of the Lee
Lumsden *Gillem Lumsden of that Ilk and Blanerne
MacAlester *William St J S McAlester of Loup and Kennox
McBain *J H McBain of McBain
Malcolm (MacCallum) Robin N L Malcolm
Macdonald Lord Macdonald *(The Macdonald of Macdonald)*
Macdonald of Clanranald Ranald A Macdonald of Clanranald
Macdonald of Sleat (Clan Husteain) *Sir Ian Bosville Macdonald of Sleat, Bt
MacDonell of Glengarry Air Cdre Aeneas R MacDonell of Glengarry, CB, DFC
MacDougall vacant
Macdowall *Fergus D H Macdowall of Garthland
MacGregor Sir Gregor MacGregor of MacGregor, Bt
MacIntyre *James W MacIntyre of Glenoe
Mackay Lord Reay
Mackenzie Earl of Cromartie
Mackinnon *Madam Anne Mackinnon of Mackinnon
Mackintosh The Mackintosh of Mackintosh
MacLachlan vacant
MacLaren Donald MacLaren of MacLaren and Achleskine
Maclean Hon Sir Lachlan Maclean of Duart, Bt

MacLennan vacant
MacLeod John MacLeod of MacLeod
MacMillan George MacMillan of MacMillan
Macnab J C Macnab of Macnab *(The Macnab)*
Macnaghten *Sir Patrick Macnaghten of Macnaghten and Dundarave, Bt
Macneacail *Iain Macneacail of Macneacail and Scorrybreac
MacNeil of Barra Ian R Macneil of Barra *(The Macneil of Barra)*
Macpherson Hon Sir William Macpherson of Cluny, TD
McTavish E S Dugald McTavish of Dunardry
MacThomas Andrew P C MacThomas of Finegand
Maitland Earl of Lauderdale
Makgill *Viscount of Oxfuird
Malcolm (MacCallum) Robin N L Malcolm of Poltalloch
Mar *Countess of Mar
Marjoribanks Andrew Marjoribanks of that Ilk
Matheson *Major Sir Fergus Matheson of Matheson, Bt
Menzies *David R Menzies of Menzies
Moffat *Madam Moffat of that Ilk
Moncreiffe vacant
Montgomerie *Earl of Eglinton and Winton
Morrison *Dr Iain M Morrison of Ruchdi
Munro Hector W Munro of Foulis
Murray Duke of Atholl
Nesbitt (or Nisbet) *Robert Nesbitt of that Ilk
Nicolson *Lord Carnock
Ogilvy Earl of Airlie, KT, GCVO, PC
Ramsay Earl of Dalhousie, KT, GCVO, GBE, MC
Rattray James S Rattray of Rattray
Robertson *Alexander G H Robertson of Struan
Rollo Lord Rollo
Rose Miss Elizabeth Rose of Kilravock
Ross David C Ross of that Ilk
Ruthven *Earl of Gowrie PC
Scott Duke of Buccleuch and Queensberry, KT, VRD
Scrymgeour Earl of Dundee
Sempill Lord Sempill
Shaw John Shaw of Tordarroch
Sinclair *Earl of Caithness
Skene Danus Skene of Skene
Stirling *Fraser J Stirling of Cader
Strange *Major Timothy Strange of Balcaskie
Sutherland Countess of Sutherland
Swinton *John Swinton of that Ilk
Trotter Alexander Trotter of Mortonhall
Urquhart *Kenneth T Urquhart of Urquhart
Wallace Ian F Wallace of that Ilk
Wedderburn of that Ilk The Master of Dundee
Wemyss David Wemyss of that Ilk

Prominent People

Sovereigns

c 843–58	Kenneth I
858–62	Donald I
862–77	Constantine I
877–88	Aed
878–89	Giric
	Eochaid
889–900	Donald II
900–943	Constantine II
943–54	Malcolm I
954–62	Indulf
962–66	Dubh
966–71	Culen
971–95	Kenneth II
995–97	Constantine III
?997–1005	Kenneth III
	Giric?
1005–34	Malcolm II
1034–40	Duncan I
1040–57	Macbeth
1057–58	Lulach
1058–93	Malcolm III
1093–94	Donald III
1094	Duncan II
1094–97	Donald III (restored)
1097–1107	Edgar
1107–24	Alexander I
1124–53	David I
1153–65	Malcolm IV
1165–1214	William I
1214–49	Alexander II
1249–86	Alexander III
1286–90	Margaret
1290–92	interregnum
1292–96	John
1296–1306	interregnum
1306–29	Robert I
1329–71	David II
1371–90	Robert II
1390–1406	Robert III
1406–37	James I
1437–60	James II
1460–88	James III
1488–1513	James IV
1513–42	James V
1542–67	Mary I
1567–1625	James VI
1625–49	Charles I
1649–85	Charles II (exiled 1651–60)
1685–89	James VII
{1689–1702	William II
1689–94	Mary II}
1702–07	Anne

Secretary of State for Scotland

**Holders of the office, and its
predecessor titles, since 1707**

Secretary of State, Scottish Department

1707	Earl of Loudon and Earl of Mar
1707	Duke of Queensberry, until his death in 1711
1713	Earl of Mar, again
1714	Duke of Montrose
1716	Duke of Roxburghe, until 1725
1741	Marquess of Tweeddale, until 1746

Secretary for Scotland

1885	Duke of Richmond and Gordon, KG
1886	G O Trevelyan (later Sir G O Trevelyan, Bt)
1886	Earl of Dalhousie, KT
1886	A J Balfour (later Earl of Balfour)
1887	Marquess of Lothian
1892	Sir G O Trevelyan, Bt, again
1895	Lord Balfour of Burleigh
1903	A Graham Murray (later Viscount Dunedin)
1905	2 Feb Marquess of Linlithgow, KT, GCVO, GCMG
1905	10 Dec J Sinclair (later Lord Pentland)
1912	T McKinnon Wood
1916	9 Jul H J Tennant
1916	10 Dec R Munro (later Lord Alness)
1922	Viscount Novar, GCMG
1924	22 Jan W Adamson
1924	6 Nov Sir John Gilmour, Bt, DSO

Secretary of State for Scotland

1926	Sir John Gilmour, Bt, DSO
1929	W Adamson

1931	Sir Archibald Sinclair, Bt, CMG (later Viscount Thurso)
1932	Sir Godfrey Collins
1936	Walter E Elliot, MC
1938	D J Colville (later Lord Clydesmuir)
1940	Ernest Brown, MC
1941	Thomas Johnston
1945	25 May Earl of Rosebery, DSO, MC
1945	3 Aug Joseph Westwood
1947	Arthur Woodburn
1950	Hector McNeil
1951	James Stuart, MVO, MC (later Viscount Stuart of Findhorn)
1957	John S Maclay, CH, CMG (later Viscount Muirshiel)
1962	Michael A C Noble (later Lord Glenkinglas)
1964	William Ross, MBE (later Lord Ross of Marnock)
1970	Gordon T C Campbell, MC (later Lord Campbell of Croy)
1974	William Ross, MBE (later Lord Ross of Marnock)
1976	Bruce Millan
1979	George Younger, TD (later Viscount Younger of Leckie, KT)
1986	Malcolm Rifkind (later Sir Malcolm Rifkind, KCMG)
1990	Ian Lang (later Lord Lang of Monkton)
1995	Michael Forsyth (later Sir Michael Forsyth)
1997	Donald Dewar
1999	John Reid

Lord Advocate

Holders of the office since 1709

1709	Sir David Dalrymple of Hailes, Bt
1711	Sir James Stewart
1714	Thomas Kennedy
1714	Sir David Dalrymple of Hailes, Bt
1720	Robert Dundas, yr, of Arniston
1725	Duncan Forbes of Culloden
1737	Charles Erskine of Tinwald
1742	Robert Craigie of Glendoick
1746	William Grant of Prestongrange
1754	Robert Dundas of Arniston
1760	Thomas Miller of Barskimming and Glenlee
1766	James Montgomery of Stanhope
1775	Henry Dundas
1783	Henry Erskine
1784	Hay Campbell of Succoth
1789	Robert Dundas of Arniston
1801	Charles Hope of Granton
1804	Sir James Montgomery, Bt
1806	Henry Erskine
1807	Archibald Campbell (afterwards Colquhoun)
1816	Alexander Maconochie
1819	Sir William Rae, Bt
1830	Francis Jeffrey
1834	John Archibald Murray
1834	Sir William Rae, Bt
1835	John Archibald Murray
1839	Andrew Rutherfurd
1841	Sir William Rae, Bt
1842	Duncan McNeill
1846	Andrew Rutherfurd
1851	James Moncreiff
1852	Adam Anderson
1852	John Inglis
1853	James Moncreiff
1858	John Inglis of Glencorse
1858	Charles Baillie
1859	David Mure
1859	James Moncreiff
1866	George Patton
1867	Edward Strathearn Gordon
1868	James Moncreiff
1869	George Young
1874	Edward Strathearn Gordon
1876	William Watson
1880	John McLaren
1881	John Blair Balfour
1885	John Hay Athole Macdonald
1886	John Blair Balfour
1886	John Hay Athole Macdonald
1888	James Patrick Bannerman Robertson
1891	Sir Charles John Pearson
1892	John Blair Balfour
1895	Sir Charles John Pearson
1896	Andrew Graham Murray
1903	Charles Scott Dickson
1905	Thomas Shaw
1909	Alexander Ure
1913	Robert Munro
1916	James Avon Clyde
1920	Thomas Brash Morison
1922	Charles David Murray
1922	Hon William Watson
1924	Hugh Pattison Macmillan
1924	Hon William Watson

1929	Alexander Munro MacRobert
1929	Craigie Mason Aitchison
1933	Wilfred Guild Normand
1935	Douglas Jamieson
1935	Thomas Mackay Cooper
1941	James Scott Cumberland Reid
1945	George Reid Thomson
1947	John Wheatley
1951	James Latham McDiarmid Clyde
1955	William Rankine Milligan
1960	William Grant
1962	Ian Hamilton Shearer
1964	George Gordon Stott
1967	Henry Stephen Wilson
1970	Norman Russell Wylie
1974	Ronald King Murray
1979	James Peter Hymer Mackay
1984	Kenneth John Cameron
1989	Peter Lovat Fraser
1992	Alan Ferguson Rodger
1995	Donald S Mackay
1997	Andrew Hardie

Solicitor General for Scotland

Holders of the office since Second World War

1945	Daniel Patterson Blades
1947	John Wheatley
1947	Douglas Johnston
1951	William Rankine Milligan
1955	William Grant
1960	David Colville Anderson
1964	Norman Russell Wylie
1964	James Graham Leechman
1965	Henry Stephen Wilson
1967	Ewan George Francis Stewart
1970	David William Robert Brand
1972	William Ian Stewart
1974	John Herbert McCluskey
1979	Nicholas Hardwick Fairbairn
1982	Peter Lovat Fraser
1989	Alan Ferguson Rodger
1992	Thomas Cordner Dawson
1995	Donald S Mackay
1997	Colin D Boyd

Queen's Counsel

Holders of the office at present

N A Sloan (1953); L H Daiches (1956); Douglas Reith (1957); D M Walker (1958); Sir Frederick O'Brien (1960); Neil Macvicar (1960); G S Gimson (1961); A A Bell (1961); Isabel L Sinclair (1964); R D Ireland (1964); A M G Russell (1965); J G Mitchell (1970); C R Macarthur (1970); James Law (1970); Neil Gow (1970); W M Walker (1971); Gavin Douglas (1971); G H Gordon (1972); W G Stevenson (1973); D B Robertson (1973); T G Coutts (1973); Professor John Murray (1974); Rt Hon Lord Macaulay of Bragar (1975); William C Galbraith (1977); N J Adamson (1979); J M S Horsburgh (1980); Ian R Hamilton (1980); R G Craik (1981); R G McEwan (1981); R E Henderson (1982); A G C McGregor (1982); C N McEachran (1982); Rt Hon W M Campbell (1982); Rt Hon Lord Fraser of Carmyllie (1982); C P C Boag-Thomson (1982); P K Vandore (1982); C G B Nicholson (1982); H H Campbell (1983); J F Wallace (1985); C S Haddow (1985); Rt Hon Lord Hardie (1985); Rt Hon Malcolm L Rifkind (1985); G N H Emslie (1986); R R Dalgety (1986); B A Kerr (1986); W J Taylor (1986); N D MacLeod (1986); T A K Drummond (1987); J L Mitchell (1987); M G Thomson (1987); P H Brodie (1987); Rt Hon Lord Mackay of Drumadoon (1987); Professor Robert Black (1987); W T Hook (1988); A C Horsfall (1988); Angus Stewart (1988); D R Findlay (1988); P G B McNeill (1988); I S Forrester (1988); R F Macdonald (1988); N M P Morrison (1988); J E Drummond Young (1988); R L Martin (1988); J S Mowat (1988); N D Shaffer (1989); E G M Targowski (1989); K N Mure (1989); M S Jones (1989); Douglas May (1989); C W McFarlane (1989); M Lynda Clark (1989); C J MacAulay (1989); M G Clarke (1989); I D MacPhail (1990); J C McInnes (1990); J C McCluskie (1990); G R Fleming (1990); C M Campbell (1990); C J M Sutherland (1990); Ann Paton (1990); R A Dunlop (1990); W G Jackson (1990); J J Maguire (1990); J W McNeill (1991); A F Wylie (1991); G C Bell (1991); Susan A O Raeburn (1991); D S Burns (1991); D A Y Menzies (1991); M C N Scott (1991); J Irvine Smith (1992); H A Kerrigan (1992); H W Currie (1992); Hugh

Matthews (1992); N D Murray (1992); E F Bowen (1992); I G Mitchell (1992); Alexander Bolland (1992); J J Mitchell (1992); Rita E A Rae (1992); D J Risk (1992); J F Wheatley (1992); C J Harris (1992); I A S Peebles (1993); R S Keen (1993); Anne Smith (1993); D I Mackay (1993); J Gordon Reid (1993); A B Wilkinson (1993); E Prais (1993); N F Davidson (1993); W S Gale (1993); G L Cox (1993); S N Brailsford (1994); Leeona J Dorrian (1994); A M Hajducki (1994); J A Peoples (1994); I R Abercrombie (1994); Deirdre M MacNeill (1994); C D Boyd (1995); Elizabeth Jarvie (1995); Sir Crispin Agnew (1995); A P Campbell (1995); P B Cullen (1995); A L Stewart (1995); Earl of Ancram (1996); P S Hodge (1996); J N Wright (1996); G R Steele (1996); A D Turnbull (1996); Fiona L Reith (1996); J C Morris (1996); Rt Hon Lord Selkirk of Douglas (1996); J R Doherty (1997); T Welsh (1997); J R Campbell (1997); J R Wallace (1997); G J Davidson (1997); G J B Moynihan (1997); I D Truscott (1997); J D Campbell (1998); Mungo Bovey (1998); Frances J McMenamin (1998); Susan J O'Brien (1998); D W Batchelor (1998); C J Tyre (1998); S E Woolman (1998); A J S Glennie (1998).

Moderator of the General Assembly of the Church of Scotland

Holders of the office since 1980
William B Johnston, Edinburgh Colinton, 1980; Andrew B Doig, National Bible Society of Scotland, 1981; John McIntyre, CVO, University of Edinburgh, 1982; J Fraser McLuskey, MC, London St Columba's, 1983; John M K Paterson, Milngavie St Paul's, 1984; David M B A Smith, Logie, 1985; Robert Craig, CBE, Emeritus of Jerusalem, 1986; Duncan Shaw, JP, Edinburgh Craigentinny St Christopher's, 1987; James A Whyte, University of St Andrews, 1988; William J G McDonald, Edinburgh Mayfield, 1989; Robert Davidson, University of Glasgow, 1990; William B R Macmillan, Dundee St Mary's, 1991; Hugh Wyllie, Hamilton Old, 1992; James L Weatherhead, Principal Clerk of Assembly, 1993; James A Simpson, Dornoch Cathedral, 1994; James Harkness, CB, OBE, Chaplain General (Emeritus), 1995; John H McIndoe, London: St Columba's lw Newcastle: St Andrew's, 1996; Alexander McDonald, General Secretary, Board of Ministry, 1997; Rev Professor Alan Main, University of Aberdeen, 1998; Rev John B Cairns, Dumbarton Riverside, 1999

Royal Scottish Academy

Holders of offices at present
Senior Academicians: Mary Armour; William J.L. Baillie, CBE; Ellen Malcolm; R Ross Robertson; Sir Anthony Wheeler, OBE.
Academicians: Elizabeth Blackadder, OBE; Gordon Bryce; Dennis Buchan; Frederick Bushe, OBE; Vincent Butler; Joyce Cairns; Alexander Campbell; Peter Collins; George Donald; David Evans; Alexander Fraser; Jake Harvey; John Houston, OBE; Ian Howard; Jack Knox; William Littlejohn; William Maclean; Andrew MacMillan, OBE; Andrew Merrylees; Isi Metzstein; David Michie, OBE; James Morris; James Morrison; Frances Pelly; Frank Pottinger; Barbara Rae; Philip Reeves; Stuart Renton, MBE; John Richards, CBE; James D Robertson; Bill Scott; Duncan Shanks; Ian McKenzie Smith, OBE; Michael Snowden; Robert R Steedman, OBE; Frances Walker
Senior Associates: A Buchanan Campbell; Derek Clarke; Earl Haig; George Wyllie
Associates: John Johnstone; James Fairgrieve; Geoffrey Squire; John G Clifford; Kirkland Main; William Brotherston; Alastair Ross; Iain R McIntosh; John Boys; Michael Docherty; John Mooney; Glen Onwin; Douglas Cocker; Arthur Watson; Roland Wedgwood; John Busby; Victoria Crowe; George Macpherson; Andrew Stenhouse; Ian Arnott; Bet Low; Fiona Dean; Ian McCulloch; Robert Black; Beth Fisher; Willie Rodger; Lennox Dunbar; Elspeth Lamb; Sylvia Wishart; David Page; Frank Convery; Adrian

Wiszniewski; Martin Rayner; Robin Webster; Alfons Bytautas; Ronald Forbes; Edward Summerton; Ric W L Russell; Stuart Duffin; Eileen Lawrence; Gordon Mitchell; Richard Murphy; Marion Smith

Chairmen, Royal Fine Art Commission

Sir John M Stirling-Maxwell, 1927-32
Lord Hamilton of Dalzell, 1932-52
Rt Hon Earl of Rosebery, 1952-56
Sir Hector Hetherington, 1957-65
Hon Lord Johnston, 1965-78
Professor Sir Robert Grieve, 1978-83
Professor A J Youngson, 1983-90
Hon Lord Prosser, 1990-95
Rt Hon Lord Cameron of Lochbroom, since 1995

Fellows, Scottish Council Development and Industry

Sir Kenneth Alexander, 1991; P E G Balfour, CBE, 1991; Professor C Blake, CBE, 1992; Hon J M E Bruce, CBE, 1993; Ian Christie, 1997; Sir William Coats, 1985; A R Cole-Hamilton, CBE, 1995; Sir James Duncan, 1992; Sir James Farquharson, KBE, 1985; J G S Gammell, MBE, 1985; W D H Gregson, CBE, DL, 1987; Dr T L Johnston, 1990; J Langan, 1987; Sir William Lithgow, Bt, 1985; W Low, CBE, 1988; I H Macdonald, OBE, 1991; Sir Robert Maclean, KBE, DL, 1985; Sir Donald McCallum, CBE, DL, 1993; D J McPherson, CBE, 1991; Sir James Marjoribanks, KCMG, 1985; Sir Peter Menzies, 1985; W C C Morrison, CBE, 1993; Brian Nicholls, 1997; K J Peters, CBE, JP, DL, 1988; Rt Hon Lord Polwarth, TD, DL, 1985; D S Reid, OBE, 1985; Dr W S Robertson, CBE, 1985; D A Ross Stewart, OBE, 1990; Lord Taylor of Gryfe, DL, 1985; R R Taylor, CBE, 1985; Professor A S Thomson, 1985; G B Young, CBE, 1985

Astronomers Royal for Scotland

Thomas Henderson, 1834-44
Charles Piazzi Smyth, 1846-88
Ralph Copeland, 1889-1905
Sir Frank Watson Dyson, 1905-10
Ralph Allen Sampson, 1910-37
Michael Greaves, 1938-55
Hermann Alexander Brück, 1957-75
Vincent Cartledge Reddish, 1975-80
Malcolm Sim Longair, 1980-90
Title in abeyance, 1991-95
John Campbell Brown, 1995-

Presidents, National Trust for Scotland

Since foundation in 1931
Duke of Atholl
Sir John Stirling Maxwell
Earl of Wemyss and March
Marquis of Bute
Duke of Atholl
Earl of Airlie

Presidents, Royal College of Surgeons of Edinburgh

Holders of the office since 1861

1861	Patrick Small Keir Newbigging
1863	Benjamin Bell
1865	James Dunsmure
1867	James Spence
1869	James Donaldson Gillespie
1871	William Walker
1873	James Simson
1875	Sir Henry Duncan Littlejohn
1877	Sir Patrick Heron Watson
1879	Francis Brodie Imlach
1882	Sir William Turner
1883	John Smith
1885	Douglas Moray Cooper Lamb Argyll Robertson
1887	Joseph Bell
1889	John Duncan
1891	Robert James Blair Cunynghame
1893	Peter Hume Maclaren
1895	Sir John Struthers
1897	John Chiene

1899	James Dunsmure
1901	Sir John Halliday Croom
1903	Sir Patrick Heron Watson
1905	Charles Watson MacGillivray
1907	Sir Joseph Montagu Cotterill
1910	Sir George Andreas Berry
1912	Francis Mitchell Caird
1914	Sir James William Beeman Hodson
1917	Robert McKenzie Johnston
1919	George Mackay
1921	Sir David Wallace
1923	Sir Harold Jalland Stiles
1925	Arthur Logan Turner
1927	Alexander Miles
1929	James Haig Ferguson
1931	John Wheeler Dowden
1933	Arthur Henry Havens Sinclair
1935	Sir Henry Wade
1937	William James Stuart
1939	Harry Moss Traquair
1941	John William Struthers
1943	Robert William Johnstone
1945	James Methuen Graham
1947	Francis Evelyn Jardine
1949	Walter Quarry Wood
1951	Sir Walter Mercer
1957	Sir John Bruce
1962	James Johnston Mason Brown
1964	George Ian Scott
1967	James Roderick Johnston Cameron
1970	Sir Donald Douglas
1973	James Alexander Ross
1976	Andrew Wood Wilkinson
1979	Francis John Gillingham
1982	Sir James David Fraser
1985	Thomas Jaffrey McNair
1988	Geoffrey Duncan Chisholm
1991	Patrick Stewart Boulter
1994	Sir Robert Shields
1997	Arnold G D Maran

Presidents, Royal College of Physicians of Edinburgh

Holders of the office since 1937

1937	Alexander Goodall
1940	Charles McNeil
1943	Andrew Fergus Hewat
1945	David Murray Lyon
1947	William Douglas Denton Small

1949	David Kennedy Henderson, Kt
1951	William Alister Alexander
1953	Leybourne Stanley Patrick Davidson, Kt
1957	Andrew Rae Gilchrist
1960	James Davidson Stuart Cameron
1963	Ian George Wilson Hill, Kt
1966	Christopher William Clayson
1970	John Halliday Croom
1973	John Wenman Crofton, Kt
1976	Ronald Foote Robertson
1979	John Anderson Strong
1982	Ronald Haxton Girdwood
1985	Michael Francis Oliver
1988	John Richmond
1991	Anthony Toft
1994	John D Cash
1997	James C Petrie

Presidents, Royal College of Physicians and Surgeons of Glasgow

Holders of the office since 1937

1937	John Henderson
1939	John Souttar McKendrick
1940	Roy Frew Young
1942	James Hogg MacDonald
1944	William Alexander Sewell
1946	Geoffrey Balmanno Fleming
1948	William Robertson Snodgrass
1950	Walter Weir Galbraith
1952	Andrew Allison
1954	Stanley Galbraith Graham
1956	Stanley Alstead
1958	Arthur Henry Jacobs
1960	Joseph Houston Wright
1962	Sir Charles Illingworth
1964	Archibald Brown Kerr
1966	James Holmes Hutchison
1968	Sir Robert Brash Wright
1970	Edward McCombie McGirr
1972	Sir Andrew Watt Kay
1974	Sir Ferguson Anderson
1976	Thomas Gibson
1978	Gavin Brown Shaw
1980	Douglas H Clark
1982	Thomas J Thomson
1984	Ian A MacGregor
1986	Arthur C Kennedy
1988	James McArthur
1990	Robert Hume

1992 Sir Donald Campbell
1994 Norman MacKay
1997 Colin MacKay

St Andrews University

Principals since 1859
1859 Sir David Brewster
1859 John Tulloch
1886 Sir James Donaldson
1915 Sir John Herkless
1921 Sir James Colquhoun Irvine
1953 Sir Thomas Malcolm Knox
1966 John Steven Watson
1986 Professor Struther Arnott

Glasgow University

Principals since 1858
1858 Thomas Barclay
1873 John Caird
1898 Robert Herbert Story
1907 Sir Donald MacAlister of Tarbert
1929 Sir Robert Sangster Rait
1936 Sir Hector James Wright
      Hetherington
1961 Sir Charles Haynes Wilson
1976 Alywn Williams
1988 Sir William Fraser
1995 Sir Graeme Davies
Rectors since 1965
1965 Lord Reith
1966 Lord MacLeod of Fuinary
1971 Jimmy Reid
1974 Arthur Montford
1977 John L Bell
1980 Reginald Bosanquet
1984 Michael Kelly
1987 Winnie Mandela
1990 Pat Kane
1993 Johnny Ball
1996 Richard Wilson
1999 Ross Kemp

Edinburgh University

Principals since 1859
1859 Sir David Brewster
1868 Sir Alexander Grant
1885 Sir William Muir
1903 Sir William Turner
1916 Sir James Ewing

1929 Sir Thomas Holland
1944 Sir John Fraser
1948 Sir Edward Appleton
1965 Sir Michael Swann
1974 Professor Sir Hugh Robson
1979 Sir John Burnett
1987 Sir David Smith
1994 Professor Sir Stewart Sutherland
Rectors since 1963
1963 James Robertson Justice
1966 Malcolm Muggeridge
1968 Kenneth Allsop
1971 Jonathan Wills
1972 Dr Gordon Brown
1975 Magnus Magnusson
1979 Dr Anthony Ross
1982 David Steel
1985 Archie MacPherson
1988 Muriel Gray
1991 Donnie Munro
1994 Dr Malcolm Macleod
1997 John Colquhoun

Aberdeen University

Principals since 1860
1860 Peter Colin Campbell
1876 William Robertson Pirie
1885 William Duguid Geddes
1900 John Marshall Lang
1909 George Adam Smith
1935 William Hamilton Fyfe
1948 Thomas Murray Taylor
1962 Edward Maitland Wright
1976 Fraser Noble
1981 George Paul McNicol
1991 John Maxwell Irvine
1996 C Duncan Rice
Rectors since 1963
1963 Rt Hon Lord Hunt
1966 Frank George Thomson
1969 Rt Hon Joseph Grimond
1972 Michael Fieldhouse Barratt
1975 Iain Cuthbertson
1978 Henderson Alexander Gall
1981 Robert John Perryment
1984 Hamish Watt
1987 Willis Pickard
1989 Colin Bell
1992 Ian Hamilton
1997 Allan Macartney
1999 Clarissa Dickson Wright

Compendium

Almanac

January

1	James Stuart (Old Pretender) died 1766
	Glasgow Chamber of Commerce incorporated 1783
2	Ibrox Park disaster, 66 supporters killed, 1971
3	O H Mavor (James Bridie) born 1888
7	Glasgow University founded 1450
8	Lord Hardie of Blackford, Lord Advocate, born 1946
10	Rod Stewart born 1945
13	Keir Hardie founded Independent Labour Party 1893
17	Compton Mackenzie born 1883
19	James Watt born 1736
20	Benny Lynch crowned world flyweight champion 1937
22	Ramsay MacDonald first Labour Prime Minister 1924
24	First train over Forth Bridge 1890
25	Robert Burns born 1759
27	Glasgow Herald first published 1783
	First public demonstration of TV by John Logie Baird 1926
28	William Burke, body snatcher, executed 1829
29	Greenwich Mean Time adopted by Scotland 1848
31	Charles Edward Stuart died 1788
	Princess Victoria, Stranraer-Larne ferry, sank 1953

February

5	Thomas Carlyle died 1881
8	Mary, Queen of Scots, beheaded 1587
9	Sandy Lyle born 1958
10	Lord Darnley, Mary Stuart's consort, assassinated 1567
11	John Buchan died 1940
13	Massacre of Glencoe 1692
20	James I assassinated 1437
	Gordon Brown, Chancellor of the Exchequer, born 1951
22	Robert II acceded to Scottish throne 1370
24	Flying Scotsman went into service 1923
	Denis Law born 1940
26	Harry Lauder died 1950
28	Robin Cook, Foreign Secretary, born 1946

March

1	Scots voted in favour of devolution, but failed to reach 40% threshhold 1979
3	Alexander Graham Bell born 1847
7	Alexander Graham Bell patented the telephone 1876
9	David Rizzio murdered 1566
11	Alexander Fleming died 1955
13	Clydeside blitz 1941
	Sixteen primary school children and their teacher murdered in Dunblane 1996

14	First television programmes broadcast in Scotland 1952
17	cotland won Grand Slam for first time in 59 years 1984
19	Tobias Smollett born 1721
	David Livingstone born 1813
	Billy Graham began All-Scotland Crusade 1955
24	Crowns of England and Scotland united 1603
25	Bruce crowned king of Scotland 1306
27	First Scotland/England rugby international 1871
31	David Steel born 1938

April

1	Robert III died 1406
2	George MacDonald Fraser born 1925
4	James VII deprived of throne 1689
	John Napier, inventor of logarithms, died 1617
6	Declaration of Arbroath 1320
7	Jim Clark killed in crash 1968
9	Lord Lovat beheaded on Tower Hill for high treason 1747
10	James V born 1512
16	Charles Edward Stuart defeated at Culloden 1746
24	Mary, Queen of Scots, married French dauphin 1558
27	Scots defeated by Edward I at Dunbar 1296
29	Andrew Cruickshank died 1988

May

1	Union of England and Scotland proclaimed 1707
	David Livingstone died 1873
5	Sir Hugh Fraser died 1987
6	Elections for Scottish Parliament 1999
7	David Hume born 1711
9	J M Barrie born 1860
10	Rudolf Hess, Hitler's deputy, descended by parachute into Scotland 1941
12	John Smith died 1994
13	Mary, Queen of Scots, defeated at Battle of Langside 1568
15	Mary, Queen of Scots, married Bothwell 1567
21	James, Marquess of Montrose, died 1650
24	Malcolm IV acceded to Scottish throne 1153
	First circulating library opened in Edinburgh 1726
	Stanley Baxter born 1928
25	John Stuart, Earl of Bute, Britain's first Scottish Prime Minister, born 1713
	Oscar Slater found guilty of murder 1909
	Celtic won European Cup 1967
28	Cheapside docks fire, Glasgow, 19 firemen killed, 1960
29	Peter Manuel sentenced to death at the High Court in Glasgow for seven murders 1958

June

1	Covenanters defeated Claverhouse at Dumclog 1679
	Pope John Paul II in Glasgow 1982
2	Helicopter crash on Mull of Kintyre, 29 anti-terrorism experts killed, 1994

4	Peru defeated Scotland 3-1 in World Cup 1978
5	HMS Hampshire sank off Orkney 1916
	Adam Smith born 1723
7	James Young Simpson born 1811
	Robert the Bruce died 1329
10	James Stuart (Old Pretender) born 1688
11	James III assassinated 1488
	Empress of Britain launched from Clydebank 1930
13	James Clerk Maxwell born 1831
14	John Logie Baird died 1946
16	Mary, Queen of Scots, recognised Philip II of Spain as her heir 1586
	Lord Reith died 1971
17	Articles of religion, introducing Anglican principles into Scottish worship, endorsed by Scottish parliament 1617
19	James VI of Scotland and I of England born 1566
	J M Barrie died 1937
20	New Tay rail bridge opened 1887
21	German fleet scuttled in Scapa Flow 1919
22	Duke of Monmouth subdued insurrection of Covenanters at Bothwell Bridge 1679
23	Mass protest in West of Scotland against closure of John Brown's shipyard 1971
24	Robert the Bruce defeated Edward II at Bannockburn 1314
25	Crofters Act passed 1886

July

1	Queen opened new Scottish Parliament 1999
	Craig Brown born 1940
2	Lord Home of the Hirsel born 1903
	Erskine Bridge opened 1971
3	Robert Adam born 1728
	John Logie Baird transmitted first colour television 1928
6	Explosion aboard North Sea oil rig Piper Alpha, 166 lives lost, 1988
7	Kelvin Hall exhibition building, Glasgow, destroyed by fire 1925
	David Steel became Liberal leader 1976
9	Madeleine Smith acquitted of murder 1857
11	Robert the Bruce born 1274
	Eric Liddell won Olympic 400 metres in Paris 1924
12	Sir Alastair Burnet born 1928
13	Scottish Reform Act passed 1868
16	Commonwealth Games opened in Edinburgh 1970
17	Adam Smith died 1790
18	John Smith became Labour leader 1992
20	Lord Reith born 1889
	Oscar Slater's conviction quashed 1928
21	Robert Burns died 1796
	Maurice Lindsay born 1918
	Sandy Lyle won Open Golf Championship 1985
22	English defeated Scots at Battle of Falkirk 1298

23	Charles Edward Stuart landed on Eriskay 1745
24	James VI acceded to Scottish throne 1567
	David Wilkie won Olympic 200 metres breaststroke 1976
25	Annie Ross, singer, born 1930
	Alan Wells won Olympic 100 metres 1980
26	Ill-fated Darien expedition sailed from Scotland 1698
28	Forth and Clyde canal opened 1790
29	Mary, Queen of Scots, married Lord Darnley 1565
	Jo Grimond born 1913

August

3	James II killed 1460
4	Harry Lauder born 1870
5	Wallace captured by the English 1305
6	Sir Alexander Fleming born 1881
11	C M Grieve (Hugh MacDiarmid) born 1892
13	John Logie Baird born 1888
15	Macbeth killed in battle 1057
	Sir Walter Scott born 1771
	Keir Hardie born 1856
17	Royal visit of George IV to Edinburgh began 1822
18	Tay Road Bridge opened 1966
21	Donald Dewar, Secretary of State for Scotland, born 1937
23	Wallace executed 1305
25	David Hume died 1776
	James Watt died 1819
	Sean Connery born 1930
	Ramsay MacDonald formed a National Government 1931
27	First balloon ascent in Britain by James Tytler, at Edinburgh, 1784

September

3	Cromwell defeated Scots at Battle of Dunbar 1650
4	Forth Road Bridge opened 1964
5	Robert Fergusson born 1750
9	James IV killed in battle at Flodden 1513
	C M Grieve (Hugh MacDiarmid) died 1978
10	English defeated Scots at Battle of Pinkie 1547
	Mungo Park born 1771
11	James Thomson, author of *Rule Britannia*, born 1700
	Referendum on Scottish Parliament 1997
13	Montrose defeated by Covenanters at Battle of Philiphaugh 1645
	John Smith born 1938
15	Charles Edward Stuart occupied Edinburgh 1745
18	Lord Rodger of Earlsferry, Lord Justice General, born 1944
20	Queen Elizabeth II launched from Clydebank 1966
21	John Home born 1722
	Charles Edward Stuart victorious at Prestonpans 1745
	John McAdam born 1756
22	Viscount Younger of Leckie (George Younger) born 1931
27	Barbara Dickson born 1948
28	Jeremy Isaacs born 1932

October

2	United Free Church merged with Church of Scotland 1929
4	Boys' Brigade founded in Glasgow 1883
9	Lord Home of the Hirsel died 1995
10	Hugh Miller born 1802
12	Ramsay MacDonald born 1866
13	Allan Ramsay, painter, born 1713
14	German submarine sank Royal Oak in Scapa Flow, 1939
15	Allan Ramsay, poet, born 1686
16	James II born 1430
	Michael Forsyth born 1954
17	George Mackay Brown born 1921
21	Clarkston Toll disaster, 12 killed, 1971
29	James Boswell born 1740
30	Caledonian Canal opened 1822
31	Alastair Hetherington born 1919

November

1	Bank of Scotland founded 1695
	Naomi Mitchison born 1897
3	Ludovic Kennedy born 1919
8	John Duns Scotus died 1308
	Neil Gunn born 1891
12	Sir James Young Simpson first used chloroform as an anaesthetic 1847
13	Malcolm III killed 1093
	Robert Louis Stevenson born 1850
17	John Baliol acceded to Scottish throne 1292
22	Tom Conti born 1942
24	John Knox died 1572
	Billy Connolly born 1942
25	Andrew Carnegie born 1835
27	Oscar Slater released from prison 1927
	First deaths from E-coli outbreak in Scotland 1996
29	Margaret, Queen of Scotland, born 1489

December

3	Robert Louis Stevenson died 1894
4	Thomas Carlyle born 1795
6	Charles Edward Stuart's entry into Derby 1745
8	Mary, Queen of Scots, born 1542
10	Charles Rennie Mackintosh died 1928
14	Mary, Queen of Scots, acceded to Scottish throne 1542
20	First General Assembly of Church of Scotland ratified Confession of Faith 1560
21	Lockerbie disaster, 270 killed, 1988
23	Hugh Miller died 1856
25	Stone of Destiny removed from Westminster Abbey 1950
26	Sir Alastair Dunnett born 1908
28	Rob Roy died 1734
	Tay Bridge disaster 1879
31	Charles Edward Stuart died 1720
	Alex Salmond born 1954

Awards and Honours

Saltire Society

(1) Civil Engineering Awards 1998

Design and Construction Award
Halcrow Crouch/Edmund Nuttall for Scalpay Bridge, Harris (commissioning authority: Western Isles Council)
Design Awards
W A Fairhurst & Partners for Forth Road Bridge tower upgrading (commissioning authority: Forth Road Bridge Joint Board)
Ove Arup/Morrison for Nigg dock upgrade (commissioning authority: Brown & Root McDermott)
Construction Award
Charles Brand Ltd for Ardveenish fish pier, Barra (commissioning authority: Western Isles Council)
Design Commendations
The Babtie Group for Stornoway ferry terminal (commissioning authority: Stornoway Pier Commission)
West of Scotland Water Engineers for Fairlie sewage treatment (commissioning authority: West of Scotland Water)
Wallace Stone & Partners for Ardveenish fish pier (commissioning authority: Western Isles Council)
Construction Commendations
Balfour Beatty Scotland for A8 Eurocentral Interchange (commissioning authority: Lanarkshire Development Agency)
Grootcon UK Ltd for Forth Road Bridge tower upgrading (commissioning authority: Forth Road Bridge Joint Board)
Conservation Commendations
Halcrow Crouch/Morrison Construction for refurbishment of Bridge of Oich (commissioning authority: Historic Scotland)
Ted Ruddock/Hunter & Clark for restoration of Nasmyth Bridge (commissioning authority: West Lothian Council)

(2) Housing Design Awards 1998

Award for New Housing
Lee Boyd Partnership: 10–26 Pitt Street for Port of Leith Housing Association

Commendations for New Housing
Chris Stewart/Vernon Managhan: O'Neil Terrace, Alexandria for Dunbritton Housing Association
Wilson Partnership: 24/26 Dock Street and 19/27 Exchange Street, Dundee for Hillcrest Housing Association
Vernon Monaghan: Stravanan Road/Castlemilk Drive, Castlemilk for Northview Housing Association
Commendation for New Housing in Rural Areas
Brunton Voight Partnership: Tulloch Wynd, Dykehead by Kirriemuir for Angus Housing Association
Commendation for Housing Restoration
Adam Dudley: 27–29 Buccleuch Street, Edinburgh for Southside Housing Improvements

(3) Literary awards 1998

National Library of Scotland/ Saltire Research Book of the Year
The Edinburgh History of the Scots Language, by Charles Jones
Post Office/Saltire First Book of the Year
The Pied Piper's Poison, by Christopher Wallace and *Two Clocks Ticking*, by Dennis O'Donnell
The Scotsman/Saltire Book of the Year
The Sopranos, by Alan Warner

Other Awards

1998 Times Educational Supplement in Scotland/Saltire Society Award for Educational Publications
Hodder & Stoughton for *Society and You*
1998 Scottish Science Award

Professor Neil A R Gow of Aberdeen University for his work in the field of biological sciences

1998 Historical Research Book of the Year
Dr William Ferguson for *The Identity of the Scottish Nation – an historic quest*

Association for Protection of Rural Scotland

Annual award scheme, instituted in 1975, encourages good planning, architecture and landscaping and recognises particularly fine examples of structures in a rural setting. It is thought essential that each work be seen to be making a definite contribution to the rural scene in Scotland.

Winners
1975 The Smiddy Bothy, Dundonell, Wester Ross
1976 Torridon Youth Hostel, Wester Ross
1977 Gigha Hotel, Isle of Gigha
1978 Little Carbeth, Killearn, Stirlingshire
1979 Parton Village, near Castle Douglas
1980 Boathouse, Loch Marlich, Inverness-shire
1981 Corrigill Farm Museum, Harray, Orkney
1982 Flotta Oil Terminal, Orkney
1983 Easter Society, Hopetoun, West Lothian
1984 Fowler Croft, Straiton, Ayrshire
1985 The Old Castle, East Saltoun, East Lothian
1986 Salen Primary School, Mull
1987 The Hanseatic Booth, Symbister, Whalsay, Shetland; Fort George, Inverness
1988 Kylesku Bridge, Sutherland
1989 Muir of Blebo, near Cupar
1990 Aonach Mor, near Fort William
1991 The Auld Haa, Fair Isle, Shetland; Shirgarton Farmhouse, Kippen, Stirling
1992 Gesto, Isle of Skye
1993 Doctor's surgery, Ballachulish, near Fort William

1994 Six cottages, Balmacara, Kyle of Lochalsh
1995 Ardgour Primary School, near Fort William; Cantraybridge Rural Skills Cottage, Cawdor; Inverewe Garden Restaurant, Wester Ross; Old Seminary, The Scalan, Glenlivet; Moray District Local Plan, 1993-98 (Housing in the Countryside)
1996 Craigend Visitor Centre, Mugdock Country Park; The Mews and Courtyard, Sundrum Castle, Ayrshire; Scalpay Community Centre
1997 Glenmore Visitors Centre, Cairngorm
1998 Conversion of stables to a dwelling at Easter Tullybannocher, Comrie; Pentlands Science Park, Penicuik

Regeneration of Scotland Award

Royal Incorporation of Architects in Scotland award, sponsored in 1998 by Scottish Enterprise and the Miller Group. Established in 1985, it recognises the enormous potential of buildings to improve everyday lives and has been given both to new buildings and existing buildings converted for re-use.

1998 results

Supreme Award
Luma Tower, Glasgow (Cornelius McClymont for Linthouse Housing Association)

Awards
New Library, University of Abertay, Dundee (Parr Partnership)
Irvine Harbourside (Department of Architecture, Irvine Development Corporation for Irvine Housing Association)

High Commendations
Princes House, Glasgow (Fletcher Joseph Architects for Teesland Developments)
Portobello Swim Centre, Edinburgh (Percy-Johnson Marshall & Partners for

Edinburgh Leisure, City of Edinburgh Council)
Art tm Gallery, Inverness (Sutherland Hussey Architects for Art tm Gallery)

Commendations
9 George Square, Glasgow (Glass Murray Architects for Co-operative Insurance Society)
Pentlands Science Park, Penicuik (Oberlanders Architects for the Moredun Foundation)
One Pacific Quay (Parr Partnership for Pacific Quay Developments)
Virginia House, Glasgow (Keith Hobbs of United Designers Ltd, for King City Leisure)
Conversion of former Argyll Motor Works, Alexandria (Page & Park Architects for Acreground)

Calor Gas
Scottish Community
of the Year 1998

Presented in collaboration with the Association for the Protection of Rural Scotland and the Association of Scottish Community Councils. The awards aim to develop awareness of community councils and highlight work being undertaken by communities throughout Scotland.

Overall Scottish Community of the Year (joint winners): Assynt Community Council and Mayfield and Easthouses Community Council
Rural Community of the Year: Assynt Community Council
Urban Community of the Year: Mayfield and Easthouses Community Council
Environment section: Newcastleton and District Community Council
Business section: Newtonmore and Vicinity Community Council
Young people section: Cromarty and District Community Council
Older people section: Langholm, Ewes and Westerkirk Community Council
Community life section: West Ardnamurchan Community Council

Taste of Scotland Awards

Set up to encourage the pursuit of excellence and by so doing to encourage others to emulate the winners.

1993
Hotel: Sheraton Grand Hotel, Edinburgh; *Country house hotel:* Balgonie Country House Hotel, Ballater; *special merit awards:* Creelers Seafood Restaurant, Brodick; Kirroughtree Hotel, Newton Stewart

1994
Hotel: Isle of Eriska Hotel, near Oban; *Country house hotel:* Ballathie House Hotel, near Perth; *special merit award for outstanding hospitality:* Lynwilg House, by Aviemore; *special merit award for enterprise:* Chatters, Dunoon; *Macallan Personality of the Year:* Andrew Radford, Atrium, Edinburgh

1995
Hotel: Balmoral Hotel, Edinburgh; *Restaurant:* Green Inn, Ballater; *Country house hotel:* Flodigarry Country House Hotel, Staffin, Skye; *special merit award for newcomers:* Braidwoods Restaurant, near Dalry; *special merit award for achievement:* Loch Fyne Oyster Bar, Cairndow; *Macallan Personality of the Year:* Christine Morrison, Handa, Lochs, Isle of Lewis

1996
Hotel: Balbirnie House Hotel, Glenrothes; *Restaurant:* Symphony Room at Beardmore Hotel, Clydebank; *Country house hotel:* Ardsheal House, Kentallen; *special merit award for best informal lunch:* East Haugh Country House Hotel and Restaurant, Pitlochry; *special merit award for hospitality:* Little Lodge, Gairloch; *Macallan Personality of the Year:* Stewart Cameron, Turnberry Hotel

1997
Hotel: Wheatsheaf Hotel, Swinton; *Restaurant:* Let's Eat, Perth; *Country house hotel:* Knockinaam Lodge, Portpatrick; *special merit award for best*

lunch: Ballathie House Hotel, Perth; *special merit award for best tea-room:* Kind Kyttock's Kitchen, Falkland; *Macallan Personality of the Year:* Alan Craigie, Creel Restaurant and Rooms, St Margaret's Hope, Orkney

1998
Hotel: Crinan Hotel, Crinan; *Restaurant (jointly):* Let's Eat, Perth, Three Chimneys Restaurant, Isle of Skye; *Country house hotel:* Kilmichael Country House Hotel, Isle of Arran; *best breakfast:* Kinloch Lodge, Isle of Skye; *best child friendly establishment:* Old Pines Restaurant, Spean Bridge; *overall excellence award and best restaurant with rooms:* The Albannach, Lochinver

Thistle Awards

Recognises and celebrates excellence in Scottish tourism.

1998 awards

Silver Thistle for Outstanding Achievement: Ian Grant, CBE
Small Company Training: Poole House Hotel, Poolewe
Large Company Training: The Glasgow Marriott
Tourism for All: Scotch Whisky Heritage Centre
Tourism and the Environment: Brighouse Bay Holiday Park, Kirkcudbright
Tourism and the Arts: Highlands of Scotland Tourist Board for *Discover the Highlands of Scotland and its art and culture*
Tourism and the Media: Nick Nairn for Island Harvest
Natural Cooking of Scotland: Harbour Inn, Isle of Islay
Serviced Accommodation: Acorn Lodge Guest House
Area Tourism Initiative: Scottish Borders Events Development Scheme
Student of the Year: Graham Hood, Perth College
Manager of the Year: Stephen Leckie, Crieff Hydro
Scotland Year-round: Farleyer House Hotel, Aberfeldy
Small Business Marketing: Loch Lomond Castle Lodges
Marketing Campaign of the Year: Stirling Initiative

Beautiful Scotland in Bloom

1999 awards

Premier Awards
Bank of Scotland Rosebowl: Perth
Rosebowl Reserve Trophy: Alness
Best Village Shield: Comrie
Class Awards
City: Aberdeen
Large Town: Perth
Medium Town: Hawick
Small Town: Alness
Country Town: Pitlochry
Urban Community: Balerno
Large Village: Comrie
Small Village: Denholm
Special Project Awards
Bank of Scotland Garden Seats for special projects in cities, towns or villages: Lovat Hotel Wall, Fort Augustus, Crieff Road Pre-school Centre, Perth
Entrant Awards
Lady Jane Grosvenor Wee Village Trophy: Rowanburn, Dumfries and Galloway
New Entrant Trophy: Monymusk, Aberdeenshire
Horticultural Award: Perth
Permanent Landscaping Award: East Kilbride
Cleanliness Award: Rowanburn, Dumfries and Galloway
Sustainable Development Award: East Kilbride
Local Authority Awards
Royal Caledonian Horticultural Society Trophy: Perth and Kinross Council
ILAM Scotland Trophy: Highland Council
IWM Scottish Centre Trophy: Highland Council
Sustainable Development Award: Dumfries and Galloway Council
Greenfingers Challenge
Scottish Winner: Glenluce Primary School, Dumfries and Galloway
Royal British Legion – Best Kept War Memorials
Champion of Champions: Forres
Memorials with Gardens (Large

Community): Tayport
Memorials with Gardens (Small Community): Glenurquhart, Drumnadrochit
Memorials without Gardens: Oban

Scottish Arts Council

1998 Spring Book Awards
Duncan McLean for Lone Star Swing
Candia McWilliam for Wait Till I Tell You
Allan Massie for Shadows of Empire
Alastair Reid for Oases
Christopher Whyte for The Warlock of Strathearn

1998 Autumn Book Awards
William Boyd for Armadillo
James Kelman for The Good Times
Dilys Rose for War Dolls
Alice Thompson for Pandora's Box
Alan Warner for The Sopranos

1999 Spring Book Awards
Michael Faber for Some Rain Must Fall
Jackie Kay for Trumpet
W N Herbert for The Laurelude
Robin Jenkins for Matthew and Sheila

First Scottish Arts Council Children's Book Awards
Joan Lingard for Tom and the Tree House
J K Rowling for Harry Potter and the Chamber of Secrets
Susan Cooper for The Boggart and the Monster
Ross Collins and Frances Thomas for Supposing
Catherine MacPhail for Fighting Back

Scottish Writer of the Year

McVitie's Prize
1987 David Thomson for Nairn in Darkness and Light
1988 Bernard MacLaverty for The Great Profundo & Other Stories; and Edwin Mickleburgh for Antarctica: Beyond the Frozen Sea
1989 Alan Bold for MacDiarmid
1990 Sorley MacLean for From Wood to Ridge
1991 William Boyd for Brazzaville

Beach
1992 John Purser for Scotland's Music
1993 John Prebble for Landscapes and Memories
1994 Janice Galloway for Foreign Parts
1995 Frank Kuppner for Something Very Like Murder
1996 Alan Spence for Stone Garden and other stories

Stakis Prize
1997 Aongoas MacNeacail for A Proper Schooling and other poems
1998 Edwin Morgan for Virtual and Other Realities; James Kelman for The Good Times

An Comunn Gaidhealach

Winners of the Royal National Mod Gold Medal 1990-98

1990 Gillian MacKenzie, Gress
Donald M MacInnes, North Bragar
1991 Wilma Kennedy, Glasgow
Donald Murray, Insch
1992 Katrina MacKellar, Auldearn
George Gunn, Inbhir Nis
1993 Mairead Stiubhart-Harding, Am Bac
Seumas Gunna, Inbhir Nis
1994 Maggie MacDonald, Inverness
Norman MacKinnon, Campbeltown
1995 Margaret J MacLellan, Mingarry
Fionnlagh MacAoidh, Goilspidh
1996 Joanne Murray, Lewis
Alasdair Barnett, Oban
1997 Alyth McCormack, Glasgow
Grahma Neilson, Edinburgh
1998 Barbara Smith, Dornie
Angus Smith, Oban

Winners of the Lovat & Tullibardine Choral Competition, 1990-98

1990 Ceolraidh Ghaidhlig Ghlaschu
1991 Largs Gaelic Choir
1992 Glasgow Hebridean Choir
1993 Glasgow Gaelic Musical Assoc
1994 Oban Gaelic Choir
1995 Coisir Ghaidhlig Inbhirnis
1996 Dingwall Gaelic Choir

1997   Glasgow Islay Gaelic Choir
1998   Coisir Ghaidhlig Inbhirnis

Scottish Press Awards
sponsored by Bank of Scotland

Winners 1999

Journalist of the Year: Joan McAlpine, Sunday Times Scotland
Scoop of the Year (joint winners): Fidelma Cook, Mail on Sunday (on the decision not to award Sean Connery a knighthood); Andrew Barr/Karen Grant/Alan Muir/ Martin Wallace, The Sun (story exposing Ian Oliver, former Chief Constable of Grampian, which was followed by his departure from the post)
Reporter of the Year: Fidelma Cook, Mail on Sunday
Journalist Team of the Year: Charles Beaton/Stuart Griffiths, Daily Record
Feature Writer of the Year: Joan McAlpine, Sunday Times Scotland
Columnist of the Year: William McIlvanney, The Herald
Campaigning Journalist of the Year: Allison McLaughlin, Daily Record
Financial/Business Writer of the Year: Gary Duncan, The Scotsman
Political Journalist of the Year: Peter MacMahon, The Scotsman
Sports Journalist of the Year: Bill Leckie, The Sun
Arts/Entertainment Writer of the Year: Ajay Close, The Herald
Cartoonist of the Year: Steven Camley, Scotland on Sunday
Anthony Finlay Award for Young Journalist of the Year: Mark Daly, Clydebank Post
Weekly Newspaper Journalist of the Year: Katherine Dearden, Galloway Gazette
Erskine Hospital David Boyle Memorial Award: Aileen Ballantyne, Sunday Times Scotland
Sgriobhadh Gaidhlig: Chrissie Dick (Criosaidh Dick), The Scotsman

Royal Scottish Academy
Annual Exhibition Awards 1999

RSA Guthrie Award: Alasdair Wallace for Field

RSA Latimer Award: Sara Gallie for Idyllic Twist
RSA Benno Schotz Prize: Colin C J Macfadyen for Nut and Bolt In Triassic Sandstone
RSA Keith Prize: Joyce Wiseman for Concept II
RSA Ottillie Helen Wallace Scholarship Prize: Lucy Poett for Laura
RSA Medal for Architecture: Paul Stallon for The Parson Street Project Townhead, Glasgow
John Murray Thomson Award: Margaret M Smyth for Puccini's Window
Maude Gemmell Hutchison Prizes: Michael Agnew for If Only They Could; Beth Fisher for Night Dogs
William J Macaulay/Scottish Gallery Award: Michael Snowden for The Triathlete
N S Macfarlane Charitable Trust Award (Painting): Caroline Baillie for Hillside, Mull
N S Macfarlane Charitable Trust Award (Sculpture): Elaine Allison for Head of a Dancer
Dunfermline Building Society Prize: William Littlejohn for Dark Colour-Wheel
Highland Society of London Award: Neil Macpherson for Life's Tender Journey
Scottish Arts Club Prize: Adrian Wiszniewski for Raspberryade
Glasgow Arts Club Prize: Jo Ganter for Monument

Royal Scottish Society of Painters in Water-colours

Prize-winners 1999

Alexander Graham Munro Travel Award: Emma S Davis for Winter's Tale
RSW Council Award: James D Robertson for Inner Harbour
Alexander Graham Munro Award: A McEwan for Big Country
John Gray Award: William J L Baillie for Winter View from Playfair Steps
Sir William Gillies Award: Kirkland Main for Lincluden
May Marshall Brown Award: Dawson

Murray for In and Out of the Garden
Scottish Arts Club Award: Alasdair Wallace for Darkfield
Glasgow Arts Club Fellowship: Caroline Bailey for The Red Field

Scottish Community Drama Association

Scottish one act festival 1999

1, Kirkton Players; 2, Atholl Players; 3, Edinburgh Civil Service Dramatic Society; *best stage decor:* Kirkton Players; *best original play:* Wick Players, A Talent for Giving by Mike Tibbetts

Scottish Museums Council

Kintore Award for Conservation 1999

Specially Commended Award Winner
Falkirk Museum for "Presents from the Past", communicating preventive conservation

Other winners
Dunblane Cathedral City Museum for the conservation of communion tokens
Groam House Museum, Rosemarkie, for the conservation of the George Bain collection of Pictish and Celtic designs
Paxton House for the conservation of a carnival costume worn by Patrick Home of Paxton House in 1750

The Queen's Awards

Instituted by royal warrant in 1976 as the Queen's Award for Export Achievement and the Queen's Award for Technological Achievement and taking the place of the Queen's Award to Industry, which was instituted in 1965. A third award, the Queen's Award for Environmental Achievement, was instituted in 1992

Scottish winners 1999

Export Achievement
Aggreko UK Limited – Manufacturing, Dumbarton
Compugraphics International Ltd, Glenrothes
Edinburgh Business School, Edinburgh
Elmar Services Ltd, Aberdeen
Glenmorangie plc, Broxburn
Hydrovision Ltd, Dyce, Aberdeen
Innovative Tooling Solutions (division of Forth Tool and Valve Ltd), Glenrothes
The Macallan Distillers Ltd, Craigellachie, Moray
MacDuff Shellfish (Scotland) Ltd, MacDuff, Aberdeenshire
McCormick Europe, Condiment Division, Paisley
Walkers Shortbread Ltd, Aberlour-on-Spey, Moray

Technological Achievement
Telecom Systems Division of Hewlett-Packard Ltd, South Queensferry

Environmental Achievement
None

Quality Scotland

The Quality Scotland Award for Business Excellence, instituted in 1994, is based on the belief that the promotion of quality and the achievement of excellence can be sustained in Scotland through the existence of a prestigious quality award.

Awards

1994 OKI (UK) Ltd, Cumbernauld
 Blue Circle Cement, Dunbar
1995 Aviall Caledonian Engine Services, Prestwick
 O.I.L. Ltd, Aberdeen
 Rank-Xerox (Scotland), Glasgow
1996 Inland Revenue Accounts, Cumbernauld
 TSB Homeloans, Glasgow
 Vesuvius, Newmilns
1997 ICI Explosives Europe
 Aberdeen College
 Govan Initiatives Ltd
1998 Honeywell Control Systems Ltd, Motherwell
 Scottish Homes

The Towns of Scotland

In official statistics prepared from the 1991 census, there appear such "towns" as Clarkston and Polmont which are suburbs rather than towns. Compiling a list of genuine towns, we have chosen to return to the self-governing structure of burghs which existed until the mid 1970s. We think we have caught all of them – but there were rather a lot! Population figure as shown.

Aberchirder *Aberdeenshire* 1,098
Aberdeen *Aberdeen* 189,707
Aberfeldy *Perth and Kinross* 1,748
Aberlour *Moray* 821
Abernethy *Perth and Kinross* 895
Airdrie *North Lanarkshire* 36,998
Alloa *Clackmannan* 18,842
Alva *Clackmannan* 5,201
Alyth *Perth and Kinross* 2,383
Annan *Dumfries and Galloway* 8,930
Anstruther *Fife* 3,650
Arbroath *Angus* 23,474
Ardrossan *North Ayrshire* 10,750
Armadale *West Lothian* 8,958
Auchterarder *Perth and Kinross* 3,549
Auchtermuchty *Fife* 1,932
Ayr *South Ayrshire* 47,962
Ballater *Aberdeenshire* 1,362
Banchory *Aberdeenshire* 6,230
Banff *Aberdeenshire* 4,110
Barrhead *East Renfrewshire* 17,252
Bathgate *West Lothian* 13,819
Bearsden *East Dunbartonshire* 27,806
Biggar *South Lanarkshire* 1,994
Bishopbriggs *E Dunbartonshire* 23,825
Blairgowrie *Perth and Kinross* 8,001
Bo'ness *Falkirk* 14,595
Bonnyrigg and Lasswade *Midlothian* 13,696
Brechin *Angus* 7,655
Bridge of Allan *Stirling* 4,864
Buckhaven and Methil *Fife* 17,069
Buckie *Moray* 8,425
Burghead *Aberdeenshire* no pop count
Burntisland *Fife* 5,951
Callander *Stirling* 2,622
Campbeltown *Argyll and Bute* 5,722
Carnoustie *Angus* 10,673
Castle Douglas *Dumfries and Galloway* 3,697
Clydebank *West Dunbartonshire* 29,171
Coatbridge *North Lanarkshire* 43,617
Cockenzie and Port Seton *East Lothian* 4,235

Coldstream *Borders* 1,746
Coupar Angus *Perth and Kinross* 2,223
Cove and Kilcreggan *Argyll and Bute* 1,586
Cowdenbeath *Fife* 12,126
Crail *Fife* 1,449
Crieff *Perth and Kinross* 6,023
Cromarty *Highland* 721
Cullen *Moray* 1,430
Culross *Fife* 470
Cumbernauld *North Lanarkshire* 48,762
Cumnock *East Ayrshire* 9,607
Cupar *Fife* 7,545
Dalbeattie *Dumfries and Galloway* 4,421
Dalkeith *Midlothian* 11,567
Darvel *East Ayrshire* 3,759
Denny and Dunipace *Falkirk* 13,481
Dingwall *Highland* 5,224
Dollar *Clackmannan* 2,670
Dornoch *Highland* 1,196
Doune *Stirling* 1,213
Dufftown *Moray* 1,750
Dumbarton *West Dunbartonshire* 21,962
Dumfries *Dumfries and Galloway* 31,136
Dunbar *East Lothian* 6,518
Dunblane *Stirling* 7,368
Dundee *Dundee* 158,981
Dunfermline *Fife* 55,083
Dunoon *Argyll and Bute* 9,038
Duns *Borders* 2,444
East Kilbride *South Lanarkshire* 70,422
East Linton *East Lothian* 1,422
Edinburgh *Edinburgh* 401,910
Elgin *Moray* 19,027
Elie and Earlsferry *Fife* 903
Ellon *Aberdeenshire* 8,627
Eyemouth *Borders* 3,473
Falkirk *Falkirk* 35,610
Falkland *Fife* 1,197
Findochty *Moray* 1,100
Forfar *Angus* 12,961
Forres *Moray* 8,531
Fortrose *Highland* 1,319
Fort William *Highland* 10,391
Fraserburgh *Aberdeenshire* 12,843
Galashiels *Borders* 13,753
Galston *East Ayrshire* 5,154
Gatehouse of Fleet *Dumfries and Galloway* 919
Girvan *South Ayrshire* 7,449
Glasgow *Glasgow* 662,954
Glenrothes *Fife* 38,650
Gourock *Inverclyde* 11,743
Grangemouth *Falkirk* 18,739

Grantown on Spey *Highland* 2,391
Greenock *Inverclyde* 50,013
Haddington *East Lothian* 8,844
Hamilton *South Lanarkshire* 49,991
Hawick *Borders* 15,812
Helensburgh *Argyll and Bute* 15,852
Huntly *Aberdeenshire* 4,230
Innerleithen *Borders* 2,515
Inveraray *Argyll and Bute* 512
Inverbervie *Aberdeenshire* 1,879
Invergordon *Highland* 3,929
Inverkeithing *Fife* 6,001
Inverness *Highland* 41,234
Inverurie *Aberdeenshire* 9,567
Irvine *North Ayrshire* 32,988
Jedburgh *Borders* 4,118
Johnstone *Renfrewshire* 18,635
Keith *Moray* 4,793
Kelso *Borders* 5,989
Kilmarnock *East Ayrshire* 44,307
Kilsyth *North Lanarkshire* 9,918
Kilwinning *North Ayrshire* 15,479
Kinghorn *Fife* 2,931
Kingussie *Highland* 1,296
Kinross *Perth and Kinross* 4,552
Kintore *Aberdeenshire* 4,347
Kirkcudbright *Dumfries and Galloway* 3,588
Kirkintilloch *E Dunbartonshire* 20,780
Kirkwall *Orkney* 6,469
Kirriemuir *Angus* 5,571
Ladybank *Fife* 1,373
Lanark *South Lanarkshire* 8,877
Langholm *Dumfries and Galloway* 2,538
Largs *North Ayrshire* 10,925
Lauder *Borders* 1,064
Laurencekirk *Aberdeenshire* 1,611
Lerwick *Shetland* 7,336
Leslie *Aberdeenshire* 3,062
Leven *Fife* 8,317
Linlithgow *West Lothian* 11,866
Livingston *West Lothian* 41,647
Loanhead *Midlothian* 5,659
Lochgelly *Fife* 7,044
Lochgilphead *Argyll and Bute* 2,441
Lochmaben *Dumfries and Galloway* 2,024
Lockerbie *Dumfries and Galloway* 3,982
Lossiemouth *Moray* 7,184
Macduff *Aberdeenshire* 3,894
Markinch *Fife* 2,176
Maybole *South Ayrshire* 4,737
Melrose *Borders* 2,270
Millport *North Ayrshire* 1,340
Milngavie *East Dunbartonshire* 12,592
Moffat *Dumfries and Galloway* 2,342

Monifieth *Angus* 7,900
Montrose *Angus* 11,440
Motherwell *North Lanarkshire* 30,717
Musselburgh *East Lothian* 20,630
Nairn *Highland* 7,892
Newburgh *Fife* 1,401
New Galloway *Dumfries and Galloway*
Newmilns *East Ayrshire* 3,436
Newport on Tay *Fife* 4,343
Newton Stewart *Dumfries and Galloway* 3,673
North Berwick *East Lothian* 5,687
Oban *Argyll and Bute* 8,203
Oldmeldrum *Aberdeenshire* 1,976
Paisley *Renfrewshire* 75,526
Peebles *Borders* 7,065
Penicuik *Midlothian* 17,173
Perth *Perth and Kinross* 41,453
Peterhead *Aberdeenshire* 18,674
Pitlochry *Perth and Kinross* 2,541
Pittenweem *Fife* 1,561
Port Glasgow *Inverclyde* 19,693
Portknockie *Moray* 1,296
Portsoy *Aberdeenshire* 1,822
Prestonpans *East Lothian* 7,014
Prestwick *South Ayrshire* 13,705
Queensferry *Edinburgh* 8,887
Renfrew *Renfrewshire* 20,764
Rosehearty *Aberdeenshire* no pop count
Rothes *Moray* 1,345
Rothesay *Argyll and Bute* 5,264
Rutherglen *Glasgow*
St Andrews *Fife* 11,136
St Monance *Fife* 1,373
Saltcoats *North Ayrshire* 11,865
Sanquhar *Dumfries and Galloway* 2,095
Selkirk *Borders* 5,922
Stevenston *North Ayrshire* 10,153
Stewarton *East Ayrshire* 6,481
Stirling *Stirling* 30,515
Stonehaven *Aberdeenshire* 9,445
Stornoway *Western Isles* 5,975
Stranraer *Dumfries and Galloway* 11,348
Stromness *Orkney* 1,890
Tain *Highland* 3,715
Tayport *Fife* 3,346
Thurso *Highland* 8,488
Tillicoultry *Clackmannan* 5,269
Tobermory *Argyll and Bute* 825
Tranent *East Lothian* 8,316
Troon *South Ayrshire* 15,231
Turriff *Aberdeenshire* 3,951
Whitburn *West Lothian* 11,511
Whithorn *Dumfries and Galloway* 949
Wick *Highland* 7,681
Wigtown *Dumfries and Galloway* 1,117

The Islands of Scotland

Population 5 or more in 1991

Inner Hebrides

Skye	8,840
Islay	3,540
Mull	2,680
Tiree	768
Seil	506
Jura	196
Luing	179
Coll	172
Raasay	163
Gigha	143
Lismore	140
Colonsay	133
Iona	130
Eigg	69
Easdale	41
Kerrera	39
Ulva	30
Rum	26
Muck	24
Canna	20
Soay	14
Isle of Ewe	12
Holy Island	10
Shona	9
Scalpay	7

Shetland Islands

Mainland	17,560
Yell	1,080
Unst	1,060
Whalsay	1,040
West Burra	817
Bressay	352
Trondra	117
Muckle Roe	115
Fetlar	90
Out Skerries	85
East Burra	72
Fair Isle	67
Foula	40
Papa Stour	33

Orkney Islands

Mainland	15,120
South Ronaldsay	943
Westray	704
Sanday	533
Hoy	450
Stronsay	382
Burray	363
Shapinsay	322
Rousay	217
Eday	166
Flotta	126
North Ronaldsay	92
Papa Westray	85
Egilsay	46
Wyre	28
Graemsay	27

Outer Hebrides

Lewis and Harris	21,680
South Uist	2,110
Benbecula	1,830
North Uist	1,400
Barra	1,240
Scalpay	382
Great Bernera	262
Grimsay (North Uist)	215
Eriskay	179
Berneray	141
Vatersay	72
Baleshare	55
St Kilda	25
Grimsay (Benbecula)	24
Flodday	8

Clyde

Bute	7,350
Arran	4,470
Great Cumbrae	1,390
Little Cumbrae	6

The Scottish Weather

Coldest day: Minimum air temperature recorded: -27.2 degrees C at Braemar, 11 February 1895

Windiest day: Fastest gust recorded: 173 mph at Cairngorm, 20 March 1986.

Wet, wet, wet: Scotland's average rainfall ranges from 22 inches to 40 inches a year, typically about 15 inches higher than England's.

Hot stuff?: Average temperature of the coldest month in Lerwick is 3 degrees C compared to -10 degrees C in Moscow, which is several hundred miles to the south of Lerwick.

The Geography of Scotland

10 highest mountains and their height in feet
Ben Nevis, 4,406
Ben Macdhui, 4,300
Braeriach, 4,248
Cairn Toul, 4,241
Cairngorm, 4,084
Aonach Beag (Lochaber), 4,060
Carn Mor Dearg, 4,012
Aonach Mor (Highland), 3,999
Ben Lawers, 3,984
Beinn a' Bhuird, 3,924

10 largest lochs and their size in square miles
Loch Lomond, 27.5
Loch Ness, 21.9
Loch Awe, 14.9
Loch Maree, 11.0
Loch Morar, 10.3
Loch Tay, 10.2
Loch Shin, 8.7
Loch Shiel, 7.6
Loch Rannoch, 7.4
Loch Ericht, 7.2

10 deepest lochs and their depth in feet
Loch Morar, 1,017
Loch Ness, 751
Loch Lomond, 623
Loch Lochy, 531
Loch Ericht, 512
Loch Tay, 508
Loch Katrine, 495
Rannoch, 440
Loch Treig, 436
Loch Sheil, 420

10 longest rivers and their length in miles
Tay, 119
Forth, 116
Clyde, 106
Spey, 96
Tweed, 96
Dee, 87
Don, 82
Nith, 70
Findhorn, 62
Deveron, 61

10 largest islands and their size in square miles
Lewis and Harris, 859
Skye, 643
Mainland Shetland, 373
Mull, 347
Islay, 247
Mainland Orkney, 207
Arran, 168
Jura, 143
North Uist, 136
South Uist, 128

5 highest waterfalls and their height in feet
Eas Coul Aulin, 658
Falls of Glomach, 370
Foyers, 205
Falls of Bruar, 200
Grey Mare's Tail, 200

The above information was compiled for us by the Royal Scottish Geographical Society

Other geographical facts

The greatest distance from north to south in mainland Scotland is 274 miles from Cape Wrath to the Mull of Galloway. The greatest width is 154 miles from Buchan Ness to Applecross. The width of the central belt between the Firths of Clyde and Forth measures 25 miles. The border with England runs 60 miles along the line of the Cheviot Hills.

Scotland has 790 islands, of which 130 are inhabited.

It has 31,460 lochs.

It has six mountains of more than 4,000 feet.

Distance in miles by road from Edinburgh
Aberdeen, 125; Ayr, 73; Berwick upon Tweed, 57; Birmingham, 292; Dundee, 56; Exeter, 450; Fort William, 144; Glasgow, 44; Land's End, 574; London, 378; Stranraer, 124; Swansea, 392; York, 194

Maximum length of the United Kingdom
787 miles from Unst to St Agnes, Isles of Scilly

Legal Notes

The first coherent statement of Scots law was published in 1681 by Lord Stair, Lord President of the Court of Session. Reflecting Scotland's close links with France and the Netherlands, where Roman law was taught, Scots law has a closer affinity to Roman law than any other system. The Act of Union in 1707 guaranteed the separate identity of the Scottish system. In both civil and criminal cases Scots law is adversarial and not accusatorial, court hearings being conducted generally on the basis of a dispute between two parties heard by an independent judge. Public prosecution is carried out by the Lord Advocate, the country's senior law officer. In criminal cases, as well as "guilty" and "not guilty" verdicts, there is a "not proven" verdict where the evidence is not sufficiently strong to justify a conviction. The final court of appeal in criminal matters is the High Court of Justiciary, from which there is no higher court of appeal. From the Court of Session, the supreme civil court in Scotland, there is a right of appeal only to the House of Lords.

The following is a brief A to Z guide to salient features of Scots law:

Adoption Petitions for adoption are made to the Sheriff Court or the Court of Session. Anyone over the age of 21 may legally adopt a child. Married couples in normal circumstances must adopt jointly. Unmarried couples may not adopt jointly, but one partner may adopt. When a child is adopted, he or she enjoys the same status as a child born to the adoptive parents.

Advocates The legal profession in Scotland has two branches – advocates and solicitors. The former are specialists in the art of advocacy, the expert presentation of a case in court, and also advise clients on every aspect of litigation. Solicitors usually carry on a more general type of legal practice and tend to practise in partnership with other solicitors, whereas advocates are sole practitioners working independently. When a person consults a lawyer his first contact is with a solicitor, who will instruct an advocate if required. It is not possible to be an advocate and a solicitor at the same time. Advocates have a right of audience before the House of Lords, the supreme courts of Scotland, the lower courts and before many tribunals and disciplinary bodies.

Children's Hearings In 1971 these took over from the courts most of the responsibility for dealing with children under 16 who commit offences or who are in need of care or protection. Children under 16 are now only considered for prosecution in court where serious offences such as murder or assault to the danger of life are in question or where they are involved in offences where disqualification from driving is possible. The children's hearing is a lay tribunal composed of three members charged with making decisions on the needs of children. Its proceedings are informal and its remit is to consider the wider picture and the long-term well-being of the child. More than 2,000 people appointed by the Secretary of State for Scotland serve on children's panels.

Court of Session Supreme civil court in Scotland consisting of 26 judges. It is divided into the Inner House and the Outer House. With a few exceptions, causes initiated in the Court of Session begin in the Outer House, while appeals are heard in the Inner House.

Jury Service For a civil case, a jury consists of 12 members in the Court of Session and seven in the Sheriff Court. For a criminal trial, a jury consists of 15 members. The maximum age for a juror in Scotland is 65 (70 in England and Wales). Among those excused from jury service are ministers of religion, persons in holy orders and those who have served on a jury in the previous five years. Anyone who has at any time been sentenced by a UK court to a term of imprisonment of five years or more is automatically disqualified from jury service, along with anyone who in the previous 10 years has served any part of a sentence of imprisonment, youth custody or detention, or who has received a suspended sentence or a community service order. A person serving on a jury knowing himself or herself to be ineligible is liable to a maximum fine of £1,000. Failing to attend for jury service without good cause is punishable by a maximum fine of £400.

Justices of the Peace First appointed throughout the country in 1609.

Legal Aid Anyone with a disposable income of £8,158 or less and disposable capital of £6,750 or less is eligible for legal aid before the Scottish courts. Disposable income is defined as income less outgoings such as tax and national insurance contributions, rent, council tax and mortgage payments. Those who qualify for legal aid are required to contribute towards their costs if their disposable income is between £2,498 and £8,158 and their disposable capital exceeds £3,000.

Liquor licensing Reforms in 1991 introduced the children's certificate permitting children under 14 to accompany adults for a meal in pubs and hotels which, in the opinion of local licensing boards, represent a suitable environment. More stringent rules were introduced for the granting of regular extensions to permitted hours. From December 1994, off-sales premises have been allowed to open on Sunday afternoons.

Lord Advocate Principal law officer of the Crown in Scotland, who is responsible for the investigation of crime and for prosecutions in the High Court, Sheriff Courts and District Courts. In addition to his role in the system of public prosecution, he is the government's constitutional and legal adviser on Scottish affairs. The office arose out of the necessity for the sovereign to have an advocate to represent him in both criminal and civil proceedings. The first person to act in the role of "King's Advocate" was John Ross of Montgrenan, who was appointed to be the king's commissioner for the hearing of a case in Stirling in 1476. It was not until 1587 that he adopted his full role as public prosecutor. As one of the great officers of state of Scotland, the Lord Advocate is one of the persons charged with maintaining and protecting the Scottish regalia. Before the Union, he was *ex officio* a member of the Scottish parliament. After the Union, he assumed for a time the powers of the (abandoned) office of Secretary of State for Scotland, along with the Home Secretary. The Lord Advocate is a member of the government.

Lord Justice General Chief judge of Scotland, the office held in combination with that of Lord President. His second in command is the Lord Justice Clerk.

Lords of Session The judges of the Court of Session, numbering 26.

Marriage, law on Proclamation of banns is not required. Each of the parties is required to complete a marriage notice form and return it to the district registrar for the area in which they are to be married at least 15 days before the ceremony. The registrar will prepare a marriage schedule which will be issued to the parties up to seven days before a religious marriage or on the day of a civil marriage. The schedule must be signed immediately after the ceremony and the marriage registered within three days. The minimum age for marriage is 16 years old on the day of the marriage. A regular marriage is a marriage which is celebrated by a minister of religion, registrar, or other authorised celebrant. Open-air ceremonies are permitted in Scotland.

Procurators Fiscal Responsible for the investigation of all sudden and suspicious deaths (there is no office of coroner in Scotland) and for the conduct of fatal accident inquiries in the Sheriff Courts on behalf of the Lord Advocate.

Property, purchase of In Scotland, property is not sold subject to contract as it is in England. As soon as there is a written offer and a written acceptance without qualification, there is a binding contract. Only Scottish lawyers can carry out conveyancing of property in Scotland.

Registration of births The birth of a child must be registered within 21 days (42 days in England and Wales). By law it must be registered at the register office of either the district in which the baby was born or the district in which the mother was living at the time of the birth.

Registration of deaths A death must be registered within eight days (five days in England and Wales) and may be registered in the registration district in which the deceased was normally resident immediately before his or her death. The person registering the death should take the medical certificate giving the cause of death. A certificate of death is issued free of charge. In Scotland a body may be buried, but not cremated, before the death is registered, though this is not the case in England and Wales where in normal circumstances a certificate for burial or cremation must be obtained from the registrar in advance.

Sheriff The first record of the office occurred in 1120. The sheriff was originally a local executive officer of the crown, with administrative and financial as well as some judicial functions. In 1747 the country was organised into principal sheriffdoms. The modern sheriff has jurisdiction in most civil actions and in criminal cases excluding murder and rape.

Solicitor General Second law officer of the government after the Lord Advocate. Originally (1587) the king's agent in actions before the civil courts.

Stipendiary magistrates Salaried appointments to the District Court bench are confined to Glasgow, where there are four stipendiary magistrates.

Wills Any person aged 12 and over and of sound mind can make a will in Scotland. One witness is required to a will. The person making the will must sign each page. In a case of intestacy, the surviving spouse has the right to inherit the matrimonial home up to a value of £110,000 and the furnishings and contents of the home up to the value of £20,000. What is left is generally divided between the surviving spouse and children, according to their legal rights.

Tables

Air travel The number of passengers using Scottish airports in 1997 was as follows:

Aberdeen	2,568,620	Benbecula	36,983
Campbeltown	8,710	Dundee	15,777
Edinburgh	4,161,337	Glasgow	6,011,792
Inverness	379,256	Islay	19,508
Kirkwall	88,701	Lerwick	4,221
Prestwick	567,338	Stornoway	96,180
Sumburgh	345,027	Tiree	5,056
Wick	25,195		

Arts The government-funded Scottish Arts Council distributed £25.5 million in grants in 1997-98. Its major clients, with their grant-in-aid, were as follows:

Scottish Opera	£4.67 million	Traverse Theatre	£0.40 million
Scottish Ballet	£2.35 million	Dundee Repertory	£0.31 million
Royal Scottish National Orchestra	£1.84 million	Perth Theatre	£0.26 million
Scottish Chamber Orchestra	£1.00 million	Pitlochry Festival	£0.23 million
Citizens Theatre	£0.64 million	Tron Theatre	£0.21 million
Royal Lyceum Theatre	£0.57 million	Wildcat	£0.20 million

Biosphere Reserves Areas nominated by national governments for inclusion in a UNESCO programme set up in 1971 to co-ordinate understanding of man's influence on the natural environment. Each reserve should conserve genetic resources, species habitats and landscapes; foster sustainable economic and human development; and support demonstration projects, research and environmental education. There are nine reserves in Scotland:

Beinn Eighe (Highland)	Rum (Highland)
Caerlaverock (Dumfries/Galloway)	Silver Flowe/Merrick Kells (Dumfries/Galloway)
Cairnsmore of Fleet (Dumfries/Galloway)	St Kilda (Western Isles)
Claish Moss (Highland)	Taynish (Argyll and Bute)
Loch Druidibeg (Western Isles)	

Football Played in Scotland since medieval times, though prohibited in 1424 and again in 1491. Ten clubs play in the Scottish Premier League:

Aberdeen, founded 1903	Hibernian, 1875
Celtic, 1888	Kilmarnock, 1869
Dundee, 1893	Motherwell, 1886
Dundee United, 1909	Rangers, 1873
Heart of Midlothian, 1874	St Johnstone, 1884

Gaelic Introduced by Irish emigrants around 500 AD. Legally defined as a national language, it is spoken by 65,978 people in Scotland according to the 1991 census, distributed as follows in the (now defunct) local government regions:

Western Isles	19,546	Central	1,612
Strathclyde	18,283	Fife	1,477
Highland	14,713	Dumfries and Galloway	515
Grampian	2,491	Borders	460
Tayside	2,479	Orkney and Shetland	197

Independent schools There are 87 independent schools in Scotland, with a total roll of 32,200 pupils. They receive no grants from public funds, earning their income by charging fees. Twenty are members of the Headmasters' and Headmistress' Conference. Boarding fees in these schools range from £9,000 to £14,000 a year; day fees from £3,500 to £9,500.
They are as follows:

	Founded	No. of pupils
Daniel Stewart's and Melville College, Edinburgh	1832	778
Dollar Academy	1818	756
Dundee High School	1239	715
Edinburgh Academy	1824	483
Fettes College, Edinburgh	1870	392
George Heriot's School, Edinburgh	1659	931
George Watson's College, Edinburgh	1741	1,265
Glasgow Academy	1845	568
Glenalmond College, Perth	1841	370
Gordonstoun College, Elgin	1934	430
High School of Glasgow	1124	644
Hutcheson's Grammar School, Glasgow	1641	1,252
Kelvinside Academy, Glasgow	1878	400
Loretto School, Musselburgh	1827	319
Merchiston Castle School, Edinburgh	1833	375
Morrison's Academy, Crieff	1860	393
Robert Gordon's College, Aberdeen	1729	940
St Aloysius College, Glasgow	1859	811
St Columba's School, Kilmacolm	1897	360
Strathallan School, Perth	1913	420

Children's names In 1976, David was the most commonly chosen boy's name in Scotland. In 1997, he had declined to ninth. Forty years ago, Ryan was nowhere: look at him now. Among the girls, Rebecca has leapt from 97th in the league table to 2nd – in less than half a century.

Boys

1. Ryan
2. Andrew
3. Jack
4. Ross
5. James
6. Connor
7. Scott
8. Lewis
9. David
10. Michael

Girls

1. Emma
2. Rebecca
3. Chloe
4. Megan
5. Lauren
6. Amy
7. Shannon
8. Caitlin
9. Rachel
10. Hannah

National Scenic Areas Nationally important areas of outstanding natural beauty, representing some of the best examples of Scotland's landscapes, particularly lochs and mountains. Originally identified by the Countryside Commission for Scotland and introduced by the government in 1980. The 40 areas extend from the Solway Firth to Shetland. They are as follows:

Assynt-Coigach	Loch Rannoch and Glen Lyon
Ben Nevis and Glen Coe	Loch Shiel
The Cairngorm Mountains	Loch Tummel
The Cuillin Hills	Lynn of Lorn
Deeside and Lochnagar	Morar, Moidart and Ardnamurchan
Dornoch Firth	North West Sutherland
East Stewartry coast	Nith estuary
Eildon and Leaderfoot	North Arran
Fleet Valley	River Earn, Comrie to St Fillans
Glen Affric	River Tay, Dunkeld
Glen Strathfarrar	St Kilda
Hoy and West Mainland, Orkney	Scarba, Lunga and the Garvellachs
Jura	Shetland
Kintail	The Small Isles
Knapdale	South Lewis, Harris and North Uist
Knoydart	South Uist machair
Kyle of Tongue	The Trossachs
Kyles of Bute	Trotternish
Loch na Keal, Mull	Upper Tweeddale
Loch Lomond	Wester Ross

Parks There are four regional parks in Scotland: Clyde-Muirshiel; Pentland Hills; Fife; Loch Lomond. Country parks, of which there are 36, are relatively small areas of countryside near to towns which are managed for public enjoyment. Most are owned or managed by local authorities with the support of Scottish Natural Heritage. They are as follows:

Aden (Aberdeenshire)	Forfar Loch (Angus)
Almondell and Calderwood (W Lothian)	Gartmorn Dam (Clackmannanshire)
Balloch (W Dunbartonshire)	Gleniffer Braes (Renfrewshire)
Balmedie (Aberdeenshire)	Haddo (Aberdeenshire)
Beecraigs (W Lothian)	Haughton House (Aberdeenshire)
Bonaly (Midlothian)	Hillend (Midlothian)
Brodick (N Ayrshire)	John Muir (E Lothian)
Calderglen (S Lanarkshire)	Lochore Meadows (Fife)
Camperdown and Temple Woods (Dundee)	Monikie (Angus)
Castle Semple (Renfrewshire)	Mugdock (Stirling)
Chatelherault (S Lanarkshire)	Muiravonside (Falkirk)
Clatto (Dundee)	Muirshiel (Renfrewshire)
Craigtoun (Fife)	Palacerigg (N Lanarkshire)
Crombie (Angus)	Polkemmet (W Lothian)
Culzean (S Ayrshire)	Pollok (Glasgow)
Dean Castle (E Ayrshire)	Strathclyde (N and S Lanarkshire)
Drumpellier (N Lanarkshire)	Townhill (Fife)
Eglinton (N Ayrshire)	Vogrie (Midlothian)

Tourism Here are the Top 10 tourist attractions with free admission in 1997-98:

Name of attraction	No of visitors
Kelvingrove Art Gallery and Museum, Glasgow,	1,128,455
Royal Botanic Garden, Edinburgh	812,574
Royal Scots Regimental Museum, Edinburgh	550,000
Museum of Transport, Glasgow	497,874
Gallery of Modern Art, Glasgow	452,678
National Gallery of Scotland, Edinburgh	442,322
People's Palace, Glasgow	442,153
Glasgow Botanical Gardens	400,000
Burrell Collection, Glasgow	343,325
New Lanark Village	304,500

And the Top 10 tourist attractions with paid admission, 1997-98:

Name of attraction	No of visitors
Edinburgh Castle	1,219,055
World Famous Old Blacksmith Shop, Gretna Green	711,480
Edinburgh Zoo	525,000
Museum of Scotland	424,320
Stirling Castle	398,828
Burns National Heritage Park, Alloway	345,000
Palace of Holyroodhouse, Edinburgh	288,000
Official Loch Ness Monster Exhibition Centre, Drumnadrochit	280,000
Urquhart Castle, near Drumnadrochit	235,745
Blair Drummond Safari and Leisure Park, near Stirling	203,195

Where do they come from? Here are the countries of origin of overseas tourists in Scotland, 1997

Name of country	Number of trips	Percentage of total
USA	429,000	20
Germany	239,000	11
Irish Republic	184,000	9
Australia	149,000	7
France	149,000	7
Canada	142,000	7
Netherlands	108,000	5
Italy	73,000	3
Spain	50,000	2
Japan	33,000	2
All other countries	544,000	26

Envy Finally, the top-earning advocates, 1997-98

These figures represent the amounts payable from the Legal Aid Fund to advocates.

1. W Gordon Jackson	£255,000	6. Ruth Anderson	£125,000
2. William McVicar	£192,000	7. Gerald Carroll	£121,000
3. Herbert A Kerrigan	£181,000	Mhairi R Richards	£121,000
4. Donald R. Findlay	£167,000	Peter L Gray	£121,000
5. Edgar Prais	£159,000	10. Neil D Murray	£120,000

Miscellany

Treasure Trove

In Scotland, all items of archaeological and historical interest as well as items of gold, silver and other precious metals fall to the Crown if they have no owner. In other parts of the UK, this "treasure trove" only includes precious metals.

If the find is claimed for the Crown, for example to display in a museum, the finder may receive a reward up to the full market value. If the Crown does not claim the item, it may be returned to the finder.

The Queen's and Lord Treasurer's Remembrancer is assisted in making these decisions by the Treasure Trove Advisory Panel, which includes leading academics and museum staff. Panel members are appointed by the Secretary of State for Scotland and receive no payment for their services. The caseload has increased significantly in recent years but the Panel continues to give careful, objective consideration to all cases.

In a recent year, 155 finds were claimed as treasure trove with 20 items allocated to the National Museums of Scotland, Edinburgh, and 120 items allocated to local museums. A further 15 finds were still being considered by the Panel. Rewards totalling £34,260 were paid to finders: the largest single reward was £4,000.

Significant finds during the year in question included a Middle Bronze Age palstave (axehead) found by a metal detectorist on farmland near Glamis, Angus. The finder waived any reward so that the axehead could be displayed in the local museum, the Meffan Institute, Forfar. A fragment of an early historic brooch, found by a metal detectorist near Anwoth, Dumfries and Galloway, is now on display at the Stewartry Museum, Kirkcudbright. The finder received a £500 reward.

Source: Crown Office

Undergraduate Awards

The following are typical examples of student awards processed by the Student Awards Agency for Scotland during 1998-99:

Case study 1

Student A is aged 19 and lives at home during term-time. She is applying for an award for year 2 of her HND accountancy course at Moray College and would therefore be assisted under the old student support arrangements. Student A's parents have a total income of £25,000 which would result in an assessed parental contribution of £771. She would therefore be entitled to a Standard Maintenance Allowance of £1,565 less parental contribution of £771, a net grant of £794. Student A would also be eligible for tuition fees of £1,000 and excess travelling expenses of up to a maximum of £3 per day plus £495.

Case study 2

Student B is a 33-year-old married student doing the third year of an LLB course at Aberdeen University and would therefore be assisted under the old arrangements. Her husband earns £29,000 which would result in an assessed spouse contribution of £1,893. Student B would not be entitled to a maintenance award as the spouse contribution exceeds the amount of £1,847 which would be payable as the Standard Maintenance Allowance. The student would be eligible to have her fees paid and she would also be reimbursed for any excess travelling expenses once the unexpired spouse contribution of £46 had been deducted.

Case study 3

Student C is a 35-year-old single student living in his own home who is studying the fifth year of a Bachelor of Medicine course at Glasgow University and would therefore be assisted under the old arrangements. He is exempt from either a parental or spouse contribution and is therefore entitled to £1,735, the maximum Standard Maintenance Allowance for his course. The student is also entitled to Mature Students' Allowance of £1,165 because he commenced the programme of studies prior to 1995-96. Student C would therefore be awarded a total grant of £2,900 plus tuition fees of £1,000 and he would also be eligible to claim up to £3 per day plus £635 in excess travelling expenses.

Case study 4

Student D is aged 18 and lives outwith the parental home during term-time. He is applying for assistance to undertake the first year of an MA course at Edinburgh University and would therefore be assisted under the new student support arrangements. His parents' total income is £18,000 which would result in an assessed parental contribution of £126. The parental contribution is applied to the tuition fee and the balance of £874 is paid directly to Edinburgh University by the agency. Student D would therefore be due a Standard Maintenance Allowance of £735. He would also be entitled to excess travelling expenses of up to £3 per day plus 6 single journeys between his home and term-time address.

Case study 5

Student E is a single parent of two children aged 12 and 15 and lives in her own home. She is studying an HNC Computing course at Glenrothes College and would therefore be assisted under the new student support arrangements. Student E would be entitled to a Standard Maintenance Allowance of £1,071, Dependants' Allowance of £2,875 and the Optional Allowance of £1,000, a total of £4,946. Excess travelling expenses up to a maximum of £3 per day plus £635 and tuition fees of £1,000 would also be paid directly to Glenrothes College by the agency.

Source: Student Awards Agency for Scotland

From the Casebook of a Children's Reporter

For every referral he receives, the Children's Reporter must investigate and reach a decision. Reports are obtained from agencies in contact with the child and family, but the process may also involve extensive inquiries and reference to specialist services. The Reporter then has the choice of referring the child's case to a Children's Hearing. If he chooses not to do so, he may refer the child and family to the local authority for voluntary support.

The following are four examples of recent cases from the Reporter's casebook:

Case study 1

An 11-year-old boy set fire to a litter bin. Investigation disclosed no other reasons for concern, but the boy's actions had to be addressed appropriately. The Reporter liaised with the Fire Service and agreed that the child and his parents should be invited to the local fire station where the dangers of playing with fire would be reinforced. The Reporter's decision was based on the need for an appropriate educational experience. It appears the arrangement worked well.

Case study 2

"Kevin", aged 14, was detained in police custody on charges of possession of a knife and breach of the peace. The Reporter referred him to an emergency Children's Hearing. Kevin attended the hearing with his mother. During discussion about what should happen pending a full hearing, Kevin stated that he had attempted suicide before and that he still wanted to kill himself. He seemed very disturbed. The hearing adjourned until later in the day. The Reporter liaised with social work and psychiatry services and arrangements were made for an initial psychiatric assessment to be carried out that day. The re-convened hearing were advised of the arrangements. They issued a warrant to keep Kevin in a place of safety pending completion of the assessment. From the point when Kevin realised that he might be placed in a residential setting, he became brighter and more settled. The preliminary psychiatric view was that he did not suffer from mental illness but that he had experienced significant losses in the past, and required continuing support to relieve his overwhelming feelings of nihilism and despair. Later in the day Kevin was placed in a local assessment unit.

Case study 3

A school referred "Diane" (aged 8) who had an absence rate of 97% despite endeavours by various education professionals. Investigation by the Reporter confirmed that she suffered a rare medical condition, but that more regular attendance would be possible. When at school she appeared bright and able. The parents hotly disputed the professional view, claiming that Diane was fit only to attend medical appointments – although many had been missed. When a Children's Hearing was arranged they initially insisted they would rather go to jail than attend it. School attendance remains poor. The parents have claimed that a wide range of needs must be met to enable Diane to attend school, and the Reporter and colleagues have extensively researched medical opinions and literature on her condition, to arrive at an objective view on these claims.

Case study 4

The Reporter arranged to meet the parents of a boy referred for committing an offence. The parents were concerned that their son was involved with a "bad crowd". The parents felt that if the boy could get involved in more constructive leisure pursuits, this would prevent the need for him to associate with those who "got him into bother". The child had begun to express an interest in some leisure activities, but the family did not seem clear about how to follow this through. The Reporter put the child and family in touch with the appropriate people in the local leisure and recreation services of the local authority, who were able to steer the child into developing new interests. To date, there has been no further offending by the child.

Source: Scottish Children's Reporter Administration

Becoming a Crofter

The crofting system regulated by the Crofters' Commission under unique legislation is largely responsible for retaining people in rural parts of the Highlands and Islands. The population density of nine people per square kilometres is one of the lowest in Europe. Without crofting, the area might now be a virtual wilderness.

Absent Crofter Initiative encourages crofters living away from the croft to return or to release the land to new entrants. Ending a tenancy is a last resort, when all attempts at reaching voluntary agreement have failed. Since April 1998, as a result of the initiative, 635 absentees have been investigated and 125 crofts released, 91 to new entrants. Twenty absentees returned to live on their croft. People interested in taking on tenancies are asked to register with the commission and make their interest known within the community.

Assignation is the permanent transfer of a croft tenancy by a crofter to a person of their choice. It is the most common entry route into crofting. Where possible the commission prefers new entrants, bringing new skills, increased vigour and greater security for schools, Post Offices, medical services and local shops. The commission encourages crofters to think about assignation as a way of sustaining the community, economically and socially. If a crofter wishes to transfer the croft to a family member, only the landlord's written consent is needed. If the proposed entrant is not a relative, the commission considers the impact on the community interest. When demand for crofts outstrips supply, rising tenancy prices often result in young people being outpriced. The commission weighs the interests of the outgoing crofter with the needs of the community, and where the price substantially exceeds the compensation value of the permanent croft improvements (fences, buildings, etc) may refuse the application in the interests of the local community.

Re-letting. When a tenant vacates or renounces a tenancy and moves away, the landlord can re-let the croft to a new entrant.

Subletting ensures croft land is used productively when the existing tenant cannot work the croft or grazings share. It is a temporary arrangement enabling the tenant to make longer-term plans for the future of the croft, and offers an opportunity for new entrants to gain crofting experience. Tenants applying to the commission to sublet retain their own security of tenure. Absentee tenants applying to sublet must satisfy the commission that they intend returning to work the croft and live within the community. Absentee sublets will normally be for three years allowing ample opportunity to plan for the long-term occupancy of the croft. Rather than agree to consecutive sublets, the commission encourages absentees to transfer the tenancy or return to the croft, at the end of the first period.

Succession. A croft is part of a crofter's heritable estate and can be passed on to anyone of their choice. The commission encourages crofters to make a will specifying their wishes for the croft. As a rule it does not interfere with these arrangements. However, if the successor to a tenancy is not a member of the deceased crofter's family, the executor must apply for consent to the transfer.

Croft purchase. Crofters can buy their croft house site for its agricultural value and their croft land for 15 times the annual rent. Since 1975, fewer than 20% of crofts have been bought.

Apportionment. A shareholder in a common grazing can apply for an apportionment, obtaining the exclusive use of part of the grazings, most commonly for improved stock management. Once the apportionment is fenced, the area becomes part of the croft and the right to graze the common is reduced.

Croft enlargement. Crofts can be enlarged by adding non-croft land, provided the new croft is no more than 30 hectares and the rent £100 or less.

Subdivision splits a croft into two or more units and can improve the viability and working of the land. Creating a new croft may keep a family in the area or bring in people with new skills. The landlord and the commission must agree to any subdivision, balancing the advantages in introducing new people against the agricultural merits of splitting the croft.

Decrofting. The commission resists the loss of land from crofting unless it offers benefits such as additional housing, road improvement or water treatment facilities for the community. In 1998 the Commission agreed to release land for a hospital, a cemetery, and a visitor centre.

Register of Crofts. The commission maintains a Register of Crofts containing the name, location, rent, and, where known, the extent of individual crofts. It also records the name of the tenant and landlord.

Source: Crofters Commission

Complaints against solicitors

The Scottish Legal Services Ombudsman is empowered to investigate the handling of complaints against legal practitioners. A complainer must first take a complaint to the Law Society of Scotland (or the Faculty of

Advocates, if appropriate) which must investigate the complaint and report on its investigations to the complainer and to the practitioner concerned. If a complainer is dissatisfied with the outcome, he or she may then refer the matter to the Ombudsman. The following are a few of the cases he dealt with in the past year:

Complaint 1

This started out as a conveyancing case, the complainer and her husband having instructed the solicitors with regard to a joint sale and purchase. She complained that the firm had accepted her husband's instructions to settle the VAT outstanding on his business without consulting her, when she had no knowledge of his business affairs. The balance of the proceeds had then been forwarded to a building society instead of to her, notwithstanding her husband's share and part of her own share having been used to pay off the arrears. The solicitors had taken the view that when dealing with what appeared to be a happily married couple, it could be assumed that her husband's instructions were with her approval. A Complaints Committee agreed with the Reporter that there had been an inadequate professional service, but that no formal notice, order or direction was appropriate. At the same time, the complainer alleged that the solicitors had failed to obtain copies of building warrants and listed building planning permission in relation to extensive works previously carried out on their new property, and no provision had been included in the missives to protect the complainer and her husband against unauthorised alterations which might have been carried out. The Complaints Committee concluded that there would undoubtedly have been a finding of inadequate professional service if the survey had referred to alterations and no appropriate clause had been included in the missives. This in itself was a bone of contention, as the complainer maintained that the survey had referred to various refurbishments and it was emphasised that the whole building had been listed. I was most critical of the confusion and various delays which had arisen.

Recommendations: compensation payment of £150 in recognition of the inconvenience caused; re-opening of the case in order to consider whether the lesser finding of unprofessional conduct, as opposed to professional misconduct which had been dismissed, might be appropriate. Recommendations accepted.

Complaint 2

A case where the solicitors' views on replying to correspondence beggared belief: the solicitors were acting on behalf of a firm which was a client of the complainers and which had gone into receivership. The complaint was about the professional discourtesy of the solicitors who had failed to respond to the complainers' letters with regard to their position as creditors. When contacted by the Law Society, the solicitors responded to the effect that their clients had been sequestrated, the complainers would hear from the interim trustee, but they themselves had no obligation to correspond. In a further response to the Law Society, the solicitors expressed the view that they need not necessarily reply to every item of mail coming into their office unless there were sufficient resources in place to do so, and that most offices lacked the resources to deal with such matters. In this particular case they had taken the view that it was unnecessary to indicate to the complainers whether or not they were under instruction from their clients. In a further exchange of correspondence the Law Society invited the solicitors to acknowledge that it would have been prudent to have advised the complainers of their position. This was grudgingly accepted by the solicitors, but only because it might avoid a fruitless exchange of correspondence with the Society!

The Law Society declined to implement a full investigation into this complaint, and I accepted that the matter was not sufficiently serious to warrant formal investigation into the individual solicitor's conduct. Nevertheless, I was highly critical of the approach adopted by the firm whose attitude with regard to common professional courtesy was so far removed from what is required by the profession today.

Complaint 3

This was a harrowing problem regarding ownership of a property, with its origins back in the 1950s. The complainer's parents had accepted the property in lieu of repayment of a debt and had moved into the property after carrying out renovations. The debtor had undertaken to arrange for a solicitor to transfer title, but by the time of his death nothing had happened and it was discovered that he did not possess title and that there were no title deeds. The debtor's brother had thereafter persuaded the local landowner to grant title to him, and the complainer's parents had been told to move out. The solicitors had sought to assist her parents, but there were subsequent allegations that they had failed to carry out their instructions with regard to the provision of a holograph will, failing to take action in respect of a family car that had been impounded, failing to reduce the title of their property when requested to do so and failing to take appropriate action when the complainer had not been allowed to re-enter the property to reclaim her possessions. The Reporter took the view that it had been a difficult case to fight and that the solicitors had stressed at the outset that the property might be lost. The complaint was dismissed.

I was critical of the time taken by the Reporter to produce his report and his failure to identify and address each of the complainer's concerns and provide explanations for his conclusions. There were indications that matters had been thought through, but the arguments had not been recorded. I recommended that the case be re-opened and that the complainer should receive compensation of £200. Both recommendations were accepted, although the Law Society clearly felt that I had been too hard on the Reporter.

Complaints against Local Authorities

The Commissioner for Local Administration in Scotland (Local Government Ombudsman) investigates complaints of injustice arising from maladministration by local authorities and related bodies. The following are a few of the cases he dealt with in the past year:

Case 1

This complaint arose from the allocation of a council house. The complainant, Mrs A, claimed that despite being top of the list for housing in the area in question, she was deprived of the tenancy as a consequence of flawed procedures. She alleged, in particular, that the actions of one councillor had led to the house being given to the mother of a former councillor who was a close friend.

This investigation brought under scrutiny a long-standing arrangement whereby individual councillors could bring 'special cases' for consideration by a House Letting and Loans Sub-Committee. This procedure was found to be seriously flawed. The Sub-Committee had no criteria against which to exercise their discretion and it became clear that they relied extensively on the judgement of the referring member. It was not unusual for a member of the Sub-Committee to sponsor a case and then take part in the decision-making process. There were occasions when the Sub-Committee allocated specific houses to individuals without any regard to other competing interests.

All of these flaws were manifest in this complaint, but, in addition, the referring member breached the National Code of Local Government Conduct by not declaring an interest in the matter.

The report concluded that, had there been no maladministration, Ms A would have been offered the tenancy of the house. To remedy the injustice, the Council agreed to grant her priority status and instructed the Director of Housing to meet her to discuss how the priority could best be used to meet her housing needs. They also agreed to pay her £250 for her time and trouble. She has now been rehoused in the area of her choice.

In view of the criticism levelled against the Councillor who was named in the Report, the Council terminated his appointment to the Housing Committee. He is no longer a serving member.

Case 2

In this case, the complainant had waited nearly six months before the Council had repaired her fire. She complained that as the fire was the only source of heating in her living room and she considered it was unsafe to use, the repair should have been dealt with as an emergency and carried out within 24 hours of it being reported. She also complained to me about the Council's handling of her formal complaint on the matter.

Whilst the Council had attributed the delay in effecting the repair to difficulties in obtaining access to the complainant's house, during my investigation I established that the complainant had not been asked for a contact telephone number when the repair had been reported. If she had it was clear that a single telephone call could have avoided the Council having to make at least six abortive visits to the property. There was also some doubt as to whether post cards had been left at the property advising of these visits and asking the complainant to contact the local repairs team to arrange an appointment. It had also not been established or recorded when the repair was reported that the fire was considered unsafe and was the only source of heating in the living room. I believe that an effective repairs system should ensure that all relevant information such as this is obtained by the Council. Had this information been obtained at the appropriate time, the repair could have been carried out far more quickly and may well have attracted emergency status – as it was, the repair had not been recorded as such.

I had no hesitation in determining that the Council's response to the repair was unsatisfactory and amounted to maladministration. In addition I found that the Council's handling of the complainant's formal complaint on the matter had fallen short of the standards I would expect.

In the event I am happy to report that the Council accepted my recommendations which included issuing a full apology to the complainant and making her a payment of £200.

Case 3

In this case involving housing benefits I could understand the Council's initial reluctance to contemplate a settlement which involved paying financial compensation to the complainants. To do so might, they felt, give out the wrong message. The complainants alleged that their benefit was stopped without notification either to themselves or their landlord, who was receiving the payments direct. As a consequence, unbeknown to them, rent arrears had accrued until they were eventually threatened with eviction. It transpired that the case had in fact been referred to the Council's fraud investigation team who established that the husband had had periods of employment which had not been declared. Benefit was eventually reinstated albeit at a reduced level. During the investigation the Council acknowledged that, in cases of suspected fraud, it remains necessary to follow proper procedures and withdrawing benefit without notice was unacceptable. They agreed to amend their procedures accordingly, apologise, and pay £200. With my agreement the payment was sent direct to the landlord to reduce the outstanding arrears and I felt obliged to point out to the complainants that they too had responsibilities under the benefit system.

Source: Commissioner for Local Administration in Scotland

For the Record (1)

Among the recent additions to the National Register of Archives (Scotland) are the following:

Fergusson of Kilkerran family, baronets, Ayrshire:
Lecture notes of 2nd Bt while a student at Leyden University, c 1709; notes of his tour through Low Countries, 1710; letter from William Adam, architect, re. marble chimneys, 1744. Papers and correspondence of 3rd Bt, including account of British Fishery Society's tour of the Hebrides, 1787, American war, 1775-79, trade with Ireland, 1778. Letters of 6th Bt from the Crimea, 1854-55, including description of battle of Inkerman, and papers concerning his appointments as Governor of South Australia and of

Bombay. Diary and letters of 7th Bt as commander of 10th and 15th Sudanese battalions, and adjutant-general, Egyptian Army, 1895-1903. Scripts of broadcast talks of 8th Bt, including his anti-Nazi propaganda, 1941-44.

Glasgow School of Art:
Programmes of School of Art Dramatic Club, 1925-70. Papers of Henry Y Alison, including specification for his glass eye, 1934. Photograph album containing photographs of "The Immortals" (Charles Rennie Mackintosh, Margaret and Frances MacDonald, Jessie M King, and others), 1893.

Marshalls Food Group Ltd., Newbridge, Edinburgh
Minutes and miscellaneous board papers of Chunky Chicks (Nichols) Ltd, 1958-62.

Mercer Elphinstone family, Lords Keith, Kincardineshire
Marriage settlement of Margaret Mercer Elphinstone, Baroness Nairne and Keith (1788-1867) with Auguste Charles Joseph, Count de Flahault (d 1870).

Orkney Archives
Collections of poems and songs by Betsy I Skea (d 1994), writer and local historian, as well as her volume containing place names in Lady parish, including an account of the wreck of the Henrietta in 1847, and of the sighting of a German submarine during World War I.

Simpson family, Aberdeen
Family correspondence, 1820-52, with descriptions of Scottish riots and embarkation of emigrants for New Zealand, 1848.

Bank of Scotland, Edinburgh
Correspondence of Dundas of Arniston family, Viscounts Melville, including impeachment of Henry Dundas, 1st Viscount Melville, while Treasurer of the Navy, 1804-05, naturalisation of foreigners through purchase of Bank of Scotland stock, 1818, and small note scare, 1826.

Fazzi Bros Ltd., grocers and wine merchants, Glasgow
Board papers, 1952-75.

Douglas-Hamilton family, Dukes of Hamilton and Brandon
Memoranda on changing the course of the River Avon near Hamilton, 1709-10. Note of expenses for improving the island of Arran, 1771-72. Letter concerning a meeting about building a new church in Shotts, 6 March, 1821.

Anstruther-Gray of Kilmany family, Fife
Correspondence, 1840-1964, on such topics as the invention of bullet-proof shields, the design of machine guns and the restoration of a John Singer Sargent painting.

For the Record (2)

The following is a complete list of acquisitions by the Scottish National Portrait Gallery between 1994 and 1997:
Sir Archibald Acheson, d 1634, by George Jamesone

William Anderson 1805-1866, by Alfred, Comte d'Orsay
Neal Ascherson, b 1932, by Alexander Moffat
Sir James Matthew Barrie, 1860-1937, by Michael Llewelyn Davies
Robert Walter Stewart, 11th Baron Blantyre, 1775-1830, by John Cox
Dillman Engleheart
Sir Thomas Brand, 1714-1761, attributed to Benjamin Arlaud
Margaret Oliver Brown, b 1912, self-portrait
The Battle of Camperdown, 11 October 1797, by George Chambers
Robert Dundas Duncan, 2nd Viscount Duncan and 1st Earl of
Camperdown, 1785-1859, by Robert Dighton
Thomas Carlyle, 1795-1881, lecturing with John Gibson Lockhart, 1794-
1854, in the audience, by Jemima Wedderburn
Andrew Carrick, 1802-1860, by Xavier Jan Kaniewski
George Lyon Carrick, b 1840, by an unknown artist
Jessie Carrick, 1810-1876, by Xavier Jan Kaniewski
Jessie Mary Carrick, b 1842, by an unknown artist
Charles I, 1600-1649, probably by Thomas Simon
The Citizens (Robert David MacDonald, b 1929; Philip Prowse, b 1937;
Giles Havergal, b 1938), by Adrian Wiszniewski
William Skeoch Cumming, 1864-1929, by James Pittendrigh MacGillivray
Study for "The House of Commons – Ramsay Macdonald 1866-1937
addressing the House", by Sir John Lavery
Robert Craigie, Lord Craigie, 1685-1766, by Allan Ramsay
William Craig, Lord Craig, 1745-1813, by Archibald Stirling
Tam Dalyell, b 1932, by Gerald Ogilvie-Laing of Kinkell
Fifteen portraits of Adam Duncan, 1st Viscount Duncan of Camperdown,
1731-1804, by John Singleton Copley, George Romney (attributed), Sir John
Gregory Hancock, James Tassie, Thomas Wyon senior (possibly), Josiah
Wedgwood and others
Unidentified naval officer, attributed to Tilly Kettle
Lieutenant Alexander Duncan, 1781-1803, by Robert Dighton
Sir Henry Duncan, 1786-1835, by Robert Dighton
Two watercolours of Henrietta Dundas, Viscountess Duncan, 1749-1832,
by Julia Janet Georgiana Haldane-Duncan, Baroness Abercromby, and by
an unknown artist
Princess Elizabeth, 1635-1650, and Princess Anne, 1637-1640, daughters of
Charles I, by Sir Anthony van Dyck
Major-General William George Keith Fullerton Elphinstone, 1782-1842, by
George Engleheart
Nicholas Hardwick Fairbairn of Fordell, 1933-95, by Janet Scrymgeour
Wedderburn
Major-General Ronald Crawfurd Ferguson, 1773-1841, by Richard Cosway
Bill Forsyth, b 1946, by Steven Campbell
Bill Gibb, 1943-88, by Michael Leonard
James Goldie, 1928-1990, by Robin Spark
Rev James Hall, 1755-1826, by William Tassie
Sir James Hall of Dunglass, 1761-1832, by Angelica Kauffman

William, 12th Duke of Hamilton, 1845-1895, by Carlo Pellegrini
Giles Havergal, b 1938, by Adrian Wiszniewski
John Hay, d 1781, by Samuel Cotes
Highland Games at Holland Park, by an unknown 19th-century artist
Two portraits of Eric Liddell, 1902-45, by Eileen Soper
Callum Macdonald, b 1912, by Victoria Crowe
Robert David Macdonald, b 1929, by Adrian Wiszniewski
Duncan Macrae, 1905-1967, by William Crosbie
William Marshall, 1748-1833, by John Moir
Unidentified Gentleman, possibly a member of the Rankin family, by George Marshall Mather
James Maxton, 1885-1946, by Joseph Southall
Sir Gilbert Elliot, 3rd Baronet Minto, 1722-1777, by an unknown artist
Jean Muir, 1928-1995, by Glenys Barton
Sir William Nicholson, 1872-1949, by James Ferrier Pryde
Sir Robin Philipson, 1916-92, by Jack Firth
A Photographer's Showroom, by A B Paton
Professor Stewart Piggott, 1910-1996, by John Craxton
Two portraits of Philip Prowse, b 1937, by Adrian Wiszniewski
James Ferrier Pryde, 1866-1941, by Sir William Nicholson
Captain Charles Robertson, 1808-1889, by Edward Robertson
John Ker, 3rd Duke of Roxburghe, 1740-1804, by Pompeo Batoni
Interior of the Rustic Art Club, by Robert Sherar
Jimmy Shand, b 1908, by George Bruce
Robert Louis Stevenson, 1850-1894, by an unknown artist
Two portraits of Prince Charles Edward Stewart, 1720-1788, by Maurice-Quentin de La Tour and Ozias Humphry
Prince James Francis Edward Stewart, 1688-1766, by Ermenegildo Hamerani
Unknown officer, by Archibald Skirving
Queen Victoria, 1819-1901, and Prince Albert, 1819-1861, leaving Granton Harbour in procession for Edinburgh, by Jemima Wedderburn
Mohamed Ali Khan Walajan, 1717-1795, by George Willison
Two portraits of Ethel Walker, 1861-1951, by Marian Kratochwil
Dr Arthur Walton, 1897-1959, by Edward Arthur Walton
Cecile Walton, 1891-1956, with her children Edward and Gavril, by Cecile Walton
George Walton, 1867-1933, by Sir William Oliphant Hutchison
George Washington Wilson, 1823-1893, by Sir George Reid
Sir David Wilkie, 1785-1841, Samuel Rogers, 1763-1855, and Sir James William Colville, 1810-1880, inspecting a portrait, by Jemima Wedderburn
Two portraits of Wendy Wood, 1892-1981, by Stewart Carmichael and William Gordon Burn Murdoch
Two portraits of Very Revd Ronald Selby Wright, 1908-1995, by Delmar Banner

Source: National Galleries of Scotland

Listed Buildings

The Government is required by law to compile lists of buildings of special architectural or historic interest. All buildings erected before 1840, where their character is substantially unimpaired, are listed, while later buildings are chosen on the basis of their individual character and quality. Buildings are assigned to one of three categories according to their relative importance:

Category "A"
Buildings of national or international importance, either architectural or historic, or fine, little-altered examples of some particular period, style, or building type. There are 3,287 listed buildings in this category.

Category "B"
Buildings of regional or more than local importance, or major examples of some particular period, style or building type which may have been altered. There are 25,793 listed buildings in this category.

Category "C"
Buildings of local importance, lesser examples of any period, style, or building type, as orginally constructed or altered; and simple, traditional buildings which group well with others in categories A or B or are part of a planned group such as an estate or an industrial complex. There are 14,732 listed buildings in this category.

Source: Historic Scotland

Training Initiatives

The three main Government initiatives at present are:

Skillseekers
This scheme offers a guarantee of a vocational training place to young people under the age of 18, leading to qualifications awarded by the Scottish Qualifications Authority. It offers broad-based vocational education and training, including planned work experience.

Modern apprenticeships
These are also available to 16 and 17 year olds. They are usually concentrated on a more specific occupation, last about three years, and are provided through contracts with independent providers of training.

Training for work
These are operated by Local Enterprise Companies (LECs) to help people who have been unemployed for more than 6 months. Training is delivered in or out of the workplace to enable trainees to gain experience and skills for employment.

In addition, the *New Deal for Young Unemployed People*, for those aged 18-24 who have been claiming Jobseekers' Allowance for at least 6 months, aims to improve employability and to find unsubsidised jobs for as many as possible.

Index of Organisations

**The song often sung of which few can remember,
if they ever knew, the words**

Should auld acquaintance be forgot,
And never brought to min'?
Should auld acquaintance be forgot,
And auld lang syne?

For auld lang syne, my dear.
For auld lang syne,
We'll tak a cup o' kindness yet,
For auld lang syne.

We twa hae run about the braes,
And pu'd the gowans fine;
But we've wander'd mony a weary foot
Sin' auld lang syne.

We twa hae paidled i' the burn,
From morning sun till dine;
But seas between us braid hae roar'd
Sin' auld lang syne.

And there's a hand, my trusty fiere,
And gie's a hand o' thine;
And we'll tak a right guid-willie waught,
For auld lang syne.

And surely ye'll be your pint-stowp,
And surely I'll be mine;
And we'll tak a cup o' kindness yet
For auld lang syne

Editor's note: the word "syne" is pronounced with an s, not a z